Luminos is the Open Access monograph publishing program from UC Press. Luminos provides a framework for preserving and reinvigorating monograph publishing for the future and increases the reach and visibility of important scholarly work. Titles published in the UC Press Luminos model are published with the same high standards for selection, peer review, production, and marketing as those in our traditional program. www.luminosoa.org

This book is freely available in an open access edition thanks to the
generous support by the University of California Davis Library.

Additional support for this book was generously provided by the
Margarita M. Hanson Fund of the American Musicological Society,
supported in part by the National Endowment for the Humanities
and the Andrew W. Mellon Foundation.

Missionaries, Anthropologists, and Music in the Indonesian Archipelago

Missionaries, Anthropologists, and Music in the Indonesian Archipelago

Edited by

Anna Maria Busse Berger and Henry Spiller

UNIVERSITY OF CALIFORNIA PRESS

University of California Press
Oakland, California

Suggested citation: Busse Berger, A. M. and Spiller, H. (Eds.). *Missionaries, Anthropologists, and Music in the Indonesian Archipelago*. Oakland: University of California Press, 2025. DOI: https://doi.org/10.1525/luminos.223

Library of Congress Cataloging-in-Publication Data

Names: Busse Berger, Anna Maria, editor. | Spiller, Henry, editor.
Title: Missionaries, anthropologists, and music in the Indonesian
    archipelago / edited by Anna Maria Busse Berger and Henry Spiller.
Description: Oakland, California : University of California Press, [2025] |
    Includes bibliographical references and index.
Identifiers: LCCN 2024024822 (print) | LCCN 2024024823 (ebook) |
    ISBN 9780520400566 (paperback) | ISBN 9780520400573 (ebook)
Subjects: LCSH: Music—Indonesia—History and criticism. |
    Missionaries—Indonesia—History. | Ethnomusicology—Indonesia—
    History.
Classification: LCC ML345.I5 M57 2025 (print) | LCC ML345.I5 (ebook) |
    DDC 780.9598—dc23/eng/20240906

LC record available at https://lccn.loc.gov/2024024822
LC ebook record available at https://lccn.loc.gov/2024024823

34 33 32 31 30 29 28 27 26 25
10 9 8 7 6 5 4 3 2 1

CONTENTS

ILLUSTRATIONS

FIGURES

MAP

MUSICAL EXAMPLES

TABLES

ACKNOWLEDGMENTS

Generous funding from the Henry Luce Foundation's Asia Program enabled us to pool our expertise—in Indonesian studies, music scholarship, ethnography, the history of comparative musicology, literature, archival research, and missionary studies—to recruit a diverse group of scholars to reconsider the history of Indonesian music, enriched by new information from often overlooked missionary sources. We are grateful to the Luce Foundation and to the foundation's program director for Asia, Helena Kolenda, who provided gentle and generous guidance even during the difficulties presented by the COVID-19 pandemic. On the UC Davis side, several individuals who were vital to the smooth administration of the grant, including Karen Bowman (then known as Karen Ostergard), Sarah Carle, Jennifer Prahl, Nancy Louks, Kathleen Carroll, and Kali Sullivan, have earned our gratitude as well. We also thank Jaimey Fisher and Molly McCarthy of the UC Davis Humanities Institute for their help in formulating the original proposal.

Most of the essays in this collection were first presented at one of the two Luce-funded conferences in Davis, CA (November 2021 and November 2022), hosted by UC Davis. We are grateful for the support of Laurie San Martin (chair, UC Davis Department of Music) and the department's excellent production staff— Phil Daley, Josh Paterson, Caitlin Sapunor-Davis, and Stephen Bingen—for their superhuman efforts to make these conferences successful, the difficulties of a global pandemic notwithstanding.

The Luce Foundation also funded Dustin Wiebe as our postdoctoral fellow as part of the project. Dustin's contributions to the project include not only his essay in this collection but also research and administration assistance and excellent work developing a proposal for the present volume.

We would like to thank Michael Ladisch of the UC Davis Library for his invaluable assistance in securing funding to make this volume open access (via UC Davis's Funding for Open Access Monographs program). Christina Nellas-Acosta (UC Davis) was helpful in providing excellent initial copy editing for the essays.

Finally, we would like to thank the contributors to the volume and the editors and staff at UC Press—LeKeisha Hughes, Raina Polivka, Nora Becker, Stephanie Summerhays, and Richard Feit—and Paige MacKay at Ubiquity Press for guiding this complex process through to completion.

Introduction

Anna Maria Busse Berger and Henry Spiller

THE INDONESIAN ARCHIPELAGO

The Indonesian archipelago, which lies north of Australia and south of mainland Southeast Asia, has been a nexus for the circulation of goods and ideas from all over the world for millennia. Beginning in the first millennium, traders and religious figures from East, South, and West Asia planted the seeds of Hinduism, Buddhism, Islam, and even some sects of Christianity there. The Portuguese brought European Catholic missionaries with them to the archipelago in the mid-sixteenth century, and Protestant missionary activity increased from the nineteenth century on.

As David Hollinger points out in his contribution to this collection, colonial Christian missionaries were once held in high esteem by the populations of colonizing countries; as the deleterious effects of colonization on indigenous peoples and cultures became clear in the mid-twentieth century, however, the entire colonial missionary project (of "civilizing" third-world communities) lost its luster. Anthropologists—and ethnomusicologists—have conventionally maligned the documentary work of Christian missionaries, assuming that their catechismal motivations eliminated any chance of producing valid ethnographic data. The pioneer ethnomusicologist Jaap Kunst, for example, was brutal in his assessment of Dutch missionaries' deleterious effects on the music of Nias: "The songs and dances of Nias were utterly eradicated; indeed the performing of the ancient songs and choral dances was made punishable, by exclusion from Holy Communion. In this manner the culture of Nias was first systematically violated and destroyed in order to then sow the seeds of Christianity."[1]

As the medical anthropologist Sjaak van der Geest pointed out in 1990, however, an anthropologist and a missionary share many traits: they are both guests in foreign lands, they gather and trade ethnographic knowledge, and they both participate in the colonial enterprise.[2] Missionaries and anthropologists are "brothers under the skin," as Geest characterizes their relationship—riffing, perhaps, on Rudyard Kipling's poem "The Ladies," which crudely suggests that all women, from prostitutes to nobility, share the same exploitative aims when it comes to their relationships with men.[3] Local populations generally see little difference between an anthropologist and a missionary. "Both appropriate a culture by understanding it in terms of their own beliefs," Geest notes. Both are ethnocentric, and both bring about cultural changes. "Anthropologists see themselves as an exception to their own definition, as human anomalies. Their relativism presents itself as a poorly reflected religion."[4] He further identifies several ways in which missionaries might have gathered more complete information. Missionaries spend longer times in communities than do anthropologists, and missionaries try to become more closely integrated. They often are more successful at learning local languages and cataloguing local customs, and they are more inclined to accept the kind of transcendental experiences that a commitment to science might lead an anthropologist to disregard.

The essays in this collection are a first attempt to scrutinize this exceptional trove of historical information. Many of the essays lend support to a realization that Christian missionaries and ethnographers/anthropologists are cut from the same cloth and that missionary activity (Christian or not) often provides a fresh lens through which to consider the history of the Indonesian archipelago. The movement of religions, traders, religious adherents, and missionaries from the outside, across both geographical space and through time, reveal new historical connections and insights that may confound conventional understandings of the region.

The region's history stretches back long before the arrival of the Christian missionaries of the nineteenth century and long before the European colonial project had begun several centuries earlier. But it is difficult to escape European hegemony in the globalized world of the twenty-first century—even when considering a place as far geographically from the so-called West.

Currently, this archipelago encompasses the modern-day nation of Indonesia, as well as Timor L'este, Papua New Guinea, parts of Malaysia, and most of the Philippines. Geographically, the entire region is unified by a common environment, characterized by "water and forest," heavy rainfall, and hot temperatures.[5] With regard to human culture, the archipelago is profoundly diverse; it is home to hundreds of related yet distinct ethnic and language groups. Modern understandings of these places are inevitably colored by the legacy of European colonialism, the arbitrary boundaries of which influenced the current division of the area into a few nation-states. Thus, this volume's geographic designation for the region—"the Indonesian archipelago"—is, from the outset, problematic.

And not just because it privileges the name of one of the region's nations in particular. The term *Indonesia* itself, derived from Greek words meaning "islands of India," is steeped in Western bias. As such, it conveys both the West's reverence for its own (dubious) cultural roots in ancient Greece and an orientalized essentialization of an expansive archipelago, covering thousands of miles, as merely an extension of India. The world maps that circulate in the "First World" reinforce this marginalization, typically relegating the archipelago to the lower right-hand corner. It was not only Europeans who marginalized the area, however.[6] For the seventeenth-century Persian diplomat ibn Muhammed Ibrahim, the archipelago was relegated to the "lands below the winds," so called because of the navigation difficulties resulting from different trade-wind patterns that troubled travel to the region.[7]

Yet this part of the world has significant claims to a position of importance throughout human history. *Homo erectus* fossils suggest that hominid populations inhabited the island of Java well more than a million years ago; some think *H. erectus* may even have arisen there.[8] *Homo sapiens* arrived in the archipelago as much as forty thousand years ago, when low sea levels provided land bridges. Additional waves of human migrations populated the area with a variety of prehistoric human groups over the millennia.[9]

Most existing populations were pushed to the margins of the area, however, during the Austronesian expansion of three to four thousand years ago, when peoples thought to have originated in present-day Taiwan used their seafaring skills to colonize the entire Pacific. Thus, the archipelago's human prehistory has a significant tilt toward Taiwan and the Pacific Ocean—the opposite direction from India—as a primary fountainhead. And languages and other cultural practices throughout the archipelago continue to reflect these Austronesian roots.

Many of the common technologies in use throughout the ancient archipelago, including diets emphasizing rice and fish and the exploitation of bamboo for buildings and tools, were a function of the common environment. Other lifeways common throughout the archipelago, such as betel chewing, cockfighting, and animistic concepts of the presence of spirits in inanimate objects, however, likely point toward common and persistent cultural roots.[10]

That is not to say there is no connection at all between India and other points to the west of the archipelago. There was significant contact back and forth between Sumatra, Java, and South Asia, including India and Africa, in what scholars now theorize as the Indian Ocean World.[11] Hinduism spread through a variety of mechanisms—Indian settlers intermarrying with local populations and ongoing economic and cultural exchanges—and became a religion of Javanese aristocrats. A slew of Hindu temple complexes, such as Prambanan near Yogyakarta, were built toward the end of the first millennium.

Buddhism also spread throughout Asia through missionary activity in the first millennium.[12] Less than fifty miles from Prambanan is the massive ninth-century

Buddhist monument called Borobudur. According to the historian Craig A. Lockard, local rulers in Southeast Asia mobilized Hindu and Buddhist notions of social hierarchy and the divinity of rulers to consolidate control over their emerging powerful polities. Often, Hinduism and Buddhism were blended with indigenous animist practices; a variety of powerful Hindu, Buddhist, and Hindu-Buddhist empires rose and fell before 1500.[13] Legacies of Indic ideas, including literacy, notions of social hierarchy, the epic stories of the *Ramayana* and *Mahabharata*, and vocabulary from Sanskrit and other South Asian languages remain in evidence throughout the archipelago, side by side with traces of Austronesian practices.

Those same trade routes brought Islam to the archipelago. Islam proliferated widely from its origins in the Middle East, primarily through trade, educational exchange, military expansion, and the adoption of the religion by powerful political leaders. Indonesian Islam hearkens back to the *wali sanga* (nine saints), semi-legendary missionaries who propagated Islam in Java as early as the fourteenth century. Early Javanese approaches to Islam involved holdovers of pre-Islamic notions of ancestor worship, Hindu gods, and Indic ideas of the ruler as a cosmic "center." The *wali sanga* purportedly embraced gamelan (tuned percussion orchestras) and wayang (puppet theatre) as tools of Islamic proselytization. Sufi approaches to Islam allowed more heterodoxy than more orthodox twentieth-century approaches.[14]

By the time European colonists arrived in the archipelago from Portugal, England, and Holland, the local governments were mostly powerful Islamic sultanates, except on the island of Bali, where some of the Hindu aristocrats managed to flee from Java, establish control, and resist Islam—and the Dutch—until the early twentieth century. The archipelago's current political boundaries solidified after the end of the Japanese colonial occupation of the entire region during World War II. Some countries established their independence through revolution, others through diplomatic means; present-day boundaries reflect the legacy of European colonialism. In any case, dismissing the rich legacy of human habitation and the myriad polities and cultures of the archipelago as merely "Indian islands" diminishes the rich variety of peoples, languages, polities, and musical practices that have invigorated the region for millennia.

MISSIONARIES IN THE ARCHIPELAGO

According to Robert Ellwood's pithy definition, missionaries are "people who attempt to convert other people to their religion."[15] As we have seen, the missionization of the Indonesian archipelago by foreign representatives of world religions has been going on for thousands of years and implicates Hinduism, Buddhism, Islam, and Christianity among other religions. It is difficult in most cases to separate exclusively missionary activities from other sorts of cultural interventions such as trade, invasion, and intermarriage. And it is misleading to imagine that each world religion is unitary; Hinduism, Buddhism, Islam, and Christianity are all characterized by multiple sects, some of which hold contradictory tenets. Thus, missionaries vary widely in their power, methods, and goals, as well as in their engagement with, opposition to, and sympathy for existing local cultures.

The essays by Kathy Foley (chapter 12) and Sumarsam (chapter 11) both touch on the legacy of Hindu and Buddhist influence in present-day Indonesian performing arts. Most of the essays in this collection, however, focus on the activities of Christian missionaries in the Indonesian archipelago. Although there is some evidence of Christian outposts in the archipelago as early as the seventh century CE, Christian missionary activity began in earnest only with European incursions into the area beginning in the sixteenth century.[16]

Portuguese expeditions beyond Europe began in the early fifteenth century and expanded to the Indian Ocean World early in the sixteenth century.[17] We can only imagine the frustration of these explorers, feeling newly empowered after finally defeating the "Moors" (North African Muslims) at home, setting off on long sea voyages to conquer new territory, and having to compete with Muslim traders literally on the other side of the world. In the eastern parts of the archipelago, they competed not only with Muslim traders but with Spanish explorers as well. The main aim of the Spanish and the Portuguese was to corner the market on the spice trade, but as good Catholics, they also were compelled to spread Christianity. In 1540, the newly formed Society of Jesus (Jesuits) sent missionaries to the archipelago under the leadership of Francis Xavier. These initial efforts met with only limited success, but they were the beginning of the long-standing presence of Catholics—first the Jesuits, then other orders—in what is now eastern Indonesia.[18] Spanish missionaries had better luck in what is now the Philippines, which has maintained a staunchly Catholic majority since these early European incursions.

The 1529 Treaty of Zaragoza, in which the Spanish and the Portuguese agreed on a division of these new territories in Asia between them, stopped them from competing. Protestant European powers, however, ignored the treaty, and soon, Dutch and English ships made their own incursions into the so-called Spice Islands. As Protestants, they were much less invested in notions of converting the locals to Christianity; indeed, Dutch priorities were economic exploitation not religious conversion, and the Dutch (and the British) did not want to antagonize their Muslim trading partners by promoting Christian missionary activity.[19] On Java, in the early nineteenth century, there were some homegrown Christian communities founded by local individuals, but systematic missionary activity did not begin until the second half of that century.[20]

To summarize, the Indonesian archipelago has experienced millennia of missionary activity from a gamut of Hindu, Buddhist, Islamic, and Christian sects, as well as trade and colonizing interactions with actors from the greater Pacific, the Indian Ocean World, the Middle East, and Europe. Making sense of this enormous region's rich, multilayered history requires consideration of many issues from many different angles.

MISSIONARIES AND MUSIC

This volume aims to corroborate documentation in assorted media from the Christian missions that took root in many parts of the East Indies in the nineteenth and twentieth centuries. Much of these data (including music-related manuscripts, recordings, photographs, films, and personal papers) are published here for the first time. This volume only scratches the surface of an enormous field; there is much more to consider, in terms of both hidden archives and theoretical approaches. *Missionaries, Anthropologists, and Music in the Indonesian Archipelago* brings together historians, musicologists, literary scholars, and ethnomusicologists from around the world to contribute to broader efforts to decolonize the project of making music history.

European missionaries produced documentation in a variety of media. There is voluminous correspondence between missionaries in the field and their home mission societies, which provide a wealth of quotidian information along with occasionally exceptional descriptions of musical activities. Missionaries created a wealth of materials for use by their local communities for worship, including hymn books and the like. Some of the best linguistic work, in the form of grammars and dictionaries of local languages, were created by missionaries. In addition, some missionaries experimented with new technologies such as sound recording and film. The present volume crafts a multitude of possible historical narratives to interrogate how histories motivate, or justify, present-day musical ideologies and activities. By putting all these sources into dialogue with one another (and with what verifiable facts exist), our goal is not to establish one "true" history—embracing or debunking previous attempts at retelling the past—but rather to reframe these as multiple historical narratives embedded within past and present musical ideologies and activities. It is worth emphasizing that the essays in this volume engage with only a fraction of the relevant materials that exist; there is much, much more to study.

ORGANIZATION OF THIS VOLUME

The first three parts of the book are organized more or less in historical order, beginning with the early modern period. Part 4 reexamines the interactions between missionaries and those with a more anthropological approach, especially the Dutch ethnomusicologist Jaap Kunst. Part 5 takes a broader view of missionization by considering how non-Christian religions were spread in the archipelago.

The final part examines more broadly some of the various technologies that have been used first to spread, and then to preserve, musical activities, including the legacy of pre-Christian missionaries.

Part I. Early Modern Music History in Indonesia

The first section of the book deals with the music of the early modern period. In chapter 1, David Irving gives an overview of the early years of colonial domination and its influence on the music and culture of the Indonesian archipelago, concentrating particularly on Portuguese and Iberian sources in the Moluccas. The Portuguese arrived in the early sixteenth century, followed by the Spanish in 1666 and then the Dutch. The orders active in this area were not only Jesuits but also Augustinians, Franciscans, and Dominicans. It is surprising how much information on music is available. Sources from the mid-sixteenth century confirm that the Jesuits had established schools in the Moluccas. Irving describes numerous mentions of the students singing chant or polyphony. The texts also include descriptions of local music and ceremonies as well as the use of musical instruments. Particularly interesting are the accounts of musical hybridity and cross-cultural influences. For example, there are reports of the singing of *cantigas* (songs) accompanied by local instruments.

In chapter 2, Estelle Joubert and David Irving discuss a little known music treatise published in 1792 in Batavia by Jan Frans Gratiaen (born 1727 in Bruges, died 1788 in Sri Lanka) titled "Arguments on Useful Musical Topics for the Investigation of Connoisseurs, for the Delight of the Practised, and for the Education of Music Lovers." The major question raised by this document is why this basic theory text was published in Batavia, a place normally not associated with Western music. Although the text was written for the upper classes, as it discusses topics such as aesthetics, genres, theory, and history, the authors show that enslaved people were involved in the performance of Western music. It is remarkable that almost the entire treatise has been copied from an earlier treatise by another theorist, Jacob Wilhelm Lustig (1706–96) without any reference to him.

*Part II. Missionaries and Local Music
in the Nineteenth Century*

Nineteenth-century missionaries were rarely sympathetic to non-Western music. Usually, the Protestants introduced Western chorales and the Catholics Gregorian chant without even considering the possibility that local music might be appropriate for the Christian service. Very few missionaries had any appreciation for local music. They regularly described it using terms such as *screaming* and *howling*. And when it came to the singing of Western songs, they usually complained that the local population was "unmusical" because they could not sing in tune. This, however, was definitely not the case with several nineteenth-century missionaries in Java. Some introduced local music into the service, and others included fascinating accounts of Javanese music that anticipated the research of twentieth-century ethnomusicologists.

In chapter 3, Henry Spiller identifies a missionary active in East Java between 1858 and 1861 who not only appreciated Javanese music but also gave detailed descriptions of what he heard. In both published and unpublished writings, the Dutch missionary Henrik Smeding (1833–91) gives accounts of gamelan music that also include a description of the construction of the instruments, the tunings, and the playing style. Most notable are his remarks on the vocal basis of gamelan, which he describes as "declamatory," by which he means free rhythm. Note, though, that Smeding never advocates the use of the Javanese style of solo singing (*tembang*) for the Christian service. But in contrast to other missionaries of the period, the reason is not that he considers it "sinful." Rather, he feels that the aesthetic requirements of *tembang* would not be fulfilled in the Christian service.

In chapter 4, Ben Arps describes nineteenth-century singing in Christian communities in Java. The vast majority of Dutch missionaries wanted their congregations to sing slow church songs if possible, exactly as they were sung in Amsterdam, and many voiced their dismay at the Javanese style of singing. But there were also local congregations, often strongly criticized by Dutch missionaries, such as the congregation of Coenraad Laurens Coolen, who sang hymns with a text translated from Dutch but with Javanese melodies. Similarly, there were numerous congregations in areas without the supervision of missionaries that followed Javanese spiritual traditions. Most noteworthy is the fact that there were several Dutch missionaries who argued early on for Javanese music in the service.

Part III. Local Church Music in the Twentieth Century

In missionary societies around the world, the twentieth century is the period when some missionaries began to appreciate local music and occasionally even tried to introduce it into the service. The attitude of these missionaries is very much dependent on their home country, and David Hollinger describes significant differences between American and Dutch missionaries (chapter 5). It should be kept in mind that at the beginning of the twentieth century, missionaries were often graduates of top institutions in the United States and much admired there. To quote Hollinger, "Missionaries were in the vanguard, taking risks to advance what were understood as the finest features of American society, spreading them out to the wider world." Of course, there were some missionaries who subscribed to what we call today racism and colonialism, but there were many others who supported nationalism and anticolonialism in the countries where they were working. Hollinger contrasts the American missionary Frank Laubach, active in the Philippines, with the important Dutch missionary Hendrick Kraemer, active in Indonesia. Laubach became one of the most important promoters of world-wide literacy (he considered this as doing Christ's work), establishing many schools and publishing language primers in 312 languages. Kraemer, on the other hand, became a critic of American liberalism and did not approve of granting autonomy to Christian converts.

In chapter 6, Julia Byl writes about missionary activities in Sumatra, more specifically the public ritual ensemble of the Tobak Batak (the drums, gongs, and shawm of the *gondang sabangunan*) and the *ende*, which refers to unaccompanied sung poetry. The *gondang* (ritual instrumental music) was forbidden by the missionaries of the Rheinische Mission from 1870 until at least 1938, and yet it came back to take its place in kinship practices and religious beliefs. The *ende*, on the other hand, was not forbidden because it did not represent a threat to Christianity, but the missionaries certainly did not think it could compare in any way with their chorales. Byl argues that as a result of the introduction of harmonized chorales accompanied by harmonium and other instruments, the separation of *gondang* and text-based *ende* was no longer relevant. Instead, a new Tobak musical genre was created, which became the foremost vehicle for musical creativity in the twentieth century.

In chapter 7, Emilie Rook discusses Catholic *musik inkulturasi* and hymnals in Indonesia that were created after the Second Vatican Council. She shows how this inculturation combines both missionary and local music, with the local music gradually gaining predominance. This new musical identity goes hand in hand with political empowerment.

Philip Yampolsky's broader historical analysis, in chapter 8, of *lagu inkulturasi* complements the detailed ethnographic account of a specific context in Rook's essay. Yampolsky also probes the often contradictory claims by the creators that *lagu inkulturasi* both acknowledge tradition and are effective as liturgical expressions.

Part IV. Missionaries and Anthropologists

Part 4 deals with the relationship between missionaries and Jaap Kunst, the most important Dutch musicologist in Indonesia. Throughout this volume, we have seen that anthropologists would not have been able to do their work without the help and support of local missionaries who knew the languages well and had close contact with the local population. Yet Kunst often makes ambiguous statements about missionaries.

In chapter 9, Dustin Wiebe concentrates on Kunst's relationship with the Catholic missionary Piet Heerkens during and after a seven-week research trip to the island of Flores in the Dutch East Indies that resulted in his 1942 book *Music in Flores*. Kunst openly acknowledges that he could never have written this book without the help of Heerkens. Moreover, Kunst was instrumental in publishing Heerkens's manuscript *Lieder der Florinesen* in 1953 after Heerkens's death. This article demonstrates in fascinating detail how close the missionary and ethnomusicologist worked together.

In his publications and lectures, Jaap Kunst was frequently highly critical of missionaries. The missionaries of the Rheinische Mission on the island of Nias, whom Kunst claimed forbade the singing of local music, came in for particularly strong scorn. After a perusal of the archives of the Rheinische Mission in Wuppertal, Germany, Anna Maria Busse Berger shows that the picture is more complicated (chapter 10). There were many missionaries who appreciated local music, one of whom became a friend and collaborator of Kunst's. It turns out that the first and second generation of indigenous Christians who became evangelists (or *panditas*) were the ones who were really opposed to local music.

Part V. Technologies of Indoctrination

The authors in part 5 examine the technologies of religious indoctrination stemming from the medieval Hindu-Javanese and Muslim polities that predate most of the Christian interventions of the previous sections.

Sumarsam, in chapter 11, examines ancient literary texts to illustrate how various histories and mythologies interact and also discourses on performing arts in old literary works—such as the nineteenth-century *Serat Tjenṭini* and the eighteenth-century *Serat Cabolek*—to uncover links between present and past cultural performances. He pays special attention to tracing antinomian aspects in a court jester cum dancer/singer figure known as *canthang balung*.

In chapter 12, Kathy Foley outlines the development of wayang shadow puppetry from its pre-Majapahit origins to explain how the genre was and continues to be a powerful medium for religious experience and proselytization. In Foley's telling, the religions and the stories change, but the use of the art to spread or teach spiritual ideas remains constant. She points out that wayang among modern Javanese and Sundanese audiences continues to reference aspects of Hindu–Buddhism, the religious tradition in which it first evolved in the ninth century. Foley also addresses more recent postcolonial experiments within Catholic, Protestant, Buddhist, and Islamic communities that continue to spur religious revivals in Indonesia.

Part VI. Technologies of Preservation: Archives

The complex histories of the phonogram archives are the subject of the part 6, the concluding section of the volume. Recordings in those archives were made by explorers, scholars, colonial administrators, and missionaries. How should we view them today? What do they tell us about the people who were recorded? Did they even understand what was going on? Would they approve of it now?

In chapter 13, Sebastian Klotz, scientific coordinator of the Lautarchiv in Berlin, provides a finely nuanced study of the background of the recordings made in New Guinea and Melanesia and asks fundamental questions about the role missionaries played in early recordings and their relationship with anthropologists. While few missionaries made recordings (and if they did, in contrast to anthropologists, they lacked protocol rules for how to make, process, collect and classify these recordings), they provided crucial help for anthropologists and scientists who made recordings for the phonogram archives. Moreover, Klotz shows how varied the interests of all participants in these cultural encounters were during the period of colonial globalization.

Barbara Titus, as director of the Jaap Kunst Archive in Amsterdam, is similarly interested in the history of the recordings there. A central topic of the volume's final chapter is the complex colonial history of the Netherlands in Indonesia and what it means for the recordings in the archive. The questions she addresses are fundamental: How were these recordings made, who was involved, and what does it mean for the people who had no say in the making of these recordings?

Readers can listen to select recordings described in this section on the companion SoundCloud website: https://soundcloud.com/uc-press/sets/missionaries-anthropologists-and-music

The current collection of essays builds on several streams of scholarly discourses variously related to Indonesian music history and theory, missionization/missionaries, and archival sources and research methods. The essays contribute to a small but growing body of research that specifically explores the contributions of mission archives to historical knowledge. *Missionaries, Anthropologists, and Music in the Indonesian Archipelago* helps to provide a more complete picture of the influence of missions around the globe. We look forward to future scholarship along these lines.

NOTES

1. Jaap Kunst, "Indigenous Music and the Christian Mission," in *Indonesian Music and Dance: Traditional Music and its Interaction with the West*, ed. Ernst Heins, Elisabeth den Otter, Felix van Lamsweerde, and Maja Frijn (Amsterdam: Royal Tropical Institute, 1994), 57–87, 62.

2. Sjaak van der Geest, "Anthropologists and Missionaries: Brothers under the Skin," *Man*, New Series 25, no. 4, 1990: 588–601. www.jstor.org/stable/2803655.

3. van der Geest, "Anthropologists and Missionaries."

4. van der Geest, "Anthropologists and Missionaries," 593, 597.

5. Anthony Reid, *Southeast Asia in the Age of Commerce, 1450–1680*, vol. 1, *The Lands below the Winds* (New Haven, CT: Yale University Press, 1988), 2–3.

6. See David R. M. Irving, "Ancient Greeks, World Music, and Early Modern Constructions of Western European Identity," in *Studies on a Global History of Music: A Balzan Musicology Project, 2013–2015*, ed. Reinhard Strohm (Abingdon: Routledge, 2018), 21–41.

7. Reid, *Southeast Asia in the Age of Commerce*, xiii, 1. See also Muhammad ibn Ibrahim [1688], *The Ship of Sulaiman*, trans. from the Persian by J. O'Kane (London: Routledge and Kegan Paul, 1972).

8. J. H. Langdon, "The Erectines of Asia," in *Human Evolution* (Cham: Springer International, 2022), https://doi.org/10.1007/978-3-031-14157-7_14.

9. Craig Lockard, *Southeast Asia in World History* (New York: Oxford University Press, 2009), 5–8.

10. Reid, *Southeast Asia in the Age of Commerce*, 5–6. See also Robert Wessing, "Bamboo, Rice, and Water," in *The Garland Encyclopedia of World Music*, vol. 4, *Southeast Asia*, ed. T. E. Miller and S. Williams (New York: Garland, 1998), 47–54.

11. See Jim Sykes and Julia Byl, *Sounding the Indian Ocean Musical Circulations in the Afro-Asiatic Seascape* (Berkeley: University of California Press, 2023).

12. Robert Ellwood, "Missionaries," in *The Encyclopedia of World Religions*, ed. Robert S. Ellwood and Gregory D. Alles (New York: Facts on File, 2007).

13. Lockard, *Southeast Asia in World History*, 23–25.

14. David D. Harnish and Anne K. Rasmussen, "Introduction: The World of Islam in the Music of Indonesia," in *Divine Inspirations: Music and Islam in Indonesia*, ed. David D. Harnish and Anne K. Rasmussen (New York: Oxford University Press, 2011), 5-42.

15. Ellwood, "Missionaries."

16. See "Christianity in Pre-Colonial Indonesia," chapter 1 in Jan Sihar Aritonang and Karel Steenbrink, *A History of Christianity in Indonesia* (Leiden: Brill, 2008), 3-9.

17. See "A Race between Islam and Christianity?," chapter 2 in Aritonang and Steenbrink, *A History of Christianity in Indonesia*, 9-21.

18. Aritonang and Steenbrink, *A History of Christianity in Indonesia*, 19–20.

19. Frances Gouda, *Dutch Culture Overseas: Colonial Practice in the Netherlands Indies, 1900–1942* (Jakarta: Equinox, 2008), 66.

20. Aritonang and Steenbrink, *A History of Christianity in Indonesia*, 641, 713.

PART I

Early Modern Music History in Indonesia

Iberian Sources for the Historiography of Musics in the Early Modern Moluccas (Maluku)

David R. M. Irving

The Moluccas, or Maluku, featured relatively rarely in musicological research on Indonesia until the 1990s. In that decade, Margaret Kartomi published a number of seminal studies on musics of the region, focusing particularly on the revival of traditional performing arts in the islands of Ternate and Tidore, where the practice of music and dance had fluctuated in its cultivation during the 1980s.[1] In the title of an article from 1994 she asked, "Is Maluku still musicological *terra incognita?*" Addressing this question, she offered a wide-ranging overview of musical knowledge and practice, drawing from Dutch colonial sources and her own fieldwork (conducted over several months in 1989–1990 and 1993), as well as other anthropological and ethnomusicological studies.[2] The earliest historical texts that Kartomi considered were eighteenth-century descriptions of music cultures in north and central Maluku made by Dutch Protestant minister and chronicler François Valentijn (1666–1727) in his five-volume work *Oud en Nieuw Oost-Indiën* (Old and New East Indies).[3] However, she also acknowledged the wealth of sixteenth- and seventeenth-century Portuguese and Spanish historiography relating to eastern Indonesia as examined by historian Leonard Andaya in his 1993 monograph *The World of Maluku*.[4] Additionally, she made an intriguing reference to Portuguese Catholic church music—introduced to the region from 1512—and its lasting impact on musics of subsequent periods, as noted by Alfred Russel Wallace (1823–1913) in Ambon in 1869.[5]

These sources are, of course, all of European origin. For any researcher delving into the music history of Maluku a major challenge for the study of the early modern period is the imbalance of surviving records written from different cultural perspectives. Extant indigenous texts from this period and region are rare.

Benjamin Moseley and other historians have pointed out that one of the few examples is the *Hikayat Tanah Hitu* (Story of the Land of Hitu) by Rijali (1590–1662),[6] which includes a brief description of the sounds of war, giving a list of musical instruments used by the Portuguese.[7] Andaya, commenting that "sources for the study of Maluku before the nineteenth century are almost exclusively European," offered a detailed and useful overview of relevant Portuguese, Spanish, and Dutch manuscripts and printed works.[8] Comprising chronicles of events, correspondence, ethnographic observations, records of trade, and other data, many of these texts contain points of interest for the musicologist.

Zooming out, it can be seen that the influence of Portugal on the music cultures of the broader Malay-Indonesian archipelago has been studied extensively.[9] Nevertheless, there remains a musicological lacuna regarding Portuguese primary sources relating specifically to the Maluku region, which some scholars have recently begun to address.[10] As demonstrated by Kartomi, musicologists and historians have drawn mostly from Dutch sources, with some mention of English voyage accounts, for the history of musical practices in Maluku before the nineteenth century.[11] This is because the Dutch became the dominant colonial presence in this spice-producing region from the final third of the seventeenth century. From around 1666, Portuguese and Spanish colonial interests, which had by then existed for approximately one and a half centuries, in the form of incursions, religious missions, and trading factories, were extinguished, although there remained a number of cultural legacies of their presence, especially music.[12] Until recently, the colonialism and religious missions of Spain in Maluku received less attention from historians, compared to those of Portugal.[13] This chapter, inspired by and building on the work of Kartomi and Andaya and informed by a range of recent studies, focuses on both Portuguese and Spanish sources and aims to address the following question: What kinds of musical data can be found in Iberian historiography of early modern Maluku? It aims to contribute to current work in this area, to look afresh at these sources, and to highlight the potential utility of data found in sixteenth- and seventeenth-century Iberian writings that mention musical practices in or of Maluku.

First, some geographical context is necessary. As is well known, this part of the Indonesian archipelago is globally significant as the source of certain spices—cloves, nutmeg, and mace—that were originally endemic to specific islands. Today Maluku consists of three main administrative regions: north, central, and south (Kabupaten Maluku Utara, Kabupaten Maluku Tengah, and Kabupaten Maluku Tenggara). The overall name has undergone changes in meaning over the last half-millennium. Andaya notes that "'Maluku' in this period [sixteenth through eighteenth centuries] referred only to the clove-producing islands of north Maluku, the most powerful of which was Ternate," with Tidore being "equally prominent"; tracing its possible historical meanings, and the way it has been inflected and interpreted in terms of collective regional identity, he notes that "the name Maluku came to be applied to all areas which acknowledge Ternate's or

Tidore's dominance."[14] Jesuit historian Adolf Heuken has also written of varying applications of the term:

> In the narrow sense of the word, Maluku is used for the islands of Tidore, Ternate, Motir, Makian, Bacan, and for a few tiny islets close to them, or for the four ancient kingdoms of Jailolo, Tidore, Ternate, and Bacan. In the wider sense, however, the Moluccas comprise all the islands between Celebes (Sulawesi) and Papua (West New-Guinea), and between Moro Island north of Halmahera, and the Banda Islands in the south.[15]

This chapter takes the latter, broad geographical view of the area. The major polities in the broader region were ruled by sultans, *sangajis* (local rulers), and rajas, while the four kingdoms just mentioned began to be perceived by Europeans as "the 'center' of an expanding Malukan world," in the words of Andaya.[16] Alliances and conversions of rulers and populations variously to Islam, Catholicism, and Calvinism punctuate the complex political picture.

In terms of chronology, the period considered here spans from the arrival of the Portuguese in the early sixteenth century (beginning in 1512) to the Spanish withdrawal from the region in the late 1670s.[17] The Portuguese established forts on Ternate from 1522, Ambon from 1569, and Tidore from 1578.[18] (During this time a number of significant Portuguese chronicles were composed.) In 1570, Sultan Hairun of Ternate—who had begun his reign in 1535 and over succeeding decades interacted intensively with Portuguese and spoke their language—was murdered by Portuguese forces, and his son Baab Ullah (d. 1583) aimed to avenge his death.[19] The Ternate base was captured by Sultan Baab Ullah in 1575, and those of Ambon and Tidore by the Dutch in 1605; in 1606, a Spanish force led by Pedro Bravo de Acuña (d. 1606) then seized the fortress of Tidore, where Spain then maintained a presence until 1663.[20] There were periodic English establishments from the 1590s until the "Ambon massacre" of 1623, when the Dutch executed English factors (a widely reported event with descriptions that include musical details), after which the English withdrew from the area.[21] It was against this complex political and economic backdrop that the Catholic missionaries operated in the sixteenth and seventeenth centuries, not only Jesuits but also members of other orders, including Augustinians, Dominicans, and Franciscans.[22] The Jesuits are particularly prominent in the documentation of this part of history, and I focus on them here.[23] By far the most detailed historiography devoted to the Jesuit mission in Maluku during this period is the three-volume set *Documenta Malucensia* (Moluccan documents, 1974–84) edited by Jesuit historian Hubert Jacobs (1909–96), presenting transcriptions of primary source materials from the archives of the Society of Jesus, with extensive introductions and contextual studies, as well as biographies of indigenous and foreign individuals.[24]

In this chapter, I offer interpretations of descriptions made by chroniclers of sonic events, contextualizing them within a broader political, social, and cultural framework. I do not claim any comprehensiveness in the following overview of sources; rather, I will give some brief snapshots of examples that demonstrate the kinds of musical and sonic elements found in Iberian historiography. I concentrate on three main areas: first, musical and other ethnographic information relevant to the performing arts in an account by a secular Portuguese writer whose work preceded the beginning of the Jesuit mission—the ca. 1544 treatise on Maluku by António Galvão (ca. 1490–1557); second, accounts and letters of the Jesuits (in Portuguese and Spanish); and third, an influential book written in Spain and published there in 1609, the *Conquista de las Islas Malucas* (Conquest of the Moluccan Islands) by Bartolomé Leonardo de Argensola (1562–1631).[25] In terms of the kinds of vocabulary that might attract the eyes of a musicologist looking at sixteenth-century Portuguese texts, Maria de São José Corte-Real has provided a useful list of terms and expressions drawn from the *peregrinação* (pilgrimage) of Fernão Mendes Pinto (ca. 1509–83), who visited China and Japan (but not Maluku). She divides them into categories of "the sound environment," "musical performance," and "musical instruments."[26] Many, but not all, of these terms can be found in Portuguese texts regarding Maluku, although orthography of the time is fairly variable. Musical details in Jesuit letters about the region—in Portuguese, Spanish, Italian, and Latin—are relatively sparse, but a great deal of context can be fleshed out from them. Situated at the geographical frontiers of Spanish and Portuguese colonial ambition, Jesuit missions were shaped by rivalry between the two Iberian nations.[27] However, they were also motivated in their work by religious and cultural competition with Islam and with Dutch Calvinism. Baptism was at the forefront of the aims and ambitions of the Society of Jesus in Maluku, as we will see.[28]

INDIGENOUS MUSICS AND OTHER PERFORMING ARTS OF MALUKU ACCORDING TO GALVÃO

A Portuguese treatise dating from ca. 1544 on Maluku and the customs of their inhabitants was found in 1928 by Jesuit historian Georg Schurhammer (1882–1971) in the Archivo General de Indias, Seville.[29] Some decades later, Jacobs attributed the text's authorship to António Galvão and in 1971 published an annotated edition (with English translation).[30] The treatise offers ethnographic and linguistic information for this era that cannot be found elsewhere.[31] Reading Galvão's treatise in tandem with the letters of missionaries from the late 1540s onward—beginning with Francis Xavier (1506–52), one of the founders of the Society of Jesus—musicologists can gain an increasingly layered understanding of how mid-sixteenth-century Iberians viewed and represented the performing arts and religious sound of local cultures.[32]

At various points in the sixty chapters of Galvão's treatise, he mentions sound-art and dancing in religious practice, warfare, celebrations, entertainment, and travel. He sometimes uses Christian terminology such as "Matins, (canonical)

Hours, Lent, Easter, Our Lady of Candlemas, Pope, to explain Mohammedan customs," as Jacobs notes, to make comparative descriptions of Islamic religious practices.[33] For example, Galvão states, "They usually have fine mosques with no image in them, but with a big drum hung up with which they call to Matins and to the ordinary Hours, which they recite five times a day."[34] The last clause refers clearly to daily Islamic prayers (*salat/salah*). Another point to note is that the mention of the drum, implicitly analogous to church bells in Galvão's sentence, is a clear reference to an instrument known in other parts of the Malay world as *beduk*; Valentijn also writes about it, calling it a *tifa*.[35] Galvão was not alone in making such comparisons; as we see later, another Iberian writer would explicitly liken this drum's function to a church bell.

Galvão has a particular focus on royal ceremonial and cultural practices of the elite, and this goes hand in hand with a discussion of instruments. For instance, he notes the importance of musical ensembles on the boats of rulers as a marker of prestige and royal identity: "When the kings sail in their boats, [bands] play for them on gongs, *tifas*, and sistra; these [bands] are royal insignia because no one else may maintain them. As soon as this *tifa* resounds, those who are on the land gather at the shore to make the *sembahjang* [Islamic prayers, now spelled *sembahyang*] and to ask if something is wanted."[36] He later repeats this observation, adding some extra details: "They carry with them drums, gongs, and sistra, this being a royal privilege, to the music of which they row and sing rhythmically as the people of Galicia do. [In singing] they mention everything they did or hope to do both in peace and in war. They recognize each other by their way of singing."[37]

Galvão's description of the enthronement or installation of a ruler includes information about musical instruments and dancing:

> They make music for him on Javanese gongs; these are like bronze basins with a kind of boss in the middle and holes at the rim, through which they pull cords. Hanging from wooden poles, they are carried along on the shoulders of two men while others beat them with wooden mallets; they produce [the pitches of countertenor and soprano] . . . , for some are larger and others smaller. They have drums similar to tambours, some of which resemble tambourines and are called tifa. Other instruments are like shawms, and they call them *saruni* [*serunai*]; they have flutes and sistrum-like instruments and many others to their liking.[38]

Besides the gongs, *tifa, serunai,* and plucked string instruments, instruments that Galvão mentions elsewhere in the text are the conch trumpet ("buzio") and nose flute ("ffrauta [*sic*] com a vemtana do naris"). The conch is described as being played alongside gongs and *tifa* in alarms or rallying cries for warfare, and the nose flute in solitary settings during periods of mourning after a bereavement.[39] In a slightly offbeat reference, Galvão also recounts an apocryphal tale regarding the insertion of bells between the foreskin and head of the penis, quoting the people of Pegu.[40]

Of dances he writes, "The *alifurus* come with their wives and daughters to the palace gate to sing and to perform a swinging dance called *lego-lego*; it is practised more by night than by day."[41] The term *alifuru* refers to ethnic groups including the Nuaulu and Huaulu, an indigenous group living in mountainous regions who worked for societies on the coasts.[42] Kartomi describes the *lego-lego* as a female court dance in which

> twenty ladies-in-waiting wearing broad European-style green skirts and matching blouses with antique metal headdresses and necklaces and red and yellow dance scarves . . . move gracefully to the accompaniment of a female *tampiang* (small frame drum) player and a female vocalist . . . who sings advice to and even criticism of the Sultan. The present [1990s] Sultan says this is the only time that his people have traditionally been allowed to criticize and advise a Sultan. . . . Such female dances may be centuries old.[43]

In this discussion of the genre, Kartomi cites Valentijn's 1724 description of a female dance.[44] Galvão's use of the name *lego-lego* in his treatise stretches its historiography back to the sixteenth century.

Galvão also describes many aspects of music within feasts. When a king makes a visit to another community for a feast, he is "preceded by a train of men armed with swords and *salawakus* [shields] and accompanied by music on the customary instruments," although Galvão does not specify which instruments.[45] Halfway through feasts the people "sing and play instruments and make jokes, riddles, and pleasantries."[46] In his description of feasts, Galvão also makes a distinction between classes in terms of their performances: "The peasantry appear with their daughters and wives in order to dance the *lego-lego*" but "the courtiers, elegantly dressed, come and perform their tournaments, which they call *carracheo*, to the sound of musical instruments."[47] The tournament is a display of strength in competitive fights. Galvão claims that if a competitor falls, the ground must be ceremonially purified, in a ritual involving gongs, amulets, herbs, and crushed stones.[48] He also notes that "the sultan of Ternate has to marry a daughter of the sultan of Tidore, since he is the most important after him."[49] In this context, he mentions later in the treatise festivities (including music) held for a marriage he claims to have brokered between the sultan of Ternate and the daughter of the sultan of Tidore.[50]

In describing social ranks, Galvão draws from the history of religious conversion and of the introduction of specific cultural practices and objects (including musical instruments). He relates that he was told of their Javanese origins, writing, "They say that they took these titles from the Javanese who made them Muslims and introduced coinage into their country, as well as the gong, the *serunai*, ivory, the *kris* dagger, and the law, and all the other good things they have."[51] He additionally writes of metal currency and other objects—again specifying gongs from Java—that "they treasure these [coins] up, and also jewels, objects of gold, Javanese gongs, copper basins, pieces of ivory, porcelain, fine silk and cotton fabrics; all this comes from abroad in exchange for clove because none of it is natural to the country."[52] The arrival of commodities in the area—including musical instruments such as gongs and *serunai*—is thus attributed to the trade in cloves.

Galvão writes of the origins and history of the inhabitants of Maluku in chapters 12 to 14 of his work.[53] He offers historiographical perspectives and information on how they transmitted their songs and ballads, not only committing them to memory but also using Chinese ink to write them on palm leaves:

> This is what I could find out of their past, because they have no chronicles nor [written] history and they keep no archives. As far as I understood from them, they commit their past to memory by way of aphorisms, songs, and rhyming ballads, of which they are very fond. They make good ones which are handed down from one to another like the Hebrews used to do: when their soldiers returned victorious they sang: "Saul slew thousands and David slew tens of thousands"; and at Caesar's triumph [the soldiers sang]: "Senators of Rome, take care of your wives"; and for Count Fernão Gonsálvez: "While the king stayed in Granada, the knights advanced in the fields of the Mondego"; and other sayings in which literature abounds. They commit their stories to memory, and so one learns but little from them of their past.[54]

Later in the text he adds the extra context that "they write upon *ola*, which are palm leaves, and on paper which is imported from India; and the pens are made of ferns, for those of ducks are not known there. And the ink comes from China."[55]

While the first thirty-six chapters focus on the people, natural history, and cultural practices of Maluku, the remaining ones introduce the Portuguese into the narrative, beginning with a short overview of Portugal's history of navigation and colonialism. The earliest Portuguese and Spanish arrivals to Maluku are described in detail, including the expedition of Juan Sebastián Elcano (ca. 1486–1526), who continued and completed the voyage of circumnavigation that had been started by Ferdinand Magellan (ca. 1480–1521). In describing his own arrival in Maluku (October 1536), a point at which the Portuguese colony was apparently in decline, Galvão gives a heroic account and states that "everyone said that António Galvão had come to rescue them, and they marched out to meet him, in procession behind the cross and [singing] *Te Deum laudamus*."[56] He also mentions trumpets and unspecified instruments of "the common soldiers," although whether the latter refers to Moluccan or Iberian individuals is not clear.[57] In his description of the Portuguese attack on (and seizing of) Tidore, he refers to "the sounding of the trumpets and of all the other instruments," which seems to suggest a binary between Portuguese trumpets and a range of indigenous instruments used in warfare (gongs, *tifa*, and conch trumpets).[58] Toward the end of his treatise, which discusses the events that followed the seizure of Tidore in the establishment of a Portuguese colony and ongoing negotiations with surrounding rulers, Galvão boasts of his work in founding an urban settlement and his support of incipient work in evangelization. Early baptisms—particularly anyone from the Moluccan elite—caused considerable controversy among the local societies, but Galvão asserts that they were celebrated with large ceremonies and feasts.[59]

MUSIC IN JESUIT LETTERS AND REPORTS

Baptisms were a fundamental aim of the Jesuit mission to the region, and music was part of the process of evangelization. The first Jesuit to arrive was Francis Xavier, who was present in Maluku from February 14, 1546, to May 1547. On January 20, 1548, he wrote from Kochi (Cochin), Kerala, to his fellow Jesuits in Rome. In his letter he described aspects of his experiences in the region of Maluku, including the following passage:

> There was reason for thanking our Lord for the fruit which was produced by God in the hearts of his creatures, who sang his praise and glory among a race [*sic: gente* (people)] newly converted to his faith. For it turned out in Maluco that the boys on the squares, the girls and women in their homes both day and night, the workers in the fields, and the fishermen on the sea, instead of their vain songs, sang sacred canticles, for example, the Creed, the Our Father and Hail Mary, the Commandments, the Works of Mercy, the *Confiteor*, and many other prayers, all in their own language, so that everyone understood them, both those who had been recently converted to our faith and those who had not. God our Lord willed that within a short time among the Portuguese of this city and the natives of the land, both Christians and infidels, *I found great favor in their eyes.*[60]

Xavier's stay in the Maluku region constituted a pivotal period for mutual engagement between two distinct cultures. The primary sources attesting to his activities are relatively scarce but have been studied in extensive detail. His own writings gloss over local customs and cultural practices giving scanty detail, focusing rather on the transculturative processes of evangelization. Andaya writes that "both Xavier and the other Jesuits quickly realized that it was the ritual of the Church, with its various ceremonies, candlelight, and music, and not the doctrine, which appealed to the local inhabitants. . . . He combined the native love of music with Catholic ritual to create a pleasant and effective way of conveying the Christian message."[61] This tendency was noted by a hagiographer of Francis Xavier, who mentioned his teaching of the singing of the doctrine in Ternate, and his evening walks evangelizing with a small bell (campanilla).[62]

Xavier had no instruments other than his voice and a little bell. Yet it is pertinent to note that in sixteenth-century Portuguese sources, the word *sino* is used to refer not only to gongs but also to bells introduced by the missionaries.[63] By extension, it seems that local gongs themselves occasionally functioned as church bells. On January 8, 1558, Fernão de Osório (ca. 1531–65) wrote to his superior Francisco Vieira (1519–ca. 1560) at Ternate, describing his mission work (in a location that Jacobs identifies as Bacan).[64] On the feast of Epiphany, Osório made a petition to a local ruler who appeared impressed by the church ceremonies performed on the previous day. The missionary asked him for wood to make crosses and for permission to evangelize among the children and women of the local population; he also asked for "a *sino* to ring on Sundays and to signal *Ave Marias*."[65] It seems that *sino* here refers to a gong, for in the next sentence the Osório notes that "I don't have any other means of attracting these children, because they are fearful of this black wolf" (the last comment presumably referring to his black robe).[66] In the letter, it seems that he is justifying to his Jesuit superior the need to use a local instrument. He goes on to say that he intends to win the confidence of the children in this way and then he will punish them.[67]

Another Jesuit who mentioned bells or gongs was Pero Mascarenhas (ca. 1532–81). Writing from Ternate to Jesuits in Goa on March 6, 1569, Mascarenhas reported on his voyage to Kolongan, Sulawesi, where he erected a large cross.[68] He recounts: "Adding more to the joy was that the playing [of gongs?] and pealing of bells started [*comessarem a tanger e a repicar sinos*] throughout the city at the time that we were adoring the cross, and the festivities lasted most of the night."[69] Although the phrase "comessarem a tanger e a repicar sinos" could certainly be interpreted simply as "bells started to be rung and pealed," it is tempting to read "sinos" in its double meaning of gongs and bells, and perhaps imagine the simultaneous playing of local gongs and ringing of imported bells.

Mass baptisms are frequently described in general terms throughout the Jesuit documentation, but on several events the conversion of individuals is emphasized. As Juan Ruiz Jiménez has recently noted, the baptism of a princess of Bacan in 1559 was reported with a number of musical details. According to a letter dated March 9 that year written by Vieira and sent to the Society of Jesus in Portugal, it took place in Ternate. The procession to the church included a "beautiful choir of singers, of whom there are many good ones here"; another version of the text specifies that they sang "canticos de Benedictus" (probably the Song of Zechariah, from the Gospel of Luke, 1:68–79).[70] There were also some players of trumpets, and at the event some boys who were "splendidly dressed" performed a dance.[71]

Additional musical references in the letters concern the singing of the doctrine in Malay and other languages, especially by children.[72] For example, in March 1559, Vieira reported (secondhand) the singing of the doctrine by children on Bacan.[73] In July 1563, Diogo de Magalhães (d. 1573) wrote to Pero Mascarenhas from Manado, Sulawesi, referring to a place he calls "Batachina" (which Jacobs suggests refers to a location in north Sulawesi); he states that the people, old and young, were very fond of singing the doctrine, and sang it continuously, whether on land or water.[74] Some decades later, in the Annual Letter of Tidore for 1602, sent to Goa, Luís Fernandes (1550–1608) wrote of the children in Labuha, Bacan: "This Christianity continued with the daily teaching of the Christian Doctrine to children, sung in church, in the Malay language; and with the Salve [Regina] in Portuguese every Saturday, sung by the boys and girls all with lighted candles in their hands, which inspired much devotion."[75]

In the same letter, he mentions that a procession took place on Maundy Thursday (Jacobs states that this was April 19, 1601), with the *sangaji* (local ruler) of Labuha holding high a cross and the priest singing litanies, which was admired by many onlookers who gathered there.[76] Another letter by Fernandes, written March 31, 1607, to the Jesuit General Claudio Acquaviva (1543–1615) in Rome, refers to the language of Ternate on the island of Morotai, used by an unnamed Jesuit father who had recently constructed a church and house, and baptized five hundred people:

> With what joy and happiness they attend the church to hear their mass and sermon, which is preached to them in their language, and the children to sing the Christian doctrine, and to discuss [argue] questions about it. All [is] in the Ternate language that all of them know very well and understand, which is something to give many praises to God for and to cry lively tears of happiness and joy.[77]

The Jesuits established their own schools in Maluku, and from the late 1540s they already had systems in place to send students to the College of St. Paul in Goa. As Jacobs and Triyono Bramantyo note, six boys from Maluku and four from Makassar appear to have already been studying there in 1546; the constitutions dating from that year allow for six students from Melaka and six from Maluku.[78] Maria Monteiro cites a letter from this same college in 1558, which mentions the musical curriculum: besides learning to read, write, and count, the boys were taught singing and participated in a *capela* (literally "chapel," but implying a musical ensemble) that sang polyphony (*canto de órgão*), doing so for "the Offices at our house on solemn days and on Sundays, as well as singing at Vespers and officiating at masses."[79] In that year there was a boy from Ambon named Dom João (described as the son of a Muslim ruler) in the college.[80] One wonders if he is the same youth mentioned in 1563 by Baltasar de Araújo (ca. 1524–73), who wrote from Ternate describing devotions in Hatiwi, Ambon, at which "an Ambonese boy who was raised [educated] in the College of St Paul in Goa spoke the litanies and everyone responded."[81]

Mascarenhas, writing on February 10, 1564, to the Jesuits of São Roque in Lisbon, describes the building of a church in Ternate, where he was based, giving details of its measurements. He states that the first mass celebrated there was sung.[82] In 1566, the viceroy of Goa, Antão de Noronha (1520–69), issued a normative document with the requirements for the maintenance of the fortress of Maluku (in Ternate). In this he mandated the employment of two choirboys—who had to be sons of Portuguese—in its church.[83] In February 1569, a stone church was proposed, since the previous one, constructed in 1563, was built of wood (with a roof of woven pandanus leaves); in June 1570, the new church was still being constructed.[84]

At this time, in Ambon, there is one intriguing mention of music in parts: the annual letter dated June 15, 1570, written again by Mascarenhas, reports the singing of litanies in polyphony ("ladainhas de cãoto d'orgão").[85] One wonders if this referred to composed or improvised polyphony. Catholic liturgical polyphony appears to have been a relatively new practice in the Malay world; in 1554, a Jesuit arriving in Melaka (from Goa) claimed that the performance of polyphony there was something "to which this land was unaccustomed."[86] This is a surprising comment, given that by that stage there had been at least four decades of Catholic observances in that Portuguese settlement (after its initial colonization in 1511). If true, it seems that the use of vocal polyphony in liturgical contexts arose in Southeast and East Asia in the second half of the sixteenth century—especially in centers with growing Catholic populations such as Macau, Manila, and Nagasaki—and perhaps not earlier, although monophonic chant (liturgical or devotional) certainly proliferated. In his letter of 1570, which includes a description of the arrival of a Jesuit in another town on Ambon, Mascarenhas also mentions *cantigas* (songs), without mentioning the style: "They sang other *cantigas* in praise of the Christians."[87] Later, he refers to the use of Moluccan instruments to accompany Christian songs, in Ulat on the island of Saparua (east of Ambon): "All [were] dancing and singing God's praises to the sound of the gongs and *tifa* that were being played by people who accompanied the father."[88]

However, some local practices were prohibited by the Jesuits. In the annual letter from Maluku (dated Ternate, April 8, 1612), Jorge da Fonseca (1558–1627) states: "Certain dances that are very popular in all Maluku have also been suppressed, [since] there are usually many offences against God, particularly when they are performed at night, which is most often the case."[89] No further details are given as to why these dances involved "offences," but based on general patterns of the description in missionary writings of this time, it is possible that these dances were perceived to have non-Christian religious connotations or that they displayed lascivious forms of expression.

Negative comments about performing arts arise elsewhere in Jesuit historiography. A visitation report by Manuel de Azevedo (1581–1650), written in Ternate in 1620 and sent to André Palmeiro (1569–1635), Visitor of the India Missions, refers to "excesses" of a number of priests, although Jacobs suggests that these reports were greatly exaggerated.[90] First was João Baptista (ca. 1557–before 1639), a *mestiço* (mixed-race) person born in Kochi. Azevedo claims that Baptista impoverished the house of the Jesuits through his lifestyle and by maintaining a number of boys as servants, "some of whom would sing to him, others to practice [music?] at night when he could not sleep, others as pages and scribes."[91] Then, two Italian Jesuits, Lorenzo Masonio (1555–1631) and Andrea Simi (1580–1634), met with his disapproval. Masonio, he wrote, raised five or six boys and dressed them in costly clothes and even saved money for their dowries.[92] He and Simi were apparently employing two Spaniards to teach boys to dance and sing, and one of these masters was being paid at great expense; the two Jesuits argued as to which of the teachers was better.[93] Azevedo claims that a salary and food were given to the two Spaniards, and that "rehearsals took place most of the day."[94]

Masonio, who later moved to Manila, appears to have been well regarded in the community; the seventeenth-century Jesuit historian Francisco Colín (1592–1660) claims that even the Dutch respected him and offered him gifts ("books, wine for masses, and other things, and gifts from Europe").[95] However, Azevedo described how both Masonio and Simi engaged in commercial trade to carry on paying for this activity.[96] Later, in a disapproving tone, he says that in the house, there were "ten or twelve *violas* and other very expensive [instruments], besides *pandeiros* [frame-drums], *cestros* [sestro, possibly implying another kind of drum] and other similar things."[97] Azevedo suggests that Simi be removed from his post and sent back to India, although Jacobs notes that this missionary remained on Ternate until 1633.[98]

The use of the term *viola* in the documents from Maluku is rare, and its meaning is ambiguous; used in this isolated instance with (as yet) no other examples for comparison in Maluku, it could perhaps mean either a plucked string instrument or a bowed viol. Yukimi Kambe, in her study of references to viols in sixteenth- and seventeenth-century Portuguese texts relating to the Jesuit missions in Japan, has shown that the terms *viola* and *viola de arco* were both used to refer to the viol but that sometimes *viola* by itself could imply another kind of instrument.[99] In another East Asian context, Corte-Real suggests that the use of the term by Mendes Pinto in the middle of the sixteenth century is "the first known reference to a Western guitar—the Portuguese viola—in China" (involving a musician named Gaspar de Meireles).[100] In the Malay-Indonesian archipelago, however, it could also more directly denote the violin, especially given that *biola* has long been a common Malay word for that instrument, which was adopted into local musical practices from the sixteenth century onward.[101] Thus, in Azevedo's 1620 letter from Ternate, we can only conclude broadly that it could be either a plucked or a bowed instrument, and possibly a violin.

The annual letter for 1623 of the Jesuit Province of Cochin describes festivities held in Maluku to celebrate the beatification of Francis Xavier (however, he was beatified in 1619 and canonized in 1622, and it is likely these festivities were held for his canonization). Although he had left Maluku in 1547, his reputation in the region was lasting and his presence was long remembered there. The author emphasized that these were the very beaches that Xavier himself walked on. A tragic play representing "some stages in the life and death of the Saint was performed with great perfection," with the costs covered by the *mestre do campo* (colonel) and the captain of the infantry. The writer continues, "That day a sung mass [*missa cantada*] was celebrated with the greatest possible solemnity, sung by the Franciscan friars. The poets of Maluku performed their hymns and songs [*letras e cançōes*] composed in praise of the Saint. Once the mass had finished, there commenced a devotional procession through the streets of Maluku, which had been appropriately adorned."[102] He gives no information about the musical structures of the mass, hymns, or songs; it is likely that the mass was celebrated in plainchant, but it is possible that polyphony was involved in other aspects of this event, given the mention of *cãoto d'orgão* (polyphony) in 1570, as discussed above. The devotional procession would surely also have been accompanied by music, vocal and instrumental, as was usual practice in Catholic missions of the time.

In an annual letter by Baltasar da Costa (1607–73), written from Kochi in November 1648 and sent to Rome, there is mention of activities in the Collegio de Maluco (Ternate). Although a secondhand description, Jacobs states that it "clearly show[s] that . . . some information had reached Cochin from Maluku."[103] The letter mentions penitential exercises and the singing of the Miserere on Fridays during Lent, followed by a "passo" procession (a Lenten procession related to the stations of the cross) "with its motet" ("com seu mutete [*sic*: motete]").[104] The next sentence continues, "There are many good voices; all the natives, soldiers, and the *mestre do campo* with the most captains come along."[105] Whether this singing involved polyphony is not specified; however, given the mention of a motet, the presence of music with multiple vocal parts is a strong possibility.

In this letter, there follows the mention of a confraternity devoted to the Child Jesus.[106] This group celebrated mass every Sunday of the year "with much solemnity of music and wax [candles], attended by all the brothers [members] with their lighted candles, which they also shared with those who were not members of the confraternity."[107] On the Feast of the Circumcision, the confraternity made "as fine, solemn, and lustrous a procession as could be seen in the most prominent cities of India."[108] Mention is made of the use of six richly decorated litters, presumably for images, among which were performed "curious dances and folias[?] etc." (*coriosas dansas e fulias ett.*); the feast concluded with games of skill.[109] Da Costa writes that the devotion of this confraternity was borne out in claims of apparitions of the Child Jesus during fighting with Muslims on Ternate, and he claims that the latter group would swear to seeing these apparitions too.[110]

Following the withdrawal of Spanish forces after 1662, a sizeable group of Christians from Ternate went in exile to the Philippines and took with them the image of the Child Jesus venerated by the confraternity; the Jesuit Pedro Murillo Velarde (1696–1753) made mention of this in 1749, observing that their devotion continued.[111] They settled in a town named Ternate (Murillo Velarde calls it Maragondong, which today is the adjacent municipality) in the province of Cavite, Luzon, where the image is still located.[112] From 1663 until today, there has been the annual tradition of ritually bathing the image on December 31 and changing its clothes on January 5, the eve of the Feast of the Circumcision.[113] The music history of this emigrant community of the Moluccan Catholic diaspora suggests potential for further research.

Even after the Spanish military left the region in 1662, there remained a Jesuit mission in operation in Siau, until 1677.[114] Apparently Francisco de Miedes (1622–74) and Diego de Esquivel (1623–65) composed linguistic treatises (*artes*) and compiled vocabularies (*vocabularios*); Jacobs notes, however, that Esquivel's writings on the language of Siau are lost.[115] According to Murillo Velarde, Miedes had to make shoes out of the covers of his books "so as not to say Mass barefoot";

in the last days of the mission in Siau, his greatest treasures were a few books and a box with papers.[116] A *relación* (report or account) written in Manila in June 1676 regarding the state of this mission the previous year mentions liturgical music, with reference to the lack of religious observance since the last official Jesuit visitation in 1670. The unnamed author points out encouragement for the increase in Catholic practice and refers to the first sung mass being celebrated at this time; from that point, various communities began to increase their religious practices, celebrating "sung masses on Saturdays and Sundays, the singing of the Salve Regina and the rosary on Saturday evenings, processions for [the Feast of] Corpus Christi, [observance of] Lent, services for Holy Week, homilies [*pláticas*], public sermons, and other [forms of devotion] that had not [yet] started."[117]

A *relación* attributed to Manuel Español (1639–84) and written a few months later—probably in Siau during August, but certainly in 1676—recounts the events of the preceding twelve months in the Jesuit mission. It asserts that onlookers had a more positive reaction to Catholic ceremony than to Calvinist rituals. The author states:

> Luckily some of the native heretics [i.e., converts to Calvinism] of these parts, having seen by chance the [Catholic] church ceremonies and the celebration of the feasts and divine offices, the pomp of the altar, and hearing the music (such as it is), have said that the Calvinist law that the Dutch teach them does not have an impression on them because they do not see anything [and the Dutch] teach them in a disorderly way, and [all] this in a strange language that the majority of the people do not understand.[118]

Writing of Talaud, the author also reports on the previous "lack of singers" ("falta de cantores") but mentions that despite this the procession for Holy Week took place, with the "Father singing the litany and his servants responding, concluding with his sermon on the Passion."[119] Intriguingly, he also makes mention of harp playing in Cayuhuse (Kauhise, Siau), in what seems to be the only reference to this instrument in the Jesuit documentation for the Maluku region in its broadest sense. Given that there is no earlier mention of the harp, we may wonder whether its use there was incipient; Español writes that "major feast days did not lack their little bit of harp music."[120] This poignant comment marks the twilight of the first period of Jesuit missions in the area.

MUSIC IN THE *CONQUISTA DE LAS ISLAS MALUCAS* (1609) BY LEONARDO DE ARGENSOLA

The manuscript sources just mentioned, produced in the final third of the seventeenth century, present a marked contrast to a triumphalist narrative printed in Spain almost eight decades earlier. In 1609, the book *Conquista de las Islas Malucas* by Bartolomé Leonardo de Argensola (1562–1632) was published in Madrid.[121] Leonardo de Argensola had been invited to write it following news of the 1606 conquest of Ternate by Spanish forces led by Pedro de Acuña.[122] This author, however, did not travel to Asia. As John Villiers has pointed out, "Although he had already established a certain reputation as a historian by that date, he had no special knowledge or first-hand experience of the region, or of recent events that had taken place in it."[123] A royally appointed historian, Leonardo de Argensola had access to many manuscript sources sent or carried to Spain and Portugal by eyewitnesses in Maluku, as well as published accounts of voyages and a range of correspondence. Carmen Nocentelli describes his work as "a synthesis of totalizing ambitions—a veritable summa of geographic, historical, and ethnographic information drawn from a vast array of sources including Barros's *Décadas da Ásia*, Maffei's *Historiarum Indicarum*, and Linschoten's *Itinerario*."[124] Around a century later, French (1706), English (1708), and German (1710) translations were published.[125]

In early modern Europe, the *Conquista* thus appeared to have functioned as a far-reaching and long-lasting piece of historiography on Maluku. Nocentelli further asserts that "thanks to this wide circulation, Argensola's *Conquista* actively participated in, and contributed to, a transnational discourse that shaped Europe's view of Asia throughout the seventeenth century and beyond."[126] The popularity of this account possibly inspired a number of theater pieces, including the Spanish play *Conquista de las Malucas* (Conquest of the Moluccas) by Melchor Fernández de León (dates unknown), published in Madrid in 1679.[127] This work, which includes numerous musical moments (with *flautas* [recorders] and *panderos* [frame drums or tambourines], and especially *caxas* [drums] and *clarines* [trumpets]), remained sufficiently popular to be republished in 1762, in Valencia, as *Comedia famosa: La conquista de las Malucas* (Famous comedy: The conquest of the Moluccas).[128]

Leonardo de Argensola's text, despite its secondhand nature, provides some intriguing data regarding sound-art practices of Maluku and descriptions of music in interactions between the Moluccans, the Spanish, and the Dutch. His book is historiographically valuable for the study of reception, in terms of demonstrating what kinds of information and discourse about Moluccan cultural practices were available to readers in early modern Europe. It is worth briefly surveying some examples here (and to retain an early modern flavor, I quote from the 1708 English translation). A remarkable level of detail emerges in the descriptions made at a far geographical remove, based on the primary sources available to the author, and reinterpreted by him. For example, Leonardo de Argensola writes: "Instead of a Bell, there hangs up the holy great flat Drum, which they beat with Sticks; tho each Mosque has a great Bell, without a Clapper, which they strike with a Stone, or piece of Iron, when requisite."[129] At the return of the Sultan of Ternate following his victories in Tidore, the text states, "At his Arrival, he was received with Trumpets, Kettle-Drums, and Basons [gongs] they beat on, and with Songs they make for such like Occasions."[130]

Of particular note was music in maritime contexts, especially the ensembles that travelled aboard the watercraft of Maluku. Leonardo de Argensola describes them as follows:

> In the *Philippine* Islands they give the Name of *Carcoas* to a sort of Vessels that use Oars, open, and bigger than our Barks, and are Steer'd by two Rudders, the one ahead, and the other astern. The *Ternates* call'd them [the boats] *Janguas*, which differ from the *Carcoas* only in having two Half-Moons of Wood, Painted, or Guilt, rising above the Keel at the Head and Poop. About 100 Men Row in each of them, to the sound of a Tabor, and a Bell.[131]

He earlier describes this kind of music as "barbarous."[132] Later in the narrative, he mentions similar craft at Ambon and Dutch reactions to Ambonese singing:

> The Admiral of *Amboyna* came with three of these Vessels full of arm'd Men, to see the *Dutch*, with a Noise of Kittle-Drums [*sic*], and Brass Basons hanging on the Musitian's Left-Shoulder, and striking them with the Right-Hand, as they do the Tabors in *Spain*. They sang their set Airs [*sus canciones acordadas*], understood by none but the Native *Amboyneses*, tho' attentively listen'd to by the *Dutch*, for their Strangeness. The Slaves also sang to the Noise of their Oars.[133]

Here the 1708 English translation gives the description "*Musick*" in the margin, although that keyword does not appear in the Spanish original. Clearly the early eighteenth-century translator or publisher thought it a passage worthy to point out to the reader with this keyword.

Later in the narrative, the author mentions a musical incident following the marriage of the Sultan of Tidore to a princess of Bacan: "When they were at Sea, they heard the new marryed King's Bagpipes, Basons, Trumpets, and Kettle-Drums."[134] Here "bagpipes" (*gaytas*) perhaps referred to *serunais*, given that both were reed instruments, with a Spanish eyewitness originally using a familiar term to describe what he heard. On another occasion, the description of the music in the sultan of Ternate's retinue is "the Noise of his Brass Basons, Flat Tabors, Guns, Shouts, and *Persian* Songs" (no explanation is given for the last category).[135] Shortly after, following a show of military strength to the Dutch (which included the firing of guns and "clattering of Bells [gongs]"), "they sang Verses, as they do to denote Peace, in the Malay Tongue, so they call the Language of Malaca, whence it was convey'd to the Moluccos."[136] Citing a Dutch author (possibly Jan Huyghen van Linschoten or a writer associated with the voyage of Jacob Cornelis van Neck and Wybrand van Warwijck), he also describes prayers in the mosque at Banda, even giving a romanized Arabic text and its translation.[137] While it is clear that this is a synthesis of ethnographic material drawn from a number of sources, further intertextual analysis of the book of Leonardo de Argensola may reveal additional points of detail about intercultural observations in this period.

It may also indicate more about the ways that data emanating from eyewitnesses were reformulated, edited, and represented in travel literature and chronicles about Maluku.

CONCLUSION

Writing in 2014, Rein Spoorman noted that "despite the Moluccan archipelago being renowned for its musical richness, to date little substantial research has been carried out on its music in context" and cited Kartomi's 1994 article for this observation.[138] While his mention of scholarly lacunae specifically concerns "music in context," a similar statement could be made about studies of archival sources for the historiography of musics in early modern Maluku, as well as that of adjacent regions. The three types of Iberian sources examined in this chapter not only demonstrate the complexity of intercultural encounters and engagements in sixteenth- and seventeenth-century Maluku but also make clear the challenges that musicologists and historians face in interpreting them. Musical practices and the performing arts in general were undergoing rapid change as multiple cultures converged in this part of the archipelago. This was especially the case for the forms of sonic expressions associated with religious devotion and observance, and with ceremonies linked to politics and social status. Further research could shed more light on the story of multiple individuals and communities who moved from Maluku to other parts of Southeast Asia (and even South Asia) in this period, including the town of Ternate in Luzon, the Philippines. The Iberian sources outlined here potentially offer new perspectives and data for ongoing critical interpretation of diverse musical pasts in early modern Maluku.

ACKNOWLEDGMENTS

This essay is dedicated to Margaret J. Kartomi in gratitude for the collegiality, friendship, and encouragement she has generously offered me and countless other scholars over the course of many years. For the present study, I am particularly inspired by the pioneering work that she and Hidris Kartomi carried out on the music cultures of Maluku in the 1990s. I also want to thank Anna Maria Busse Berger and Henry Spiller sincerely for inviting me to participate in their project "Toward a Music History of the Indonesian Archipelago," funded by the Henry Luce Foundation's Asia Program, and Dustin Wiebe for his enthusiasm and support. Research for this chapter has been carried out within the framework of the project "Poder y Representaciones Culturales en la Época Moderna," financed by the Agencia Estatal de Investigación, Government of Spain (PID2020–115565GB-C21).

NOTES

1. See the following works by Margaret J. Kartomi: "Appropriation of Music and Dance in Contemporary Ternate and Tidore," *Studies in Music* 26 (1992): 85–95; "Revival of Feudal Music, Dance and Ritual in the Former 'Spice Islands' of Ternate and Tidore," in *Culture and Society in New Order Indonesia*, ed. Virginia Matheson Hooker (Kuala Lumpur: Oxford University Press, 1993), 184–211; "Is Maluku Still Musicological *Terra Incognita?* An Overview of the Music-Cultures of the Province of Maluku," *Journal of Southeast Asian Studies* 25, no. 1 (1994): 141–71; and "Maluku," in *The Garland Encyclopedia of World Music*, vol. 4, *Southeast Asia*, ed. Terry Miller and Sean Williams (New York: General Music, 1998), 812–22.

2. Kartomi, "Is Maluku Still Musicological *Terra Incognita?*" Kartomi also produced a sound recording, *Music of Indonesia: Maluku and North Maluku*, released in 2003 by the CD label Celestial Harmonies (0000DKFZ7). Kartomi referred to publications from the late nineteenth century by Baron G. W. W. C. van Hoëvell (1882) and W. Joest (1892), an encyclopedia article by J. F. Snelleman (1918), and work on the Kai Islands by Jaap Kunst (1945) in "Is Maluku Still Musicological *Terra Incognita?*," 144. Tilman Seebass later pointed out another example, an article of 1840 on musics of the islands of Sunda and Maluku in the *Allgemeine musikalische Zeitung*: G. W. Fink, "Notizen über Musik und Gesänge der malaiischen Eingebornen auf den sundischen und molukkischen Inseln (Ostindien)," *Allgemeine musikalische Zeitung* 52 (December 23, 1840): cols 1057–63. See Tilman Seebass, "Presence and Absence of Portuguese Musical Elements in Indonesia: An Essay on the Mechanisms of Music Acculturation," in *Portugal and the World: The Encounter of Cultures in Music*, ed. Salwa El-Shawan Castelo-Branco, 245 (Lisbon: Publicações Dom Quixote, 1997). Seabass lists the authorship of this work as anonymous.

3. François Valentijn, *Oud en nieuw Oost-Indiën, vervattende een naaukeurige en uitvoerige verhandelinge van Nederlands mogentheyd in die gewesten, benevens eene wydluftige beschryvinge der Moluccos, Amboina, Banda, Timor, en Solor, Java, en alle de eylanden onder dezelve landbestieringen behoorende, het Nederlands comptoir op Suratte, en de levens der Groote Mogols*, 5 vols (Amsterdam: J. van Braam en G. Onder de Linden, 1724–26). See Kartomi, "Is Maluku Still Musicological *Terra Incognita?*," 144; and Kartomi, "Maluku," 812. The second volume of Valentijn's work contains an extensive description of music on Ambon, based on his first-hand observations—including two engravings of music and dance performance, with detailed depictions of instruments—and some secondhand descriptions of music in north Maluku. He treats "musical instruments, dances and songs" of Ambon in vol. 2, 162–65. The illustrations are in figure 38, on two plates: one between 164–65 and the second at the top of 165. During his two periods of employment with the Vereenigde Oostindische Compagnie (VOC, Dutch East India Company) in 1686–94 and 1705–13, Valentijn was based mostly in Ambon. Leonard Y. Andaya notes that "although he had never been to north Maluku, he relied on travel descriptions, VOC documents, and personal contacts to write his extensive account." Andaya, *The World of Maluku: Eastern Indonesia in the Early Modern Period* (Honolulu: University of Hawai'i Press, 1993), 20. As Siegfried Huigen has pointed out, Valentijn was an antiquarian and well versed in literature of comparative ethnography; on Ambon, he even related the name of the local drum *tifa* to the Hebrew word *toph*. See his chapter "Antiquarian Ambonese: François Valentyn's Comparative Ethnography," in *The Dutch Trading Companies as Knowledge Networks*, ed. Siegfried Huigen, Jan L. de Jong, and Elmer Kolfin (Leiden: Brill, 2010), 188; Valentijn, *Oud en nieuw Oost-Indiën*, vol. 2, 162. Ian Woodfield also highlighted that Valentijn was a musician and had a violin with him in Ambon. Woodfield, *English Musicians in the Age of Exploration* (Stuyvesant: Pendragon Press, 1995), 247–48.

4. Kartomi, "Is Maluku Still Musicological *Terra Incognita?*," 144.

5. Kartomi, "Is Maluku Still Musicological *Terra Incognita?*," 155. Alfred Russel Wallace writes of the "old Christian population" in Ambon: "Though now Protestants, they preserve at feasts and weddings the processions and music of the Catholic Church, curiously mixed up with the gongs and dances of the aborigines of the country. Their language has still much more Portuguese than Dutch

in it, although they have been in close communication with the latter nation for more than two hundred and fifty years." Alfred Russel Wallace, *The Malay Archipelago: The Land of the Orang-Utan and the Bird of Paradise. A Narrative of Travel, with Studies of Man and Nature*, 2nd ed., 2 vols (London: Macmillan, 1869), 1:300. Kartomi also wrote of "court arts in times past" on Ternate and Tidore—about which she learnt from her informants that "soldiers who performed military or protocol dances wore yellow coats, white trousers with side stripes, with Portuguese-style plumes in their red-trimmed yellow hats." Kartomi, "Revival of Feudal Music, Dance and Ritual," 191–92.

6. Benjamin L. Moseley, "An Ambonese Account on the Arrival of the Portuguese" (blog post), November 8, 2019, https://benjaminlmoseley.com/2019/11/08/an-ambonese-account-on-the-arrival-of-the-portuguese/. A bilingual Malay–Dutch edition of this is Ridjali, *Historie van Hitu: Een Ambonse geschiedenis uit de zeventiende eeuw*, ed. and trans. Hans Straver, Christiaan van Fraassen, and Jan van der Putten (Utrecht: Landelijk Steunpunt Educatie Molukkers, 2004). See also G. L. Koster, "How Malay Is the Ambonese Chronicle Hikayat Tanah Hitu?," Research Gate, July 7, 2021, www.researchgate .net/publication/353039754_How_Malay_is_the_Ambonese_chronicle_Hikayat_Tanah_Hitu. On the question of language, Galvão writes in ca. 1544 that "at present the Malayan language has come into vogue; and most of them speak it and avail themselves of it throughout the entire region, where it is like Latin in Europe." Hubert Jacobs, ed., *A Treatise on the Moluccas (c. 1544): Probably the Preliminary Version of Antonio Galvão's Lost História das Molucas Edited, Annotated, and Translated into English from the Portuguese Manuscript in the Archivo General de Indias, Seville by Hubert Th. Th. M. Jacobs* (Rome; St. Louis: Jesuit Historical Institute; St. Louis University, 1971), 74 (Portuguese), 75 (English). Ridjali's work has been studied by Zacharias J. Manusama, G. L. Koster, Jan van der Putten, and others; a Dutch translation was published in 2004 (cited above), and an English translation is forthcoming. Zacharias J. Manusama, "Hikayat Tanah Hitu: Historie en sociale structuur van de Ambonse eilanden in het algemeen en van Uli Hitu in het bijzonder tot het midden der zeventiende eeuw" (PhD diss., University of Leiden, 1977); Koster, "How Malay Is the Ambonese Chronicle Hikayat Tanah Hitu?"; Koster, "*Hikayat Tanah Hitu*: A Rare Local Source of 16th and 17th Century Moluccan History," *Review of Culture* 28 (2008): 133–42; Jan van der Putten, "In the Fringe of the Page: The Malay Tale of Hitu from Its Margins," in *Teks, naskah dan kelisanan: Festschrift untuk Prof. Achadiati Ikram*, ed. T. Pudjiastuti, T. Christomy, and A. Ikram (Depok: Yayasan Pernaskahan Nusantara, 2011), 399–416; Jan van der Putten, "A Collection of Unstandardised Consistencies? The Use of Jawi Script in a Few Early Malay Manuscripts from the Moluccas," in *Creating Standards: Interactions with Arabic Script in 12 Manuscript Cultures*, ed. Dmitry Bondarev, Alessandro Gori, and Lameen Souag (Berlin and Boston: De Gruyter, 2019), 217–36.

7. "Then he [i.e. Dom Duarte] landed and entered the battlefield as fifes, drums and shawms played a variety of tunes. And [the Portuguese] then hoisted their banners and the Muslim warriors did likewise. Their commanders and paladins took up their positions. And the two sides stood facing each other like people who are praying turned in the direction of Mecca. And then both sides raised a battle-cry which sounded like the rumbling of thunder in the sky." English translation in Koster, "How Malay Is the Ambonese Chronicle Hikayat Tanah Hitu?," 18 (the square brackets and their text are from Koster). For original Malay text see Ridjali, *Historie van Hitu*, Mal. [Malay] 20–29, quoted in Koster, 18n29. It includes a rare use in Malay classical texts of the word *caramela*, which appears to be adopted directly from the Portuguese term for shawm: *charamela*. Ridjali's use of this term seems to be unique within the corpus of pre-modern Malay texts compiled in the Malay Concordance Project, Australian National University: https://mcp.anu.edu.au/, consulted May 29, 2022.

8. Andaya, *The World of Maluku*, 9–22, "The Sources" (quotation on 9). An earlier survey of Portuguese sources was given by Charles Ralph Boxer, "Some Portuguese Sources for Indonesian Historiography," in *An Introduction to Indonesian Historiography*, ed. Soedjatmoko, Muhammad Ali, G. J. Resink, and G. McT. Kahin (Ithaca: Cornell University Press, 1965), 217–33.

9. See Seebass, "Presence and Absence of Portuguese Musical Elements in Indonesia"; Margaret Kartomi, "Kapri: A Synthesis of Malay and Portuguese Music on the West Coast of North Sumatra," in *Cultures and Societies of North Sumatra*, ed. Rainer Carle (Berlin: Dietrich Reimer Verlag, 1987),

351–93; Kartomi, "Portuguese Influence on Indonesian Music" in *Festschrift Christoph-Hellmut Mahling zum 65. Geburtstag*, ed. Axel Beer, Kristina Pfarr, and Wolfgang Ruf (Tutzing: Hans Schneider, 1997), 657–66; and Kartomi, "A influência portuguesa na música da Indonésia e da Malásia," *Revista de Cultura* 26 (1997): 27–38, www.icm.gov.mo/rc/viewer/30026/1846. Seebass's 1997 chapter included a useful bibliography of ninety-eight scholarly and reference works published from 1840 onward that related to "Portuguese influence on Indonesian music": Seebass, "Presence and Absence of Portuguese Musical Elements in Indonesia," 245–51. Studies in the last two decades include a number of essays by Christian Storch; see "The Influence of Portuguese Musical Culture in Southeast Asia in the Sixteenth and Seventeenth Centuries," in *Portuguese and Luso-Asian Legacies, 1511–2011*, vol. 2, *Culture and Identity in the Luso-Asian World: Tenacities and Plasticities*, ed. Laura Jarnagin (Singapore: Institute of Southeast Asian Studies, 2012), 208–22; "Wege portugiesischer Musikkultur nach Südostasien im Kontext der europäischen Expansionspolitik des 16. und 17. Jahrhunderts," in *Migration und Identität: Wanderbewegungen und Kulturkontakte in der Musikgeschichte* (Kassel: Bärenreiter-Verlag, 2013), 69–83; and "How the Pagans Became 'Convinced' about Christianity: Four Conclusions on the Relationship between Music and the Missions in Early Colonialism," in *Música discurso poder*, ed. Maria do Rosário Girão Santos and Elisa Maria Lessa (Ribeirão: Edições Húmus, 2012), 221–34.

10. Triyono Bramantyo has pointed to the significance of the area, writing about liturgical music in sixteenth-century Maluku and treating it in comparison with the Jesuit mission in sixteenth-century Japan; see his article "Early Acceptance of Western Music in Indonesia and Japan," *Arts and Social Sciences Journal* 9, no. 5 (2018): 2. Recently, Juan Ruiz Jiménez has discussed music at the baptism ceremony of a princess of Bacan in 1559 as part of his Interconnected Cities series for the website *Paisajes sonoros históricos (c.1200–c.1800)*. See his "Bautismo de la princesa de Bacan en la isla de Ternate (1559)," *Paisajes sonoros históricos (c.1200–c.1800)*, January 8, 2021, http://historicalsoundscapes .com/evento/1256/ternate/es.

11. See Kartomi, "Is Maluku Still Musicological *Terra Incognita?*," 144; and Kartomi, "Maluku," 812. Also see Woodfield, *English Musicians in the Age of Exploration*, 247–48. Stretching the historiography of music in the region back to the late sixteenth century, Woodfield examined English sources as well as Dutch texts, considering especially the ways in which music framed Sir Francis Drake's (ca. 1540–96) encounters with the rulers of Ternate in 1579 (see 5–6, 103); he also identified a detail of an engraving from 1601 that shows a trumpeter with the Dutch expedition of Jacob van Neck (1564–1638) to Ternate in 1598 (see 173).

12. As described by Margaret Kartomi in 1993, Ibu Syahrinsad Syah (daughter of the forty-seventh sultan of Ternate) informed her that the name of a hunting dance, *betiado*, "is based on a forgotten Portuguese word." Kartomi, "Revival of Feudal Music, Dance and Ritual," 195, 209n22. This word is yet to be traced.

13. Historians including Antonio C. Campo López, Jean-Noël Sánchez Pons, Jorge Mojarro, Bondan Kanumuyoso, and others, have recently offered new perspectives on primary texts relating to Spanish activities in the "Spice Islands." See chapters and editions of primary source documents in Javier Serrano Avilés and Jorge Mojarro Romero, eds., *En el archipiélago de la especiería: España y Molucas en los siglos XVI y XVII* (Madrid: Desperta Ferro, 2021).

14. Andaya, *The World of Maluku*, 7; see also 47.

15. Adolf Heuken, SJ, "Catholic Converts in the Moluccas, Minahasa and Sangihe-Talaud, 1512–1680," in *A History of Christianity in Indonesia*, ed. Jan Sihar Aritonang and Karel Steenbrink (Leiden: Brill, 2008), 23.

16. Andaya, *The World of Maluku*, 58.

17. Interestingly, the Bolognese traveler Ludovico di Varthema (ca. 1470–1517) writes of visiting Maluku some years earlier. His travelogue, published in 1510, does not mention music or sound in his brief account of "the Spice Islands," although he does describe music and sound in other places. See Paola Dessì, "L'itinerario sonoro di Lodovico di Verthema," in *Per una storia dei popoli senza note*, Heuresis. XIII: Sezione Di Arti, Musica, Spettacolo, No. 9 (Bologna: Cooperativa Libraria Universitaria

(CLUEB), 2010), 105–11. From 1666, the Dutch, as Andaya states, were "the sole surviving European nation in Maluku." Andaya, *The World of Maluku*, 156.

18. Hubert Th. Th. M. Jacobs, *Documenta Malucensia: I (1542–1577)* (Rome: Jesuit Historical Institute, 1974), 11*–12*.

19. Andaya, *The World of Maluku*, 58.

20. Jacobs, *Documenta Malucensia*: I, 11*–12*.

21. Kartomi, "Revival of Feudal Music," 186; Woodfield, *English Musicians*, 232.

22. See Heuken's detailed study of the history of Catholic conversion in the Maluku region in the sixteenth and seventeenth centuries. Heuken, "Catholic Converts," 23–72. See also his book *Be My Witness* to the Ends of the Earth! The Catholic Church in Indonesia before the 19th Century (Jakarta: Cipta Loka Caraka, 2002).

23. Francisco Colín gave a description of the Maluku region in his *Labor evangelica* (originally published Madrid, 1663). Colín and Pastells, *Labor evangélica*, 1:105–15.

24. Jacobs, *Documenta Malucensia: I; Documenta Malucensia: II (1577–1606)* (Rome: Jesuit Historical Institute, 1980); *Documenta Malucensia: III (1606–1682)* (Rome: Jesuit Historical Institute, 1984). From here I will refer to these three volumes as *DM I*, *DM II*, and *DM III*. See also his overview in "Indonesia: Antigua CJ (1546–1677)," in Diccionario histórico de la Compañía de Jesús: biográfico-temático, ed. Charles E. O'Neill and Joaquín María Domínguez (Rome and Madrid: Institutum Historicum, S. I. [Societatis Iesu], Universidad Pontificia Comillas, 2001), 2015–17.

25. I am not considering here the three French texts and one Italian text that survives of the account of Antonio Pigafetta (ca. 1491–ca. 1531), from his visit in 1521, as I discuss that elsewhere. See David R. M. Irving, "Global Soundscapes from the First Voyage of Circumnavigation, 1519–1522," in *Soundscapes of the Early Modern Hispanophone and Lusophone Worlds*, ed. Victor Sierra Matute (New York: Routledge, 2025), 287–312. Nor will I discuss another well-known sixteenth-century text, the *Boxer Codex* (written in Spanish in 1590s Manila), as it contains only one tiny mention of the music of Maluku, citing gongs (*campanas*) and drums (*tambores*) in festivities for Eid al-Fitr, following Ramadan. See Jorge Mojarro, "Los molucos en el *Códice Boxer*, 1592," in *En el archipiélago de la especiería: España y Molucas en los siglos XVI y XVII*, ed. Javier Serrano Avilés and Jorge Mojarro Romero (Madrid: Desperta Ferro, 2021), 293. For critical studies of the source from various perspectives, see Manel Ollé and Joan-Pau Rubiés, eds., *El Códice Boxer: Etnografía colonial e hibridismo cultural en las Islas Filipinas* (Barcelona: Publicacions i Edicions de la Universitat de Barcelona, 2020). The famous *Suma Oriental* (1512–15) of Tomé Pires (c. 1468–1524/40) contains interesting ethnographic details in his description of the Maluku region but no data specifically on music. Tomé Pires, *The Suma Oriental of Tomé Pires: An Account of the East, from the Red Sea to Japan, Written in Malacca and India in 1512–1515*, ed. and trans. Armando Cortesão, 2 vols (London: Hakluyt Society, 1944), 1:205–22.

26. Maria de São José Corte-Real, "Music in Fernão Mendes Pinto's *Peregrinação*," in *Portugal and the World: The Encounter of Cultures in Music*, ed. Salwa El-Shawan Castelo-Branco (Lisbon: Publicações Dom Quixote, 1997), 195–200.

27. See Jean-Nöel Sánchez Pons, "Misón y dimisión: Las Molucas en el siglo XVII entre Jesuitas portugueses y españoles," in *Jesuitas e imperios de Ultramar: Siglos XVI–XX*, ed. Alexandre Coello de la Rosa, Javier Burrieza, and Doris Moreno (Madrid: Sílex, 2012), 81–101.

28. Maria Odete Soares Martins has distinguished between coerced and voluntary baptisms in her book *A missionação nas Molucas no século XVI: Contributo para o estudo da acção dos Jesuítas no Oriente* (Lisbon: Centro de história de Além-Mar, Universidade Nova de Lisboa, Faculdade de Ciências Sociais e Humanas, 2002). See also Brett Charles Baker, "Indigenous-Driven Mission: Reconstructing Religious Change in Sixteenth-Century Maluku" (PhD diss., Australian National University, 2012).

29. See George Schurhammer's preface to Jacobs, *A Treatise on the Moluccas*, viii.

30. Jacobs, *A Treatise on the Moluccas*.

31. Jacobs asserts, for instance, that "the catalogue of Malay and Moluccan words that can be composed [i.e., extracted] from this document may be one of the earliest extant, or even *the* earliest

extant," noting that Pigafetta's earlier wordlist was not representative of vocabulary from the Maluku region; *A Treatise on the Moluccas*, 25. Jacobs gives a glossary of "Indonesian and other Asian words" in this source, with cross-references to Galvão's text, on 367–76. Giuseppe Marcocci has pointed out that other chroniclers of the sixteenth century, including João de Barros and Garcia de Orta, clearly relied on the work of Galvão. Giuseppe Marcocci, *The Globe on Paper: Writing Histories of the World in Renaissance Europe and the Americas*, trans. Richard Bates (New York: Oxford University Press, 2020), 60.

32. Other Portuguese chroniclers who wrote about Maluku include Fernão Lopes de Castanheda, João de Barros (who did not travel to Asia), Gaspar Correia, Diogo do Couto, and Gabriel Rebelo. For a recent overview of these texts, see Baker, "Indigenous-Driven Mission," 15–26. Rebelo, who arrived there after Galvão had left, wrote a report titled "Informação sobre as Malucas," which survives in two manuscript sources. Andaya, *The World of Maluku*, 15; and Boxer, "Some Portuguese Sources for Indonesian Historiography," 222. The two texts appear in Artur Basílio de Sá, ed. *Documentação para a história das missões do padroado português do Oriente. Insulíndia 3.º vol. (1563–1567)* (Lisbon: Agencia Geral do Ultramar: Divisão de Publicações e Biblioteca, 1955), 192–343 and 345–508. However, there are fewer mentions of music or the performing arts in Rebelo's account. See, for instance, descriptions of festivities and instruments on 356, 357, and 384.

33. Jacobs, *A Treatise on the Moluccas*, 335n2.

34. Jacobs, *A Treatise on the Moluccas*, 86 (Portuguese), 87 (English).

35. Kartomi, "Is Maluku Still Musicological *Terra Incognita?*," 158.

36. Jacobs, *A Treatise on the Moluccas*, 149 and 151 (English), 150 (Portuguese). The square brackets are given by Jacobs.

37. Jacobs, *A Treatise on the Moluccas*, 158 (Portuguese), 159 (English). The square brackets are given by Jacobs. Many decades later, in the 1590s, Francis Drake described a similar kind of waterborne royal greeting on his arrival at Ternate and mentioned that the sultan "seemed to be much delighted" by the English musical performance. See Woodfield, *English Musicians*, 103.

38. Jacobs, *A Treatise on the Moluccas*, 110 (Portuguese), 111 (English). Insertions in square brackets are mine. The original text regarding the pitch of the gongs states, "ffazem [*sic*] comtratenor e tipre." I differ from Jacobs's speculation on the designation of pitch ranges. He writes: "We suppose that, instead of *contratenor*, *contrabaixo* was meant, this being the opposite of *tipre*; thus the phrase fits in better with the following *mores . . . e menores*" (339).

39. Jacobs, *A Treatise on the Moluccas*, 166 (Portuguese), 167 (English), 182 (Portuguese), 183 (English).

40. Jacobs, *A Treatise on the Moluccas*, 118–21. Such a claim was also made by Pigafetta several decades earlier, with reference to Java, in his account of the Magellan/Elcano voyage. See Irving, "Global Soundscapes."

41. Jacobs, *A Treatise on the Moluccas*, 111 (Portuguese), 112 (English).

42. Kartomi states that they were "known in colonial times as the Alifuru people." Kartomi, "Is Maluku Still Musicological *Terra Incognita?*," 141; Jacobs, *A Treatise on the Moluccas*, 367.

43. Kartomi, "Revival of Feudal Music, Dance and Ritual," 202. A recording by Kartomi is available on YouTube: "Tari Lego-Lego—Music of the Court of Ternate," YouTube video, September 25, 2014, https://youtu.be/IJBhuUV65nU (accessed June 11, 2022). This is from the album *Music of Indonesia*, cited above.

44. Kartomi, "Is Maluku Still Musicological *Terra Incognita?*," 151.

45. Jacobs, *A Treatise on the Moluccas*, 142 (Portuguese), 143 (English).

46. Jacobs, *A Treatise on the Moluccas*, 144 (Portuguese), 145 (English).

47. Jacobs, *A Treatise on the Moluccas*, 146 (Portuguese), 147 (English).

48. Jacobs, *A Treatise on the Moluccas*, 146 (Portuguese), 147 (English).

49. Jacobs, *A Treatise on the Moluccas*, 114 (Portuguese), 115 (English).

50. Jacobs, *A Treatise on the Moluccas*, 304–7.

51. Jacobs, *A Treatise on the Moluccas*, 104 (Portuguese), 105 (English). Jacobs notes that "*sinos* generally means *bells*, but here it evidently stands for the famous Javanese *gongs*" (338).

52. Jacobs, *A Treatise on the Moluccas*, 140 (Portuguese), 141 (English). The point about cloves being exchanged for commodities is also mentioned in chapter 24, 130 (Portuguese) and 131 (English).

53. Jacobs, *A Treatise on the Moluccas*, 74–85.

54. The square brackets and the text they contain in the English translation are given by Jacobs. Jacobs, *A Treatise on the Moluccas*, 84 (Portuguese), 85 (English). See also Marcocci, *The Globe on Paper*, 60.

55. Jacobs, *A Treatise on the Moluccas*, 122 (Portuguese), 123 (English).

56. Jacobs, *A Treatise on the Moluccas*, 230 (Portuguese), 231 (English).

57. Jacobs, *A Treatise on the* Moluccas, 236 (Portuguese), 237 (English); 242 (Portuguese), 243 (English).

58. Jacobs, *A Treatise on the Moluccas*, 248 (Portuguese), 249 (English).

59. Jacobs, *A Treatise on the Moluccas*, 296–99.

60. English translation from Francis Xavier, *The Letters and Instructions of Francis Xavier*, trans. and ed. M. Joseph Costelloe (St. Louis, MO: Institute of Jesuit Sources, 1992), 171. For original Spanish text, see *DM I*, 35. The last seven words, given in italics in the translation, are originally in Latin ("inveni magnam gratiam coram oculis eorum"). Jacobs suggests that the reader compare this quotation to Genesis 18:3 in the Bible (*A Treatise on the Moluccas*, 35n16).

61. Andaya, *The World of Maluku*, 127, 128.

62. Francisco García, *Vida y milagros de San Francisco Xavier, de la Compañia de Jesus, apostol de las Indias* (Madrid: Iuan Garcia Infanzon, 1672), 113.

63. This is also noted by Corte-Real, "Music in Fernão Mendes Pinto's *Peregrinação*," 200.

64. *DM I*, 224. For biographies see *DM I*, 31*–32* (Vieira) and 33*–34* (Osório).

65. *DM I*, 226.

66. *DM I*, 226.

67. *DM I*, 226. See also Baker, "Indigenous-Driven Mission," 255n110.

68. For his biography, see *DM I*, 37*–38*.

69. *DM I*, 537.

70. Ruiz Jiménez, "Bautismo." One text reads: "Diante a cruz hia huma boa capella de cantores que aqui hay muyto bons"; the other reads: "mais avante huma capella de boa musica com canticos de Benedictus competente à festa." *DM I*, 272. For a description and critique of the two texts see *DM I*, 250–51.

71. *DM I*, 272. See also Ruiz Jiménez, "Bautismo."

72. For studies of the singing of the Christian doctrine and catechism in early modern Catholic evangelization (especially by the Jesuits), see Daniele V. Filippi, "A Sound Doctrine: Early Modern Jesuits and the Singing of the Catechism," *Early Music History* 34 (2015): 1–43; and Daniele V. Filippi, "'Catechismum Modulans Docebat': Teaching the Doctrine through Singing in Early Modern Catholicism," in *Listening to Early Modern Catholicism: Perspectives from Musicology*, ed. Daniele V. Filippi and Michael Noone (Leiden: Brill, 2017), 129–48.

73. Baker, "Indigenous-Driven Mission," 255, citing *DM I*, 268.

74. *DM I*, 416. For a biography of Magalhães see *DM I*, 40*–41*.

75. *DM II*, 547. For a biography of Fernandes see *DM II*, 39*–41*.

76. *DM II*, 547.

77. *DM III*, 64.

78. *DM I*, 122n12; Bramantyo, "Early Acceptance of Western Music," 2. On the roll, Jacobs cites Josef Wicki, *Documenta Indica I* (1540–1549) (Rome: Monumenta Historica Societatis Iesu, 1948), 120.

79. Maria Isabel Lopes Monteiro, "Instrumentos e instrumentistas de sopro no século XVI português" (Master's thesis, Universidade Nova de Lisboa, 2010), 99. Monteiro cites Josef Wicki, *Documenta Indica IV (1557–1560)* (Rome: Monumenta Historica Societatis Iesu, 1956), 191.

80. *DM I*, 216.

81. *DM I*, 387. For a biography of Araújo see *DM I*, 34*.

82. *DM I*, 417.

83. *DM I*, 493.

84. *DM I*, 521, 589; see also 547 (July 1569). For information on the previous church, constructed in 1563, see 417.

85. *DM I*, 597.

86. In Jesús López-Gay, *La liturgia en la misión del Japón del siglo XVI* (Rome: Libreria dell'Università Gregoriana, 1970), 159; for a transcription of the letter see Joseph Wicki, ed., *Documenta Indica III (1553–1557)* (Rome: Monumenta Historica Societatis Iesu, 1954), 134.

87. *DM I*, 600.

88. *DM I*, 601.

89. *DM III*, 222. Jacobs speculates that this was "presumably a dance after the style of the well-known *wela-wela*" (222n36). For a biography of Fonseca see *DM II*, 48*–49*; *DM III*, 24*.

90. Azevedo was in Maluku from 1620 to 1624. See *DM III*, 32*. Jacobs suggests that criticism of one Jesuit (Lorenzo Masonio, discussed below) was "severe and apparently undeserved," and comments that Azevedo "passed . . . a sharp criticism on nearly every Jesuit." *DM III*, 22*, 32*.

91. *DM III*, 416. For a biography of Baptista, see *DM III*, 27*–28*.

92. *DM III*, 417.

93. *DM III*, 417–18. For a biography of Masonio see *DM II*, 44*–45*; *DM III*, 21*–22*; of Simi, see *DM III*, 26*–27*.

94. *DM III*, 418.

95. Colín and Pastells, *Labor evangélica*, 3:90.

96. *DM III*, 417, 420.

97. *DM III*, 421. On the etymology of sestro see Rafael Bluteau, Vocabulario portuguez, e latino (Coimbra; Lisbon: Collegio das Artes da Companhia de Jesu; na officina de Pascoal da Sylva, 1712–28), vol. 7 (1720), 622. Available at Wellcome Collection, https://wellcomecollection.org/works/qkm8aczp.

98. *DM III*, 426n22.

99. See Yukimi Kambe, "Viols in Japan in the Sixteenth and Early Seventeenth Centuries," *Journal of the Viola da Gamba Society of America* 37 (2000): 31–67.

100. Corte-Real, "Music in Fernão Mendes Pinto's *Peregrinação*," 193–94.

101. See, for example, Kartomi, "A Malay-Portuguese Synthesis on the West Coast of North Sumatra," in Portugal and the World: The Encounter of Cultures in Music, ed. Salwa El-Shawan Castelo-Branco (Lisbon: Publicações Dom Quixote, 1997), 313. See also: Brigitta Scarfe and Muhamad Hasbi, "The Significance of Place in the Musical Practice of Two Biola Players in Riau Islands Province," in Performing the Arts of Indonesia: Malay Identity and Politics in the Music, Dance and Theatre of the Riau Islands, ed. Margaret Kartomi (Copenhagen: NIAS Press, 2019), 152–68; and Kartomi, *Musical Journeys in Sumatra* (Urbana: University of Illinois Press, 2012), 244–45.

102. *DM III*, 453.

103. *DM III*, 560n2.

104. *DM III*, 561. The last word is clearly meant to be *motete*. The tradition of the "Santos Passos and Motets" is still practiced in Goa, India, today. See Deepti Coutinho, "Santos Passos & Motets / Tradition of Christian Sacred Music for Lent," Goa Roots, March 9, 2016. https://goaroots.com/santos-passos-motet-tradition-of-christian-sacred-music-for-lent/.

105. *DM III*, 561.

106. For a discussion of an earlier confraternity in Maluku in the Jesuit documents, that of the Confraternity of the Blessed Sacrament in Ternate (mentioned in a letter of February 24, 1563), see *DM I*, 382n3.

107. *DM III*, 561.

108. *DM III*, 561.

109. *DM III*, 561–62.

110. *DM III*, 562.

111. Pedro Murillo Velarde, *Historia de la provincia de Philipinas de la Compañía de Jesús*: Segunda parte, que comprehende los progresos de esta provincia desde el año de 1616 hasta el de 1716 (Manila: En la Imprenta de la Compañía de Jesús, por D. Nicolas de la Cruz Bagay, 1749) f. 284v.

112. *DM III*, 562n9. See also Manuel Lobato, "Os *mardicas* de Ternate e os crioulos de origem portuguesa nas Filipinas: Um olhar interdisciplinar sobre as relações entre identidade e língua," in Tópicos transatlânticos: Emergência da Lusofonia num mundo plural, ed. Silvério da Rocha-Cunha, Noémi Marujo, Cláudia Teixeira, Marco Martins, Paulo Rodrigues and Maria do Rosario Borges (Évora: Universidade de Évora—Escola de Ciências Sociais, 2012), 55–67.

113. See "Santo Niño de Ternate—Ternate's Watchful Patron," *Pintakasi: Chronicles on Filipino Popular Piety and Ecclesiastical History* (September 26, 2017), https://pintakasi1521.blogspot .com/2017/09/santo-nino-de-ternate-ternates-watchful.html, accessed June 10, 2022. See also Esteban A. De Ocampo, *The Ternateños*: Their History, Language, Customs and Traditions (Ermita, Manila: National Historical Institute, 2007).

114. Horacio de la Costa, *The Jesuits in the Philippines*, 1581–1768 (Cambridge, MA: Harvard University Press, 1961), 438.

115. For biographies of Miedes and Esquivel, see *DM III*, 40*–43*. See also Murillo Velarde, *Historia de la Provincia*, ff. 284r, 352v–53r.

116. Murillo Velarde, *Historia de la Provincia*, f. 353r.

117. *DM III*, 689–90.

118. *DM III*, 702. For Español's biography, see *DM III*, 45*–46*.

119. *DM III*, 703.

120. *DM III*, 708.

121. Bartolomé Leonardo de Argensola, *Conquista de las Islas Malucas* (Madrid: Alonso Martin, 1609). For a contextual overview see Fernando Sánchez Marcos, "*Conquista de las Malucas* (1609): Texto y contexto de una historia marítima," in El mar en los siglos modernos, ed. Manuel-Reyes García Hurtado, Domingo L. González Lopo, and Enrique Martínez Rodríguez (Santiago de Compostela: Xunta de Galicia, 2009), 685–97.

122. Andaya, *The World of Maluku*, 19.

123. John Villiers, "'A Truthful Pen and an Impartial Spirit': Bartolomé Leonardo de Argensola and the Conquista de las Islas Malucas," Renaissance Studies 17, no. 3 (2003): 449–73.

124. Carmen Nocentelli, *Empires of Love*: Europe, Asia, and the Making of Early Modern Identity (Philadelphia: University of Pennsylvania Press, 2013), 91. For an overview of the text, see also Donald F. Lach and Edwin J. Van Kley, *Asia in the Making of Europe*, 3 vols in 9 books (Chicago: University of Chicago Press, 1965–93), 3:311–12.

125. Villiers, "'A Truthful Pen and an Impartial Spirit,'" 454. For example, see Bartolomé Leonardo de Argensola, *The Discovery and Conquest of the Molucco and Philippine Islands: Containing Their History, Ancient and Modern, Natural and Political: Their Description, Product, Religion, Government, Laws, Languages, Customs, Manners, Habits, Shape, and Inclinations of the Natives. With an Account of Many Other Adjacent Islands, and Several Remarkable Voyages through the Streights of Magellan, and in Other Parts. Written in Spanish by Bartholomew Leonardo de Argensola, Chaplain to the Empress, and Rector of Villahermosa. Now Translated into English: And Illustrated with a Map and Several Cuts* (London: 1708).

126. Nocentelli, *Empires of Love*, 92.

127. Melchor Fernández de León, "La gran comedia, Conquista de las Malucas," in Primavera numerosa de muchas armonias luzientes, en doce comedias fragantes parte quarenta y seis, impressas fielmente de los borradores de los mas célebres plausibles ingenios de España (Madrid: Francisco Sanz, 1679), ff. 174v–97v; Antonio C. Campo López, "Molucas y España en el siglo XVII," in En el archipiélago

de la especiería: España y Molucas en los siglos XVI y XVII, ed. Javier Serrano Avilés and Jorge Mojarro Romero (Madrid: Desperta Ferro, 2021), 52.

128. Melchor Fernández de León, *Comedia famosa*: La conquista de las Malucas (Valencia: en la imprenta de la Viuda de Joseph de Orga, 1762). For musical indications in the work, see Fernández de León, "La gran comedia, Conquista de las Malucas," ff. 177v–78r, 180v–81r, 182r–83r, 185v–86r, 187v, 188r–v, 191r, 193r–94r, 195r, 196v, 197r; Fernández de León, *Comedia famosa*, 6, 10–14, 18–19, 22, 27, 31, 33, 36–37.

129. Leonardo de Argensola, *The Discovery and Conquest*, 55; Leonardo de Argensola, *Conquista de las Islas Malucas*, 80.

130. Leonardo de Argensola, *The Discovery and Conquest*, 99; Leonardo de Argensola, *Conquista de las Islas Malucas*, 149.

131. Leonardo de Argensola, *The Discovery and Conquest*, 17; Leonardo de Argensola, *Conquista de las Islas Malucas*, 24.

132. Leonardo de Argensola, *The Discovery and Conquest*, 10; Leonardo de Argensola, *Conquista de las Islas Malucas*, 14.

133. Leonardo de Argensola, *The Discovery and Conquest*, 167; Leonardo de Argensola, *Conquista de las Islas Malucas*, 250.

134. Leonardo de Argensola, *The Discovery and Conquest*, 241; Leonardo de Argensola, *Conquista de las Islas Malucas*, 356.

135. Leonardo de Argensola, *The Discovery and Conquest*, 170; Leonardo de Argensola, *Conquista de las Islas Malucas*, 255.

136. Leonardo de Argensola, *The Discovery and Conquest*, 170; Leonardo de Argensola, *Conquista de las Islas Malucas*, 255.

137. Leonardo de Argensola, *The Discovery and Conquest*, 161; Leonardo de Argensola, *Conquista de las Islas Malucas*, 240–41. Lach and Van Kley noted that Leonardo de Argensola cites "las relaciones de Hugo" (Jan Huyghen van Linschoten) but that "some of it appears to have come from the published reports of the second Dutch voyage under [Jacob] Cornelis van Neck and Wybrand van Warwijck." Lach and Van Kley, *Asia in the Making of Europe*, 3:311, 1148, 1399–408, 1427.

138. Rein Spoorman, "Tradition and Creative Inspiration: Musical Encounters of the Moluccan Communities in the Netherlands," in *Recollecting Resonances: Indonesian-Dutch Musical Encounters*, vol. 288 of *Verhandelingen van het Koninklijk Instituut voor Taal-, Land- en Volkenkunde*, ed. Bart Barendregt and Els Bogaerts (Leiden: Brill, 2014), 282.

2

A European Music Treatise Published in Late Eighteenth-Century Batavia (Jakarta)

Estelle Joubert and David R. M. Irving

In 1792, the sixth volume of the *Verhandelingen van het Bataviaasch Genootschap van Kunsten en Wetenschappen* (Proceedings of the Batavian Society of Arts and Sciences; figure 2-1) was published in colonial Batavia (Jakarta). It included a 302-page treatise on music, titled "Redeneeringen over nuttige Muzikaale Onderwerpen, Tot onderzoek van Kenners, tot verlustiging van Geoeffende en tot onderrichting van weetgierige Muziek-liefhebbers" (Arguments on useful musical topics, for the investigation of connoisseurs, for the delight of the practiced, and for the education of curious music lovers; figure 2-2).[1] Discussing diverse aspects of European music aesthetics, genres, theory, and history, as well as considering music's place in (European) society, it takes up some two-thirds of the volume and is attributed to "Johannes Vranciscus [*sic*] Gratiæn" (Jan Frans Gratiaen).[2] This person was employed for most of his life by the Dutch East India Company (Vereenigde Oostindische Compagnie, or VOC). Born in Bruges in 1727, he moved to Ceylon (Sri Lanka) in 1747 and resided there (apart from a brief period in southern India) until his death in 1788. The work bearing his name was printed posthumously. It appears to be the most extensive literary text on European music published in Southeast Asia before the nineteenth century.

The "Redeneeringen over nuttige Muzikaale Onderwerpen," although concerned solely with European music, is relevant for Indonesian music historiography to the extent that it demonstrates the concerns of the colonial elite in late eighteenth-century Batavia (as well as other settlements of the VOC) and the networks of musical thought and discourse that enabled its publication.[3] It has remained somewhat obscure since its first appearance but has not gone unnoticed in musicology.[4] In her doctoral dissertation of 2001, Els Strategier made a startling

FIGURE 2-1. Title page of the sixth volume of the *Verhandelingen van het Bataviaasch Genootschap van Kunsten en Wetenschappen* (Batavia [Jakarta]: Pieter van Geemen, 1792). © The British Library Board 438.k.13–27

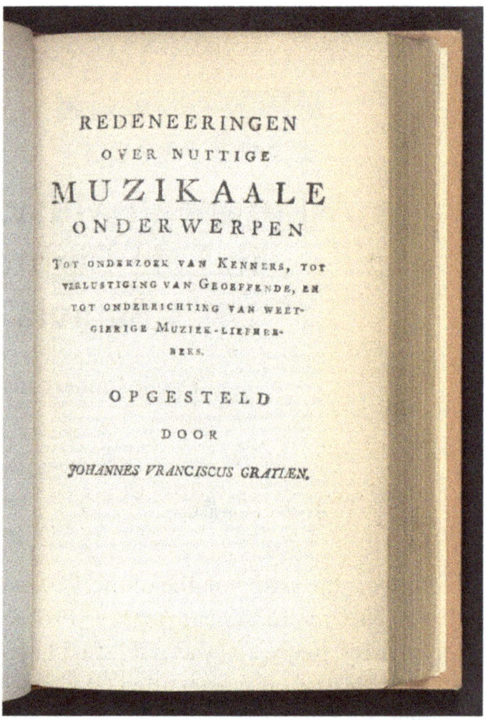

FIGURE 2-2. Johannes Vranciscus Gratiaen, "Redeneeringen over nuttige Muzikaale Onderwerpen, Tot onderzoek van Kenners, tot verlustiging van Geoeffende en tot onderrichting van weetgierige Muziek-liefhebbers," *Verhandelingen van het Bataviaasch Genootschap van Kunsten en Wetenschappen* 6 (1792): seventh section, title page. © The British Library Board 438.k.13–27

observation about it. She found that Gratiaen's text is a paraphrase of two treatises by Jacob Wilhelm Lustig (1706–96), a musician born in Hamburg who later became organist at the Martini church in Groningen.[5] Lustig was a prolific writer who produced, in Dutch, a large corpus of writings on music, including translations of historical writings by Charles Burney (1726–1814) and of treatises by Johann Joachim Quantz (1697–1773), Andreas Werckmeister (1645–1706), Friedrich Wilhelm Marpurg (1718–95), and Nicolò Pasquali (ca. 1718–57)—as well as his own works. The last category includes Lustig's *Inleiding tot de Muziekkunde* (Introduction to the study of music, 1751, reprinted 1758; second edition, 1771) and *Twaalf redeneeringen over nuttige Muzikaale Onderwerpen* (Twelve arguments on useful musical topics, 1756), the two texts that Gratiaen plundered for his "Redeneeringen."[6] According to Strategier, there is no mention of Lustig's name anywhere in the Batavian document of 1792; she further observes that Gratiaen claims authorship of the entire work in a fourteen-page preface ("Voorreeden"). In that portion of the text, occasional mentions of the "East Indies" or "Indies" might indeed lead one to believe that Gratiaen had composed at least this introductory section, even if the chapters that follow are taken from Lustig. Closer examination shows, however, that this preface was also adapted and pasted together from snippets of multiple editions of Lustig's *Inleiding* and *Twaalf redeneeringen*, published between 1751 and 1771.

These features raise many questions. The present chapter investigates the circumstances surrounding this curious publication that emanated, perhaps rather unexpectedly, from the VOC's press in Batavia in 1792 (and again in a reprint of 1827, which used updated Dutch orthography). We begin by examining the wider context for music in colonial Batavian society, leading up to the establishment of the Bataviaasch Genootschap and establishment of the *Verhandelingen*. Subsequently, we investigate issues pertaining to authorship, intended audience, chronology of the text's production, and the relation of the contents to Lustig's writings. To close, we offer some thoughts about the possible reception of the document.

COLONIAL BATAVIA AND THE BATAVIAASCH GENOOTSCHAP VAN KUNSTEN EN WETENSCHAPPEN

The settlement established by the Dutch at the Javanese port of Jacatra and named Batavia (after the ancient Roman term for the low countries) in 1619 became a major hub in an extensive network of knowledge transfer mediated by VOC shipping. Its routes spread eastward through the Southeast Asian archipelago and as far as Japan, west across the Indian Ocean to Ceylon and southern Africa, and to the Netherlands.[7] Within the ranks of the VOC (which employed only men, although it permitted a limited number of women to travel from the Netherlands to the colonies), there were various people who were practitioners and patrons of art music. A prominent example is Ferdinand Dejean (1731–97), a German-born surgeon for the company based in Batavia from 1759 to 1767 and an amateur flute player. During his time in Asia, he traveled as a surgeon on ships running routes that extended from the Bay of Bengal through the Malay-Indonesian archipelago; he also amassed considerable wealth. Once back in Europe, he commissioned Wolfgang Amadeus Mozart (1756–91), whom he met in Mannheim in 1777, to write concertos and quartets for the flute, offering a handsome fee.[8]

For certain long-term residents of the colony, the practice of music from Europe was a desirable activity and one associated with social prestige. Jean Gelman Taylor, who has authored an extensive study of cultural life in seventeenth- and eighteenth-century Batavia, points out that tuition in this art from an early age was part of the education of the local elite.[9] However, it must be noted that much labor of music in wealthy households was performed by enslaved people, about whom relatively little is yet known but whose activities can occasionally be glimpsed in the archive. For instance, the Dutch lady Cornelia van Beek, writing from Batavia in 1689, described a group of enslaved musicians who "played on the harp, viol and bassoon at mealtimes."[10] Such groups, performing for domestic and public entertainment, were patronized by a number of Europeans and other wealthy residents. They sometimes appear in pre-1800 iconography; for example, four musicians playing cello, flute, and two violins are depicted in a drawing by the Dutch (Lutheran) minister and artist Jan Brandes (1743–1808) of a wedding celebration in Batavia around 1779–85.[11] One of the more extravagant patrons of art music was the Eurasian Augustijn Michiels (ca. 1769–1833), who adopted a "musical mixture" of Javanese and European traditions; in his city house and country estates, Michiels patronized various ensembles of musicians and dancers who performed in Javanese or European styles.[12] After his death, an ensemble of enslaved musicians—listed as playing fiddle, French horn, bassoon, sackbut, clarinet, flute, and bass violin, together with "music of the latest editions, imported from Europe"—were advertised for auction in Batavia.[13]

Michiels was a leading member of the community known as Mardijkers, people claiming descent from earlier generations of Portuguese colonialists in South and Southeast Asia who had married among the local population.[14] They spoke Portuguese and made up a sizeable community of the Dutch Reformed Church in Batavia.[15] At the beginning of the eighteenth century, a major music publication was produced by the VOC Press in Batavia for their use: a Portuguese translation of the entire Genevan Psalter, printed complete with staff notation.[16] For the Calvinist contexts of Dutch colonial society, the singing of monophonic psalms was one of the most prominent forms of Christian sacred music. Nevertheless, there were at least three church organs in the late eighteenth century, as noted by book historian and hymnologist Katharine Smith Diehl (1906–89).[17] One was in the Evangelical Lutheran Church (constructed in 1747–49 and demolished in 1833 because of disrepair), in which Brandes served as minister in the years 1779–85.[18] Imported from the Netherlands in 1746, this instrument (with *rückpositiv*, a small auxiliary organ placed behind the organist), is visible with considerable detail (from the left) in a watercolor-over-pencil depiction of the church made at that time (beneath the organ appears the pulpit holding the preacher, possibly Brandes himself); the front-on view also appears in an earlier watercolor of 1753.[19] Regarding secular contexts, Diehl also observes that there was an "opera house . . . completed before 1800" and that during the British occupation of 1811–16, there was constructed a new building named the Harmonie, "a combination of large auditorium and dining room at which all sorts of pleasant events, banquets, and other functions could be held."[20]

Beyond these contexts for cultural life, however, Taylor observes that for most of the eighteenth century in Batavia, "there were still no coffee houses or other places where upper class men could gather informally, as there were in Dutch cities."[21] This situation changed with the establishment of the Bataviaasch Genootschap van Kunsten en Wetenschappen (Batavian Society of Arts and Sciences) in 1778. The organization owes its foundations to Jacobus Cornelis

Mattheus Radermacher (1741–83), who also donated a house for the meetings.[22] A Dutchman who had arrived in Batavia as a teenager, Rademacher had risen quickly through the ranks of the VOC; he married a stepdaughter of a councilor extraordinary of the city and in 1762 established the city's first Masonic Lodge.[23] After a stint in the Netherlands studying law between 1763 and 1767, he returned to Batavia full of inspiration from new scholarly movements in the Netherlands and founded the society in 1778, by which stage his father-in-law Reynier de Klerk (1710–78) was governor general.[24]

From its beginnings the Bataviaasch Genootschap—described by Taylor as "the first association for intellectual pursuits established in a tropical European settlement"—had almost two hundred members, with more than half based in Batavia.[25] The charter of the society stated that it would "attempt to stimulate all arts and sciences and will eagerly receive anything which deals with the natural history, antiquities, customs and mores of the peoples"; it prioritized studies of subjects that could "be beneficial to the agriculture, trade, and particular welfare" of the colony.[26] Rademacher donated a number of items that, according to Diehl, laid "the foundation for both library and museum"; as well as books and specimens of natural history, they included coins and "Javanese musical instruments."[27] The library of the Bataviaasch Genootschap experienced several vicissitudes over the first half of the nineteenth century relating to damage inflicted by insects (and likely humidity) as well as deliberate damage and loss, but it began to grow from the time its first catalog was made (in 1846).[28] A new site for the society, next door to the Harmonie building, was established during the British occupation and another home for it built in 1862-68.[29] The last edifice was ultimately incorporated into the Perpustakaan Nasional Republik Indonesia (National Library of Indonesia), as were its bibliographic holdings.[30]

The *Verhandelingen*, first issued in 1779 and published (with some breaks) until 1950, promoted learning and research in the colony and concerned itself mainly with history, culture, and natural sciences of the region.[31] Reflecting the aims of the society, its contents included articles on such topics as "agriculture, fisheries, local manufactures, water control, medicine, and languages."[32] Diehl estimates that the print run of the first volume was no greater than 225 copies.[33] The extent to which this periodical was read by Asians is unknown; for instance, it was only around 1860 that the first Indonesian members of the Bataviaasch Genootschap are noted.[34] The journal's first four volumes (dated 1779, 1780, 1781, and 1786) contained sixty articles—a quarter by Radermacher himself—which are mostly on topics related to the archipelago. Volumes 5 and 6, published respectively in 1790 and 1792, on the other hand, "constituted only a pale shadow of accomplishment," in the words of Lian The and Paul W. Van der Veur.[35] According to Hans Groot, the inclusion of Gratiaen's treatise in volume 6 was, for lack of other content, something of a stopgap measure, and it was unusual since it did not address the kinds of local subjects that were the focus of articles in previous volumes.[36] What, then, is the story behind this text? What do we know about Gratiaen, and how did his writings come to be published in Batavia?

JAN FRANS GRATIAEN

Relatively few details are known about this writer's life and less still about his musical training. In 1888–91 a short entry was published in a biographical dictionary by J. G. Frederiks and F. Jos. van den Branden, stating the following:

> Gratiaen (*Jan Frans*), musician from the early eighteenth century, was born in Bruges, [and] settled in Paris, where he became a pupil of J. M. Leclair [Jean-Marie Leclair (1697–1764)], musician at the French court, in 1731. He subsequently traveled to the East Indies, where already in 1750, he was engaged with an important work entitled: Arguments on useful musical topics, for the investigation of connoisseurs, for the delight of the practiced and for the instruction of curious music-lovers.[37]

Details in this entry can be challenged by data drawn from recent research. Articles published in 2012 and 2013 by, respectively, Peter de Baets, an archivist familiar with sources in the Brugge Stadsarchief (Bruges City Archive), and Lutgard Mutsaers, a scholar of Indonesian music and popular music, revisited the life and times of this man.[38] De Baets, for instance, confirms that Gratiaen was born on March 1, 1727.[39] Therefore, he cannot realistically have been studying with Leclair in 1731. However, his studies may well have occurred later; in the "Voorreeden" of the 1792 treatise, Gratiaen does mention his time in Paris and his studies with Leclair, as both de Baets and Mutsaers have noted.[40]

According to VOC records, Gratiaen left the Netherlands on the ship *Zeelandia*, departing January 10, 1746.[41] It appears that he changed to another vessel in southern Africa (the ship arrived at False Bay on June 9), since it was on the *Krabbendyk* (*Krabbendijke*) that he landed at Ceylon in 1747, according to a genealogy of the Gratiaen family published in Colombo in 1913.[42] He married Anna Aletta Kokaart (1733–85) the year after his arrival; they had seven children and were the founders of a local family dynasty.[43] Among their direct descendants is the well-known author Michael Ondaatje (b. 1943), whose mother's surname was Gratiaen, a fact that de Baets and Mutsaers have highlighted.[44] In the 1750s to 1780s, Gratiaen held a range of VOC posts in Ceylon and also for some time in southern India. These included *ambtenaar* (civil servant) and *consumptie boekhouder* ("clerk in the consumer goods registration office") in Calpetty (now Kalpitiya) from 1758.[45] Mutsaers notes that "in 1770 he oversaw the arreek [betel nut] trade in Colombo, involving the buying, storing and selling of areca palm tree nuts."[46] He then took up the post *fiscaal en secretaris* (treasury official and secretary) from 1772 in Tutucoryn (now Thoothukudi), Tamil Nadu.[47] Returning to Ceylon, he held in Galle the post of junior merchant from 1776, then *fiscaal* and cashier from 1783.[48] He died there in 1788.

Mutsaers speculates that Gratiaen's son-in-law Willem Sebastiaan Boers (d. 1792), who was then a member of the Batavian Society and listed as an *onderkoopman en dispensier* (junior merchant and dispenser [of grain]) based in Colombo, may have suggested the treatise as content for the 1792 volume of the journal.[49] However, whether he saw it in print before his death in November that year is unknown, and whether he traveled to Batavia is also yet to be established. As Mutsaers comments, "It would have been too late for Boers to check the origins of his father-in-law's manuscript. Or perhaps Boers was instructed by the Gratiaen family in Ceylon. In any case, Batavia's learned men were unable to recognize an existing text."[50] The frontmatter of the 1792 volume of the *Verhandelingen* offers the following statement pertaining to its inclusion, describing the contents as follows:

> One part of a Discourse on Music, [created] while he was in Ceylon by the junior merchant Johannes Franciscus Gratiaan, member of this society. [It is on] a subject which does not directly belong to the society's plan, yet it is not entirely foreign and not deemed unworthy to fill out the present mix of more unusual materials, to which end the sequel will be set aside for a subsequent edition.[51]

Although Gratiaen is mentioned here as a member of the Bataviaasch Genootschap, his name never appears in the detailed membership lists published in volumes 1–3 or in 5–6 (published after his death in 1788). However, the name and occupation of his son-in-law Boers does appear in volumes 5 and 6.[52] Despite the promise of a continuation of this article being published in subsequent volumes of the *Verhandelingen*, there is no evidence that this stated intention was ever followed through. The treatise's table of contents, headed "Hoofd deelen in dit werk vervat" (Main parts contained in this work), lists a total of twenty chapters (as we discuss below and reproduce in the appendix), but only twelve chapters are included in the 1792 publication. It seems that the remaining eight were kept for "the sequel." This raises the question of who "set aside" the complete manuscript of Gratiaen: Was it kept by family members or deposited in the library of the Bataviaasch Genootschap, and how many copies of the manuscript existed? One also wonders whether the readers realized the extent to which it reused the texts of Lustig and whether the society may have refrained from printing the promised continuation for that reason. Further research may shed light on such matters.

AUTHORIAL APPROPRIATION AND QUESTIONS ABOUT GRATIAEN'S INTENDED READERSHIP

Lustig ended his preface in the 1751 and 1758 editions of his *Inleiding* by quoting a passage from Cicero's *Tusculan Disputations*: "I am not inventing, I am not misrepresenting, am I? I long to be refuted. For why am I exerting myself except to get the truth in every problem unravelled?"[53] Intriguingly, Gratiaen chose not to reproduce this quotation. Instead, he elected to finish his preface with the quotation used in Lustig's new preface to his 1771 edition of the same treatise (not the previous versions), this time taken from the biblical apocrypha, the book of Ecclesiasticus, also known as the Book of Sirach (chapter 18, verse 6): "When a man hath done, then shall he begin: and when he leaveth off, he shall be at a loss."[54] In his use of this verse it seems possible to detect something of Gratiaen's religious perspective. While he reproduces verbatim the verse in the *hoogduitsche* (High German) wording of Martin Luther, exactly as used by Lustig, Gratiaen prefaces this by quoting the translation given by the Synod of Dordrecht, thus perhaps revealing to the reader an adherence to the Dutch Reformed Church. Personal interventions such as this are relatively few and far between, but unraveling the true extent to which Gratiaen copied and adapted Lustig's writings is still a painstaking task. In what follows, we will highlight a few representative instances of invention and misrepresentation to illustrate the complex relationship between the texts of the two men.

As mentioned earlier, one might assume Gratiaen's authorship of his foreword because of occasional mentions of "India," "the Indies," and "the East Indies" (to where Lustig, by contrast, did not travel). However, a closer examination reveals that even this part of the publication is a collage of passages, many taken verbatim from the two editions of Lustig's *Inleiding* (1751 [apparently reprinted in 1758] and 1771). Some are rearranged, others adapted to the contemporary context, and a few invented to glue the stolen passages together. The risk of deception is particularly grave when passages are examined in isolation, rather than alongside the relevant passage in Lustig's treatises. Consider, for example, the most substantive comment on musical life in Ceylon in Gratiaen's preface:

> After all, we here in the Indies know nothing of church and stage music, and we say we know little even of delightful concerts and vocal music, and thus because of an absence of exchange we are unaware of any fashions. So one should not stretch the bow too wide [in other words, set the bar too high], since there is much opportunity for the advancement and cultivation of music.[55]

This comment might easily be taken at face value as an honest assessment of music in his immediate environment, if it were not for its very close resemblance to the corresponding passage in Lustig's 1751 treatise: "After all, since we in this country know nothing of church and stage music, yes, even of so-called vocal music, we know little, and thus, due to lack of exchange remain unaware of any fashions. One should not stretch the bow too wide [set the bar too high], since the advantage of gallant readers of music is great."[56] Given such a close likeness to Lustig's passage, Gratiaen's comment on the apparent state of music in "the Indies" cannot be taken completely seriously. The only element that might be considered plausible in this passage is the writer's desire to cultivate music in colonial outposts such as Ceylon (or even southern India during his posting there, given that Gratiaen must have written this preface after 1771). For this purpose, Lustig's writings were the perfect models to appropriate, as they were written in the Dutch language and were aimed primarily at educated readers who were not professional musicians.

One of the more interesting subtle adaptations of Lustig's writings in the preface involves a consideration of the glory of the Dutch empire and a perceived lack of concomitant global recognition of the nation's musical contributions. To this end, Gratiaen again subtly adapts a passage from Lustig's *Inleiding*, albeit with a shift of context from a national to an international perspective. Lustig writes:

> Being pleased with the glory of the educated Netherlands, it began to dawn on me that the learned Brossard, compiler of a certain renowned *Dictionaire* [*sic*] *de Musique*, printed in Amsterdam, after having counted 900 musical authors, from all kinds of nations, boldly declared that he had never been able to discover any musical treatise in the Dutch language, much less in Danish, Swedish, Polish and Hungarian.[57]

In light of this comment, Lustig's wide range of writing on music can be viewed as a response to Brossard's observation concerning the paucity of Dutch musical texts during the eighteenth century.[58] Gratiaen refashions this passage as follows (with the sentence immediately prior including the comment that "I find myself here in India [used generically, which could include Ceylon], after many years firmly engaged outside the bustle of the great world"):

> Being pleased with the glory of the Netherlands, so in Europe as in the East Indies, it began to grieve me that the learned Brossard, compiler of the well-known *Dictionaire* [*sic*] *de Musique*, printed in Amsterdam, after nearly 900 musical authors, from all kinds of nations, added up on page 361, boldly dared to declare never to have discovered a musical investigation in the Dutch language, much less in Swedish, Polish and Hungarian.[59]

Gratiaen thus seems to imply that he is addressing this lacuna identified by Brossard—almost a century later and in the wake of Lustig's works, some of which were issued in multiple editions. This statement is daring and risky to the point of appearing curious. Does it suggest a brazen confidence that none of his readers will have come across Lustig's writings? Or does he think that close emulation is the highest form of flattery? Perhaps more revealing is his change of emphasis from the Netherlands' national identity within a European context to praise of the Dutch colonial enterprise around the globe, as seen in his phrase "so in Europe as in the East Indies." Might it suggest that those living in colonial outposts, like Gratiaen, were much more aware of and concerned with maintaining the expansive networks and power of the Dutch empire, than were domestic readers in Amsterdam, Haarlem, and other cities of the Netherlands and Europe?

Taking a broader, even global, perspective on this issue works well when put into dialogue with questions of the text's potential audience. As mentioned above, the *Verhandelingen* often included a list of members of the society, offering unusual clarity pertaining to the social composition of the audience receiving the print. One such list is found in volume 6. It is divided by type of member, listing for each person (all men) his occupation and location, the latter presumably current, to the best of local Batavian knowledge, at the time of publication. Categories of members include "Ordinaire Leden" (ordinary members); "Extra-Ordinaire Leden" (extraordinary members), living in other places, which include Ambon, Banda, Makassar, Melaka, the Coromandel Coast, Ceylon, the Cape of Good Hope, "Java's northeast coast," Bengal, Surat, "Sumatra's west coast," Malabar, Banten, Japan (which must imply the Dutch trading factory at Deshima), Cirebon, Timor, and Palembang; "Correspondeerende Leden" (corresponding members) in the Netherlands; and "Buitenlandsche Correspondenten" (foreign correspondents) in other parts of the world. The last category included the famous naturalists Joseph Banks (1743–1820) and Carl Peter Thunberg (1743–1828), both of whom had musical interests and had visited Batavia, as well as "supercargos" in China and "the missionaries [presumably Jesuits] in Beijing" (these last two entries do not give individual names or an indication of numbers).[60]

The 1792 membership of the society stretched from the Malay–Indonesian archipelago to Japan and China, to Ceylon and southern Africa, and to countries in Europe. Its intercontinental reach suggests that Gratiaen's text was not published by the society solely for a local Batavian audience, even though the latter constituted the majority of the journal's intended readership. Many members of the society were based in other outposts in Asia (see map 2–1). This point about reception plays into questions of the text's utility and application in social contexts. (The "utility of music" is, incidentally, the topic of one of the chapters in the treatise, as discussed below.) As with Lustig, Gratiaen's concern was the cultivation of music not among specialists but among people like himself, those employed as merchants, government clerks, lawyers, medical personnel, seafarers, and others—all people broadly involved in setting up Dutch colonies and trading posts across several continents—who were also music enthusiasts.

With so much of the treatise paraphrased from Lustig's writings, one might wonder whether there remains anything substantive within the prose to be gleaned about Gratiaen's personal life. To this end, a passage detailing Lustig's early musical training that Gratiaen adapted to showcase his own musical background is worth noting. Lustig originally writes in his *Inleiding*:

> In order to find and present something useful, in the days of my youth, in Hamburg, alongside the constant enjoyment of beautiful church, stage, and chamber music, I researched not only various old and new musical writings, but even attended a private colloquium on the study of music (de Scientia melodica) with the universally renowned Mr. Kapellmeister *Matheson* [sic; Johann Mattheson (1681–1764)]. But, not finding absolute certainty anywhere, I found myself powerfully engaged, outside the bustle of the great world, though in a lower musical rank than perhaps I might have wished for, to consider the whole matter thoughtfully, and in a manner, as though it had never been studied before.[61]

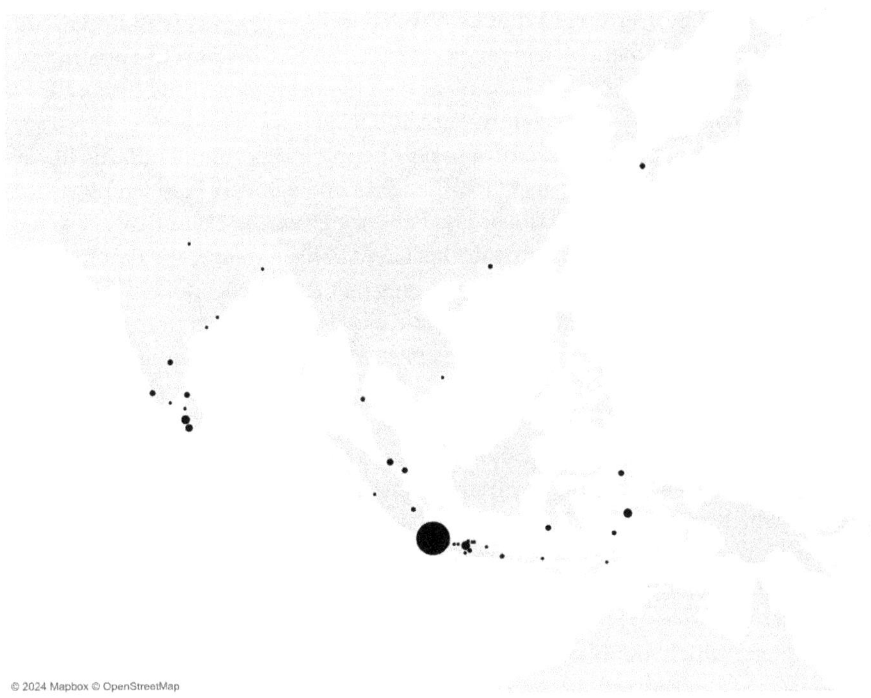

MAP 2-1. Members of the Bataviaasch Genootschap van Kunsten en Wetenschappen based in Asia, according to the "Naam lyst" in *Verhandelingen* 6 (1792): 25–50, weighted by number of members resident in any given location. © 2024 Mapbox © OpenStreetMap

Gratiaen adapts this passage to offer details concerning his own musical biography (if true):

> In order to discover something new about music and musical knowledge, the burning desire for knowledge in the days of my youth, in Bruges in Flanders, the town of my birth, [I went] eventually to Paris, where I enjoyed a steady stream of delightful church, stage and chamber music, and researched not only various old and new musical texts, but even [studied] with the famous Mr. Le Clair, who was a disciple of the great Somis [Giovanni Battista Somis (1686–1763)] at the court of Sardinia, [who held] a private collegium of musical science of Scientia Melodica.[62]

Somis, a student of Arcangelo Corelli (1653–1713), was based at the court in Turin and gave violin lessons to Leclair (widely considered the founder of the French violin school).[63] It does seem plausible, then, that Gratiaen would have had the opportunity to study with Leclair in Paris (but not in 1731, as claimed in the late nineteenth-century dictionary of Frederiks and van den Branden, cited above). As Neal Zaslaw notes, Leclair was invited by Anne, Princess of Orange (1709–59), to her court in the Netherlands, where he was based three months of each year from 1738 to 1743.[64] From 1740 to 1743, he spent the remaining nine months in The Hague, where he was appointed maestro di cappella to François Du Liz.[65] Thus, if we were to take Gratiaen's word that he traveled to Paris to study with Leclair, this may have happened when Leclair returned from the Netherlands to Paris in 1743. Gratiaen departed for the Cape in 1746, and so the most likely time frame for his claimed musical study with Leclair in Paris is between 1743 and 1746.

We see, then, that the few extant sources offering insight into Gratiaen's life are brief and often in conflict. For instance, Frederiks and van den Branden must have assumed an earlier birth date (as discussed above), given the claim that his studies with Leclair began in 1731; they also state that after Gratiaen went to the East Indies he was, by around 1750, already engaged in working on the "Redeneeringen."[66] However, given that Gratiaen's "Voorreeden" in that source clearly reuses text from the prefaces in both the 1751 and 1771 editions of Lustig's *Inleiding* (the latter containing new material), it follows that Gratiaen must have worked on the "Redeneeringen" between 1771 and his death in 1788. Gratiaen's selection and adaptation of specific editions of Lustig's works are thus helpful in verifying and resolving conflicting biographical details.[67]

Table 2-1 shows how Gratiaen carefully selected and rearranged the chapters—some of which are taken verbatim from Lustig's works and others adapted in a manner similar to that used in the preface—to form this new text. (For the purposes of initial comparison, we use the 1751 edition of the *Inleiding*.) Four thematic clusters emerge from the topics listed in the table of contents: first, the initial two chapters, which are much more heavily adapted from the *Twaalf redeneeringen*, treat vocal music and the origins of music (chapters 1–2); second, a series of six chapters (3–8) are on philosophical approaches to musical practice (four on the effects, utility, value, social purpose, and essence of music followed by two on church music, pleasure and displeasure in music); third, a series of ten chapters (9–18) deal with more technical aspects of music, such as the properties of intervals, harmony, forms, and other themes (the treatise describes musical sound in prose, including names of notes, and does not include any examples in staff notation). Finally, the last two chapters (19 and 20) discuss the scope and utility of the study of music. As mentioned above, only twelve chapters were published in 1792, despite twenty chapter titles being listed in the table of contents. We are nevertheless able to extrapolate from Gratiaen's titles of the unpublished chapters the parts of the Lustig texts from which they would have drawn, and these are also indicated in the table.

Of Gratiaen's chapters, the most heavily adapted texts (as opposed to the ones copied more or less verbatim) offer insight into his biases and approach in constructing the treatise. The first two are drawn from Lustig's *Twaalf redeneringen*, a work that is divided into "Samenspraaken" (literally "dialogues"), in which the text is set up as a conversation between two imaginary characters, Musander and Aurelia, to debate various ideas related to music. Gratiaen, however, dispensed with this dialogic form, adapting his text to the first person, presumably to be consistent with the rest of the treatise and possibly also to hide his plagiarism. In chapter 1, treating the use of song in community, he omits two large portions of Lustig's text. One of these is a section outlining the "Golden Verses" of Pythagoras, including comments on the value of song in ancient Greek tragedy and (pagan)

TABLE 2-1 Content of "Redeneeringen over nuttige Muzikaale Onderwerpen, Tot onderzoek van Kenners, tot verlustiging van Geoeffende en tot onderrichting van weetgierige Muziek-liefhebbers," attributed to Gratiaen, and its relationship with Lustig's texts

(UNPUBLISHED CHAPTERS OF GRATIAEN'S TEXT, THE TITLES OF WHICH ARE KNOWN FROM THE 1792 TABLE OF CONTENTS, ARE INDICATED IN BOLD.)

Gratiaen, "Redeneeringen over nuttige Muzikaale Onderwerpen, Tot onderzoek van Kenners, tot verlustiging van Geoeffende en tot onderrichting van weetgierige Muziek-liefhebbers" (Batavia, 1792)	Lustig, *Inleiding tot de muzykkunde* (Groningen, 1751)	Lustig, *Twaalf rede-neeringen over nuttige Muzikaale Onderwerpen* (Amsterdam, 1756)
1. Het rechte gebruik der Zangmuziek [The proper use of vocal music], 1–19		Chapter 5, 207–41 (heavily revised by Gratiaen)
2. Den oorsprong der Muziek [The origin of music], 20–37		Chapter 6, 259–85 (heavily revised by Gratiaen)
3. De werking en nuttigheid der Muziek in 't gemeen [The effects and utility of music in the community], 38–58	Chapter 11, 263–83	
4. De waarde der Muziek [The value of music], 59–64	Chapter 12, 284–88	
5. Het oogmerk der Muziek [The purpose of music], 65–75	Chapter 13, 289–96	
6. Het weezen der Muziek-kunst [The essence of musical art], 76–93	Chapter 14, 297–310	
7. De Geestelyke of Kerk-Muziek [Spiritual or church music], 94–106	Chapter 15, 311–22	
8. Het Muziekaal begaagen den mishagen [On musical pleasure and displeasure], 107–21	Chapter 16, 323–33	
9. De Muziek in 't gemeen [On music in general], 122–44	Chapter 1, 1–18	
10. De Muziek-kunde of Theorie[1] [The science of music, or theory], 145–63	Chapter 2, 19–33	
11. De Toon-kunde [On musical art], 164–255	Chapter 3, 34–93	
12. De Muziekaale stoffe [On musical materials], 256–86	Chapter 4, 94–121	
13. **De eigenschappen der gebruikelykste Intervallen [On the properties of the most common intervals]**	Chapter 5, 121–47	
14. **De tempering der Muziekaale Intervallen [On tempering musical intervals]**	Chapter 6, 148–52	
15. **Den Muziekaalen Geest [On the musical spirit]**	Chapter 7, 153–67	
16. **De Muziekaale Harmonie in 't gemeen [On musical harmony, in general]**	Chapter 8, 168–86	
17. **Het vormelyke der Muziek [On musical forms]**	Chapter 9, 187–208	

(Continued)

---

[1] This is the title in the table of contents, but the chapter title on page 145 is simply given as "De Muziek-kunde."

TABLE 2-1   (Continued)

Gratiaen, "Redeneeringen over nuttige Muzikaale Onderwerpen, Tot onderzoek van Kenners, tot verlustiging van Geoeffende en tot onderrichting van weetgierige Muziek-liefhebbers" (Batavia, 1792)	Lustig, *Inleiding tot de muzykkunde* (Groningen, 1751)	Lustig, *Twaalf redeneeringen over nuttige Muzikaale Onderwerpen* (Amsterdam, 1756)
18. **De Muziekaale geschied-kunde** [On music history]	Chapter 10, 209–62	
19. **Den geheelen omtrek der Muziek en Muziek-kunde [On the entire scope of music and the study of music]**		"Over de Muziek en de Muziek-kunde in 't gemeen," 7–37
20. **De nuttigheid der Muziek-kunde** [On the utility of the study of music]	Chapter 17, 334–40	

worship services. Gratiaen also excludes large portions of the same chapter by Lustig that focus on instrumental musical expression, as well as sections on Italian opera seria. One might surmise that Gratiaen carefully considered his audience with these amendments; he was writing for Dutch settlers, most of whom would have participated in Dutch Calvinist worship traditions and probably had varying degrees of access to musical instruments. While evidence of musical instruments has yet to be discovered for Batavia, it is known that in Cape Town, a music store was operating by 1780.[68] Of course, performances of opera seria were unlikely to interest his readership, particularly since this repertory required highly specialized singers whose skills may not have been easily found among enthusiasts in colonial outposts.

Even when chapters are less heavily revised, Gratiaen appears to have selected musical topics that would have been of interest or perhaps deemed useful. His third chapter, dealing with the effects and utility of music in the community, offers insights on the potentially positive and adverse effects of music on the nervous system. Practical applications of these ideas are then referenced, including examples from biblical times, which would have been familiar to Dutch settlers. For instance, the treatise suggests that during the time of Moses, instrumental music could be used to cultivate courage in the face of war or that it could assist in the healing of insanity, using the example of David and Saul.[69] Music's uses also include "restoring mental and physical strength after labor," restoring the human spirit, and offering delightful amusement.[70] The choice to focus on these themes suggests that Gratiaen was interested in cultivating amateur and community music making rather than professional performances in local settings. Discussions of the value of music in chapter 4, in which he states that "music is a mirror of order" and that "music is a sign of a blossoming, well-governed Republic," reveal ideals of music as a means of cultivating well-functioning political and social structures.[71]

Following an investigation of music for church, stage, and chamber (in chapter 6), "Spiritual or Church Music" receives its own chapter (7), which includes a historical commentary dating back to the singing of the Psalms of David and music in early Egyptian Christian communities and ranging to musical practices such as antiphons in the early medieval church at the time of Ambrosius (Ambrose), Athanasius, and Hieronymus (Jerome), going on to consider Gregorian chant. Musical forms such as Lutheran hymns and other Dutch and German musical practices of the Reformation are covered, as are descriptions of Jewish music for worship, leading to discussions of instrumental music for church use by composers such as Mattheson. This eclectic history of church music provides the reader with an overview of the rich and varied possibilities for music in worship, including the use of instrumental music.

Explorations of "music in general" (including theoretical aspects of musical sound) and "The Science of Music" (chapter 10) must, according to Gratiaen/ Lustig, have practical outcomes: "All musical arts must have a use in practice."[72] The section on "acoustical properties of sound" in chapter 12 explains basic principles of sound production, for example using the metaphor of ripple effects in water to explain sonic vibrations, thus rendering this information accessible to the general reader.[73] This is followed by discussions of bells, trumpets, and the construction of organ pipes, keyboard instruments, and the like; then, crucially, it factors temperature into sound production on string instruments: "The warmer a music room becomes, the more the tension dissipates, which causes strings to move more slowly, as though they are less stretched, thus producing lower tones."[74] One wonders if Gratiaen may have considered it useful for inhabitants of the tropics to include Lustig's detailed remarks on the impacts of humid weather and climates as they pertain to keyboard instruments. The text states that strings maintain their tuning best in cooler weather, though "excessive dryness causes the wood to shrink, which, with regard to organ registers, cannot be stopped, and thus some pipes join [in sounding] uninvited. There is no better remedy for this than patience to wait for humidity to return."[75] This practical information would have been relevant to music making in the varied and more extreme climates inhabited by the widely dispersed members of the Batavian Society. Chapter 12, "On Musical Materials" ("De Muziekaale [S]toffe"), is clearly aimed at enthusiasts, as it offers basic instruction in understanding music notation: "one counts musical letters from the bottom to the top, or from lower tones to higher ones."[76] A description of the various types of musical intervals follows, and with this the published text ends abruptly.

CONCLUSION: SPECULATION ON RECEPTION

While Mutsaers has already pointed out the unlikelihood of scholars in Batavia recognizing the inherent intertextuality (or more plainly, plagiarism) of Gratiaen's text, one wonders whether some other contemporaneous readers of the *Verhandelingen* elsewhere, especially those in the Netherlands, may have identified its contents as the work of Lustig.[77] Given that Lustig was still alive in 1792—he died in Groningen in May 1796—it is theoretically possible that even he might have been aware of this Batavian publication. Certainly, two of the Bataviaasch Genootschap's corresponding members were based in the same city as he.[78] However, any evidence of literary reception—in Asia, Europe, or elsewhere—has yet to emerge. For now, we can comment only on the existence of copies that were separated from the *Verhandelingen* and that became part of various library collections. A self-standing copy of Gratiaen's text was apparently contained in the British Library; the catalog lists the date in square brackets as "1780" but notes that it was destroyed (at a time not specified).[79] Nevertheless, a set of the journal volumes belonging to Joseph Banks remains there; the volume in question has his stamp of ownership on the reverse of the title page (its bleed-through is visible in figure 2–1) but has no annotations or visible signs of his having read it.[80] The 1877 published catalog of the library of François-Joseph Fétis (1784–1871) lists a copy that was likewise seemingly detached from the journal.[81] Its publication details are given as "s. l. n. D." ("sans lieu ni date," without place or date); however, the second name of the author is spelled "Vranciscus," which implies that it was probably the 1792 edition, since in the reprint of 1827, it appeared as "Franciscus."[82] The same catalog includes a copy of Lustig's *Twaalf redeneeringen over nuttige Muzikaale Onderwerpen*, so a comparison by Fétis or another reader would theoretically have been possible.[83] Another separatum of the first edition is held in the Bibliothèque nationale de France.[84] The 1893 catalog of the music library of Dutch musicologist Daniel François Scheurleer (1855-1927) lists a copy of the 1827 version of Gratiaen's text within a section headed "Algemeene Beschouwingen.—Aesthetik" (General ideas—aesthetics).[85] Like Fétis, Scheurleer possessed a copy of each edition of another work of Lustig—in this case the *Inleiding* (1751 and 1771 editions)—and one wonders whether he also could have noted their similarity with the work of Gratiaen.[86]

Despite the author's plagiarism, it can be acknowledged that Gratiaen was responsible for reordering and restructuring Lustig's work in a unique way, and presumably through a process that was meaningful and useful for him in his local context—even if at the same time disingenuous. It is not clear whether Gratiaen ever intended the "Redeneeringen" for publication, given its posthumous production and the role of his son-in-law in delivering the manuscript. At the same time, one must ask why he would have taken the trouble to assemble and adapt the segmented portions of Lustig's text, deliberately changing biographical details in the process, if he did not mean to claim the work as his own (whether in printed form or as a manuscript for private use or circulation). For musicologists and cultural historians looking at the complex societies of colonial Batavia and Colombo, the history of the production and publication of the treatise nevertheless invites new ways of thinking about long-distance intellectual and musical connections that existed between people involved with a transnational company such as the VOC. It also inspires us to look further into vestiges of their musical activities that can be drawn from archives dispersed around the world. In these senses among others, Gratiaen's text becomes a useful and inspiring source to provoke additional questions about the place of music within VOC society, and the ways in which its members attempted to transplant their cultural practices to diverse outposts along their trading routes.

NOTES

1. Johannes Vranciscus Gratiaen, "Redeneeringen over nuttige Muzikaale Onderwerpen, Tot onderzoek van Kenners, tot verlustiging van Geoeffende en tot onderrichting van weetgierige Muziek-liefhebbers," *Verhandelingen van het Bataviaasch Genootschap van Kunsten en Wetenschappen* [hereafter Verhandelingen] 6 (1792): seventh section, "Voorreeden" (1–14), contents (1–2), and main text (1–286); 95–299 in the reprint of the volume published in Batavia in 1827.

2. Extant source documents use varying spellings of his name. The Flemish spelling, Gratiaen, appears on the document and is used by his many descendants today. The Dutch spelling, Gratiaan, is used in the VOC documents, among other sources. We are grateful to Rebekah Ahrendt for clarifying this distinction.

3. This is not the only extensive music treatise from the late eighteenth century to be printed by Europeans in Asian cities. In 1792, the famous essay by Sir William Jones "On the Musical Modes of the Hindoos" appeared in the journal *Asiatick Researches*, published in Calcutta. See Sir William Jones, "On the *Musical Modes* of the *Hindus*: written in 1784, and since much enlarged—By the President," *Asiatick Researches: Or, Transactions of the Society, Instituted in Bengal, for Inquiring into the History and Antiquities, the Arts, Sciences, and Literature of Asia* 3 (1792): 59–87.

4. An early mention of it in anglophone scholarship is in Katharine Smith Diehl, *Printers and Printing in the East Indies*, vol. 1, *Batavia* (New Rochelle, NY: Aristide D. Caratzas, 1990), 166.

5. P. E. M. Strategier, "De taal der hartstochten: De visie van drie achttiende-eeuwse Nederlandse schrijvers op muziek en haar relatie met de dichtkunst" (PhD diss., University of Amsterdam, 2001), 16.

6. Strategier, "De taal der hartstochten," 16.

7. On the establishment of this Dutch colonial outpost, see Jean Gelman Taylor, *The Social World of Batavia: Europeans and Eurasians in Colonial Indonesia*, 2nd ed. (Madison: University of Wisconsin Press, 2009), 3–19. On networks, see Siegfried Huigen, Jan L. de Jong, and Elmer Kolfin, eds., *The Dutch Trading Companies as Knowledge Networks* (Leiden: Brill, 2010).

8. Such a request provides an example of European musical patronage possibly connected to wealth drawn from colonial contexts. On Dejean, see Otto Bleker, "Ferdinand Dejean (1731–97): Surgeon of the Dutch East-India Company, Man of the Enlightenment, and Patron of Mozart," *The Historian* 78, no. 1 (2016): 57–80; J. S. Jenkins, "Mozart's Indian: Dr Ferdinand Dejean," *Journal of Medical Biography* 2, no. 1 (1994): 53–58; Stephen Martin, "The Symbolic Portrait of Mozart's Patron Dr. Ferdinand Dejean," *Hektoen International: A Journal of Medical Humanities* 10, no. 4 (2018), https://hekint.org/2018/04/12/symbolic-portrait-mozarts-patron-dr-ferdinand-dejean/. Mozart, for his part, referred to Dejean as "the Indian Dutchman, that true friend of humanity," with the last comment probably referring to Dejean's medical work. Jenkins, "Mozart's Indian," 56.

9. Taylor, *The Social World of Batavia*, 139–40.

10. In Charles Ralph Boxer, *The Dutch Seaborne Empire 1600–1800* (London: Hutchinson, 1965), 270.

11. See the drawing (with watercolor) held in the Rijksmuseum (object number NG-369) by Jan Brandes, "Hollands bruidsfeest te Batavia, Jan Brandes, 1779—1785," *Rijksmuseum*, www.rijks museum.nl/en/collection/NG-369, accessed March 2, 2023. Reproduced in Taylor, *The Social World of Batavia*, 65. Brandes traveled widely and produced artworks depicting everyday scenes—some including music—in Dutch settlements within Java, Sri Lanka, and southern Africa. See reproductions and extensive discussion in Max de Bruijn and Remco Raben, eds., *The World of Jan Brandes, 1743–1808: Drawings of a Dutch Traveller in Batavia, Ceylon and Southern Africa* (Zwolle: Waanders, 2004).

12. Danielle Fosler-Lussier, *Music on the Move* (Ann Arbor: University of Michigan Press, 2020), 22–23; Taylor, *The Social World of Batavia*, 61.

13. Fosler-Lussier, *Music on the Move*, 24–25. The list of people to be sold, along with their birthplaces and occupations, is transcribed in C. A. Gibson-Hill, "Documents Relating to John Clunies Ross, Alexander Hare and the Early History of the Settlement on the Cocos-Keeling Islands," *Journal of the Malayan Branch of the Royal Asiatic Society* 25, no. 4 (1952): 168–69.

14. See Taylor, *The Social World of Batavia*, 47–49, 61.

15. Hendrik E. Niemeijer, "The Free Asian Christian Community and Poverty in Pre-Modern Batavia," in *Jakarta–Batavia: Socio-Cultural Essays*, ed. Kees Grijns and Peter J. M. Nas (Leiden: KITLV Press, 2000), 85.

16. For discussion of this source, see David R. M. Irving, "The Genevan Psalter in Eighteenth-Century Indonesia and Sri Lanka," *Eighteenth-Century Music* 11, no. 2 (2014): 239–41.

17. Diehl, *Printers and Printing*, 146. Diehl undertook pioneering archival research in Jakarta in the early 1970s and connected the history of printing in this city to its urban musical past.

18. Max de Bruijn, "The Lutheran Church," in *The World of Jan Brandes, 1743–1808: Drawings of a Dutch Traveller in Batavia, Ceylon and Southern Africa*, ed. Max de Bruijn and Remco Raben (Zwolle: Waanders, 2004), 182.

19. Brandes's watercolor over a pencil sketch, now in a private collection, is reproduced in Max de Bruijn, "Interior of the Lutheran Church," in The World of Jan Brandes, 1743–1808: Drawings of a Dutch Traveller in Batavia, Ceylon and Southern Africa, edited by Max de Bruijn and Remco Raben (Zwolle: Waanders, 2004), 185; for the front-on view from the earlier watercolor of 1753, see 186, and for context about the organ, see 187.

20. Diehl, *Printers and Printing*, 179.

21. Taylor, *The Social World of Batavia*, 86.

22. Lian The and Paul W. Van der Veur, *The Verhandelingen van het Bataviaasch Genootschap: An Annotated Content Analysis* (Athens: Ohio University, Center for International Studies, 1973), 3; Diehl, *Printers and Printing*, 155; Taylor, *The Social World of Batavia*, 86. As Huib J. Zuidervaart and Rob H. van Gent point out, however, the immediate inspiration for its foundation had been the astronomical observations of clergyman Johan Maurits Mohr (1716–75) from the 1760s. Huib J. Zuidervaart and Rob H. van Gent, "'A Bare Outpost of Learned European Culture on the Edge of the Jungles of Java': Johan Maurits Mohr (1716–1775) and the Emergence of Instrumental and Institutional Science in Dutch Colonial Indonesia," *Isis* 95, no. 1 (2004): 21–25.

23. Taylor, *The Social World of Batavia*, 85–86.

24. The and van der Veur, *The Verhandelingen*, 1–2.

25. Taylor, *The Social World of Batavia*, 85–86. See also Diehl, *Printers and Printing*, 154.

26. Translation in The and van der Veur, *The Verhandelingen*, 3.

27. Diehl, *Printers and Printing*, 155.

28. See discussion in The and van der Veur, *The Verhandelingen*, 13.

29. Diehl, *Printers and Printing*, 158.

30. S. W. Massil, "The History of the National Library of Indonesia: The Bibliographical Borobudur," *Libraries & Culture* 24, no. 4 (1989): 475–88. Diehl points out that the Bataviaasch Genootschap later "had its own printing establishment" and that it produced work for other organizations; she gives the example of a program for a cantata performed "at Willems Kerk (now Immanuel Church [Gereja Immanuel]) on 16 July 1843 celebrating the newly installed pipe organ (in excellent condition in 1972)." Diehl, *Printers and Printing*, 160.

31. For an overview of the journal, see The and van der Veur, *The Verhandelingen*. For a discussion of content in the early volumes, see Taylor, *The Social World of Batavia*, 86.

32. Diehl, *Printers and Printing*, 153.

33. Diehl, *Printers and Printing*, 154; The and van der Veur, *The Verhandelingen*, 3. Further research is required to understand the circumstances and practicalities of its distribution.

34. The and van der Veur, *The Verhandelingen*, 16.

35. The and van der Veur, *The Verhandelingen*, 5.

36. Hans Groot, *Van Batavia naar Weltevreden: Het Bataviaasch Genootschap van Kunsten en Wetenschappen, 1778–1867* (Leiden: KITLV Uitgeverij, 2009), 120.

37. Johannes Godefridus Frederiks and F. Jos van den Branden, *Biographisch Woordenboek der noord- en zuidnederlandsche Letterkunde*, 2nd revised ed. (Amsterdam: L. J. Veen, 1888–1891), 294. Transcription at www.dbnl.org/tekst/bran038biog01_01/bran038biog01_01_1599.php.

38. Peter de Baets, "Michael Ondaatje: Een Brugse connectie," *Biekorf: West-Vlaams Archief voor Geschiedenis, Archeologie, Taal- en Volkskunde* 112, no. 2 (2012): 169–70; Lutgard Mutsaers, "Jan Frans Gratiaen: Michael Ondaatje's Ancestor from Flanders," *The Low Countries* 21 (2013): 284–85.

39. De Baets, "Michael Ondaatje," 169.

40. De Baets, "Michael Ondaatje," 170; Mutsaers, "Jan Frans Gratiaen," 285.

41. Nationaal Archief, VOC, Opvarenden (passengers), Nummer toegang: 1.04.02, inventarisnummer: 13017, folio 242, www.nationaalarchief.nl/onderzoeken/index/nt00444/c638724c-c864–11e6–9d8b -00505693001d, accessed February 28, 2023. Many thanks to Rebekah Ahrendt for pointing out this source. See also Huygens Instituut, "The Dutch East India Company's Shipping between the Netherlands and Asia 1595–1795: Details of voyage 3347.1 from Rammekens to Batavia," https://resources .huygens.knaw.nl/das/detailVoyage/94420, accessed February 28, 2023.

42. F. H. de Vos, "Genealogy of the Family of Gratiaen of Ceylon," *Journal of the Dutch Burgher Union* 6, no. 1 (1913): 16. That ship set out from the Cape on January 18, 1747, and arrived at Ceylon on August 17, 1747; see Huygens Instituut, "The Dutch East India Company's Shipping between the Netherlands and Asia 1595–1795: Details of Voyage 3368.3 from Texel to Ceylon," https://resources .huygens.knaw.nl/das/detailVoyage/94441, accessed February 28, 2023.

43. De Vos, "Genealogy of the Family of Gratiaen of Ceylon."

44. De Baets, "Michael Ondaatje"; Mutsaers, "Jan Frans Gratiaen." Ondaatje is renowned for a number of prize-winning novels, including *The English Patient* (1992). He has written about his family in the book *Running in the Family* (London: Picador, 1984).

45. De Baets, "Michael Ondaatje," 170.

46. Mutsaers, "Jan Frans Gratiaen," 285.

47. De Baets, "Michael Ondaatje," 170; Mutsaers, "Jan Frans Gratiaen," 285. These appointments are also found in the annual *Naam-boekje*, a catalog of VOC employees and officials, in which he is listed variously as "Johannes François Gratiaan" and "Johannes Franciscus Gratiaan." See, for example, *Naam-boekje van de wel. ed. Heeren der Hooge Indische Regeeringe, gequalificeerde persoonen, enz. en bedienden op Batavia; Mitsgaders de Respective Gouverneurs, Directeurs, Commandeurs en Opperhoofden op de Buiten Comptoiren van Nederl. India, zoo als dezelve ultimo September 1759. in wezen zyn bevonden. Als meede alle de Gouverneurs Generaal, zedert het jaar 1610. Nevens de hooge en mindere Collegien en Bediendens op de Buyten Comptoiren van Nederlands India* (Amsterdam: Cornelis Wilt, 1760), 71, where "Johannes Francois Gratiaan" is listed as "*Consumptie Boekhouder*" with the date of commencement given as 1758.

48. De Baets, "Michael Ondaatje," 170.

49. According to de Vos, Gratiaen's daughter Johanna Gerardina (1768–1836) married de Boers (who was from Gouda) on October 28, 1787. See de Vos, "Genealogy of the Family of Gratiaen of Ceylon," 16.

50. Mutsaers, "Jan Frans Gratiaen," 285.

51. "Voorberigt," *Verhandelingen* 6 (1792): first section, 2–3.

52. In "Naam lyst der heeren Directeuren, Dirigeerende en andere Leden van het Bataviaasch Genootschap der Kunsten en Weetenschappen &c." (dated February 7, 1791), *Verhandelingen* 5 (1790): first section, 53; also in a list with the same title (dated February 17, 1792), *Verhandelingen* 6 (1792): first section, 40.

53. Translation in Cicero, *Tusculan Disputations*, translated by J. E. King, Loeb Classical Library 141 (Cambridge, MA: Harvard University Press, 1927), 281. The original Latin (280) is: "Num fingo, num mentior? Cupio refelli; quid enim laboro nisi ut veritas in omni quaestione explicetur?" Lustig adapts it as follows, citing Cicero: "Si mentor, si fingo, refelli cupio; quid enim laboro, nisi ut veritas in omni quæstione explicetur. Cicero. Quæst. tusc. 3." Jacob Wilhelm Lustig, *Inleiding tot de muzykkunde: uit*

klaare, onwederspreekelyke gronden, de innerlyke geschapenheid, de oorzaaken van de zonderbaare uit-werkselen, de groote waarde, en 't regte gebruik der muzykkonst aanwyzende (Groningen: printed for the author by Hindrik Vechnerus, 1751), page 9 of unnumbered "Voorrede." Coincidentally, Johann Mattheson had also used this quote in his *Der musicalische Patriot* (Hamburg, 1728), 203–4. Lustig, who studied with Mattheson in Hamburg, is likely paying homage to his teacher here.

54. Gratiaen, "Redeneeringen," "Voorreeden," 14.

55. Gratiaen, "Redeneeringen," "Voorreeden," 6.

56. Lustig, *Inleiding*, page 6 of unnumbered "Voorrede."

57. Lustig, *Inleiding*, pages 4–5 of unnumbered "Voorrede."

58. See Sébastien de Brossard, *Dictionnaire de musique, contenant une explication des termes grecs, latins, italiens & françois les plus usitez dans la musique* (Paris: Christophe Ballard, 1703), page 3 of unnumbered section titled "Catalogue des auteurs qui ont écrit en toutes sortes de Langues, de Temps, de Païs &c.," under "Cinquième classe."

59. Gratiaen, "Redeneeringen"; "Voorreeden," 4–5.

60. "Naam lyst," in *Verhandelingen* 6 (1792), first section, 49.

61. Lustig, *Inleiding*, page 4 of unnumbered "Voorrede."

62. Gratiaen, "Redeneeringen," "Voorreeden," 4.

63. Neal Zaslaw, "Leclair, Jean-Marie," *Grove Music Online*. Retrieved 28 Feb. 2023, from www.oxfordmusiconline.com/grovemusic/view/10.1093/gmo/9781561592630.001.0001/omo -9781561592630-e-90000380313.

64. Zaslaw, "Leclair, Jean-Marie."

65. Zaslaw, "Leclair, Jean-Marie."

66. Frederiks and van den Branden, *Biographisch Woordenboek*, 294.

67. The information offered in Frederiks and van den Branden's *Biographisch Woordenboek*, including their proposed date for Gratiaen's study in France, is reproduced without comment by De Baets in his short essay on Gratiaen. See De Baets, "Michael Ondaatje," 169.

68. Jan Bouws, *Solank daar musiek is . . . Musiek en musiekmakers in Suid-Afrika (1652–1982)* (Cape Town: Tafelberg, 1982), 33.

69. Gratiaen, "Redeneeringen," 45, 49.

70. Gratiaen, "Redeneeringen," 53.

71. Gratiaen, "Redeneeringen," 59, 60.

72. Gratiaen, "Redeneeringen," 161.

73. Gratiaen, "Redeneeringen," 189–93.

74. Gratiaen, "Redeneeringen," 212.

75. Gratiaen, "Redeneeringen," 230–31.

76. Gratiaen, "Redeneeringen," 263.

77. Mutsaers, "Jan Frans Gratiaen," 285.

78. They are listed as J. A. Engelhard and N. G. Schroeder. "Naam lyst," *Verhandelingen* 6 (1792): first section, 46.

79. British Library, General Reference Collection D-7898.l.26.

80. British Library, General Reference Collection 438.k.13–27.

81. Bibliothèque royale de Belgique, *Catalogue de la bibliothèque de F. J. Fétis, acquise par l'état belge* (Brussels: Librairie Européenne C. Muquardt, 1877), 813 (no. 6915).

82. This same copy is held in the Koninklijke Bibliotheek / Bibliothèque royale (Royal Library of Belgium), and the catalog entry for it lists "Batavia" and "1792" in square brackets. It also gives a reference to RISM (Répertoire International des Sources Musicales) B VI, 375.

83. Bibliothèque royale de Belgique, *Catalogue de la bibliothèque de F. J. Fétis*, 811 (no. 6891).

84. Bibliothèque nationale de France, V-25231.

85. Daniel François Scheurleer, *Catalogus der muziekbibliotheek van D. F. Scheurleer* (The Hague: printed by Gebr. Giunta d'Albani, 1893), 38.

86. Scheurleer, *Catalogus*, 25.

PART II

Missionaries and Local Music in the Nineteenth Century

3

___

"I am in no way surprised that the Javanese can listen to it all night long"

A Nineteenth-Century Dutch Missionary
on Javanese Music

Henry Spiller

In the early 1600s, when the Dutch East India Company (Vereenigde Oostindische Compagnie, hereafter VOC) began its economic exploitation of Java and the other islands of what is now the modern state of Indonesia, the Dutch merchants who ran the VOC showed little concern for the lives of the indigenous population beyond their economic potential. Although they happily transferred European technologies such as weaponry—not to mention European diseases—to Java, they did not think it desirable, as did the Spanish and Portuguese colonialists, to try to convert the locals to Christianity. As Frances Gouda wrote, "During its nearly 200 year presence in Java, evangelical activity had not really constituted a 'priority' of the Dutch East India Company."[1]

Most of the VOC's interests were taken over by the British during the Napoleonic Wars in the early nineteenth century and then handed off to the new Dutch Republic in 1814. Like the VOC, however, those controlling Dutch economic interests in the Indies remained reluctant to jeopardize their commerce with Javanese Muslims by promoting Christian missionary activity.[2]

Christianity in Java was marginal, at best, around the beginning of the nineteenth century. Sartono Kartodirdjo reports that there were about seventy thousand indigenous Christians serviced by only five preachers in Java in 1797; but according to Aritonang and Steenbrink, "In 1800 there were virtually no native Christians in Java" and no coordinated and continuing missionary efforts, either.[3]

Early Christian conversions were local, bottom-up affairs. Around 1820, for example, Coenraad Laurens Coolen (1775–1873), who had a Russian father and an aristocratic Javanese mother, established a village, Ngoro, not far from Surabaya. There, he and his followers practiced a syncretic version of Christianity that incorporated aspects of Javanese mysticism, including hymns in "traditional Javanese style" as well as *wayang* and dance.[4] Another early Christian missionizer was the German-born Johannes Emde (1774–1859), who originally came to Java as a watchmaker and was married to a Javanese woman. In contrast to Coolen, Emde's goal was to thoroughly Westernize his Javanese converts.[5] Emde even formulated a list of "ten commandments" for his Javanese flock that explicitly forbade gamelan, wayang, and *tembang*.[6]

Leaving aside for the moment the question of precisely how many Javanese subscribed to these homegrown forms of Christianity at the beginning of the nineteenth century, one thing is clear: there was no dogmatic, one-size-fits-all answer for whether traditional Javanese arts are compatible with Christianity. These early approaches to Javanese Christianity either embraced *or* forbade Javanese arts—just as the competing Dutch missionary societies would do as the nineteenth century progressed, as we shall see.

Once the semiofficial Dutch "hands off religion" policy ended in the early nineteenth century, a dizzying array of Protestant sects established as many as twenty-one mission societies in Holland with the aim to proselytize local populations in the Indies—"convert the 'heathens and Mohammedans,'" as one group stated their goals—but it was only by the 1830s that Dutch missionaries came to Java in any significant, yet still very small, numbers, never more than about twenty in the second half of the nineteenth century, according to Arps.[7] According to Maryse J. Kruithof, it was not until the 1850s that the Nederlandsch Zendeling Genootschap (Netherlands Missionary Society, NZG) initiated concentrated missionizing efforts in Java.[8] The Dutch government continued to discourage interference with the practice of Islam, which limited the areas in which missionaries could work; but the government saw advantages in using missionaries for education and research, especially into local languages and traditions, which could help advance Dutch economic goals.[9]

Indeed, many of the most prolific documentarians of the languages and cultures of nineteenth-century Java were first and foremost missionaries, who, as the anthropologist Rita Smith Kipp puts it, effortlessly wove "anthropology and evangelism into one seamless life."[10] Kipp echoes James Clifford, who sees what he calls a "common cultural heritage" in the putative rivalry between godless, relativist anthropologists and the anti-science, ethnocentric missionaries: he writes that they both are "an amalgam of Greek rationality and Christian universalism. . . . Both participate in a restless Western desire for encountering and incorporating others, whether by conversion or comprehension."[11] Clifford's view of the commonalities between anthropology and Christian missions runs counter to the received secular humanist wisdom that anthropological relativism is a neutral position; but it helps to make more sense of missionaries' sometimes sympathetic engagement with Javanese culture.

In this chapter, I examine some of the work of one such individual, Henrik Smeding (1833–91), who was a missionary in Kediri, East Java, between 1858 and 1861. Most of Smeding's peers were not favorably disposed to the Javanese arts. Smeding's successor in Kediri, Carel Poensen (1836–1919), for example, a noted linguist and documenter of Javanese culture in his own right, described Javanese music as "noise" (*herrie*).[12] And J. L. Zegers, a missionary in Indramayu, in 1876 mentioned several reasons why a particular church property was undesirable, including the "proximity of the screams of the ronggengs (dancing girls) and the monotonous sound of the gamelan (Javanese music orchestra)."[13]

Smeding, in contrast, praised the Javanese arts. He sums up his first encounter with gamelan music with a poetic compliment: "The gamelan sounds are, especially heard from a distance, a pleasant rain, a soft feeling caressing sound, and I am by no means surprised that the Javanese can listen to it all night long."[14]

Like most of his fellow Protestant evangelists, however, he did not think Javanese artistic practices, including singing, were suitable for Christian worship services. Using James Clifford's terms, it is clear that Smeding privileged conversion over comprehension. Nevertheless, his contributions to comprehension are worthy of our attention in that they represent the clear, careful descriptions of a fresh eye and ear in a time and place for which not much such evidence survives. Furthermore, examining Smeding's complicated engagements with Javanese music provides some insight into the related dilemmas of both the anthropologist *and* the missionary.

SMEDING AS ANTHROPOLOGIST

The Dutch mission societies regularly published the ethnographic and linguistic scholarship of the missionaries. In particular, the NZG included detailed accounts, written by missionaries, in its periodical, *Mededeelingen* (Notices).[15] The 1861 edition includes an account, written by Smeding, of a trip he took early in his time in Java with another missionary, S. E. Harthoorn, to Kediri, Madiun (Madioen) and Mojokerto (Modjokerto), in July, 1859.[16]

According to his account, upon arriving in Kepanjen (Kĕpandjèn, near Malang) after a long day of travel, Smeding "suddenly became aware of the sweet melancholic sounds of a gamelan." His Javanese host, noticing his interest, took him to the place where the gamelan was being played. Smeding ascertained, by questioning those in the house, that they were celebrating Javanese New Year. Smeding provides a detailed account of the information he gleaned through what we might, in retrospect, call "ethnographic method": he "got to know about gamelan through asking questions and observation."[17]

What follows are some of Smeding's observations. The gamelan in question, he writes, is called a *nénéngah* or *panĕngah*, a "middle sort" (*middelste soort*). In modern parlance, such a designation could refer to the size of the instruments, the tessitura of its tuning, or even the quality of its materials and craftsmanship.[18] Smeding says the term refers to the set's *omvang* and *grootte*, both multivalent Dutch words which might refer to the number of instruments as well as their actual size. Curiously, the aforementioned Poensen later includes "De gamĕlan-panĕngah" in his encyclopedic list of various kinds of gamelan, misinterpreting Smeding's description as a reference to a fully fledged genre of gamelan ensemble rather than as a simple descriptive qualifier.[19]

Smeding notes that the human voice plays a leading role in gamelan music, while the instruments provide accompaniment (a point to which I will return shortly). He then proceeds to describe the instruments in considerable detail. First, the *rebab* (spike fiddle), which he calls a "Javanese violin."[20]

The description is rather long, and here I highlight only a few specific spots that demonstrate the acuity of his descriptions. Regarding the construction, he reports that the instrument's body is similar "to an ostrich egg cut in half" and is "made of nangka wood (a yellow, very hard wood), with a bladder stretched over the open side." About tuning, he notes that "the lowest string in tone corresponds to the main tone of the saléndro [tuning system]. . . . The second string differs with the first one by a pure fifth." Describing the playing technique, he makes the keen observation that "the fingers touch the strings, but do not press them against the neck of the instrument; in this way even the vibrato, which occurs so frequently in Javanese singing, can easily be imitated by a slight movement of the fingers." Finally, he indicates that the rebab player is the "orchestra master (*pĕmbateg*), and plays the melody, which is [also] sung. All the other parts are based on him, and thus on the singing."[21] It is clear from this description that Smeding was not only a keen observer but also skilled—or at least relentless—in asking questions and processing the answers.

Smeding's emphasis on a vocal basis for gamelan music is particularly noteworthy. Later in the article, he takes to task existing authorities—Thomas Stamford Raffles and J. A. Wilkens—for their insistence that gamelan music is metrical.[22] Smeding instead characterizes the music as "declamatory," by which he means that the vocal (and rebab) parts are in free rhythm (*een vrije tijdmaat gebruikt*): "The orchestra therefore adheres to a measure, but it is only the subjective feeling of the singer whereby it is indicated and controlled; so it can be said at the same time, Javanese music knows no meter."[23]

Such a view contradicts not only Raffles and Wilkens, but subsequent twentieth-century scholarship on gamelan music by Western specialists such as Jaap Kunst and Mantle Hood.[24] But Smeding's emphasis on gamelan music's basis in vocal music foreshadows the groundbreaking scholarship of the Javanese ethnomusicologist Sumarsam, who makes the case that the metrical surface structures of gamelan music derive from an unperformed "inner melody," and that vocal melodies provide the "melodic precedent" for gamelan pieces.[25] I am tempted to

FIGURE 3-1. Raffles's drawing of *bonang* (1817).

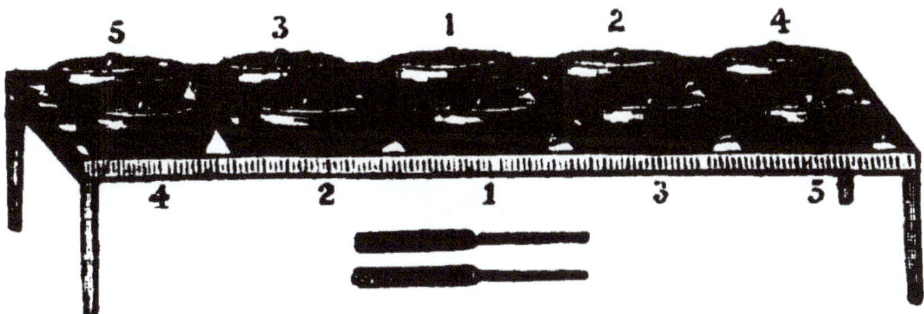

FIGURE 3-2. Smeding's drawing of *bonang* (1861).

furthermore make another contrarian interpretation of these comments about rhythm. Perhaps Smeding was trying to characterize the end-weightedness of Javanese understandings of meter, in which "the stress or accent comes at the end of a unit, rather than the beginning, and any subdivisions of a beat precede (rather than follow) the beat itself," a phenomenon for which no nineteenth-century European musician would have the vocabulary to explain.[26]

He may have consulted Raffles for information (figure 3-1), but Smeding's bonang illustration (figure 3-2) provides additional information.[27] A bonang typically has two rows of five kettles each; the row farthest from the player consists of pitches that are one octave higher than the row closest to the player. Smeding labels the kettles in each row with the numerals 1 to 5 to indicate which kettles in the farther row are octave equivalents to kettles in the closer row. He makes the canny observation that the layout he documents facilitates playing octaves without having to cross arms—and indeed the octave pairs he indicates correspond to modern practice. The numbering system he uses, however, is obscure.

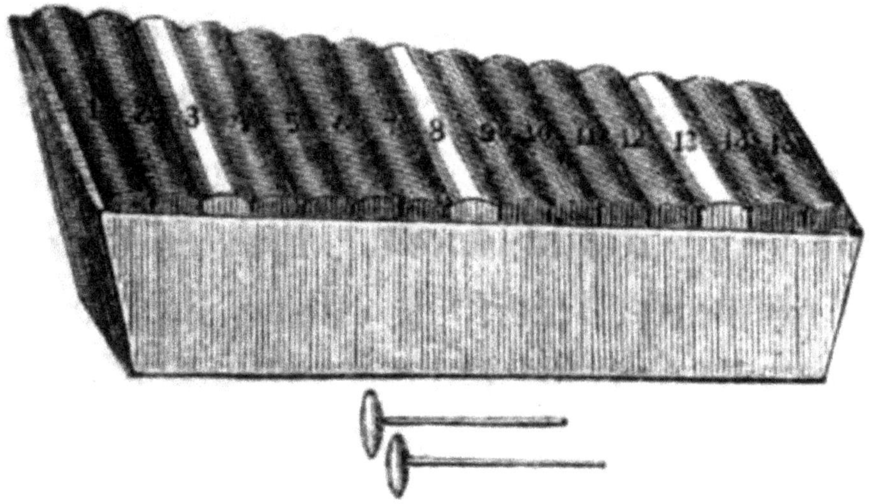

FIGURE 3-3. Smeding's drawing of *gambang* (1861).

The article also includes a description and illustration of "*gambang kajoe*" (*kayu*; figure 3-3). The details Smeding provides about the instrument's construction are for the most part consistent with modern instruments. Smeding makes much of the fact that the gambang has only five pitches/keys per octave; he notes that in the resultant scale, "the second and seventh are missing. It is therefore semitone intervals that this instrument lacks." He further remarks that this pentatonic tuning is consistent with the tendency of his congregants in Malang to replace any semitones with a pitch either "a half tone higher or one whole tone lower."[28]

Smeding's gambang illustration numbers each of the keys, and Smeding calls attention to three keys (3, 8, and 12), "which are lighter in color than the others and differ in pitch by an octave."[29] It is not clear from the prose, however, whether those three keys were actually lighter in color on the model instrument or were lightened only in the drawing for the purpose of illustration. It is unlikely that the instrument on which he based the drawing had numbers painted on the keys—this is uncommon in modern practice, and his bonang illustration (see figure 3-2) also added number labels, sequentially numbering all keys regardless of any octave duplications. (Unfortunately, this numbering system only makes the bonang illustration's numerals more puzzling.)

Smeding's descriptions are at times whimsical. He compares the shape of the various kettle gongs to "old-fashioned gentlemen's hats" (*oudmodische heerenhoeden*). After describing the large gong as a "bass instrument [*basspeeltuig*]," he goes on to compare the *kethuk* to the orchestral viola; given that the *kethuk* plays only a single note, one can't help but wonder if perhaps Smeding's comparison was the world's first viola joke.[30]

Some of Smeding's comments suggest that he misunderstood the differences between salendro and pelog tunings, and that gamelan music was not necessarily limited to the accompaniment of vocal music. He characterized *gending* as "declamatory," by which I think he means that the choral vocal parts (known in the present as *gerong*) for gamelan pieces were simple (relative to the *tembang* singing that he engages with later). And his own apparent bias toward vocal music may have led him to mistakenly characterize gamelan music as completely ametrical because the singing did not seem metrical to him. Nevertheless, in its accuracy, objectivity, and attention to descriptive detail, this encounter with a gamelan showcases the relativist anthropologist side of Smeding.

SMEDING AS MISSIONARY

Smeding devotes several pages of this same account to discussions with Javanese Christians about the propriety of gamelan music. At another stop on his journey, he is delighted to learn that one of the Christian residents there, named Matthew, had a reputation as a skilled gamelan player. Matthew was a former resident of Ngoro, the aforementioned Christian village led by Coolen, who advocated the use of gamelan and wayang in Christian worship. Smeding was disappointed to learn, however, that Matthew no longer had a gamelan. Smeding quotes Matthew as responding, "It is not proper for Christians to play gamelan." Smeding countered that Dutch Christians are allowed to play the "'Dutch gamelan' (piano) and the 'Dutch rebab' (violin)," and that Smeding himself "loves to hear the beautiful sounds of the Javanese gamelan."[31] Smeding asks Matthew to identify a place in scripture that forbids Dutch or Javanese music, and (of course) Matthew cannot.

However, Matthew mobilizes an argument that Smeding finds difficult to rebut: "If one has a gamelan, it isn't long before dancers are also involved." Smeding suggests to his readers that he is not convinced that dancing is inherently sinful, either, but acknowledged to Matthew that getting rid of his gamelan was probably the right thing to do: "There are many things in the world which are by no means evil in themselves, and therefore also are not forbidden by God; but if anyone knows that by such practice he comes to real sins, and if he does not abstain from it, he has already sinned against his conscience as a result." Here Smeding refers Matthew to the epistle of St. Paul to the Romans, chapter 14, which admonishes believers to respect the consciences of others, specifically in matters of food restrictions, but more generally as well. Smeding goes on, in his account, to cite a recent event, reported by another missionary, of a visit by a gamelan with *talédhék* dancers, which many of the local Christian men patronized; Smeding ultimately concedes that "gamelan is a trap for the Christian Javanese."[32]

As we saw earlier, Smeding is capable of being a relativist when considering gamelan music in the abstract. But here, the missionary in him seems to acknowledge that gamelan's associations with public dancing are a bridge too far, and any commitment to cultural relativity must take a back seat to promoting Christian moral values. Here we see the missionary taking precedence over the anthropologist.

SMEDING AS ANTHROPOLOGIST *AND* MISSIONARY

A third case makes a little more sense of this clash between his missionary and anthropologist sides. In a later article, published in 1862, Smeding provides a retrospective view of his ethnographic and linguistic work with his Javanese congregants as part of an effort to guide future missionaries. He also contributes to an ongoing discourse among Dutch missionaries about the potential for traditional Javanese music in worship, as foreshadowed by the different approaches of Coolen and Emde mentioned earlier.[33]

Smeding was convinced that Javanese music, including much gamelan music, was in essence vocal-based. Smeding, like most other Dutch scholars and missionaries, appears to have used the term *tembang* as a generic term for Javanese "song." Smeding's colleague, Harthoorn, with the assistance of his Javanese choirmaster (named Johannes), experimented with creating Christian *tembang* and advocated their use on a broader scale.[34] Smeding himself claims that he learned to sing some *tembang* from Johannes while he was teaching Harthoorn's congregation Dutch choral singing.[35]

As he did with the gamelan, he makes some pertinent and accurate observations about *tembang* performance practice. He notes that there are regional styles of singing *tembang*. *Tembang*, he asserts, is a solo performance, and the songs "are by their nature unsuitable for being sung more than one voice at a time, or they lose their peculiar character." What Javanese listeners admire about *tembang*, he writes, is its calm expression of deep emotions; despite the ornamentation in the singing, *tembang* are not "wild or voluptuous," and, furthermore, their calm expression reflects the Javanese character.[36]

Regarding *tembang* melodies, Smeding insists that they defy staff notation, in their pitch vocabulary, their ornamentation, and in the variability of individual performances.[37] He comments on F. W. Winter's set of transcriptions of twenty-eight *tembang* (1874): "I must admit that I do not know how to reproduce [the Javanese] ways of singing, completely freely figured by the singer, from [this] notation." Finally, he observes, *tembang* texts are obscure, written in what Smeding calls "Kawi Miring, the language of the poets."[38] He notes that many Javanese do not understand the language without some explanation.

According to Jaap Kunst, "To the Javanese, singing and poetry are one and the same thing," and the term *tembang* refers to "purely vocal compositions" and includes songs/poems in various *macapat* meters.[39] In contemporary practice, each *macapat* meter is defined by a specific number of lines, each with a specific number of syllables and ending with specific vowel sounds. Each meter is associated with one or more basic melodic forms, which provides an abstract melodic outline that guides individual performances of poem. And most significantly, each *macapat* meter expresses an affect or mood, which is hinted at in the name of the poetic meter.[40]

To demonstrate the flexibility of both themes and style in *tembang* songs, as well as the very specific nature of these performances' expression of affect, consider a very recent *macapat* song, in the *pocung* meter, presented on YouTube by one of the four central Javanese royal palaces, Kraton Ngayogyakarta Hadiningrat, in Yogyakarta, as part of a series of *macapat* videos that the palace posted as one of its responses to the COVID-19 pandemic.[41]

The palace official who introduces the video describes the affect of *pocung* as "careless, humorous, flexible, but giving advice."[42] He specifies that the *pocung* verses have four lines, each of which has a specific number of syllables and ends with a particular vowel sound:

line 1: 12 syllables, ending with an 'u' sound
line 2: 6 syllables, ending with an 'a' sound
line 3: 8 syllables, ending with an 'i' sound
line 4: 12 syllables, ending with an 'a' sound

The Javanese text of the poem, as presented in subtitles on the video and published in *Balungan*, follows these conventions precisely—each line has the prescribed number of syllables and ending vowel sound:

Kang tuwajuh nindakake keh pituduh
Ngadhepi Korona
Manut dhawuhing pangarsi
Aja kendhat dhedhepe marang Hyang Suksma[43]

I find it rather charming, even humorous, that the requisite "a" vowel at the end of the second line is fulfilled with the word *korona*, referring to the virus. The flexibility of the form is apparent in the poet's capacity to bring the *pocung* form to bear on a very immediate problem, namely the COVID-19 pandemic. The tone of the poem (as rendered in English by translator Nyi MJ. Reninawangmataya) expresses the requisite affect of *pocung* by providing practical advice in a light, humorous manner:

Follow the instructions earnestly
To combat the corona virus outbreak
Follow all of the orders from the leader (government)
Never stop relying on God[44]

From Smeding's writings, it appears that he was only dimly aware of how very specific were the formal and stylistic details of *macapat*: "The so-called matja matja of the Javanese," he writes, "the singing-reading of everything his literature offers him, takes place according to some kind of terminology, which is indicated at the top of the piece, and there seems to be more taste and suitability than content in this." In fact, the "terminology . . . at the top" (i.e., the specification of the form *pocung*) is quite specific, and many ordinary Javanese listeners would immediately comprehend the details and subtleties of such poems.[45]

But while he praises the practice of *tembang* singing, he ultimately advocates against Harthoorn's push to incorporate *tembang* into Christian worship—not because it is sinful or pagan, as asserted by other missionaries, but because adapting it to the requirements of Christian worship would compromise *tembang*'s aesthetic integrity. The characteristics he describes, Smeding argues, are inconsistent with the role of congregational singing in Christian worship. Referring to Harthoorn's attempts to promote *tembang* with Christian themes, he writes, "I hope that I will not be misunderstood to underestimate the value of Christian *tembang*. This is so far from what I mean that I intend, if I have the opportunity, to use *tembang* in schools. Here they can provide excellent services for training the converts. Perhaps there are other related examples that I will come to know, with more knowledge and experience, but [as for now] I consider [*tembang*] to be certainly unsuitable for singing of the congregation in religious gatherings."[46]

Determining whether Javanese music was suitable for Javanese Christians strained the relationship between Smeding's anthropologist and missionary selves. His anthropologist self found gamelan music to be delightful in the abstract, but his missionary self recognized that for Javanese congregants, gamelan music's associations with dancing girls and prostitution made it difficult to redeem for Christian contexts. In the case of *tembang*, Smeding's anthropologist and missionary selves found common ground. His advocacy for Dutch, rather than Javanese, singing was based both on an anthropologist's understanding of the relationship between musical style and social function and a missionary's confidence in the worshipful nature of group choral singing. He even cites one of his Javanese consultants to validate his opinion: "The above-mentioned Johannes, a great lover of tembang, said to me plainly: 'the tembang are beautiful, but if they are sung equally by more than one person, they are ugly. They are not intended for that. . . . The Dutch songs are very much more beautiful, because they can be sung by many at once.'"[47]

CONCLUSION

"I am convinced that a thorough knowledge of music and song of the Javanese would open to us a rich source of knowledge about the nature and character of this people," Smeding wrote to the board of the NZG in response to their question about the music education of missionaries.[48] His statement echoes the sentiment of generations of ethnomusicologists, who believe, as Bruno Nettl puts it, "that the teaching of their subject will . . . promote intercultural—maybe even international—understanding."[49]

Ethnomusicologists would likely insist that their motives are more objective than those of a missionary. As James Clifford points out, however, missionaries and anthropologists express the same "restless Western desire for encountering and incorporating others, whether by conversion or comprehension."[50] Clifford is pointing out that the power differentials between missionaries and their Others are essentially the same as the power differentials between foreign anthropologists—along with ethnomusicologists—and those same Others.

There is little doubt that missionaries such as Smeding, whatever their motivations, have left behind a trove of otherwise irretrievable lore about Javanese language, culture, and performing arts. This "rich source of knowledge about the nature and character of [a] people," as Smeding puts it, has the potential to augment modern understandings of Javanese history—indeed, of global history—and contribute in the present to counterbalancing the injustices of the past.

NOTES

1. Frances Gouda, *Dutch Culture Overseas*: Colonial Practice in the Netherlands Indies, 1900–1942 (Jakarta: Equinox Publishing, 2008), 66. See also Rita Smith Kipp, *The Early Years of a Dutch Colonial Mission, The Karo Field* (Ann Arbor: University of Michigan, 1990), 25.

2. Gouda, *Dutch Culture Overseas*, 66.

3. Gouda, *Dutch Culture Overseas*, 639–40.

4. Jan Sihar Aritonang and Karel Steenbrink, "Christianity in Javanese Culture and Society," in chapter 14 of *A History of Christianity in Indonesia*, ed. Jan Sihar Aritonang and Karel Steenbrink (Leiden: Brill, 2008), at 641.

5. Aritonang and Steenbrink, "Christianity in Javanese Culture and Society," 713.

6. Bernard Arps, "De Kwestie van het Javaanse Kerkgezang," In *Woord en Schrift in de Oost: de betekenis van zending en missie voor de studie van taal en literatuur in Zuidoost-Azië* (Leiden: Opleiding Talen en Culturen van Zuidoost-Azië en Oceanië, Universiteit Leiden, Semaian 19, 2000), 1–32, at 9.

7. Kipp, *The Early Years of a Dutch Colonial Mission*, 28; Arps, "De Kwestie van het Javaanse Kerkgezang," 7.

8. Maryse J. Kruithof, "Zaaiers, zaait in Gods naam voort!, Carel Poensen, het leven van een zendeling-etnoloog (1836–1919)" (PhD diss., Erasmus Universiteit Rotterdam, 2010), 4.

9. Gouda, *Dutch Culture Overseas*, 66, 67.

10. Kipp, *The Early Years of a Dutch Colonial Mission*, 8.

11. James Clifford, *Person and Myth: Maurice Leenhardt in the Melanesian World* (Durham, NC: Duke University Press, 1992), 126.

12. See Kruithof, "Zaaiers, zaait in Gods naam voort!," 78.

13. Papers of J. L. Zegers (1870-1890 zendeling te Indramajoe) in Utrecht Archive, letter written January 5, 1876, to his superiors, https://hetutrechtsarchief.nl/onderzoek/resultaten/archieven?mivas t=39&mizig=210&miadt=39&micode=1102-1&milang=nl&mizk_alle=zegers%20j.l.&miview=inv2, 220–21.

14. Henrik Smeding, "Bezoekreis naar de gemeenten in Kediri, Madioen en Modjokerto, gedaan van 9 tot 29 Julij 1859, door de zendelingen S.K Harthoorn en H. Smeding," *Mededeelingen van wege het Nederlandsche Zendelinggenootschap 5* (1861): 120–50, 245–86, 134.

15. Kipp, *The Early Years of a Dutch Colonial Mission*, 9.

16. Smeding, "Bezoekreis naar de gemeenten in Kediri," 00.

17. Smeding, "Bezoekreis naar de gemeenten in Kediri," 128.

18. Midiyanto, personal correspondence with author, October 22, 2022.

19. Carel Poensen, "De Wajang," *Mededeelingen van wege het Nederlandsch Zendelinggenootschap* vol. 16 (1872): 59–115, at 81.

20. Smeding, "Bezoekreis naar de gemeenten in Kediri," 128.

21. Smeding, "Bezoekreis naar de gemeenten in Kediri," 128.

22. Thomas Stamford Raffles, *The History of Java: In Two Volumes* (London: Black, Parbury, and Allen, 1817); J. A. Wilkens, "Séwåkå,een Javaansch gedicht met eene vertaling en woordenboek," *Tijdschrift voor Nederlandsch-Indië*, 2 (1850): 381–461.

23. Smeding, "Bezoekreis naar de gemeenten in Kediri," 133.

24. Kunst, *Music in Java*, 3rd enlarged ed., 2 vols. (The Hague: Martinus Nijhoff, 1973); and Mantle Hood, *The Nuclear Theme as a Determinant of Patet in Javanese Music* (Groningen: J. B. Wolters, 1954).

25. Sumarsam, "Inner Melody in Javanese Gamelan Music," *Asian Music* 7 (1975): 3–13; Sumarsam, *Gamelan: Cultural Interaction and Musical Development in Central Java* (Chicago: University of Chicago Press, 1995), 161.

26. Henry Spiller, "University Gamelan Ensembles as Research," in *Mapping Landscapes for Performance as Research: Scholarly Acts and Creative Cartographies*, ed. Shannon Rose Riley and Lynette Hunter, 171–77 (Hampshire: Palgrave Macmillan, 2009), at 174. See also Spiller, "Lou Harrison's Music for Western Instruments and Gamelan: Even More Western than It Sounds," *Asian Music* 39 (2009): 31–52.

27. Raffles, *The History of Java*; Smeding, "Bezoekreis naar de gemeenten in Kediri."

28. Smeding, "Bezoekreis naar de gemeenten in Kediri," 131.

29. Smeding, "Bezoekreis naar de gemeenten in Kediri," 131.

30. Smeding, "Bezoekreis naar de gemeenten in Kediri," 131.

31. Smeding, "Bezoekreis naar de gemeenten in Kediri," 131.

32. Smeding, "Bezoekreis naar de gemeenten in Kediri," 131.

33. See Arps, "De Kwestie van het Javaanse Kerkgezang."

34. Smeding, "Enkele Opmerkingen env rage over het zendingswerk op Java," 248–49.

35. Smeding, "Enkele Opmerkingen env rage over het zendingswerk op Java," 238.

36. Smeding, "Enkele Opmerkingen env rage over het zendingswerk op Java," 248, 250–51, 252.

37. Smeding, "Enkele Opmerkingen env rage over het zendingswerk op Java," 250–53.

38. Smeding, "Bezoekreis naar de gemeenten in Kediri," 250.

39. Kunst, *Music in Java*, 122.

40. See Wedana Susilomadyo, "Macapat from the Kraton Yogyakarta: Classic Poems for a Contemporary Catastrophe," transl. Nyi MJ. Reninawangmataya, *Balungan* 14 (2020): 49–53; Margaret J. Kartomi, *Matjapat Songs in Central and West Java* (Canberra: National University Press, 1973).

41. Susilomadya, "Macapat from the Kraton Yogyakarta," 49. The video is available at www.youtube.com/watch?v=FcwPdRXzMnE

42. Susilomadya, "Macapat from the Kraton Yogyakarta," 49.

43. Susilomadya, "Macapat from the Kraton Yogyakarta," 52.

44. Susilomadya, "Macapat from the Kraton Yogyakarta," 53.

45. Smeding, "Enkele Opmerkingen env rage over het zendingswerk op Java," 254.

46. Smeding, "Enkele Opmerkingen env rage over het zendingswerk op Java," 254.

47. Smeding, "Bezoekreis naar de gemeenten in Kediri," 253.

48. Letter from Smeding to the NZG dated February 7, 1862, Het Utrechts Archief, 1102–1, 1.2.2.7.2.2.4.

49. Bruno Nettl, *The Study of Ethnomusicology: Thirty-Three Discussions* (Champaign: University of Illinois Press, 2015), 18.

50. Clifford, *Person and Myth*, 126.

4

The Issue of the Javanese Church Songs

Bernard Arps

A key component of Protestant worship is congregational singing.[1] Imagine a church service in mid-nineteenth-century Amsterdam. Solemn-looking citizens, dressed in sober black, intone a psalm at the top of their voices to organ accompaniment, slowly paced and deliberate, from memory or a hymnal, in a vast stone building that resounds majestically.[2] Despite the difference in climate, the Willemskerk in Weltevreden or the Protestant Church in Surabaya looked and sounded much the same. Decades after the event, Javanese villagers who had discovered Christianity in the remote countryside but received baptism in the latter church in 1843–46 still cherished a lively recollection of their experience that night:

> For one person, as he entered that glorious building with its lighting, it was as if he entered the portal of heaven, filling him with holy reverence and timidity; for another those solemn organ tones, later coupled with the singing of the gathered multitude, were like hearing songs of praise from the saints in heaven, collectively lauding God's greatness and love.[3]

A service in the village church of rural Swaru, Karangjasa, or Waru Jayeng was a different matter. The walls and ceiling of bamboo matting were hardly conducive to stately resonance. An organ was lacking, as were hymnbooks. The women wore ankle-length wraparound skirts and blouses with a sash over the shoulder, the men the same kind of lower garment and high-collared jackets, often without headcloth and never with a kris—preferably no covered heads and certainly no weaponry in the house of God. If the turnout was good, some of the congregation sat on mats on the floor. Even so, the liturgical procedure differed little from the Dutch one. This is how Reformed (*Gereformeerd*) preacher F. Lion Cachet describes the first

FIGURE 4-1. Protestant mission house and church in Plaosan, Purwareja. Cachet, *Een jaar op reis in dienst der Zending*, 255.

Javanese service he attended during his "year on the road in Mission service" on Sunday, May 31, 1891, in the ward of Plaosan (figure 4-1) in the town of Purwareja, southern Central Java:

> Dressed simply in a black coat, Brother Wilhelm takes his place behind a lectern, raised somewhat above the ground, . . . and the religious service commences with *"Doeh Råmå kawoelå hingkang wontĕn hing swargå"* ("Our Father, Who art in Heaven. . . ."). After the prayer, a psalm verse was sung, rendered into Javanese from our rhymed version, retaining the ordinary melody. Every line was prompted rather loudly by a native assistant, which was indeed necessary because, apparently, only a few adults could read, and both Bibles and Psalters were almost completely absent. After the reading of the Law and Articles of Faith, there was again prayer and song, after which a sermon followed, to be concluded with thanksgiving and a final hymn, and a benediction. All of this approximately as is usual during the service in our Churches in the Netherlands, although lasting not much longer than an hour.[4]

Although they did sing, Javanese Christians were not easily persuaded to burst into jubilant melody. In fact their singing became a controversial point of contention among the missionaries who felt responsible for the Christian–Javanese rite. These people were well aware that Javanese—of whatever denomination—sang, and that some even liked to. But how and what should they have them sing during Christian worship?

That the texts had to be in Javanese was beyond dispute. It was only in this language that Javanese could experience the texts in the way they should. But regarding the musical side, opinions varied. In the 1830s and 1840s, the early days of Christianization in rural East Java, European observers had been quite accepting of native singing styles. This may be illustrated by the impression of Brumund, pastor in Surabaya, of a service around 1850 in a remote community that stood under the tutelage of "the apostle of Java," Protestant missionary J. E. Jellesma (in Java 1848–58):

> I could note a few innocent, perhaps even good remnants of their earlier faith among the new converts. The speaker's amen repeated every time by the entire congregation, and the hands folded together and held at mouth's height during prayer. The hymns were raised to a Javanese mode of singing; this was certainly not as pleasant sounding as ours, but, I believe, nonetheless more pleasant sounding than ours— entirely different from theirs—would have sounded if raised by them. Moreover it was national, and they must be allowed to keep everything among them that is a national good and unharmful.[5]

Key features of communal ritual and its esthetics were persistent: the audience punctuating an Arabic prayer with *āmīn*, the cupping together of one's raised hands with the palms facing upward during prayer, and Javanese voicing and melody. Jellesma was tolerant of this, at least initially. It was different, however, with most of the other trained and accredited Protestant missionaries sent by European missionary societies who began to operate on Java from mid-century. Some found it difficult to imagine anything other than the melodies of Dutch psalms and hymns in the house of God. Yet as predicted by Brumund, it was painfully easy to hear that these melodies were quite un-Javanese. The Reverend Lion Cachet reports about a Sunday service led by a Javanese officiant in the village of Benca, not far from Purwareja:

> Such "singing"! As if all had a cold, and in addition each individual *must* produce something entirely distinctive in the field of song, in a different tonality, with a tune thus far unknown. It would have been cause for screams of laughter, had it not cut through the heart in such a pathetically painful way. Poor people; they truly cannot help it; of the music that is chorale, so totally different from theirs, they have no understanding.[6]

Lion Cachet voiced a widespread sentiment among the missionaries. According to some, therefore, more Javanese-sounding tunes were to be preferred. But where should these come from? Could existing Javanese types of song, particularly the common traditional sung stanzaic verse forms known as *tembang*, be allowed in church?[7] Another possibility might be to have new Javanese-style melodies composed specially for Christian worship. But this option brought practical problems: Who should create them?

A DEBATE IN 1901–1902

The issue of the Javanese church singing was discussed in writing repeatedly. By far the most detailed treatment, and because of its lively character also the most gripping, is found in a series of polemical articles by two anonymous authors in the missionary periodicals *De Getuige* (The witness) and *De Opwekker* (The arouser) of 1901 and 1902. This polemic was clearly considered important, for two years later, the articles from *De Opwekker* were reprinted in book form under the title of *Iets over gĕnḍing en tĕmbang en over Javaansch kerkgezang* (A little about *gendhing* and *tembang* and about Javanese church singing). Taking, in good philological fashion, this discussion as the starting point, in this chapter I examine the question why the Protestant missionaries, and possibly Javanese Christians themselves as well, found the Javanese church singing so problematic.[8]

First, a brief characterization of the polemic. Someone writing under the pen name of "een Indo" (a Eurasian) had expressed himself disparagingly in *De Getuige* about an attempt to have a Christian Javanese text sung to the accompaniment of a gamelan piece (in Javanese, a *gendhing*). This experiment, he wrote, could only fail, "for never ever has a Javanese sung to gendhing." In this connection "a Eurasian" had claimed that "the Javanese's sense of hearing and his *adat* [customs] have been violated and mutilated" and "his property destroyed and rendered unrecognizable."[9]

"Een leek" (a layperson) responds to this. The response is devastating. The experiment was not odd at all, because choral singing to gamelan accompaniment does exist, although perhaps not in the place where "a Eurasian" is stationed. Musically it works perfectly well. The accusation of mutilation and violation is therefore groundless. However, this kind of music does not appeal to the congregation of "a layperson." He sketches what in his view is the best form of church singing: "melodies composed specially for the Native or modified after the nature of Javanese music."[10] This is not urgent, however, because the way the European melodies—which are widespread—are sung is actually not bad.

This discussion is followed by a reply in six parts by "a namesake of 'a layperson'" (*een naamgenoot van 'een leek'*), followed in turn by an extensive six-part rejoinder from "a layperson."[11] In the course of the exchange, it transpires that "a Eurasian" is the reformed missionary L. Adriaanse (on Java 1895–1902). As successor to J. Wilhelm, whom we met in Lion Cachet's first quotation, Adriaanse was based in Purwareja. In his controversial book *Sadrach's kring* (Sadrach's circle, 1899) Adriaanse had spoken with some approval about the person and practices of Sadrach Surapranata (ca. 1835–1924), spiritual leader of a large number of Christian congregations in western Central Java, who was in bad repute with most missionaries because of what they felt were his Javanese syncretistic ideas.[12] Adriaanse made overtures to Sadrach but without much success.[13] "A layperson" considers "a Eurasian," "a namesake of 'a layperson,'" and Adriaanse as a "trinity" (Dutch: *drieëenheid*).[14]

"A layperson" manages to hide his identity more effectively, but circumstantial evidence suggests that he was P. Anth. Jansz (1853–1943), the Mennonite missionary teacher who is best known as founder of the mission colony of Margareja in the residency of Japara (north coast of Central Java).[15] Jansz founded this village in 1883 in accordance with the idea propounded by his father, P. Jansz (1820–1904), known among other things as a translator of the Bible into Javanese, that evangelization was best accomplished in combination with the clearing and settling of land. The Javanese in Margareja were not obliged to be Christians, but they did have to promise to obey a number of rules, including "to abandon all idolatrous and superstitious customs" and "to attend loyally the religious gatherings."[16] With his brother-in-law and several Javanese teachers, P. Anth. Jansz gave mandatory Christian school lessons to the local youth. This included instrumental and vocal music. Jansz Jr., who spoke Javanese fluently, also led Sunday service, and as noted by Lion Cachet, "the singing was very good."[17]

Let me return to the discussion and henceforth (at the risk of being proven wrong) refer to "a layperson" as Jansz Jr. and "a namesake of 'a layperson'" (and "a Eurasian") as Adriaanse. Apparently somewhat intimidated by Jansz's passionate argument, Adriaanse states in the conclusion of his reply that he, too, awaits new songs in Javanese style. In his rejoinder, Jansz Jr. declares that his opponent has not convinced him of the desirability of using familiar Javanese forms of song for church services. The most important reason is that—according to Jansz—the Javanese themselves reject them: "The serious-minded part of the congregation is . . . *against* existing tĕmbang and gĕnding and gamĕllan in church."[18] Their opinion is not prompted by the author (Jansz) or other missionaries. As long as no suitable melodies have been created by or for Javanese Christians, one can safely continue to use Dutch ones. The congregation likes to sing them and does so well.

JAVANESE CHRISTIANS AND THEIR SONGS

Although in the second half of the nineteenth century there were never more than twenty Protestant missionaries at work in Java at any one time, circumstances in Javanese Christendom were complicated, not to say chaotic.[19] Besides the congregations led by envoys of the various Dutch and foreign missionary corporations, hundreds of Javanese Christians lived outside the direct supervision of missionaries. These people, sometimes referred to as *Kristen Jawa* in contrast to the *Kristen Landa* (Dutch Christians) of the missionaries, followed Javanese spiritual guides like Sadrach, mentioned above.

Little is known about the liturgical viewpoints of Javanese Christians outside the missionaries' sphere of influence, but there do exist a few brief descriptions of their worship. The founder of what may be identified as the first community of Javanese Christians was a man with a Russian father, a Javanese mother, a Dutch wife, and a Javanese wife. He was Coenraad Laurens Coolen (ca. 1785–1873), a former civil servant and military man who settled in Ngara, south of Jombang in East Java, probably in 1828.[20] Coolen cleared land for rice fields and established an estate of which he was granted the leasehold by the regional colonial authorities. Among the Javanese who settled and worked on his estate, Coolen propagated Christianity.

FIGURE 4-2. "Coolen begins to give moral instruction from the Gospel." Rijksmuseum RP-T-oo-3930-12.

Sunday service in Ngara involved the communal melodic reciting of formulas and prayers at several junctures.[21] After Coolen read from the Bible and gave a short explication (figure 4-2), the congregation sang hymns that, according to Van Akkeren had been translated by Coolen from a Dutch hymnbook. Their melodies were Javanese.[22]

Rituals clearly modeled on Muslim devotional practices were prominent in the religiosity established in Ngara, also outside the church. Every weekday evening, for instance, the (male) inhabitants gathered in (or outside) a community member's home, selected by rotation. The officiant—usually the host—sang Coolen's Javanese rendition of the Creed line by line, alternating with the participants' joint chanting of "There is no Deity but God / Jesus Christ is the Spirit of God" (*La ilaha illaloh / Yesus Kristus ya Rohullah*). This call-and-response recitation of the articles of faith ended with a phase where the participants continuously chanted "Indeed Jesus, indeed the Christ, indeed Jesus, indeed the Christ" (*Lha Yesus, lha Kristus, lha Yesus, lha Kristus* etc.), while rhythmically nodding the head in turn to the left and the right. This ritual was still remembered decades later under the name of *dhikiran*.[23] Not only did the procedure emulate devotional sessions in Muslim environments, which, moreover, went by the same name (derived from Arabic *dhikr*, "remembrance" of God), the refrain was a Christian variation on the Islamic profession of faith, and the movements were like those made during Muslim *dhikr* gatherings. After an interval, the participants sang hymns, ending the session by chanting the Lord's Prayer. Afterward, they sometimes continued to chat deep into the night.[24]

Coolen's fame and his practices and teachings attracted spiritual seekers, some of whom converted to Christianity. This is how the texts and tunes of his liturgy reached other parts of Java. One of these seekers was Pak Dasimah (d. 1848), who established a small Christian community in Wiyung near Surabaya, East Java. Dasimah was initiated into the main doctrines and liturgical formulas by Coolen around 1838 and stayed in contact with his teacher afterward.[25] Having come into contact with a group of European promoters of Christianity in Surabaya, in 1843 Dasimah was baptized in the city's Protestant Church (described in the beginning of this chapter). Christian worship in Dasimah's community became something of a curiosity.[26] Even decades later, members recalled that "sometimes on Sundays European ladies young and old [*nyonyah-nyonyah lan nonah-nonah*] from Surabaya would attend the congregation in Wiyung."[27] A brief account of a service "in a bamboo shed" by an observer from the Netherlands in 1846 described the scene:

> An old man positioned himself before a table, on which Bible and hymnbook were laid out; the others arranged themselves on benches, men and women and a few children, 27 in number. In a kindhearted, confident tone the aged officiant uttered a short prayer; thereupon he raised a song, in which all those present joined, that is to say those who understood it, for it was a Javanese Christian song with a Javanese melody, monotonous to our ears.[28]

We learn from other sources that what Van Rhijn called a hymnbook was in fact a proselytizing tract.[29] Dasimah had learned his church songs from Coolen but must have switched to texts from such pamphlets later.[30] They probably came from the

Surabaya-based Christian Society, founded ca. 1815, that circulated handwritten and printed tracts in Malay and Javanese.[31]

Coolen's worship made an impression, but not a favorable one, also on the accredited missionaries. Among other things, the fact that his songs were sung in Javanese style incurred their disapproval. Sources about Coolen invariably report that his religious formulas and hymns were cast in *tembang*. The term *tembang* denotes a category of melodic-metrical verse forms. Stanzas in *tembang* are versified according to complex metrical principles and read (usually aloud) with tunes that are intrinsically connected to the meters.[32] In this period, a great many Javanese genres, including lyrical, mystical, and magical texts, were versified in *tembang*. Of course, this made *tembang* suspect in missionaries' eyes. On a Christian estate where some of Coolen's followers settled after their baptism (not endorsed by Coolen), ten Christian commandments were in force, including "7. Thou shalt not read Javanese verse."[33] But it is doubtful that Coolen's songs indeed used *tembang* verse forms. The verb *nembang*, derived from the base *tembang*, could be used for all singing in Javanese scales, including if the texts did not have the metrical form of *tembang* in the strict sense. At any rate, the texts sung by Coolen's followers that I have seen are not in *tembang* but in free verse forms not known from elsewhere.[34]

Objections against Javanese song and related performing arts became widespread among Protestant missionaries. Only a few had a positive opinion of church singing in Javanese style and actively employed it. S. E. Harthoorn, who was active in the environs of Malang from 1854 to 1863 and whom we also meet elsewhere in this volume, was such an exception. According to his pupil Smeding, Harthoorn was the only one (read: the only missionary?) who used *tembang* for church songs. This was *tembang* proper, learned by Harthoorn's Javanese officiant Johannes in the royal city of Surakarta, Central Java. Still, Harthoorn used *tembang* only for the sake of variety; most of his church songs had Western melodies.[35]

In the same period, P. Jansz the elder, who would later deliver a passionate plea against *tembang* tunes, also toyed with the idea of basing the Javanese versions of psalms and hymns on the established literary tradition. As revealed in his diary, in 1858 and 1859 he rendered several dozen psalms "in Jav. Poetic meter" (*in Jav. Dichtmaat*). He wanted to have them printed in a small run "in order initially to be only in the hands of the missionaries etc." He also entertained the idea of selecting "ten to fifteen of the most easily intelligible psalms" and "having them printed with some of the most common church hymns along with the music in a special volume, to serve for general use in church and home."[36] The former collection was published in 1865 in Amsterdam; a greatly expanded version of the latter followed in Leiden twenty years later.[37] It turns out that with "Jav. Poetic meter," Jansz did not mean the existing *tembang* forms. The meters he used were his own creations. He seems to have thought he had designed them according to *tembang* principles, but he had misunderstood the structure of *tembang*.[38] Jansz limited his experiment to texts. Inasmuch as they are indicated in these volumes, the melodies are those of Dutch psalms and evangelical hymns.

Not all Javanese Christians outside missionary control sang like the followers of Coolen and Dasimah. The congregation of Tunggul Wulung (early 1800s–85) shows a rapprochement between Dutch and Javanese styles. Tunggul Wulung was an evangelist and spiritual leader who traveled around a lot but eventually settled with his followers in 1875 not far from where the Jansz family was stationed. Various accounts exist of Tunggul Wulung's conversion in the 1850s. He visited Coolen, but it seems that Jellesma played the most important role.[39] Tunggul Wulung's followers sang Javanese melodies, though not in church.[40] There they used spiritual texts versified by Jellesma:

> And doing this they sang, in their own manner, imitated chorale tunes with Javanese intervals, above all very drawn-out and very drawled (that is how it is supposed to be, they probably thought) and with the requisite Javanese twists or turns in between. And everyone followed their own musical feeling and had their own variation (*cengkok*), which they belted out as loudly as possible.[41]

Jansz describes a remarkable conjunction of old-fashioned churchly Dutch and traditional literary Javanese singing styles. In various places on Java and neighboring islands there were (and are) ways of singing texts where the solo reciter is joined at the end of a verse line by other participants, intoning approximately the same melodic contour, slowly, each with individual vocal embellishments, in neither textual nor melodic unison but heterophonically and very loudly.[42] Judging by Jansz's description, this is what Tunggul Wulung's congregation did. Meanwhile, Jansz was undoubtedly correct in believing that they self-consciously sang chorales. In this period in the Netherlands, the old-fashioned way of Protestant Church singing was isometric and slow.[43] Dutch ministers and early missionaries had promoted this style in the East as well. Congregational singing in Dutch- and Malay-language churches in north Sulawesi, the Moluccas, and Sri Lanka had an "utterly slow, drawling tone," as Van Rhijn observed in 1847, "so that on every note a few others, waving up and down, were sung in between."[44] Of course, Christianity was associated with the colonial oppressors. Once missionaries made their entrance, many Javanese Christians followed their new mentors also where the design of the liturgy was concerned. But they did not go all the way, and they may have been unwilling to. Certain facets of Javanese musical aesthetics continued to prevail with them. In all likelihood, the congregational singing in Benca, a community that followed Sadrach, was performed according to the same Javanese aesthetic standards. The vocal timbre that Lion Cachet heard there was not caused by a virus but by the manner of voice production that belongs to Javanese singing, which may appear nasal to unaccustomed ears.

Jansz adds to his description of divine service among Tunggul Wulung's followers that their singing truly sounded to European and Javanese musical ears alike as "the howling of dogs."[45] It is unlikely that the singers themselves would have described it in this way. But it was of key importance for the further development of the musical dimension of the Protestant Javanese religious service that the missionaries considered their performance as an undesirable abomination of Dutch choral singing. Luckily, the mission schools provided them with the means to teach Javanese children to sing well in European style.

THE PROTESTANT MISSIONARIES' DISCUSSIONS ABOUT JAVANESE CHURCH SONGS

In a word, the Javanese Christian liturgy in the nineteenth century showed musical diversity. At one extreme, there were independent groups that to different degrees gave a Javanese form to their church songs; at the other, there were communities under the tutelage of missionaries that, with varying success, sang in Dutch style. As the end of the century approached, an awareness of this plurality grew in Protestant missionary circles. Initially, there had been relatively little communication among the envoys of the different missionary corporations. To a certain extent, all the missionaries, who often operated in regions that were distant from each other, went their own way, including where the design of the liturgy was concerned.[46] However, in the last two decades of the century, circumstances changed. An important factor was the founding, in 1881, of the Netherlands–Indies Protestant Missionary Association (Nederlandsch–Indische Zendingbond), a platform for collaboration between the envoys of, in principle, all Protestant missionary societies.[47] It was this association that published *Gĕnḍing en tĕmbang* in 1904. *De Opwekker*, the periodical in which the polemic of Jansz Jr. and Adriaanse first appeared, served as this organization's organ from 1881, and it informed the missionaries about each other's practices and ideas.[48] The association's mission conferences (*zendingsconferenties*) convened every two to four years and provided a forum for seeking consensus. Papers were read about issues of consequence, and discussion, motion, and decision followed. Javanese church singing was on the agenda at the fourth (1885) and tenth (1900) conferences, the former with a paper read by P. Jansz Sr., the latter with one by schoolmaster J. Kats.

As noted, my central point of interest for analytical purposes is the debate reproduced in *Gĕnḍing en tĕmbang* 1904. This had been preceded, however, by several decades of discussion, incipient in Brumund's remark about an unharmful "national" mode of singing, but truly started from Smeding's principled treatment, written in 1860, of the pros and cons of Javanese and European song forms.[49] Jansz Jr. and Adriaanse's exchange of thoughts is best understood against this background; indeed, they make frequent reference to earlier sources.

A number of the missionaries' ideas and feelings about Javanese church songs have already been mentioned in passing. Basically, they saw three possibilities for the musical side of things: using Javanese song types, using European psalm and hymn melodies, or composing new melodies in Javanese style. The arguments raised in the debates after 1860 revolve around six themes. I will review them briefly in the following order: the formal aspects of the various types of singing, musical esthetics, musical and religious experience, ideological connotations of the different types of singing, the future of Javanese music, and the fact that a tradition of Javanese church singing had already been established.

In *Gĕnḍing en tĕmbang* 1904, Jansz Jr. argues vehemently against Adriaanse's use of an archaic category of *tembang* for church songs. He was against this, he claims, because Javanese are never heard singing in unison; in fact, this is impossible, because no two people realize a *tembang* melody in exactly the same way.[50] Jansz's argument was not new; Smeding had noted this forty years earlier. According-ing to Smeding, the problem was technical. *Tembang* lacked a steady musical rhythm and because each singer applied his or her own melodic ornamentation, the melodies simply could not be sung in unison. This was why the Javanese offici-ant Johannes—the one who had studied *tembang* in Surakarta in order to bring it into practice under Harthoorn—disapproved of *tembang* for religious service, preferring Dutch church songs.[51]

The missionaries' discussions about Javanese church songs tell us about arro-gance and misconceptions but also about Javanese musical practices, forms, and aesthetics of the time, including information and insights unrecorded in other sources. In his lecture at the mission conference two decades later, Jansz Sr. had even stated that in his experience, all Javanese singing was solo.[52] Possibly this was so in the north coast region where he was stationed, at least for singing in the Javanese language and by adults. In *Sadrach's kring*, Adriaanse had provided a range of counterexamples: the choral singing that goes with *bedhaya* and *srimpi* female group dances at the Central Javanese courts; the courtly praise songs sung to gamelan accompaniment by a chorus (the so-called *panembrama*); the genre of *slawatan*, which consists of Arabic songs of praise for the Prophet Muhammad, accompanied by frame drums and often using Javanese melodies; and the songs sung a cappella in children's games. Moreover, the situation in Sadrach's circle proved that Javanese choral singing in religious services was not only possible but unproblematic for those involved.[53] Ultimately, Jansz Jr. is obliged to admit that Javanese do sing in groups, but his notion of choral singing, like that of Smeding, requires melodic and rhythmic uniformity. Moreover, choral singing to gamelan accompaniment is rejected by Jansz's congregation, while unaccompanied *tem-bang* singing will result in the use of different melodies in different communities and even within the same community, and know-it-alls will either not sing along or will try to drown out the others.[54] In his response, Adriaanse considers this lack of geographical uniformity unimportant. It is not an issue in the Netherlands, where local differences also occur. Moreover, the use of notation will produce more sameness in the long run.[55] Jansz Jr. continues to insist that the variants in a *tembang* melody are so different that *tembang* cannot be used for choral singing.

Of course, a congregation can be taught a single version, but if they must be taught anyhow, why not European tunes? He claims that his pupils find it more difficult to learn *tembang* melodies than some European melodies.[56]

Not all arguments advanced in the discussions about Javanese church singing were in favor of Western melodies. At the ninth mission conference, Tiemersma had complained at length about the deficits of the Malay psalters. He thought that word stress in the Malay texts and the rhythm of the Dutch melodies to which they were sung often did not agree.[57] Kats, speaking at the tenth conference, felt that composing new melodies with matching texts was the best solution.[58] But overall, this issue was considered unimportant. In fact it had been efficiently disposed of by Jansz Sr., for whom the wrong rhythm did not matter because "the Natives do not feel or understand anything about it anyhow: owing to their own *pantuns* [sung quatrains in Malay and other languages] and *tembangs*; those who can sing keep to the cadence, but they do not bother about the stress of the words."[59] The phrasing was derogatory, but Jansz was right. Word stress is irrelevant to Javanese (and Malay) song.[60]

Other points made in the discussion between Jansz Jr. and Adriaanse concerned musical aesthetics. At the 1885 conference, Albers had argued that in mission schools, much attention should be paid to "the Christian song," because the native religious vocal genres sounded so terrible: "In a land where the *tukang adan* shouts; where *dikir* equals roaring; *nembang* equals screaming; prayer equals buzzing, in such a land all care must necessarily be devoted to song, if possible to singing in parts. The influence of Christian, melodious singing is simply beyond measure. It arouses the best possible sensations in the human being."[61] Fifteen years later, Jansz Jr. and Adriaanse no longer speak about Javanese singing in this manner. Even Jansz is remarkably relativistic about the aesthetic value of Javanese song—though not without rhetorical ulterior purpose, as it allows him to declare that Javanese have the same attitude to Western music: "Just as *we* may consider *well*-performed *native* choral singing or gamelan playing lovely and melodious but still rank our own music higher, thus a *native* who has a feeling for music in general may consider many a *European* melody, if *well* executed, beautiful, yet still put his own music above it."[62] And, Jansz continued, even if the alternatives are musically on a par, from a moral viewpoint Western church music must be preferred.

A related issue lay in tonality. It was noted frequently that many congregations sang out of tune. Undoubtedly correctly, Smeding attributed this to the influence of Javanese scales.[63] But Jansz Jr. disagrees. In his experience, the singing in Javanese congregations and mission schools is often better than in the Netherlands, especially if singing is part of these schools' curriculum.[64]

The verbal duel between Jansz and Adriaanse, this succession of idea and attenuation, of argument and rebuttal, concerned not only externalities like whether or not certain ways of singing existed, their exact form, and their musical worth. More important still was what happened in the Javanese mind. The discussants also devoted attention to the musical experience of singing and, linked to this, its moral and religious experience, as well as a still less tangible issue, namely that of its ideologies, thought to be apparent from the immorality and godlessness of kindred artistic forms.

Years earlier, Jansz the elder had already attempted to bring *tembang* into disrepute. In his lecture against the use of *tembang*, he alluded to the characters (*watak*) of the verse forms, which, according to him, were about "battle and war," "love stories," "sadness, primarily . . . frustrated love," and "lust and pleasure."[65] Jansz was selective in his choice of examples and biased in how he represented them. He conveniently forgot to note that not all *watak* identified in Javanese poetics have the kind of sensual nature that would immediately appear reprehensible to Calvinists. Two of the most common *tembang*, for instance, are felt to be "charming, captivating" and "friendly, sociable." And "lust and pleasure" is unknown as a verse form character; the term that Jansz translated in this way was probably *nepsu*, but in poetics, this means "angry."[66]

The missionaries drew psychological conclusions from the way the Javanese congregations sang the Dutch melodies. The idea that the Javanese did not understand Dutch music, that they were incapable of identifying with it, was widespread (see, for instance, the end of the second quotation from Lion Cachet). Adriaanse and initially also Jansz Jr. held the same opinion.[67] Most missionaries considered it self-evident that Javanese did identify with their own music, but it was doubtful that it had the correct ethos. According to Smeding, for instance, *tembang* lacked "that expression of mental elevation to the grand and exalted which is needed by the religious mind." Also, Smeding wrote, *tembang* had a passive character in accordance with the Javanese national character.[68] Additionally, Jansz Jr. saw signs that the Javanese do not feel more at home in their own music: "I have never noticed the children in school here having a better understanding of tĕmbang melodies with lyrics by Javanese poets, or singing them with more feeling, in a livelier manner, with greater enthusiasm than the European melodies of their school and Sunday school songs."[69] The way the psalm was sung in Benca—probably without much ardor—made Lion Cachet wonder whether the singers actually understood the text.[70] Jansz and Lion Cachet passed over the fact that a *con brio* singing style is extremely rare in Java. Textual comprehension cannot be measured by how fiery the delivery is.

Both Jansz and Adriaanse present themselves as advocates of their Javanese congregations. According to Adriaanse, they want church songs in *tembang*; according to Jansz, absolutely not. It gradually becomes clear that the reason for rejection by Jansz's congregation is ideological. *Tembang* is associated with heathen and sensual art forms like wayang shadow play and *tayuban*, a dance event in which a professional singer-dancer, usually female, known inter alia as *tledhek* or *ronggeng*, dances with male guests (figure 4-3).[71] This association had been posited by Jansz Sr. in his conference lecture:

FIGURE 4-3. Two *ronggeng* and a gamelan ensemble (c. 1910). Leiden University Libraries, KITLV 27411, http://hdl.handle.net/1887.1/item:801808.

> But the biggest objection [against using *tembang* for church singing] for most among you is likely to be that the song tunes in question have everywhere been heard from olden times until the present particularly from the mouths of those who have chosen Venus's service as their profession, which situation will continue to obtain in the future until it has been fully defeated by Christianity.[72]

Jansz Sr. was convinced that in the past, *tledhek* used to be priestesses in the service of "the Indian Venus or Sukra." The *tembang* tunes must originate from this idolatry as well, "So even their birth would have been in uncleanness." The conclusion is evident: "It appears to me that it would be unethical, indeed horrible, if in our Christian meetings the same tunes were sung that were heard yesterday and will be heard tomorrow from the mouths of public whores under the influence of opium."[73]

Jansz got it seriously wrong. *Tembang* verse was seldom sung by *tledhek*. Albers pointed this out in a footnote to Jansz's claim: *tembang* is primarily used in literature. He even called Jansz's statement "a gross error." Jansz Sr., who had been working among Javanese for thirty-one years, had composed a Javanese grammar and dictionaries, had re-versified psalms and hymns in Javanese, and was busy translating the Bible—in short, who had developed into a Javanese *littérateur* himself—should have known better. Apparently, he did not *want* to know better. His attempt to debar *tembang* goes back to fear of the unknown, not only the unknown in contemporary Javanese society (of course he did not mingle with dancing girls) but also the unknown in the past; his idea of the origins of *tembang* was pure speculation. Perhaps he was deceived by the ambiguity of the word *tembang*.

It is not only the alleged connection with *tledhek* that disqualifies *tembang* for Christian worship. For Jansz Jr., who is more knowledgeable than his father was a decade and a half earlier, *tembang* is tainted especially by the fact that it is sung by the puppeteer (*dhalang*) in wayang performances.[74] He presents this as the opinion of his flock; they feel an aversion to *tembang* tunes, he asserts, "which perhaps at the very moment when the congregation praises God in the house of prayer, a small distance away are being sung by a dhalang during a wayang."[75] Wayang, after all, depicts heathen stories.

Opposite the ideological unsuitability of Javanese song stood the proven suitability of the Dutch rite. Adriaanse tries to undermine this argument in favor of European church songs by claiming:

> I have . . . repeatedly heard people working in the mission field express the opinion that the Western song tunes belong with Christianity and therefore *must be introduced to the Javanese along with Christianity*. . . .
>
> If one bears in mind that the Javanese have *first* been given such an impression, it is unsurprising if *later* the Javanese Christians go a step further and claim that the Dutch chorale tunes were sung in this way already by Israel in the Temple and *therefore* must now also be used by the Javanese congregation.[76]

Jansz parries the attack with an insinuation addressed to Adriaanse's *Gereformeerd* church. He has never come across this idea among missionaries, but he does "recall once having heard in the Netherlands that such an opinion is sometimes found there, for instance among rigidly *Gereformeerd* farmers on the Veluwe. Might the esteemed writer perhaps be confusing the one with the other, and now think by mistake that he has observed said assertion coming from a *Javanese* mouth?"[77]

Along with the present and the past, the future of Javanese singing is of concern as well. Jansz's and Adriaanse's disputation took place in the beginning of the so-called ethical policy era. The basic political idea was that after a long period of economic exploitation, it was the moral obligation of the Dutch to elevate the Indigenous population of the Netherlands East Indies from its underdeveloped condition. We find this idea reflected in the discussion between Adriaanse and Jansz. Both agree that Christendom has the duty to raise Javanese music from its primitive level of development. In Adriaanse's words, "In my modest opinion the Protestant mission is called, inasmuch as this concerns its work, to contribute to the further development and ennoblement, indeed Christianization, of Javanese musical and poetic art."[78]

At the 1885 conference, Jansz Sr. had asked his audience whether one should

> try to obtain compositions for church song which, at any rate as much as possible, resemble their tonality more than ours do, taken either from the same school [i.e., that of Javanese tradition] or from the European school; albeit arranged in such a way that monotony is avoided and that they clearly prove to be tunes different from those performed by the popular songstresses, as well as, of course, more suited to the purpose.[79]

Jansz Sr. thought that the monotonousness of Javanese song could be explained by its level of development. The "musical scale" of the Javanese, according to Jansz, is

> that of childhood in music, which [in Europe] was brought to greater perfection as time progressed and civilization increased, so as to meet the requirements of euphony and harmony.
>
> These peoples have not come along with civilization but have remained with the old, primitive scale, which is why naturally their melodies bear a characteristic trait of monotony—I would almost say, of naivety—to some passages of which our more practiced hearing, accustomed as it is to greater luxuriance, is attracted, but in the totality of which it finds little other than boredom in the longer run.[80]

Consequently, Jansz queried if it was advisable to invite one or more European composers to create some pieces of music in Javanese style by way of experiment. It was suggested in the discussion following the lecture that the current situation should not be conserved. Javanese song had to develop. Nonetheless, Jansz's proposal, while "not undesirable," was deemed unrealistic. The motion was carried to stimulate the use of European melodies.[81] It was very convenient, of course, that, as the chairman noted, Jansz had just published his collection of Javanese psalms and evangelical hymns, which represents such tunes with staff notations and often identifies a Dutch psalm or hymn as the source of the tune.[82]

As we have seen, the results of the missionaries' decision were disappointing. It is hardly surprising, then, that at the tenth conference fifteen years later, the issue was revisited. In an extremely long-winded exposition, J. Kats, teacher at a European school in Batavia who had a special interest in singing, sketched how contemporary European harmonic music was the perfect end of a unilinear musical evolution.[83] Javanese music was closest to that of the ancient Greeks, albeit inferior in several respects. This explains why European church song was not appreciated. The Javanese should not be given music "for which he is far from ripe, and which, following the ordinary course of development, he will only comprehend and understand in several centuries."[84] The "productive artistic capacity of the Native" must be aroused and strengthened. The mission's task is clear: "Not to preserve the current situation, as the conference of '85 feared, but to build on and develop what exists by initiating it."[85] Kats came with two alternative proposals: set up a test with songs suitable for choral singing, in Javanese verse forms and tunes, or, if this was impossible, a test "with a singing method designed specially for the Native and with Native songs, for which melodies have been composed in the manner of our chorale tunes, which agree with the existing music as much as possible and satisfy Native ears."[86] The former was rejected in the discussion. An earlier experiment along these lines had not gone down well with the Javanese congregation.[87] Ultimately, Kats was asked to carry out the latter proposal himself.[88] This was basically the same proposal as Jansz the elder's fifteen years earlier. Attitudes toward it had changed under the influence of the ethical ideas that began to circulate in the colony. Jansz Jr. and Adriaanse both refer approvingly to Kats's proposal. But it has not been realized, and each advocates his own provisional solution.[89]

This brings us to the last topic of debate between Adriaanse and Jansz Jr.: the status quo. Adriaanse's explanation of the fact that Jansz's congregation rejects *tembang* is that Javanese Christians have been told for years that European chorale belongs to Christianity and *tembang* is sinful. Prior to that, several Javanese congregations in East Java knew church singing in *tembang*, but this was suppressed by the missionaries, beginning with Jellesma. In response, Jansz gives the impression that the Javanese form of church song faded away of its own accord under Jellesma.[90] In any case, during the latter half of the nineteenth century, the missionaries had already established a tradition of Javanese church singing. This is why the discussion following Jansz Sr.'s lecture in 1885 concerned the *introduction* of *tembang* for church singing, while in the discussion of Kats's 1900 lecture, *tembang* merited no mention at all.[91] European-style church song was the rule.

The exception were those Javanese Christian communities that had managed to stay outside the missionaries' control. Adriaanse demonstrated in *Sadrach's kring* (1899) that "for almost fifty years already, attempts have been made to obtain a *Javanese* style of church singing."[92] Jansz Jr., however, suggests that the texts produced in this context do not pass muster. He discusses a rather obscure text from Tunggul Wulung's congregation and adds, "Now here we have sample of a *tembang* song that was 'gripping.' It enables one to figure out approximately what would be the nature of Javanese church singing if the Javanese Christians, left to their own devices, would have had to create a Javanese *tembang* church singing for themselves."[93] Jansz Jr. captures the prevalent mood among the Protestant missionaries. Javanese cannot be trusted to give shape to a Christian liturgy. This yields defective choral singing, sung unevenly and out of tune, uncomprehended, immoral, idolatrous, and primitive.

A BROADER VIEW

In conclusion, to clarify the situation of Javanese church song, let us take a little more distance and try to formulate the politics of religious singing in nineteenth-century rural Java in general terms. A religion was gaining some ground among a large ethnic group that formerly did not adhere to it, a religion that was historically cognate and morphologically similar to the dominant one among this group and that was considered akin by some and adverse by others. Two major sets of insider perspectives obtained. Those who promoted the new complex of spiritual beliefs, mythic narratives, and ethical sensibilities knew it in intimate association with a category of practices, prominently including ritual. Their acts of worship showed certain formal similarities with ritual and artistic genres among the target group. These genres in their turn were connected with realms of spiritual, mythological, and ethical thought that corresponded only in part to those of the new religion. In theory, therefore, there was the possibility of facilitating adoption of the rites of worship that were key to the new religion by fashioning them according to familiar ritual and artistic practices. For most bringers of the new religion, however, the ideological baggage of these practices was an objection.

If this was the situation in contextless terms, in the concrete this meant that in missionaries' eyes, the ideal Javanese church songs were aligned closely with the motherland's Protestant liturgy, could be sung with feeling by Javanese, and were free from un-Christian stains. The most important factor governing the actual development of the Javanese Christian liturgy was the position of the missionaries among those who were receptive to evangelization. As authorities in Christendom and as Europeans in a Dutch colony, they enjoyed religious and social prestige and therefore power. As the recognized mentors of communities of Christians, they could afford to direct the behavior—including the ritual behavior—of those who joined their flocks in particular directions.

The missionaries considered it their task to give shape to a ritual genre. In principle, their position allowed them to be creative or let others be creative. In the rectangle formed by Dutch Protestant rites of worship, Javanese ritual-artistic genres, Javanese realms of ideas, and Christian realms of ideas, there was ample latitude. For people like Coolen, Dasimah, and other Javanese spiritual leaders and Adriaanse the ideological connections of Javanese forms of song were not an insurmountable objection. Coolen had foregrounded facets of Christianity with Javanese (and thus Islamic) counterparts. His congregational singing was modeled after *tembang* and Muslim devotional chant. Adriaanse assumed that Javanese connotations, if at odds with Christianity, would in due course become Christian.

But in Adriaanse's times, the creative space that existed in principle had already been restricted to a considerable degree. Mutual contacts among Protestant missionaries had increased and intensified. The majority felt, on the one hand, a close link between the Christian faith and Dutch liturgical practice, and on the other hand fear of the strange and unknown. When in 1900 a compromise was reached in the form of new compositions in Javanese style—an ideologically untarnished but still Javanese form of song—it was too late. The missionaries were unwilling to realize that the religious songs of people like Coolen, Dasimah, Tunggul Wulung, and Sadrach had in fact been new compositions in Javanese style, precisely what Kats had in mind. At this time, these forms of Javanese congregational singing were, however, looked upon as essentially suspect, as they had come into being outside the missionaries' sphere of influence. They were illegitimate because they were deemed to be *tembang* and accordingly heathen, or a mockery of European sacred song.

Around the turn of the century, a different tradition of church singing was well underway, one endowed with greater prestige and authority. It had been called into being after ca. 1850 by individual missionaries like Jellesma and Jansz Sr. and consolidated through the decision at the 1885 conference to stimulate the introduction of European melodies. By 1900, in some places, Dutch psalm and hymn tunes had already been sung weekly by three generations of Javanese Christians. In a tradition-observing society like the Javanese of that time, it must have been difficult to transmute such liturgical habitus, especially if the missionaries who would have to force the breakthrough were actually reluctant to do so.

The discussions I have reviewed and the ultimate compromise were among missionaries.[94] Thus, the temptation is strong to attribute the historical course of Javanese church singing to sheer force, applied by narrowminded colonialist bigots. But not taking into consideration the other major set of insider perspectives—those of Javanese Christians—results in a distorted image. The few known Javanese opinions about church singing were documented by missionaries. Unfortunately, it is difficult to trace to what extent they projected their own feelings on the members of their congregations. The following, however, is clear.

Javanese perspectives changed over time. Before mid-century, in those Javanese places where it was known, Christianity could be sensed to be a new and interesting variety of Javanese–Islamic religiosity. Javanese Islam was an Islam of quest, and Christianity fitted this paradigm well. The cognateness of Christianity and Islam in basic doctrine and ritual genres facilitated the embracing of Christianity. After 1850, a more rigid, originally external, perspective—grounded in Calvinism, missionary, institutionalized, to a considerable extent concerted (still more strongly after 1881), inimical to Islam, and colonial—gained presence.

The Javanese who embraced Christianity in this context took a radical step. By breaking with a familiar complex of concepts and practices including Arabic prayers, listening to and reciting the Qur'an, the *slametan* (ritual communal meal, a recurrent feature of Muslim Javanese community life), and circumcision, they incurred the disapproval and opposition, sometimes even aggression, of family members, neighbors, and leaders.[95] Inevitably, they placed themselves outside their community. Guillot has demonstrated that the considerations that nevertheless led them to this step were not only of a religious and ethical but also an economic nature.[96] Hefner added to this the importance of political motivations, especially resistance against a rising Islamic orthodoxy, while Ricklefs emphasized that those varieties of Christianity that allowed space for Javanese identity were most successful.[97]

There are compelling indications that an interest in ritual performance, including not only its social but also its aesthetic dimensions, played an important role as well.[98] Muslim rites had to be renounced. The same went for *tayuban* and often also wayang and other forms of epic drama, performed at ceremonies for the entertainment and edification of guests and hosts. Javanese who took the leap to Christianity entered a new community. Abandoning these familiar group rituals meant cutting major holes in social life. These gaps had to be filled. Rituals expressing mutual solidarity were required.

For many early converts the vast terrain of Christian doctrinal detail, the intellectual intricacies, were less important than the novel religious practices that caught the eye at once. Holy Scripture, the doctrine's charter, was difficult to access owing to illiteracy, except of course when read out, thus especially during religious services. Congregational worship filled the ritual void that loomed upon acceptance of Christianity. Choral singing was the most concrete performative embodiment of the cohesion of a group of Christians.

The rite was new, and where accredited missionaries were in charge, it was un-Javanese to boot. This was not a deterrent; it aroused curiosity and attracted people.[99] If Christianity was unlike familiar religiosities—a point stressed by the missionaries to counter syncretism—thus too the concomitant ritual. If this religion was European—as indeed it was from the converts' point of view—so would be its performance.

NOTES

1. This chapter is an updated, refocused, and trimmed translation of Bernard Arps, "De kwestie van het Javaanse kerkgezang," in Willem van der Molen and Bernard Arps, eds., *Woord en Schrift in de Oost: de betekenis van zending en missie voor de studie van taal en literatuur in Zuidoost-Azië* (Leiden: Opleiding Talen en Culturen van Zuidoost-Azië en Oceanië, Universiteit Leiden. Semaian 19, 2000), 1–32.

2. As in the final scene of Rademakers's 1976 movie *Max Havelaar.*

3. All translations from Dutch and Javanese are mine. Carel Poensen, "Mattheus Aniep (Eene Bijdrage tot de kennis der geschiedenis van de zending op Oost-Java)," *Mededeelingen van wege het Nederlandsche Zendelinggenootschap* 24 (1880): 333–91, at 364.

4. F. Lion Cachet, *Een jaar op reis in dienst der Zending* (Amsterdam: Wormser, 1896), 256–57.

5. J. F. G. Brumund, *Berigten omtrent de evangelisatie van Java* (Amsterdam: Van der Heij, 1854), 7.

6. Cachet, *Een jaar op reis in dienst der Zending,* 342.

7. Bernard Arps, *Tembang in Two Traditions: Performance and Interpretation of Javanese Literature* (London: School of Oriental and African Studies, 1992).

8. That is, approaching the discussion as the focal artifact in a study of worldmaking, attending to the discussion's artifactuality, apprehensibility, compositionality, contextuality, and historicity. Bernard Arps, *Tall Tree, Nest of the Wind: The Javanese Shadow-Play* Dewa Ruci *Performed by Ki Anom Soeroto: A Study in Performance Philology* (Singapore: NUS Press, 2016), 41–62.

9. As quoted in *Gĕnḍing en tĕmbang, Iets over gĕnḍing en tĕmbang en over Javaansch kerkgezang,* Door een leek. Met re- en dupliek overgedrukt uit "De Opwekker" van 1901 en 1902, Uitgegeven door den Nederlandsch-Indischen Zendingbond (Batavia: Albrecht, 1904), 3. I have not seen the articles in *De Getuige.*

10. *Gĕnḍing en tĕmbang,* 15.

11. *Gĕnḍing en tĕmbang,* 24–57 and 57–161, respectively.

12. On Sadrach, see also C. Guillot, *L'Affaire Sadrach: Un essai de christianisation à Java au XIXe siècle* (Paris: Éditions de la Maison des sciences de l'homme. Études insulindiennes—Archipel 4,

1981); Soediman Partonadi Sutarman, *Sadrach's Community and Its Contextual Roots: A Nineteenth Century Javanese Expression of Christianity* (Amsterdam: Rodopi, 1990); and numerous documents in H. Reenders, ed., *De gereformeerde zending in Midden Java, 1859–1931: een bronnenpublicatie* (Zoetermeer: Boekencentrum, 2001).

13. S. Coolsma, *De zendingseeuw voor Nederlandsch Oost-Indië* (Utrecht: Breijer, 1901), 184–86; see also Guillot, *L'Affaire Sadrach*, 277. Adriaanse's work and ideas feature extensively in Reenders, *De gereformeerde zending in Midden Java*.

14. *Gĕnḍing en tĕmbang*, 155; see also 57–58, 86, 88, 138. I believe that "a layperson" is right, at least concerning "a namesake of 'a layperson.'" The latter is of the Reformed (*gereformeerd*) persuasion and continually refers to Purwareja and Yogyakarta, where Adriaanse worked. Moreover, there are striking similarities between the writing style of "a namesake of 'a layperson'" and Adriaanse in *Sadrach's kring*, and between the opinions about Javanese church singing of "a namesake of 'a layperson'" and those in L. Adriaanse, *De nieuwe koers in onze zending, of Toelichting op de zendingsorde* (Amsterdam: Kirchner, 1903), 55–56.

15. See Arps, "De kwestie van het Javaanse kerkgezang," 6, for the data in support of this identification.

16. Coolsma, *De zendingseeuw voor Nederlandsch Oost-Indië*, 215.

17. Cachet, *Een jaar op reis in dienst der Zending*, 715–16.

18. *Gĕnḍing en tĕmbang*, 144.

19. Guillot, *L'Affaire Sadrach*, 51.

20. Much has been written about Coolen; see especially Brumund, *Berigten omtrent de evangelisatie van Java*, 23–33; H. Smeding, "Bezoekreis naar de gemeenten in Kediri, Madioen en Modjokerto, gedaan van 9 tot 29 Julij 1859, door de zendelingen S. E. Harthoorn en H. Smeding," *Mededeelingen van wege het Nederlandsche Zendelinggenootschap* 5 (1861):120–50, 245–86, 258–59, 275–80; S. E. Harthoorn, *De evangelische zending en Oost-Java: eene kritische bijdrage* (Haarlem: Kruseman, 1863), 27–28, 32–34, 149–71, 181–82; Poensen, "Mattheus Aniep," 340–54, 360–62, 366–70; C. W. Nortier, *Van zendingsarbeid tot zelfstandige kerk in Oost-Java* (n.p.: uitgegeven vanwege den Zendingsstudie-Raad door de Drukkerij van de Stichting Hoenderloo, 1939), 1–24; Nortier, *Een horlogemaker en een landheer: de eerste Christus-getuigen in Oost-Java* (Den Haag: Voorhoeve, 1954), 17–36; Philip van Akkeren, *Sri and Christ: A Study of the Indigenous Church in East Java* (London: Lutterworth Press, 1970), 54–87; and Guillot, *L'Affaire Sadrach*, 71–87. The most detailed account of Coolen's activities before 1848, based on research by Nortier into unspecified Dutch and Javanese sources clearly including oral history, was published in 1928 in a booklet in Javanese script titled *Serat Ngulati Toya Wening* (Book of the quest for the limpid water). It describes more cultural intricacies than the other writings and reproduces certain interactions among key figures. See *Serat Ngulati Toya Wening, Inggih Punika Wiwitanipun Agami Kristen Dipun Tampeni Dening Bangsa Jawi* (Bandoeng: Nix,1928).

21. *Serat Ngulati*, 52–54; summarized in Sutarman, *Sadrach's Community*, 134.

22. The drawing (figure 4-2), one of a series of twelve held in the Rijksmuseum, Amsterdam (RP-T-oo-3930-1 to RP-T-oo-3930-12), is attributed to Coolen himself (Nortier, *Van zendingsarbeid tot zelfstandige kerk in Oost-Java*, opposite p. 8). Van Akkeren, *Sri and Christ*, 65; Smeding, "Bezoekreis naar de gemeenten in Kediri," 281; Adriaanse, *Sadrach's kring*, 8–9, 22. According to *Serat Ngulati*, the singing of these hymns was known as *gaiban* (*Serat Ngulati Toya Wening, Inggih Punika Wiwitanipun Agami Kristen Dipun Tampeni Dening Bangsa Jawi*, 53, 54), meaning something like "doing profundity, mystery, esoterics."

23. *Serat Ngulati*, 54–55, briefly and partly summarized in English in Sutarman, *Sadrach's Community*, 136.

24. *Serat Ngulati*, 56.

25. *Serat Ngulati*, 5–19, 60–87; Nortier, *Van zendingsarbeid tot zelfstandige kerk in Oost-Java*, 3–5; van Akkeren, *Sri and Christ*, 69–70; Guillot, *L'Affaire Sadrach*, 59.

26. More generally, van Rhijn notes that "their walk and the purity of their mores" were being keenly watched by European Christian stakeholders and Javanese authorities, "sometimes with

suspicious eyes"; L. J. van Rhijn, *Reis door den Indischen Archipel, in het belang der evangelische zending* (Rotterdam: Wijt, 1851), 166.

27. *Serat Ngulati*, 80.

28. Van Rhijn, *Reis door den Indischen Archipel*, 161. Those who did not understand were van Rhijn and possibly other Dutch members of the visiting party. Adriaanse identifies the old man as Dasimah and the song as *tembang* (*Sadrach's kring*, 14–15).

29. Semarang-based missionary Gottlieb Brückner, who visited in 1842, mentions only that "when they met together for worship, they chanted one or two pages out of some tract" (van Akkeren, *Sri and Christ*, 94). The short description of a visit by van Hoëvell in 1847 confirms that they sang from a printed pamphlet. He also states that "the melody was soft, with much feeling, not unpleasing to the ear, but did not lack the character of all Indian music, that of monotony." Pak Dasimah clarified each verse line to his European guests; van Hoëvell, "Javaansche christenen te Soerabaija," *Tijdschrift ter Bevordering van Christelijken Zin in Neêrland's Indië* 1(4) (1847), 164–73, at 163, reproduced in van Hoëvell, *Reis over Java*, 193. Thus, he involved them in the communal performance event in a customary way; oral interlinear paraphrase is common in traditional literary recitation in several parts of Java, Madura, Bali, and Lombok (Arps, *Tembang in Two Traditions*, 24).

30. According to Nortier (*Van zendingsarbeid tot zelfstandige kerk in Oost-Java*, 5, 16), Dasimah followed Coolen's liturgy entirely.

31. Van Hoëvell, "Javaansche christenen te Soerabaija," 164; Van Rhijn, *Reis door den Indischen Archipel*, 166; Brumund, *Berigten omtrent de evangelisatie van Java*, xviii. In the 1830s, Bruckner also produced Christian tracts in Javanese, which were printed in India (van Akkeren, *Sri and Christ*, 55; van der Molen, *Woord en Schrift in de Oost*, 145, 147) and later Batavia (W. H. Medhurst, *China: Its State and Prospects, with Especial Reference to the Spread of the Gospel* [London: Snow, 1838], 580). As Bruckner refers to the text used by Dasimah as "some tract," it was probably not his own.

32. Arps, *Tembang in Two Traditions*.

33. Van Akkeren, 80; Guillot, *L'Affaire Sadrach*, 62.

34. These are the full Apostles' Creed (the twelve articles of faith) (*Serat Ngulati*, 10; Sutarman, *Sadrach's Community*, 134–35n90), a short version showing the communal refrain sung in *dhikiran* sessions (*Serat Ngulati*, 55), elsewhere provided with a cipher notation of the melody: Nortier, *Van zendingsarbeid tot zelfstandige kerk in Oost-Java*, 13; S. T. Handojomarno Sir, *Suatu Survey Mengenai Gereja Kristen Jawi Wetan* (Malang and Jakarta: Gereja Kristen Jawi Wetan and Lembaga Penelitian dan Studi Dewan Gereja-Gereja di Indonesia, Benih yang Tumbuh 7, 1976), 29; several textually inter-related prayers (*Serat Ngulati*, 34; van Akkeren, *Sri and Christ*, 92); and a hymn of the type called *gaiban* (*Serat Ngulati*, 54).

35. Henrik Smeding, "Enkele opmerkingen en vragen over het zendingswerk op Java," *Mededeelingen van wege het Nederlandsche Zendelinggenootschap* 6 (1862): 235–264, here 248–50, 253, 56; see also Smeding, "Bezoekreis naar de gemeenten in Kediri," 122–23.

36. A. G. Hoekema, ed., *"Tot heil van Java's arme bevolking": Een keuze uit het dagboek (1851–1860) van Pieter Jansz, doopsgezind zendeling in Jepara, Midden-Java* (Hilversum: Verloren. Manuscripta Mennonitica 1, 1997), 151.

37. P. Jansz, *Kitab Isi Masmur Papethingan Sawatawis*, Tinembangaken Jawi (Amsterdam: Sepin, 1865; *Kitab Masmur Katembangaken Miwah Repen Greja* (Leden: Bril, 1885).).

38. That Jansz thought he was composing according to *tembang* principles can be inferred from the first volume's title—in translation, "Book Containing Several Choice Psalms, Set to Javanese Tembang"—and the expression "Jav. poetic meter" (*Jav. dichtmaat*) in his diary. As in *tembang*, each stanza has a fixed number of verse lines, each with a fixed number of syllables, but instead of a fixed vowel in each line-final syllable, Jansz employed vowel-rhyme with the same rhyme scheme for each stanza. Jansz was not the only Western observer who misunderstood the form of *tembang*. There were others too who thought that rhyme played a role in it (Arps, *Tembang in Two Traditions*, 19).

39. Guillot, *L'Affaire Sadrach*, 89–90.

40. Jansz Jr. in *Gĕnḍing en tĕmbang*, 149–50. According to Adriaanse (*Sadrach's kring*, 366), Tunggul Wulung's people also sang a text with Javanese melody at baptism.

41. Jansz Jr. in *Gĕnḍing en tĕmbang*, 149.

42. For instance, the *celukan* (calling) style in sung reading of the Islamic story of Joseph in Banyuwangi, East Java (Arps, *Tembang in Two Traditions*, 163, 311–17). Similar verse reading styles on Madura and northern Central Java are heard on the CD *Jemblung and Related Narrative Traditions of Java* (Body and Yono Sukarno, 1997), tracks 7 and 8.

43. Smelik, "Orgelgebruik in de protestantse kerkdienst," 3–11.

44. Van Rhijn, *Reis door den Indischen Archipel*, 313–14.

45. *Gĕnḍing en tĕmbang*, 150. According to Adriaanse (*Sadrach's kring*, 363), "howling of dogs" was a Javanese way of characterizing, among other things, the singing of psalms by Dutch people. J. Kats, "Het godsdienstig lied in de zending, uit een muzikaal oogpunt beschouwd," in *Overzicht van de Tiende Zending-Conferentie, gehouden te Buitenzorg en te Depok van 25 Augustus tot 2 September 1900* [Batavia: Kolff, 1901], 103–42, at 126) returned to this in "Het godsdienstig lied in de zending," 126, as did Adriaanse in *Gĕnḍing en tĕmbang*, who related it to "the drawling, the slowness, the protractedness in the Dutch psalm-tunes" (28).

46. The same applied to western Java; Th. van den End, *De Nederlandse Zendingsvereniging in West-Java, 1858–1963: Een bronnenpublicatie* (Leiden: Brill: 1991), 28n2, 272–73.

47. Coolsma, *De zendingseeuw voor Nederlandsch Oost-Indië*, 184.

48. It began to be published in 1855, as one of the first periodicals in the Netherlands East Indies. Ahmat B. Adam, *The Vernacular Press and the Emergence of Modern Indonesian Consciousness (1855–1913)*, Studies on Southeast Asia (Ithaca, NY: Southeast Asia Program, Cornell University, 1995), 17, 183; see also 15n69.

49. Smeding, "Enkele opmerkingen en vragen over het zendingswerk op Java," 248–56.

50. *Gĕnḍing en tĕmbang*, 9–10.

51. Smeding, "Enkele opmerkingen en vragen over het zendingswerk op Java," 250–53.

52. Jansz Sr., "Kerkgezang in Javaansch têmbang ten dienste der Inlandsche gemeenten," 11.

53. Adriaanse, *Sadrach's kring*, 365.

54. *Gĕnḍing en tĕmbang*, 11.

55. *Gĕnḍing en tĕmbang*, 43–44.

56. *Gĕnḍing en tĕmbang*, 76–77, 123–27. Smeding had preceded him in this opinion (253).

57. L. Tiemersma, "Het kerkgezang en de Maleische psalmbundels," In *Overzicht van de Negende Zending-Conferentie, gehouden te Buitenzorg en te Depok van 20 tot 28 Augustus 1898* (Batavia: Kolff, 1898), 26–55.

58. Kats, "Het godsdienstig lied in de zending, uit een muzikaal oogpunt beschouwd," 131.

59. Tiemersma, "Het kerkgezang en de Maleische psalmbundels," 46, quoting a letter from P. Jansz Sr.

60. Arps, *Tembang in Two Traditions*, 20, 299–301.

61. Albers, "De Zendingschool en hare betekenis," 127. *Adan* (Ar. *adhan*) is the call to Islamic prayer; *tukang adan* means "muezzin." *Dikir* (Ar. *dhikr*) was mentioned above. As noted earlier, *nembang* means "sing (esp. *tembang* verse)."

62. *Gĕnḍing en tĕmbang*, 78.

63. Smeding, "Bezoekreis naar de gemeenten in Kediri," 131.

64. *Gĕnḍing en tĕmbang*, 22–23.

65. Jansz, "Kerkgezang in Javaansch têmbang," 13.

66. Arps, *Tembang in Two Traditions*, 422–24.

67. Adriaanse's entire polemic is based on this opinion. For Jansz's opinion, see, for instance, *Gĕnḍing en tĕmbang*, 72.

68. Smeding, "Enkele opmerkingen en vragen over het zendingswerk op Java," 250.

69. *Gĕnḍing en tĕmbang*, 20.

70. Cachet, *Een jaar op reis in dienst der Zending*, 342.

71. *Tayuban, tledhek*, and analogous genres and roles continued to have dubious moral connotations. See, for instance, Hughes-Freeland, "*Golék Ménak* and *Tayuban*, 102–17; and Spiller, *Erotic Triangles.*

72. Jansz, "Kerkgezang in Javaansch têmbang ten dienste der Inlandsche gemeenten," 12.

73. Jansz, "Kerkgezang in Javaansch têmbang ten dienste der Inlandsche gemeenten," 12. 13.

74. *Gĕnḍing en tĕmbang*, 144.

75. *Gĕnḍing en tĕmbang*, 71.

76. *Gĕnḍing en tĕmbang*, 50–51.

77. *Gĕnḍing en tĕmbang*, 142. The Veluwe region has a high concentration of orthodox Gereformeerd communities.

78. *Gĕnḍing en tĕmbang*, 47. For Jansz Jr.'s opinion, see especially *Gĕnḍing en tĕmbang*, 135–37.

79. Jansz, "Kerkgezang in Javaansch têmbang,"14.

80. Jansz, "Kerkgezang in Javaansch têmbang," 10–11.

81. Jansz, "Kerkgezang in Javaansch têmbang,"16.

82. Kitab Masmur, *Kitab Masmur Katembangaken Miwah Repen Greja.*

83. Kats, "Het godsdienstig lied in de zending," 105–26. Kats died in 1945 and must have been quite frustrated at the "evolution" of European music in his later years. He would make an intervention in Javanese poetic theory as well; see Arps, "The Regulation of Beauty."

84. Kats, "Het godsdienstig lied in de zending," 130.

85. Kats, "Het godsdienstig lied in de zending," 129.

86. Kats, "Het godsdienstig lied in de zending," 140–41.

87. This test triggered the series of articles by "a Eurasian" (Adriaanse) in *De Getuige.*

88. Kunst, *De Inheemsche muziek en de zending*, 24n17, suspects with relief that Kats's proposal was never realized, but this was probably wishful thinking as Kats did provide a singing method (Poeze, "J. Kats 1875–1945," xiv–xv, xxvii). From 1903 to 1908 and 1910 to 1913, he was director of the teacher training school in Majawarna, the center of a large number of missionary-led Christian communities in East Java, where he may have tried this method on his trainees. I do not know to what extent the melodies were Javanese and whether they impacted church singing. The same applies to a collection of musical notations of religious songs that appeared in 1914 (Poeze, "J. Kats 1875–1945," xxviii).

89. Jansz Jr. in *Gĕnḍing en tĕmbang*, 15–16, 141; Adriaanse in *Gĕnḍing en tĕmbang*, 56.

90. Adriaanse in *Gĕnḍing en tĕmbang*, 52; Jansz Jr. in *Gĕnḍing en tĕmbang*, 145–47.

91. Jansz, "Kerkgezang in Javaansch têmbang,"15; Kats, "Het godsdienstig lied in de zending," 141–42.

92. Adriaanse, *Sadrach's kring*, 366.

93. *Gĕnḍing en tĕmbang*, 150.

94. Among the sixty men and women listed as attendees of the 1900 conference (*Overzicht van de Tiende Zending-Conferentie*, 5–6) there was not a single Indonesian. The conference photo does show three Indonesians, identified as "two native servants and furthermore the Native schoolteacher Martinus" (1). Martinus taught in Depok near Batavia, a Malay-speaking area.

95. See, for instance, Guillot, *L'Affaire Sadrach*, 234–36.

96. Guillot, *L'Affaire Sadrach*, 296–308.

97. Robert W. Hefner, "Of Faith and Commitment: Christian Conversion in Muslim Java," in *Conversion to Christianity: Historical and Anthropological Perspectives on a Great Transformation*, ed. Robert W. Hefner, 99–125 (Berkeley: University of California Press, 1993), 118–22; M. C. Ricklefs, *Polarising Javanese Society: Islamic and Other Visions* (c. 1830–1930) (Leiden: KITLV Press, 2007), 105–25.

98. Among these indications are Brumund's detailed response to the accusation from a Javanese quarter that unlike Islam, Christianity lacks external, ritual forms, which he counters by referring to

prayer and religious song (Brumund, *Berigten omtrent de evangelisatie van Java*, 137–38), how in a fictional discussion among Javanese Muslims the absence of performance at a Christian wedding is singled out with amazement (Harthoorn, *De evangelische zending en Oost-Java*, 74), and the prominence in *Serat Ngulati* of early Javanese-Christian ritual, including the observation that the Christians in Ngara "had no shortness of diversion in the corporeal as well as the spiritual realm" (*Serat Ngulati*, 56).

99. See, for instance, the impressions of baptism in Surabaya's Protestant church reported by Poensen in "Mattheus Aniep," two of which were quoted above. Compare an 1895 report by Tiemersma, stationed in Tangerang near Batavia, where the congregation consisted of Chinese and Malays: "Now what for is this singing? Partly . . . to draw people. It is nice to see how they flock together in response to our singing. It has happened repeatedly that initially I had only four or five listeners. But as soon as we started to sing, the room filled up" (van den End, *De Nederlandse Zendingsvereniging in West-Java*, 243).

Local Church Music
in the Twentieth Century

5

The Heathen in His Blindness?

Missionaries, Empire, and Anti-colonialism

David A. Hollinger

One day in 1923, John R. Mott, the undisputed leader of American Protestant missionary efforts throughout the world, spent the morning with former president William Howard Taft, who was then chief justice of the US Supreme Court. Mott then went to the White House for lunch with President Calvin Coolidge. In the afternoon, Mott called on his old friend, the ailing former president, Woodrow Wilson. Three presidents in one day. Mott's social calendar reveals the public standing of missionaries a hundred years ago.[1]

In 1925, there were ten thousand American missionaries abroad, primarily in China, Japan, Korea, and India but also distributed elsewhere across the globe beyond the North Atlantic West.[2] The cultural role of missionaries in the United States at that time was much greater than their numbers would imply. To be a missionary was to have accepted a challenging and honored calling. The missionaries sent out by the major denominations were anything but marginal socially. Often they were graduates of Princeton, Yale, Oberlin, Mt. Holyoke, or Amherst. Missionaries were in the vanguard, taking risks to advance what were understood as the finest features of American society, spreading them out to the wider world. They were the bullfighters of Protestantism.

The American excitement about foreign missions was in part a response to the relative novelty of sustained contact with Indigenous peoples beyond North America. The old European imperial powers, especially the Spanish and the Portuguese among the Catholics and the British and the Dutch among the Protestants, had a long history of intimate contact with peoples beyond the North Atlantic West. Around 1890, the Americans began to think of themselves as a major actor in world history and perhaps even as an empire based on the European model.

103

This new sense of global importance led to a huge increase in missionary activity abroad and in commentary on its meaning.

There had been a handful of American missionaries abroad since the 1830s, especially in China and what was then called the Near East. But in the 1890s, the missionary project expanded greatly in size and scope, advancing into Japan, India, Africa, the Pacific Islands, and especially the Philippines. A distinctive feature of the Philippine mission field was its relation to the government of the United States. At the turn of the century, the Philippines became an American colonial possession, by far the largest the United States had acquired and would ever acquire. Unlike in the rest of the globe, where the American missionaries were more or less guests of the European imperial powers, as in India, or of local governments, as in China, Japan, Siam, and the Ottoman lands, the American missionaries dealt with the Filipino population as colonial subjects. In their new role as imperial overlords, or instructors, as they preferred to say, American missionaries were in a position more like the British in India and the Dutch in the East Indies.[3] To be sure, Americans often acted imperialistically when working in China and India and elsewhere, but in the Philippines, it was their own game.

And it was in a missionary spirit, after all, that President McKinley had announced his prayer-inspired decision to take those Pacific Islands following the American navy's victory in the Spanish American War. And it was in an overwhelmingly missionary spirit that imperialism's greatest poet, Rudyard Kipling, wrote "The White Man's Burden" as a gesture of welcome to the Americans, specifically as they joined the company of mature men and women who accepted the responsibility of world power to "serve their captives need," fully expecting to be unappreciated by the native populations it was their divine duty to guide toward a more civilized state of being.

> Take up the White Man's burden
> And reap his old reward,
> The blame of those ye better,
> The hate of those ye guard[4]

This outlook was similar to the English hymns about missions that were popular throughout the nineteenth century and were commonly sung in American and British churches well into the twentieth century. The most popular of these was written in 1819:

> From Greenland's icy mountains,
> From India's coral strand,
> Where Africa's sunny fountains
> Roll down their golden sand,
> From many an ancient river,
> From many a palmy plain,

> They call us to deliver
> Their land from error's chain.
> In vain with lavish kindness
> The gifts of God are strown;
> The heathen in his blindness
> Bows down to wood and stone.
> Shall we, whose souls are lighted
> With wisdom from on high,
> Shall we to men benighted
> The lamp of life deny?[5]

But that is far from the whole story. A great many of the American missionaries to the Philippines and elsewhere ended up, after several years of experience in the field, as anti-imperialists, as critics of all the colonial empires, and as vociferous opponents of white supremacy. The experience of living with peoples really different from themselves changed their understandings of themselves, of their country, and humanity, much to their own surprise. Missionaries were expected to make the rest of the world "more like us," more like American Protestants. But by the 1920s, a steady stream of missionary writings insisted that this old aspiration was a mistake.

The gospel ended up working like a boomerang, thrown across the sea but not staying there. It returned, carrying unexpected baggage: a more cosmopolitan sense of religious duty. The rest of humanity was much, much more than a needy expanse awaiting the benevolence and supervision of American Protestants.[6] Foreign cultures might even have something to teach American Protestants living in Hartford and Memphis and Des Moines.

So transformed, many of the returning missionaries—not all; some retained traditional racist parochialism—tried to get folks in the Methodist and Baptist and Presbyterian churches of Pennsylvania and Tennessee and Nebraska to stop singing about Indigenous peoples bowing down to wood and stone and to adopt instead a very different hymn, which appeared in 1908:

> In Christ there is no east or west,
> in him no south or north,
> but one great fellowship of love
> throughout the whole wide earth.
> In Christ shall true hearts ev'rywhere
> their high communion find.
> His service is the golden cord
> close binding humankind.
> Join hands, then, people of the faith,
> whate'er your race may be.
> All children of the living God
> are surely kin to me.[7]

To illustrate this American drift toward a more critical perspective on the missionary project and its relation to colonialism, I will describe the career of the most famous American missionary to the Philippines, Frank Laubach. I will compare Laubach briefly to his great contemporary, the influential Dutch missionary Hendrick Kraemer. In the 1920s and 1930s, Kraemer was a major figure in the debates of the international Protestant community about the character of Christianity and its role in world history and about the theoretical basis for the missionary project itself. Kraemer was by far the most prominent contemporary opponent of Americans like Laubach, who were liberalizing the missionary project.

Laubach is forgotten today, but for many decades, he was a household name. He is the only missionary to be memorialized with a postage stamp in the United States.

Laubach had spent fifteen frustrating years as a Congregationalist missionary in the Philippines, making very few converts, when he went to a mountaintop near his village on Mindanao to pray and meditate. There, God spoke to him, and bluntly. Laubach later reported that he felt that God was chastising him for secretly negative feelings about the Moros, the people among whom he lived. "You have failed because you do not really love" the people you are trying to serve, God scolded him. "You feel superior to them because you are white." God told Laubach that "if you can forget" your American whiteness and think only of love for the Moros, "they will respond."[8]

The troubled missionary decided that loving the Moros meant something very dramatic in a missionary context: stopping all proselytizing. God wanted Laubach to study the Quran, to engage in sympathetic dialogue with the predominantly Muslim local inhabitants, and to find ways to actually help the Moros live better lives. Soon Laubach hit on the idea of teaching the Moros how to read. This was a practical tool, useful without reference to any religion. The inspiration was mystical—Laubach wrote as if he were Saul being struck down on the road to Damascus—but the outcome was decidedly down to earth. Laubach went on to become the twentieth century's most illustrious promoter of literacy, rivaled only by the much younger Brazilian educational reformer Paulo Freire, who surfaced shortly before Laubach died.

Starting with the rendering of the Moro tongue into Roman characters and establishing many schools designed to teach people to read in it, Laubach and the organizations he created eventually produced language primers in 312 languages. By the time he died in 1970, he was popularly credited with enabling several million people to read in more than one hundred countries and had been awarded honorary degrees by Columbia, Princeton, and other universities. He wrote forty-three books.[9]

Laubach was absorbed into the missionary endeavor at the time of its highest confidence. Like so many in his cohort, he was well educated and committed to the social gospel. When Laubach went to the Philippines in 1915, he had recently earned a PhD in sociology from Columbia. His dissertation, a study of the social and economic causes of the large population of homeless men seen on the streets of New York, was written in the classic social gospel mode of the period.[10]

There is no doubt that his experience in the field had a deep effect on him. In the 1920s, Laubach wrote several popular books about the Filipino people and about the wrongheaded character of traditional missionary activities directed toward them. He introduced his five-hundred-page volume of 1925, *The People of the Philippines: Their Religious Progress and Preparation for Spiritual Leadership in the Far East*, with confidence that the Filipinos were capable of sharing global leadership with other peoples. Laubach looked to them and other Asian peoples to take over Christianity. He said Asians should take over from Americans and Europeans the leadership of the Christian project. In a clever provocation, he liked to describe Jesus of Nazareth as "an Asian."[11]

Laubach contrasted Christianity to communism but differed from many of his religion-invoking contemporaries in identifying poverty and injustice as the chief causes of communism's appeal. He held the privileged white peoples of the West responsible for the inequities that rendered communism one of the few options available to the world's poor. Laubach criticized American imperial authorities; he wrote in missionary publications of the predatory nature of American corporations who were gaining control over arable land that Laubach believed should be reserved for Filipino farmers and their families.[12]

Laubach remained based in the Philippines until the Japanese occupation early in World War II prevented his return from a furlough in the United States. By that time, he and his coworkers had managed to spread a phonetic-centered, highly individualized method of literacy instruction throughout many regions of the islands. This "each one teach one" method was more labor intensive than the traditional classroom approach, but Laubach was able to inspire hundreds and eventually thousands to devote themselves to do it voluntarily, even while engaged in other vocations.

Laubach always regarded the advancement of literacy as the doing of Christ's work and thus a direct extension of his missionary calling, even if literacy itself was without particularistic religious meaning. His work was appreciated beyond the Protestant company he kept. His 1938 book, *Toward a Literate World*, was published with an enthusiastic foreword by Edward L. Thorndike—John Dewey's successor as the leading educational theorist in the United States—of Columbia Teacher's College.[13] For several decades, he was a sought-after church speaker for Sunday nights, holding aloft in his hands a globe on which he had indicated by brightly colored markers exactly where the greatest concentrations of illiterate persons in need of his program could be found.[14]

Exactly during the 1920s, years when Laubach's life was being changed by his experiences in the Philippines, the Dutch missionary Hendrik Kraemer was working in the Dutch East Indies. Kraemer had been a very pious youth who decided at sixteen to become a missionary. In adulthood, he became an officer of the Netherlands Bible Society and, while based primarily on the island of Java, traveled widely and earned respect as one of the most well informed of the colonial community's students of the many Indigenous peoples of the Dutch East Indies. He was a staunch conservative, theologically. He was aware of the increasingly liberal views of American missionaries in the Philippines, China, and India.[15]

In 1928, at the meeting of the International Missionary Council in Jerusalem, Hendrik Kraemer emerged as the most articulate critic of the American liberals. The naive Americans, Kraemer insisted, do not know how dangerous it is to give up on the uniqueness of the Christian gospel as we from the Christian heartland of the North Atlantic West understand it. The Americans, Kraemer alleged, were much too willing to respect non-Christian faiths and to envisage a kind of peaceful coexistence with them. Supported by many of the British and German missionaries, also colonial powers, at this and other meetings of the international missionary community, Kraemer accused the Americans of going native, in effect being too sympathetic with the ideas and practices of the people Kraemer was still quite willing to call heathens and pagans.[16]

Consistent with this view, Kraemer was critical of the decision of American missionaries to grant more and more autonomy to the communities of Christian converts. Those souls needed the continuing supervision and juridical oversight of the Western Christians, based on their ostensibly much deeper grounding in the gospel. Communities of Christian "natives" Kraemer considered insufficiently spiritual and too concerned with their material well-being. Kraemer continued to push this outlook for the next decade, and at the next conclave of the Protestant missionary leadership at Madras in 1938, he was roundly condemned by the increasingly numerous and well-established communities of Protestant converts from throughout Asia, who had been brought into global missionary leadership by the American liberals and given voting rights.

During World War II, Kraemer changed his mind about colonial supervision. By the end of World War II, he had even become an advocate of Indonesian independence from the Netherlands. He never deviated from his conviction of the unique superiority of the Christian religion, but he became more tolerant of other faiths. But as he witnessed the growing nationalist movement, he expected all nationalist leaders to adopt Christianity and was shaken to find that so many of them, including those educated in missionary schools, became Muslims. Kraemer also found himself obliged to become more accommodating of the varieties of Christianity, often syncretistic, that emerged in almost every mission field. Still, his writings were banned by the new Indonesian government after 1948, and he continues to be remembered as a vociferous opponent of the American-led liberal movements of the 1920s and 1930s. Indeed, conservative missionary theorists have returned to Kraemer again and again for inspiration, and today he remains a giant in the history of missionary theory.[17]

An incident at the 1945 founding of the United Nations brings out dramatically the difference between the American liberal missionaries and the more conservative missionaries from the European colonial powers. The British pushed very hard for a provision of the UN charter that would guarantee the liberty to proselytize, a liberty the British justified under the rubric of "religious freedom." The American delegation, led by former missionaries, opposed this on the grounds that it would be insulting to non-Christian religions. Remarkably, the American missionary lobby won out over the missionary lobby of the European imperial powers.[18]

When I refer to the "American missionary lobby," I refer to the ecumenical denominations, especially the Congregationalists, of whom Laubach was a distinguished representative, but also the Methodists, the Presbyterians, the Disciples of Christ, the Northern Baptists, and several other Lutheran and Anabaptist bodies. But there was of course a whole different side of American Protestantism, the Fundamentalists, who during the 1940s suddenly renamed themselves "evangelicals." These more conservative Protestants had views much more like Kraemer's. The American evangelicals were very critical of the United Nations itself, complaining that the new organization failed to acknowledge God and Jesus. These evangelicals had their own missionary operations, which rejected vociferously the liberalization exemplified by Laubach.

During the quarter century following World War II, the rivalry between ecumenical and evangelical Protestants was manifest in many domains, especially missions, where most of the ecumenicals, having decided that traditional missions were an enterprise in cultural imperialism, pulled back or replaced preaching with social service programs. The evangelicals held firm to the idea that anyone not converted to Christianity was eternally damned, and it was therefore imperative that millions who had yet to hear the gospel be exposed to it as soon as possible.[19]

The ecumenical/evangelical divide was also apparent in Cold War politics and in American domestic affairs. The National Council of Churches, the ecumenical trans-denominational organization, was by far the largest American organization to lobby for the diplomatic recognition of Communist China in the 1950s, while the National Association of Evangelicals, the rival organization, castigated ecumenical leaders as dupes of the communists if not secret members themselves. The National Association of Evangelicals also proposed a constitutional amendment that would write God and Jesus directly in the Constitution of the United States. The ecumenicals were among the earliest and most vociferous opponents of the Vietnam War, which evangelicals overwhelmingly supported. The ecumenicals attacked Jim Crow, and as early as 1940 refused to hold meetings in cities where the hotel associations would not guarantee equal service to Black delegates, while the evangelicals mocked such initiatives as "meddling in politics."[20]

The political coordinates of the ecumenical/evangelical divide in 1963 were vividly etched by Billy Graham, who when asked to comment on the "I Have a Dream" speech Martin Luther King gave at the Lincoln Memorial spoke to the press in crisp and clear language: "The little white children of Alabama will walk hand in hand with the little black children of Alabama only when Christ comes again."[21]

That takes us pretty far from Indonesia, so I want to move back toward that part of the world by attending to the remarkable career of the most important of the American missionaries to any part of Southeast Asia, Kenneth Landon, a Presbyterian missionary to Thailand.

Landon had left the mission field to become a college professor and scholar by the time he was called to Washington in 1941 because the US government could not find anyone else who knew anything about Thailand. The Japanese were invading that country, and President Roosevelt was wondering what plans the United States should make about Thailand in the event that it entered the war against Japan. Landon was instantly made an intelligence officer in the Office of Strategic Services, the predecessor of the CIA, and when asked to review the government's intelligence file on Thailand, he was handed a manila folder containing two reprints of articles he himself had written. He went over to the Library of Congress to see what they had on Thailand, and he found a whole room full of Thai-language books and periodicals that had been tossed there because the Library of Congress had no one who could read the Thai language.[22]

Soon the ex-missionary found himself the head of the State Department's Southeast Asia Desk, indeed its first and only inhabitant, and in constant warfare with the nearby desk officers for Europe. The State Department during these war years considered Southeast Asia the domain of the British, French, and Dutch. Those desk officers largely accepted the colonialist perspective on all of Southeast Asia, were aware of British designs on Thailand, and were massively resistant to Landon's memoranda about French Indochina. One memo that made its way up to FDR, however, was returned with FDR's firm handwriting in the margins saying that he agreed with Landon and wanted to be sure that the French were not allowed to reoccupy Indochina after the expected defeat of the Japanese. That's not the way it worked out, of course.

By the end of the war, Landon was a formidable figure in American diplomacy and is credited by historians today for single-handedly creating the postwar alliance with Thailand and thwarting a British effort to take over that country as an extension of British-held Malaya. More striking yet, there being nobody in Washington who knew the first thing about Vietnam, Landon was dispatched—in spite of what the European desk officers said—to see what was happening there. Landon walked up to Ho Chi Minh's residence in Hanoi and knocked on the door. Ho was thrilled to have a sympathetic American ear. Ho insisted on having Landon as a dinner guest night after night. Landon's dispatch to Truman ended up, many years later, as the document with the earliest date in the Pentagon Papers. This is the legendary dispatch about the possibility of the United States taking over

Vietnam as a protectorate on the Philippine model. Truman never responded and was soon, as we all know, fully supportive of the French. Landon was highly critical of the French, predicted a communist victory over the French and later over the Americans, and spent his later years lamenting the Vietnam War as an entirely avoidable loss of life on every side.

I have been emphasizing the tendency of American missionaries to sympathize with anticolonial revolts and the tendency of the European Protestant missionaries to accept an imperial framework. Of course, there were exceptions to this, and I want to acknowledge that there were plenty of American missionaries, especially of the more evangelical persuasion, who matched the traditional image reinforced yet again in Barbara Kingsolver's novel of 1998, *The Poisonwood Bible*.[23] There, a stereotypically bigoted Southern Baptist male missionary shows himself entirely incapable of understanding the local culture of Black inhabitants of Central Africa. Yet in an irony missed by most of Kingsolver's readers, as well as by the author herself, a chapter of this novel titled "The Anti-missionary" gives eloquent voice to a non-invidious, service-centered, Indigenous-appreciating outlook on Africa that for many years was expressed by ecumenical Protestant missionaries themselves. This outlook was not so much anti-missionary as revised missionary.

James A. Michener was less hostile to missionaries in his best-selling epic of four decades earlier, but his *Hawaii* also emphasized the ethnocentrism of missionaries.[24] Mischa Berlinski's more recent *Fieldwork* develops a more ethnographically accurate picture of evangelical missionaries in Thailand, even as Berlinski emphasizes the limitation of their capacity to appreciate the culture of the Indigenous peoples they try to convert.[25] In earlier years, the most frequently mentioned representation of missionaries in popular culture was "Rain," a story by W. Somerset Maugham about a married, stereotypically repressed South Seas missionary who converts a prostitute but then commits adultery with her, and, overcome with guilt, kills himself while the woman, struck with the missionary's hypocrisy, renounces her new faith and returns to her trade.[26] This story was the basis for several films, including a 1932 Hollywood film of the same title that featured Joan Crawford as the prostitute in one of her most celebrated roles.

What happened to the missionaries who tried to persuade the US government that American interests, in the long run, were aligned with the interests of non-white, decolonizing Indigenous populations? They lost the argument more often than not. That they were defeated so crushingly in debates about Vietnam and elsewhere no doubt reflects that lack of unity and the limits of their political skills, but these defeats followed also from the strength of the opposing forces.

Despite these defeats, however, the missionaries of the most cosmopolitan orientation had careers that strongly support the "contact theory" developed by social psychologist Gordon Allport. The notion that social contact can change attitudes may seem a truism. "Unless we make ourselves hermits," the philosopher Charles

Peirce observed casually, "we shall necessarily influence each other's opinions." Social contact enables us to "see that men in other countries" hold "very different doctrines," perhaps just as sound as those we "have been brought up to believe."[27] But this insight, to which Peirce alluded in 1877, did not achieve currency as a formal theory in social science until 1954, when Allport developed it in his now classic work of 1954, *The Nature of Prejudice*.[28]

It is not clear how Allport's own brief missionary experience affected him. As a young Methodist, Allport met Muslims while spending a year as a teacher at Robert College in Istanbul. Later in life, he was an active Episcopalian and a regular speaker at religious events on his Harvard University campus. In his influential study of prejudice, Allport argued that an empowered group's prejudice toward a stigmatized group could be reduced by close contact, provided the groups were proximate in social standing.[29]

The missionary case qualifies Allport's proviso. Missionaries, driven by a radically egalitarian ideology, engaged sympathetically with a range of peoples of low status abroad and championed their interests in international politics. At home, missionary-connected individuals and groups were conspicuous among privileged Anglo-Protestants in defending confined Japanese Americans during World War II, in campaigning against Jim Crow, and in bringing African Americans into the leadership of major ecumenical organizations.

Did the cosmopolitan-striving missionaries, their children, and their supporters do as much as they might have to diminish racism, sexism, imperialism, Orientalism, homophobia, and anti-intellectualism? Certainly not. But I have not put a fine point on this obvious truth because so little reflection is required to discover that a given cast of historical actors fails to measure up to today's sense of how people should behave. The ease with which we can answer this morally *structural* question—is someone within our ethical community, or not?—accounts for the question's copious and confident answers all around us, including the renaming of schools and the reevaluation of public statuary.

Morally *developmental* questions are more challenging. What conditions have facilitated the expansion of our ethical community? What has enabled equality, inclusion, and democracy to make what gains they have made? Ecumenical Protestant missionaries did more than most of their white Christian contemporaries in the United States to advance these values. They managed to do what they did not because of purity of heart, although some did have great generosity of spirit. They lived in a force field where descent and doctrine, wealth and war, trade and travel, science and sentiment, and a host of other elements in motion made them into the relatively educated, relatively global individuals they became. The missionary cosmopolitans were less heroic agents than historic witnesses to the power of the forces that shaped and directed them and to the soundness of contact theory.

Mark Twain's sense that "travel is fatal to prejudice, bigotry, and narrow-mindedness" does not always apply.[30] But it did for thousands of missionaries.

NOTES

1. C. Howard Hopkins, *John R. Mott, 1865–1955* (Geneva: Eerdmans, 1985), 665.

2. Harland P. Beach and Charles H. Fahs, eds., *World Missionary Atlas* (New York: Institute of Social and Religions Research, 1925), 82–86. The most substantial mission fields in 1925 other than China, India, Japan, and Korea were the Belgian Congo, Brazil, Egypt, Lebanon, Mexico, Persia, Turkey, and the Philippines. More than forty denominations and trans-denominational societies sponsored these missionaries.

3. For a revealing example of American attitudes toward the Filipinos at the time of colonization, see Woodrow Wilson's famous address, "The Ideals of America," *Atlantic* (December 2002), in which Wilson defends hierarchy and declares that the reason Americans had proven to be so able at self-government is that they had once been subject to the rule of a king: "No doubt a king did hold us together until we learned how to hold together of ourselves. No doubt our unity as a nation does come from the fact that we once obeyed a king." The United States would be king to the Filipinos until they reached the maturity necessary for self-government.

4. Kipling's poem was published in 1899 and immediately reprinted throughout the English-speaking world.

5. This hymn was written in 1819 by the Anglican missionary to India, Reginald Heber.

6. I have analyzed this major consequence of the missionary project in David A. Hollinger, *Protestants Abroad: How Missionaries Tried to Change the World but Changed America* (Princeton: Princeton University Press, 2017).

7. The lyrics to this hymn, applied to the melody of a traditional African American spiritual, were written in 1908 by William Dunkerley, an English poet and clergyman, who published this hymn under his pseudonym, John Oxenham.

8. Laubach's description of this experience is found in Peter G. Gowing, "The Legacy of Frank Charles Laubach," *International Bulletin of Missionary Research* (April 1983): 59–60.

9. Laubach's role in the history of the advancement of literacy is recognized routinely in histories of literacy campaigns; see, for example, Mary Hamilton, Bryan Maddox, and Camilla Addey, *Literacy as Numbers* (New York: Cambridge University Press, 2015); Andrew J. Kirkendall, *Paolo Feire and the Cold War Politics of Literacy* (Chapel Hill: University of North Carolina Press, 2010); and Barbara J. Guzzetti, *Literacy for the New Millennium*, ed. Barbara J. Guzzetti (Westport CT: ABC-CLIO, 2007).

10. Laubach's dissertation was published as "Why There Are Vagrants" (Columbia University, New York, 1916).

11. See Frank Charles Laubach, *The People of the Philippines: Their Religious Progress and Preparation for Spiritual Leadership in the Far East* (New York: George H. Doran, 1925), one of many works he produced on these themes.

12. Laubach has yet to attract a serious scholarly biographer, but details of his life are available in David E. Mason, *Frank C. Laubach, Teacher of Millions* (Minneapolis: T. S. Denison, 1967).

13. Frank C. Laubach, *Towards a Literate World* (New York: Columbia University Press, 1938).

14. For an excellent account of Laubach's role as a cultural hero for ecumenical Protestants, see Matthew Hedstrom, *The Rise of Liberal Religion: Book Culture and American Spirituality in the Twentieth Century* (New York: Oxford University Press, 2013), 216–17.

15. For Kraemer's life and career, see Libertus A. Hoedmaker, "The Legacy of Hendrik Kraemer," *International Bulletin of Missionary Research* 4 (1980): 60–64.

16. A succinct account of Kraemer's role in the missionary disputes of the 1920s and 1930s is William R. Hutchison, *Errand to the World: American Protestant Thought and Foreign Missions* (Chicago: University of Chicago Press, 1987), 180–83. For a more detailed analysis, see J. Wesley Robb, "Hendrik Kraemer versus William Ernest Hocking," *Journal of Bible and Religiion* (April 1961): 93–101.

17. A thorough account of Kraemer's enduring influence is Tyler Lenocker, "The Mission Theory of Hendrik Kraemer."

18. Hollinger, *Protestants Abroad*, 102.

19. Hollinger, *Protestants Abroad*, 72–91.

20. For an account of the ecumenical/evangelical divide in domestic as well as foreign politics from World War II to the present, see David A. Hollinger, *Christianity's American Fate: How Religion Became More Conservative and Society More Secular* (Princeton: Princeton University Press, 2022).

21. Graham's remarks of 1963 are quoted in Anthea Butler, *White Evangelical Racism: The Politics of Morality in America* (Chapel Hill: University of North Carolina Press, 2021), 34.

22. For an account of Landon's career, see Hollinger, *Protestants Abroad*, 187–213.

23. Barbara Kingsolver, *The Poisonwood Bible* (New York: Perennial, 1998).

24. James A. Michener, *Hawaii* (New York: Fawcett, 1959).

25. Mischa Berlinski, *Fieldwork* (New York: Atlantic, 2007).

26. W. Somerset Maugham, *Rain and Other Stories* (New York: Grosset and Dunlap, 1921).

27. Charles Peirce, "The Fixation of Belief," in *Writings of Charles Peirce: A Chronological Edition*, vol. 3, *1872–1878*, ed. Christian W. Kloesel et al. (Bloomington: Indiana University Press, 1986), 250, 252.

28. Gordon W. Allport, *The Nature of Prejudice* (New York: Addison-Wesley, 1954), especially 261–81.

29. This theory of Allport's has gained popularity in recent decades specifically in regard to attitudes toward religion and sexual orientation. Individuals and families who had earlier felt contempt for same-sex intimacy were changed upon learning that a respected friend or a member of their own family was gay. Robert Putnam and David Campbell established that tolerance for religious difference increased dramatically when adherents of one faith experienced sustained contact with person of another faith with the same class position; see Robert Putnam and David Campbell, *American Grace: How Religion Divides and Unites Us* (New York: Simon and Schuster, 2010). Putnam provides one of the most lucid of recent social scientific discussions of "contact theory" in his "*E. Pluribus Unum*: Diversity and Community in the Twenty-First Century: The 2006 Johan Skytte Prize Lecture," *Scandinavian Political Studies* 30 (2007).

30. Mark Twain, *Innocents Abroad* (New York: American Publishing, 1869), 493.

6

"Sing, Choirs of New Jerusalem"

Hymnody and Sincerity in the Christian Tobalands

Julia Byl

INTRODUCTION

The public ritual ensemble of the Toba Batak—the drums, gongs, and shawm of the *gondang sabangunan*, whose sounds can carry through the highland valleys of North Sumatra for miles—is the most documented musical target of the Sumatra mission of the Rheinische Missiongesellschaft (RMG). The RMG missionaries prohibited the ensemble among converts from the 1870s and were soon assisted by the Dutch with a civil ban that was lifted only in the year 1938.[1] Gradually, the *gondang* resumed its formal place at the locus of kinship practices and religious beliefs; its repertoire is surprisingly unaltered by the now overwhelming Christian beliefs of its practitioners.[2] Indeed, the place of *gondang* within scholarship on Toba music is largely owing to the tradition's resilience after independence in 1949 and in its eventual use within Catholic and Protestant congregations.[3]

In contrast, consider the musical category of unaccompanied sung poetry, in the recollection of M. Joustra, a Dutch missionary who was working in the Karo Batak region to the north of the Tobalands in 1899. Joustra recounts the words of a non-converted villager who walked into a hymn-singing lesson the missionary was leading to "protest the racket":

> "You must not make these noises like crying people, like crazy people. You'll go crazy yourself if you do!" . . . Then I said, "Listen Father! I am teaching the people here, not so they will have misfortune, but for their welfare! You do not fully understand the use of this singing! Don't the Batak sing also? During the day, and in the evenings, in the men's house, on the path, in the villages—I have heard them singing at the top of their lungs. But the singing that I am teaching is prettier and more useful."[4]

The RMG was a Pietist Lutheran group with roots in the Prussian (German) province of Rhineland, and Joustra a representative of the Nederlandsch Zendeling

Genootschap (Dutch Missionary Society, or NZG), but both societies, from nations sharing borders, prized the accessibility of congregational singing and its cultivation of the individual believer's scriptural knowledge and piety. So, too, in precolonial times, the tradition of sung poetry—called *ende* in Toba, *ende-enden* in Karo—enlivened the daily life of people, crossing the territories of the inland Batak communities in a wide-ranging web of culturally rich music and poetry.

As the account suggests, in 1899 the *ende-enden* tradition was sung everywhere and encoded aesthetic preferences for vocal sounds, to which the unfamiliar range, intervals, or motion of the mission songs clearly did not conform. These transgressions were in turn interpreted within the precolonial Batak religious and psychological discourse of the soul (*tendi* in Karo, *tondi* in Toba), in which mental illness ("crazy") and ungovernable emotions ("crying") were understood as "soul loss."[5] But by the time of writing, in 2024, the most predominant use of the word *ende* in Sumatra is in the title of the Toba Batak Christian songbook, *Buku Ende*. And the most common use of the word *tondi* is within the rhymed stanzas of the hymns found within, where the term now references the "soul" of 1 Corinthians 15 and Psalm 103 and is carried by the diatonic melodies of the mission.

Unlike *gondang, ende* did not threaten the fragile souls of new converts with its ancestral associations and was unrestricted by the mission, at least by law. However, recall Joustra's assessment of Christian hymnody as not just "more useful" but "prettier." Hegemony works not only through legal prohibitions but through subtle, arbitrary, and sometimes unexamined means—for example, in the aesthetic judgment that governs a choice of repertoire for a songbook and the constant repetition of these values through the regular and pleasurable acts of communal singing. This power of aesthetics was all the clearer in the Toba Batak areas under the German RMG. Here, the aesthetic preference for, and pride in, the German sacred choral tradition simultaneously spurred investments in the musical education of Bataks while making it virtually impossible for the missionaries to value Toba Batak song at all. Today, the original *ende* tradition is difficult to find; when Toba Bataks are touted as Indonesia's best singers, it is usually because of open vocal tone, wide range, and facility with multipart harmony.[6]

In this essay, I discuss the transformative role of the hymnody of the RMG and, later, of the independent Huria Kristen Protestan Batak (HKBP), in altering the musical assumptions of Toba Christians. I begin with *ende* because its history reveals three elements: the fine-grained significance of precolonial Toba concepts, sometimes held intact; the process by which older traditions were forcibly excised, changes normalized, and all traces of this substitution erased; and the expanded world of knowledge offered by missionaries that spurred musical innovation among Toba Christians. Through research into the mission period, I arrive at the conclusion that the precolonial Batak division of text-based unaccompanied song (*ende*) from ritual instrumental music (*gondang*) was fundamentally, if unintentionally, transformed by the German habits of singing accompanied by harmony, keyboard, or instrumental ensembles, and that this intervention in turn caused musical arrangement to become a sphere for Toba Batak creativity in the twentieth century.

The lamentable loss of the traditional worlds of *ende* and *gondang* is directly connected to colonial interventions and erasures, but such a conclusion should not foreclose the agency of Tobas who reveled in the new musical worlds revealed by these ruptures.[7] As a telling corollary, consider the RMG's recruitment of rich local language practices and rhetorical techniques, a strategy responsible for the Sumatra mission's reputation in missiology as an exemplar of a humane and effective mission practice.[8] And yet the missionaries were not the only ones who exercised persuasion; key was the conversion of important individuals within the Toba *marga* system (a term related to both geographical networks of villages and family lineages). As the decades passed—from early mission work in the 1860s, to the consolidation of a church as an institution in the 1880s, to greater engagement with the parallel process of Dutch colonization around the turn of the twentieth century, to the development of an autonomous Batak church from 1940 and into the period of Indonesian nationalism—these individuals would become the pastors, choir directors, Sunday school teachers, and even the bishops of the church; their persuasive tools were the theology, the liturgy, the Toba Batak Bible, and the hymnbooks transmitted through the Lutheran tradition.[9] For of course, the embeddedness of language cut both ways. When animated by a well-translated Toba phrase, these new Christian texts could also participate in a pervasive Toba expressive culture, speaking to new converts in a way they were conditioned to understand. And when set to song—written down for easy reference, practiced regularly, reinforced through social worship—the result reframed both the Toba interface with the spirit world and the musical language that supported it.

A primary source for this essay is the Toba hymnbook, *Buku Ende di Huria Kristen Batak Protestan*, the direct beneficiary of musical practice from Wuppertal–Barmen. Since 1923, it has been published in interior Sumatra, first at the mission publication house in Laguboti and then by the HKBP seminary in Pematang Siantar.[10] It can count at least twenty-two editions and is available at almost any urban market, often flanked by supplements and arrangements for choir and keyboardists. The book I am flipping through right now, published in 2009 and emblazoned with the words "Jubileum 150 Tahun HKBP" (150th anniversary of the HKBP), runs to 954 pages with 864 discrete entries, a topical guide, an alphabetical index of titles, and a list of twenty-six hymnals that have served as sources, many titles in German and Dutch.[11] Each item provides a monophonic melody rendered in both cipher (number) notation and Western notation, with legible and variable time and key signatures; most list between four and nine printed verses in Toba. Beside me are two more sources—the *Buku Logu HKBP*, a book providing four-part harmony for each hymn tune, and a well-thumbed miniature hymnbook that I bought at the market in 1999. Between the three sources, it is often possible to learn the name, author, and date of the hymn text ("Tochter Zion, freue dich," Friedrich Heinrich Ranke, 1820), the person who translated it into Toba ("Drs T Manurung"), the composer and date of the hymn tune (George Friedrich Handel, 1747), and the Bible verse most relevant to its content (Zacharias 9:9, Matthew 21:9).

This is a source for an entire dissertation, one that I hope someone will take on in the future. But for this essay, although I do pay some attention to the denominational genesis of this varied hymn repertoire and its permutations over more than 150 years, I have chosen to adopt a more stripped-down sense of the hymns: I am simply interested in how these religious songs serve as a musical manifestation of the Toba language and voice, and through it, the transformation or continuity, through music, of Toba Batak social experience and religious thought. Sometimes, these hymns are imbued with vocabularies drawn from older Toba spiritual worlds, including specific religious and cultural terms with a clearly non-Christian genesis. At other times, they participate within a remade world of Judeo–Christian texts and narratives, and police the gap between the acceptable and the unacceptable Toba Christian beliefs. Over the course of this essay, I offer windows into Toba musical life over the first period of conversion in the latter decades of the nineteenth century, trace a history of the musical repertoire and the implications of Toba hymnbooks, and discuss the role of the *Buku Ende* in instilling the musical skills and sensibilities of Toba Batak musicians and innovators who have secured their place in Indonesian music history. But to better understand the positions of the missionaries vis-à-vis the linguistic and musical systems they found in the Tobalands in the 1860s, I turn first to a curious coincidence that I found in the archives of the RMG in Barmen, Germany, in 2022.

A STRANGE PAIRING IN THE ARCHIVE

In 1861, Ludwig Ingwer Nommensen did something that probably would have startled and concerned the board of the Rheinische Missionsgesellschaft: he asked the *datu* (Toba: magic practitioner) Guru Sinangga ni Adji to write down his knowledge of a broad variety of traditional practices and foundational narratives.[12] These writings, filling seven European notebooks in miniscule Toba Batak script, were donated to the Leiden University Library in 1896 after the death of Hermannus Neubronner van der Tuuk (1824–94), the pioneering scholar of Indonesian languages.[13] This collection was later catalogued in Leiden by the Dutch philologist Petrus Voorhoeve (1899–1996), who suggested that Nommensen himself send them to van der Tuuk, a worthy custodian of Toba knowledge.[14] After all, Nommensen had prepared for his mission for two years by studying the Toba Batak language with van der Tuuk himself.

Van der Tuuk, born in Malacca of European and Eurasian ancestry, had undertaken a study of the Toba Batak language a decade earlier, with the support of the Nederlandsch Bijbelgenootschap (Dutch Bible Society, or NBG).[15] The scholar was not a missionary but a linguist who viewed Bible translation as an adequate means for reaching his true goal: showing how Toba Batak grammar, literature, and vocabulary could expand universal linguistic knowledge.[16] Practically, it was this linguistic and cultural knowledge, gathered over seven years, that would allow Nommensen to translate hymns, frame theology lessons, and prepare sermons in the Toba language. Nommensen replicated van der Tuuk's methodologies as well, living in interior Toba settlements and inviting free access and social discourse without restrictions.

Years later, the RMG's Sumatra mission would jettison van der Tuuk's Biblical translations because the scholar was deemed "a humanist, not a Christian."[17] But the thin line between knowledge as a mission tool and knowledge as scientific inquiry is clear throughout the history of Batak studies; prominent among the early scholarly works on indigenous Toba Batak cosmology, state craft, law, and ritual work are the names of many RMG missionaries, Johannes Winkler, Johannes Meerwaldt, and Johannes Warneck among them. Warneck claims a doubly scholarly lineage, as he himself was the son of the pioneering missiologist, Gustav Warneck—apparently, inhabiting non-Christian religious worlds, though perhaps unadvisable for a theologian, was permissible within this lineage. This dynamic explains why Nommensen commissioned these notebooks; understanding indigenous religious and mythological systems was necessary for a well-crafted strategy of conversion.

In May 2022, I visited the RMG archives in Wuppertal–Barmen, where a copy and transliteration of the original 1871 manuscript was housed (A/W 8b27). I had been alerted by anthropologist Sandra Niessen—who, at Voorhoeve's urging, had used Guru Sinangga ni Adji's writing in her own work on traditional weaving—that two of the forty-five sections referred to music, one on "The Origins of Ende" (Toba: poetic song) and the other on "The Origins of Tataganing" (the tuned drum that plays ritual *gondang* music).[18] Such specificity is rare in the Toba corpus, so I had high hopes. But reading Toba Batak manuscripts can be difficult; the *datu* filled them with specialized knowledge that could be dangerous if read by the wrong person, so easy access was never an aim.[19] Certainly the notebooks were no *pustaha*, the most prestigious of Toba Batak bark books of magic diagrams and divination. Despite working in ink on European paper, Guru Sinangga ni Adji nevertheless marked the beginning of each section with a *bindu*, an efficacious device of Sanskrit origin that also serves as a practical bookmark.[20] I found each *bindu* and rapidly photographed as many pages as was practical to decipher further at home, moving through the repeated, obscure words in the *ende* piece, through to the prose of the creation narratives, to lists of the parts of the *gondang*, until I was brought up short by a small bundle of paper, with narrower lines and in a different hand, tucked in the very end of the last notebook (figure 6-1).

But the religious change these words heralded was clear at the top, in transliterated Toba Batak: "In the name of God the Father, the Son, and the Holy

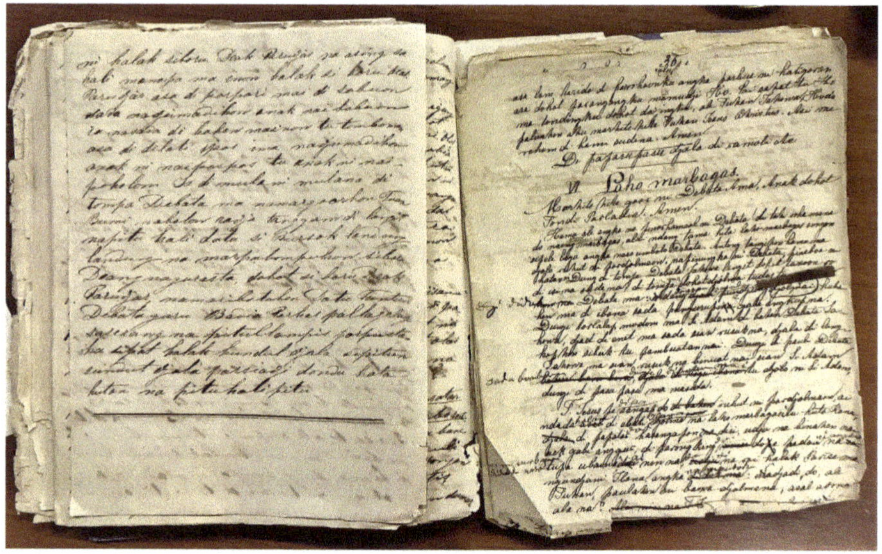

FIGURE 6-1. Guru Sinangga ni Adji's notebook with church notes. Archive and Museum Foundation of the UEM, RMG 1.340, Nachlass Nommensen, Ingwer Ludwig, Mappe 9.

Spirit. Amen." This invocation began a piece of writing with the calligraphic words "*Lao Marbagas*," "On Marriage," followed by "On Burial," "Protocol for Emergency Burials," "On the Burial of a Child," and, most tantalizing, "Protocol for Readmitting a Member into the Church." More than anything, these sections resembled the backmatter of a hymnbook, the part after the creeds and before the index that contains marriage vows and responses for the congregation to read during a baptism. Indeed, if you look at the topical list of songs in the back of a Toba Batak hymnbook now, you'll see the subheading "*Harajaon ni Debata: Lao Marbagas*" (The kingdom of God: On marriage), pointing out three hymns fit to sing during such a covenant.

Yet the writings also read by turns as sermon notes (with requisite quotations from the Bible), as liturgy (with congregational answers spelled out, often "*Olo!*," "Yes!"), as reminders for an officiating preacher, and a rhetorical device for conversion. For instance, the portion "On Marriage" begins,

Hamu ale angka na pinahamaol ni Debata! Di tahe hamuna na naeng marbagas, alaindang tama hita marbagas songon sipele begu angka na so imboto Debata. Antong tangihon ma hamuna jolo suhut ni parjolmaon, na pinaboa ni Debata i, pinaboa na hatana i. Dung di tompa ma Debata langit dohot tano on.[21]

Oh you, who are protected by God! You have been called to marry, but let us not be like the ghost worshippers, those who do not know God. Therefore, hear you the core of humanity, as told by God, told by these words. After God created heaven and earth.

The story of Adam and Eve follows, then John 2:1–11, where Jesus turns water into wine at the marriage feast, followed by congregational singing, the Lord's Prayer ("*Ale amanami na di banua ginjang*," etc.: "Our father who art in the upper world," etc.), and the celebration of "*ulaon na badia*" (the exalted ceremony): Communion. The text offers constant invitations to sing—at times, the general command "*Ende*" and other times specific instructions, such as a song performed by the school children's choir or a time of silence for reflection following a hymn. Sometimes, the Bible texts themselves suggest song, as in the protocol for the death of a child, where Luke 18:15–17 ("Suffer the little children to come unto me") is followed by a large, capitalized "Halleluya!" At other times, a specific hymn text is stipulated, the abbreviation suggesting that the song was likely known at the time: "*Ma hehe ma sogot dagingkon*" ("Tomorrow my flesh will be raised," likely Job 19:25–17.)

These twelve pages of writing, then, offer a window into the early stages of the new mission just as surely as the notebook it was slipped into reveals the comprehensive knowledge system that preceded it. It may be difficult to pinpoint the document the pages belong to, but I suspect that it came from the mission's first twenty years, that is, when liturgies and protocol were still in development but institutions like the children's choir were already self-standing. Hymns and singing were clearly a part of weekly if not daily life at this stage but not yet codified to become a number in a hymnal; and indeed, I have not yet been able to match the text above to one of the hundreds of hymns in the *Buku Ende*.

The presence of non-Christian belief systems in the vicinity of the congregation is also key. Consider the discussion of the Christian interpretation for marriage—one of the most important ceremonies in the traditional Toba ritual world—as well as the necessity of reintroducing a sinner (lapsed convert?) into the congregation. In fact, you can find both religions coexisting in our single archival image (figure 6-1); on the first line of the last page of Guru Sinangga ni Adji's notebook, you can see the name of Boru Deak Parujar and the story of her creation by Debata Guru Badia (God the Exalted Teacher) and how she subsequently lowered the world on a string she used for weaving—followed on the facing page by Genesis 1, and the creation of the heavens and the earth by Debata Jahowa (God Jahova).

In some ways, the connection between these epistemologies is logical; both van der Tuuk and Nommensen translated Genesis 1:1–31, using the cultural and language knowledge gained from indigenous scholars like Guru Sinangga ni Adji. Many of the words within the Christian service come from the vocabularies of magical literature and *adat* work. *Debata* is related to the Sanskrit *dewa* (god) and describes aspects of Shiva (called Debata Barata Guru in Toba).[22] The word for the Biblical heaven is *banua ginjang*, or upper world, referencing the tripartite Batak cosmology on which were transposed heaven, earth, and hell. And a quotation from Revelations 14:13— "After that, I heard a voice from heaven saying, 'Write: blessed are the dead who die in the Lord from now on'"—made me question whether I was reading scripture or a Toba genealogical narrative, many of which begin "*Dung ni*," or "After that."[23]

Naturally, a Protestant missionary would endeavor to translate God's word into the vernacular, but there seems to be something more going on here. The creation of affective links with elements of the religious Toba language and the exploitation of similarities to frame new theological concepts are hallmarks of the work of the Rheinische Missiongesellschaft in Sumatra and the reason that you will find Nommensen's name at the back of the *Evangelical Lutheran Worship*, commemorated on November 7 in the Calendar of Saints (Evangelical Lutheran Church in America, 2006). And yet for the individuals in the RMG congregations, who were taught Biblical knowledge and doctrine through the hymnbook, the proximity of these worlds was progressively hidden within the lexical meaning of the words, partitioned by force from the rituals that would have given them meaning: *tondi* was meant to refer only to Paul's concept of soul; the only acceptable *debata* was Jahowa. It is equally clear that for the RMG of the nineteenth century, a musical ecumenism, too, was seen as aesthetically misguided and detrimental to the spiritual welfare of the new Sumatran converts.

TRANSLATING WORDS, REPLACING MUSIC

In his description of the history of Christian conversion in East Java during the nineteenth century, anthropologist Robert Hefner describes the reticence of the Dutch to allow missionary activity in the East Indies, instead "devoting its political resources to economic programs."[24] Even the Dutch Mission Society, founded to proselytize in the colony, was stymied until the mid-nineteenth century, by which time, in Java, a mestizo community had sprung up with a Euroasian leader who "peppered his sermons with mystical terms, employed Sufi-style *dzikir* chanting for the Christian confession of faith, and sponsored such esteemed Javanese arts as gamelan music and *wayang* shadow theater, usually just after sabbath worship."[25] At this point, the Dutch, facing opposition to the expansion of military and political control in the interiors of islands, dropped their resistance to missions and accepted Western-aligned help in any form rather than countenance such a hybridization. It was in the context of this decision that the Prussian Lutheran RMG was allowed to open missions in Borneo (1838), Sumatra (1861), and Nias, off Sumatra's west coast (1865).

I begin with this description from Java because although such musical syncretism is quite familiar within the early history of Islamic proselytism in Indonesia, the situation in North Sumatra and, indeed, in the majority of Dutch and German mission stations was different.[26] Instead, Nommensen, Johannsen, and others made the decision to outlaw all use of the *gondang sabanungan*, the ritual ensemble of drums, gongs, and double reed that had long served to officiate public ceremony.[27] Brass bands from Germany were substituted in the *adat* ceremonies of church members.[28] This approach was decided upon at the earliest stages of the mission; even the gong, which had been used in the early 1860s to call the faithful to church, was soon replaced by a bell brought from Europe.[29]

Why was *gondang sabangunan* singled out by the church leaders as virtually the only indigenous component of worship to require a full-scale replacement by Western imports? After all, Nommensen was able to work with Guru Sinangga ni Adji, and "only mutual respect between the indigenous guru and the Christian missionary" could explain the connection.[30] One answer can be drawn from the third year of the ministry in the Silundung valley, to the south of Lake Toba. Church historian Paul Pedersen narrates a story in which Nommensen was threatened during a ceremony aimed at elevating the status of an ancestor, with the threat escalating as the spirit medium entered a possessed state brought on by the beating of the *gondang* drums.[31] Nommensen left unharmed, but such a sensory experience would have left an impression, especially considering the earlier murder of American missionaries Henry Lyman and Samuel Munson in 1834, in the same vicinity where Nommensen worked.[32]

Certainly, once the missionaries became aware that *gondang* was associated with ancestor worship and trance, they were eager to sever ties that might cause new converts to return to their previous ways; *gondang* was seen as too powerful to be converted. Mauly Purba points to the importance of this musical tradition in not just accompanying but substantially forming precolonial religious and political practices: "Gondang music is definitely not a subordinate constituent of *adat* and religious practices; it is essential for—indeed, inseparable from—the ritual practices involved and may not be performed unless it accompanies a ritual ceremony."[33] If the ensemble's ritual language makes a ceremony efficacious, then silencing it would weaken both religious work and the polity that sponsored it. This outcome suited both the Dutch colonial government and the German missionaries, who worked in tandem, and a ban in 1872 on the *gondang sabangunan* for Toba Christian converts, on pain of exclusion from the sacrament of Communion, became in 1879 a full-scale civil ban for Christians and non-Christians alike, enforced by colonial might.[34]

It is within this silencing that we must understand the introduction of hymn melodies and the innovations that accompanied it: the harmonium, the box organ, and the introduction of polyphonic voices itself. We know something about how this music was brought to Sumatra from Georg Zimmer, an RMG missionary who worked in the first Sumatran mission field of Borneo.[35] In 1866, upon visiting Nommensen's settlement Huta Dame ("peace village") in Silindung, he made a report to the society's newsletter, *Berichte der Rheinische Missionsgessellschaft*, on what he found: "I've been teaching seven children to read and write in Dutch, over eight days. Organist duties are also linked with the teaching post, and Brother Nommensen has translated some songs into Batak: 'Jerusalem, du hochgebaute Stadt,' 'Ich bin's voll Zuversicht,' 'Herz und Herz vereint zusammen.'"[36] In his retrospective on the music of the RMG, Ernst Quentmeier adds more detail: "Of course things went slowly. At first, [Nommensen and second missionary P. H. Johannsen] did not dare to compose songs themselves, but translated German chorales."[37] Nine hymns were completed first and results given to "native helpers"

TABLE 6-1 Growth of the church in rough number of converts during each stage
of hymnal publication

Year	Stage of hymn printing	Place of publication	Number of converts
1867	9 hymns, manuscript	Silindung	115
ca. 1881	90 hymns, book	Barmen	5,988
1911	278 hymns, book	Barmen	103,538
1923	331 hymns, book	Laguboti	210,416
1940	375 hymns, book	Laguboti	429,321

(*eingeborenen Gehilfen*) assisting in worship. Quentmeier then lays out an overview of hymn publishing: in the early 1880s, a hymnal of ninety songs was published in Germany, though the songs were "bumpy and stumbling" (*holperig und stolperig*).[38] In 1905, the missionary J. H. Meerwaldt edited a book of 278 hymns, with single melodies, again published in Germany; 1923 brought the first edition to the mission's Sumatran printing press in Laguboti, with an additional fifty-three hymns—but at the expense of musical notation. Finally, in 1936, a triumphantly integrated six thousand hymnals of 275 songs and melodies were published in Sumatra, followed by an additional ten thousand copies in 1938. As Quentmeier explains, "The fact that the entire edition was completely sold out in one year demonstrates that the members of the congregation felt they needed their own hymnbook."[39]

Quentmeier's narrative covers a good deal of time, spanning the early years of the ministry, the consolidation of the church as an institution, Nommensen's death in 1919, the ascendancy of Johannes Warneck as Ephorus (church leader), and support for Toba control of the church, which became an independent body, the Huria Kristen Batak Protestan (HKBP), in 1940. But a bird's-eye view is helpful here; adapting a chart by Andar Lubantobing, we can see the growth of the church in the rough number of converts during each stage of hymnal publication (table 6-1).[40] At present, the HKBP counts around 4,500,000 members, suggesting that the story does not end with Quentmeier in 1941; the 864 hymns of the current hymnbook concur. But before turning to more recent developments, I'd like to consider in more depth the musical details of the compositions that comprised the Toba Batak hymnbooks.

OPEN YOUR HYMNALS: "JERUSALEM," GENEVA 42, *SANKEY LIEDER*

In his report, Quentmeier details the types of compositions that comprised the 375 hymns of the *Buku Ende*, many of them by name. The majority, some 250 songs, were described as "German chorales." The list includes four by Martin Luther ("the most important": "Ein feste Burg," "Vom Himmel hoch," and "Aus tiefer Not"), seventeen by theologian Paul Gerhardt (1607–76), four by German Reformed hymnist Joachim Neander (1650–80), and seven by the aristocratic reformer

Nikolaus Zinzendorf (1700–60). In comparison to the Reformed tradition, in which all 150 Psalms would be obligatory, the Lutheran hymnal included only ten, unspecified, but rounded out thirty English hymns with sixty "rather spirited" German folk tunes, to which poetry was set.[41] To those in his readership who might have objected to the use of a secular musical source, Quentmeier reminds them of two old secular tunes, "Innsbruck, ich muss dich lassen" and "Flora meine Freude," set as melodies for hymns they themselves likely sang in their own German churches (respectively, Gerhardt's "Nun ruhen alle Wälder" and "Jesu, meine Freude," by Johann Franck and J. S. Bach).[42]

Quentmeier is careful to say that "very few are new creations," but on balance, the hymnbook is a vital blend of words and melodies meant to minister to a sensitive, moral Christian.[43] This can be seen in one of the first songs that Nommensen himself decided to translate (example 6-1): "Jerusalem, hochgebaute Stadt," or BE (*Buku Ende*) 343: "Jerusalem, Huta na Timbo" (Jerusalem, city on high), whose lyrics were penned by Johann Matthäus Meyfart, a preacher who had worked with Melchior Franck, both denizens of the seventeenth century.[44] This dating is important, because it means that the song predates the First Great Awakening (German: *Erweckungsbewegungen*), the period of religious revival that swept from England and Scotland through to Germany and the Americas in the eighteenth and early nineteenth centuries.[45] When we say that the RMG was a Pietist Lutheran society, the piety referenced not a theological movement from the older Protestant foundations but a renewal of moral urgency on a swell of personal sensibility. Indeed, the conversion narrative was as important a trope in eighteenth-century Germany as it was in nineteenth-century Sumatra.[46] The emotional expanse found in both the lyrics of the German and translated Batak hymn, then, is more important than its actual textual source in Revelations: the hymn doesn't shore up a sermon but narrates a change of heart. Although Meyfart's dates (1590–1642) predated by a hundred years those of the major Lutheran Pietist leader—Nikolaus Zinzendorf, the author of another of Nommensen's chosen three hymns—his position as an educator who strove to move the hearts of his students through sermons and hymns aligns him with the sort of persuasive work Nommensen himself was doing in the Bataklands. And the hymn's melody matches the energy of the text, with the bold octave of its opening phrase, linked by an arpeggiated chord (example 6-1).

EXAMPLE 6-1. "Jerusalem, Huta na Timbo," adapted from *Buku Ende* no. 343.

EXAMPLE 6-2. "Sai torop dope parbegu," adapted from *Buku Ende* no. 134, Buku Logu 176.

The harmonic modulations to the dominant, the repetition, and the return to tonic all mark the hymn's German compositional lineage, especially when played in four-part harmony on the keyboard. But even when sung in unison, the musical setting matches the aspiration of the text and its authors.

In contrast, consider one of the older pieces in the hymnal, with a surprising rhetorical twist. Buku Ende 134 begins (Example 6-2):

Sai torop dope parbegu	There are so many of the heathen (*parbegu*)
na di haholomon i	Living in darkness
Jesus, ro ma Ho patibu	Jesus, come quickly
mandasdasi angka i	To summon them to you

The hymn text, I thought, set as it was in a section on "Missions," was of relatively recent vintage, or at the least seemed to narrate precisely the perceived challenges of the young church. I was surprised, then, when I recognized the melody as Psalm 42 from the Calvinist Genevan Psalter, "Ainsi qu'on oit le cerf bruire" (As the hart about to falter; example 6-2). Louis Bourgeois's name is at the bottom of the piece, but strangely, a flip to Psalm 42 itself (one of the ten psalms Quentmeier referenced) showed an entirely different melody, one that was not cited and one that I did not recognize. In addition, printed above the hymn were the words "Ale Tuhan Amanami"—an entirely different hymn text that happened to share the Bourgeois melody.

The initial confusion was resolved when I considered that many hymn texts share hymn tunes—as is certainly the case in the Toba hymnal. From my own Dutch Calvinist upbringing, I could pair Psalm 42 with the psalmist's panting deer, but I also connected it to the advent hymn "Comfort, Comfort ye my People" (in German, "Tröstet, tröstet meine Lieben"). Indeed, the movement of the tune from a psalm to a hymn related to evangelism had roots in the seventeenth, not the nineteenth, century, when Johann Olearius used the tune (a rather jaunty one for a psalm of lamentation) for the festival of St. John the Baptist in mid-June, and J. S. Bach sealed the association in his cantata *Freue dich, erlöste Schar* BWV 30.[47]

Considering that John the Baptist's role was to prepare the way for the gospel, the Toba text's image of Jesus dispelling the Sumatran darkness fits; and calling someone of another religion a "parbegu," or "ghost worshipper," seems about right for John, who once referred to the Pharisees as a "brood of vipers." The version of Geneva 42 in the *Buku Ende*, then, demonstrates how that melody's flexible associations, as it moved across Protestant denominations, allowed it to fit within the key projects of the RMG while modeling some degree of flexibility for the Toba church itself as it moved to pair melody, text, and teaching in optimal ways.

In telling the story of the *Buku Ende*, I nearly missed one such movement—and I am hardly the first one. In the 1930s, about the time that the full hymnal was being printed in Sumatra, more than two-hundred hymns were being sung outside of formal church services, existing in a sort of shadow hymnal that was printed by the RMG but not numbered with the official hymnal.[48] That the songs of an "unofficial" hymnal were compiled and sung by women is not surprising, as the leadership of both the RMG mission and the independent HKBP church was, and remains, resolutely male. Yet the institution of the Frauen-Bibelschule, run by and ministering to women from 1934 to 1940, at the heart of the RMG mission in Laguboti, is crucial to understanding the expansion of the number and character of the hymn songs in the mid-twentieth century.

In 1985, the HKBP decided to formalize these 282 hymns, circulating informally in Christian social gatherings for around fifty years. The new section of the *Buku Ende* made room for *Haluaon na Gok* (Freedom in full), a work edited by Zuster Elfriede Harder sometime in the 1930s, as she served in the RMG mission from 1931 until the ouster of German personnel in 1940, at the commencement of World War II. Harder was not the only woman in the mission; other European women worked in hospitals and schools, as midwives and teachers of young girls.[49] Hester Needham, an English missionary who visited the RMG mission field in the 1890s, is rather famous among ethnomusicologists for her erroneous assertions that Toba Bataks "never sang a note 'til the Europeans came."[50] But as well as supervising the female teachers, Harder compiled a group of songs that were quite different from the character of the official hymnal: they included a large number of songs from Dutch and German hymnals that were inspired by the Second Great Awakening, this time on American soil.

This revival movement began in the rural areas of the United States between 1800 and 1830 and was spread through the country by itinerant preachers and word-of-mouth tent services.[51] One of the most famous female song composers was Fanny Crosby, whose energetic hymns, filled with dotted rhythms, invigorated the Chicago-based ministry of Dwight Moody and Ira Sankey. Moody's charismatic preaching would form the theological foundation of the meetings, which drew thousands, while Sankey would lead the singing with the hymns by Crosby and Phillip Bliss that were "Christ-centered, expressing and cultivating a type of piety."[52] Although Harder included songs by Crosby and Bliss in her Bibelschule supplement, many of the songs in the supplement were by Sankey himself, who began to compose hymns during the duo's tours to Europe.

In the sources that Harder lists (now written on the last page of the *Buku Ende* proper), it is clear that her knowledge of the American gospel songs was channeled through a number of Dutch and German evangelical hymnals: *Sankey Lieder, Siegeslieder, Singet dem Herrn*, as well as the Dutch *Zoeklicht* and the American *Fellowship Hymns*. According to Tobing, the RMG's head missionary, Johannes Warneck, did not approve of the songs—likely from an aesthetic point of view—and decided to number them differently, partitioning them from the formal worship. This interpretation is strengthened by Anna Maria Busse Berger's account of Franz Rietzsch a German Lutheran missionary in East Africa, whose loathing of Sankey hymns on an aesthetic level moved him to make graver allegations: that singing these hymns occasioned a "moral lapse" on the part of two African choir conductors.[53]

The *Buku Ende* underwent a final expansion in 2003, when a supplement, called *Sangap di Jahowa* (Hope in Jahowa), added a further 405 songs. This process was overseen by a Batak graduate of the HKBP seminary, Reverend J. A. U. Doloksaribu; in addition to his translations, credited on the majority of the songs, Doloksaribu was also responsible for the curation of the whole. These new songs ranged through the full repertoire initiated by the two earlier iterations: from Handel's "Tochter Zion," to Maranatha Music's "Heavenly Father, I Appreciate You," from "Be Still My Soul," set to Sibelius's *Finlandia*, to Doloksaribu's own composition, "Oikumene" (Ende UEM), the very last song in the book, which commemorated the United Evangelical Mission (the modern name of the RMG). Perhaps nobody would be as surprised by this last entry into the hymnbook as Quentmeier himself, our writer of the 1941 report on Sumatran hymnody, who stated unequivocally, "It should be noted that not a single song by a Batak is included. They are not that far. For now, the European still has to do all of the work."[54]

EINGEBORENEN GEHILFEN: TOWARD A TOBA BATAK COMPOSITIONAL PRACTICE

The presence of Toba Batak composers and arrangers within the *Buku Ende* is not at all surprising considering that by 1919, the RMG was boasting to the Dutch "that the superiority of the Batakmission/HKBP schools was in their use of the Batak language, especially in singing."[55] Indeed, it *is* surprising—and it turns out, untrue—that "native helpers" made no strides toward musical autonomy. From the 1860s, Toba Bataks were described as extraordinarily avid listeners. Zimmer, the visiting missionary from Borneo, describes how "the *poti marende* [box organ] seems to be a magic thing for all of them, and they come from afar to hear its magical tones [*zaubertöne*]." Not just hear, but sing with—for he continues, "so we sing with them at morning and evening prayers as well as on Sundays accompanied by the harmonium."[56]

It was a certain strategy to train the elastic minds and voices of young students, instilling musical knowledge that would filter up into the general congregation with each new class (hence Zimmer's quasi-complaint, cited earlier, that all teachers must be organists). Such seriousness about musical training is clear in Aritonang's description of the curriculum of the RMG seminary in Sipoholon at the beginning of the twentieth century: the lower classes began with two hours of singing and four hours of instrumental music, including harmonium, violin, and trumpet; the upper classes continued this practice, with the six hours of musical training outweighing the requirements for the study of the New Testament, history, arithmetic, and reading (including Latin), each of which was slated for four hours. The Dutch colonial government, which had begun to subsidize this school, actually stepped in to mandate a full twenty-six hours of general (nonreligious) education; music pointedly did not count toward this quota.[57]

By 1909, then, the mission had been training young singers for almost fifty years. The varied nature of the RMG hymns alone—requiring modulation, part reading, and the learning of new hymns from notation—attests to this training. In addition, SATB choirs sang sacred choral music of Bach and Mozart, prime exemplars of the Austro-German compositional tradition.[58] Indeed, Warneck boasted in a newsletter that "the elementary school pupils of the Batakmission were superior in Biblical knowledge (and in singing) to their German counterparts."[59] Why, then would Quentmeier, or other RMG missionaries like Meerwaldt or Beilefeld, categorically deny that Batak musicians were able to participate as musical actors in the development of hymnody, with Batak or even European style melodies? This seems especially strange since Aritonang asserts that Batak composers already *were* creating music by this time, writing that "Pastor Johannes Siregar, a Batak church worker, was actively composing hymn melodies using Batak rhythms and reported with pleasure that the school children thoroughly enjoyed singing them." In fact, according to Siregar, those songs were very effective in attracting the "heathen" to attend school.[60]

In fact, in the Angkola Batak mission, slightly to the south of the Toba territory, a children's music book was published in 1928, in a collaboration between a Dutchman, A. Van der Bijl, and a Toba Batak, Arsenius Tobing. Reportedly, the book included songs exhibiting traditional melodic and rhythmic material as well as arrangements of Western songs by Tobing.[61] This book now seems to be lost, so we are unable to verify the quality of the tunes, yet judging from the extraordinary florescence of Toba Batak musical innovation in the twentieth century, I doubt that there was a dearth of talent. Rather, I imagine that Quentmeier's doubt is partially animated by a fear that Batak Christian beliefs were unverifiable and shallowly held; at the end of his report, he muses, "Does the Christian Batak understand the songs in their depth, as we German Pietists understand them, or does the Christian Batak still think too superficially?"[62]

For the missionary, a new convert's aesthetic preference for Toba Batak music, despite all strictures and teachings to the contrary, would likely confirm the latter. Yet we should recognize that Quentmeier's ideas are themselves formed by the thought of Johann Gottfried Herder, the eighteenth-century Enlightenment thinker whose work extolled the particular genius of vernacular languages and stories. It is Herder at work when Johann Warneck's father, Gustav, coined the term *Volkskirche*—a "folk church" or "territorial church" and when Quentmeier himself argued for the validity of "Innsbruck ich muss dich lassen" in the hymnal.[63] Even for those who moved to include non-elite musical repertoires, some *völkisch* traditions were seemingly better than others. Listen to the backhanded way in which Herder himself describes the Psalms in *The Spirit of Hebrew Poesy* in 1787: "Could one refer to such a people as barbarian, even if they had just a few such national songs? And how many of the same kind do this people have?"[64] If this is how Psalms 120–34, the "songs of ascent," are described, what hope do Toba Batak violinists or singers have?

ENDE, LOGU, AND ARRANGEMENT

The too hasty prohibition of Toba traditional music prevented the missionaries from truly understanding the subtlety of the Batak tradition of sung poetry. This tradition, when transformed by new skills, would allow Toba musicians to further develop a robust and sincere Christian practice while also integrating traditional forms that had been discouraged in the past. Perhaps the missionaries would have been cheered had they concentrated on the native concept of *ende*, distinguishing it from the ritual music of the *gondang*. Indeed, the concept of *ende* was to be irrevocably transformed by the missionary project. Of course, we have used this word for "song" all along (it is in the *Buku Ende*, the word chosen to translate *hymn* in the Toba language), but a brief analysis of the term and its relation to Toba musical fundamentals might allow us to marry the world of the European hymnbook with the sonic universe of Sumatra before 1861—in other words, to bring the book of Guru Sinangga ni Adji and the pages of sermon notes in helpful contact. For despite the statements to the contrary, Toba Bataks most definitely sang before the Europeans came.

At its heart, the word *ende* refers to the voice of one entity, whether the voice of one person, one instrument, or even a whole group of people singing as one (in unison). The root is used in the general-purpose verb "to sing": you can *marendei* or *mangendei* a pop song, the melody of a hymn, or a tune in the shower. Even instruments can *marende* at times; the box organ, the *poti marende* ("box that can *marende*") is a single entity with one voice, even if that voice is split up into multiple sounds; the double-reed *sarune* is said to speak words with its instrumental voice. Similarly, in the *gondang hasapi* music, the two lutes (*hasapi*) are distinguished by their roles of melody carrying (*hasapi ende*) and gong imitation (*hasapi doal*). And this is the most import aspect: *ende* is always connected with the voicing of text, and most often, poetry. (Quentmeier actually knew this well, as he avers, in the only bit of unalloyed praise in his report, that "the Batak attach particular importance to beautiful rhymes, since many of his old proverbs are euphonious and powerful because of the rhyme."[65])

A canvas of precolonial Toba writings bears out this distinction; the manuscripts compiled by van der Tuuk contain many categories of *ende*—songs for collecting firewood or for cutting specific trees, caregiver songs (including lullabies), songs of bad luck, mourning songs, and songs of blessing. One entry describes *ende gas-gas*, a series of verses traded between young men and women as they leveled a field that needed to lay fallow.[66] Indeed, the piece of writing that I sought from Guru Sinangga ni Adji's notebooks purported to describe the origins of *ende*. Of course, the manuscripts give texts but do not lay down melodies.[67] Yet "euphony" is suggested by rhyme and repetition, and "power" by the complex construction of the stanza, with grammatical infixes and euphemistic descriptions of plants and animal life, designed to emphasize their respective spirits:

> Tinimpal ma anduhur, anduhur so la bona / Luhut do hita julma, masieit tu djolona

> Throw a rock at the mourning dove, the mourning dove named so la bona / All human beings, we have the tendency to take what we can get.[68]

The *ende* above, which sets out general truths from a Batak perspective, is related to a tradition of proverbs and blessings (*umpama* and *umpasa*) from Toba ceremonial oratory, where they are now intoned but not sung. Yet the one tradition of *ende* still practiced—*ende mangandung*, or mourning songs, extensively described in a dissertation by W. Robert Hodges—suggests the likely vocal practice for *ende*: equal phrases with patterns that move up or down a narrow range of pitches, with a stylized ending (transformed into chains of ornamentation in laments).[69] Regardless, the complexity is lodged in the construction of the poetry, as is the cultural significance.[70]

Equally important to recognize is that in contemporary Toba practice, the *ende* tradition and the instrumental tradition of *gondang* stand apart: in Toba ritual, even speech stops when the *gondang* music begins. In all my years studying *gondang*, I have on only one occasion heard my teacher set words to the melody and rhythm played by the *tataganing* and *sarune* (as each song in this repertoire *does* carry a melody, played on the tuned drums and double reed, although this was often missed by Europeans who coded the *gondang* as "monotonous"). To be clear, *ende*, *gondang*, and the related tradition of *tonggo-tonggo* (incantations) clearly share formal and melodic structures; the melodies of early popular music pieces followed *gondang* contours, and the gong cycle that underpins *gondang* can easily animate other genres. Moreover, it is impossible to reanimate the precolonial *ende* from the archival record, as a voice is not as durable as a gong or a drum. But it is likely that at the advent of the missionary project, voice and instrument were not paired within the formal ritual realm. *Gondang* and *ende* may have been made of the same musical stuff and might have been played or sung by the same person, but they were likely distinct musical traditions.

This difference explains why in the hymn publications of the HKBP, there are two distinct books and lists: *Buku Ende*, providing a hymn's stanzas, and *Buku Logu*, indicating the tunes and their realization in four-part harmony. The *Buku Ende* serves its purpose whether or not the melodies are notated; the *Buku Logu* usually has no words (though it does provide a title), but plenty of notation. The logic of this distinction is carried through in all sorts of places. For instance, Nahum Situmorang's popular song "Molo Margitar Ahu Ito" (When I play the guitar) uses the general verb *mangendei*: "*Molo mangendei ahu ito/ mambege nan hata nai*" (When I sing, sister, hear my words). However, when the singer suggests that the two lovers sing together in harmony, the verb changes: "*Molo hubaen marlogu sada* (the first logu)/*ihuton ahu marlogu dua* (the second logu)" (When I sing the low part / follow me and sing the high part). Although the singing is obviously done with the voice, the effect is no longer about the words but about the arrangement of two voices together. As a result, this music would not be described as an *ende* but rather as a *logu*.[71]

As the twentieth century progressed, another musical genre developed using this new conception of music: Opera Batak, a musical theater troupe that moved from village to village, led by composer Tilhang Oberlin Gultom (1896–1973). Gultom used the *ende* tradition of narrative song in his own compositions, pairing it with some of the instruments from the ritual genres.[72] Because Gultom began his composing in the 1920s, it is difficult to use his work as an exemplar of musical activity before the mission, although his music maintains the most traditional elements of any popular music played today. What is clear, however, is that as his compositional practice progressed, he gradually added more instruments to the arrangement, including instruments that did not normally play together, such as the lute paired with the bamboo flute. In the first track of a Folkways Records recording from 1976 (FE 4357), Gultom introduces his group with each of its eight members playing his instrument in turn—a surprising choice if they are merely supporting *ende* but a logical one if Gultom is laying out an arrangement for his new *logu* (or in Indonesian, *lagu*). Rita-ony Hutajulu remarks that over the fifty years of his career, the range of Gultom's melodies moved from the constrained five-tone range of precolonial Batak music in the beginning, to a diatonic range in the 1960s and '70s.[73] The Folkways recording also features flutes playing in parallel thirds and other harmonic incursions.

The influence of the music introduced by the RMG, then, is clear, even well outside of its religious sphere. I believe that a direct line can be drawn between the musical preferences of the nineteenth-century German church—the composite effect of choral song supported harmonically by an accompanying instrument or set of instruments—and the wide variety of Toba musical expressions that have been created since. Almost all popular genres with roots in the twentieth century take this configuration as natural—the Toba Batak recordings of Hawaiian music from the 1920s, the popular trios sung with guitar in the palm liquor stand, the songwriters of the 1960s who wrote out instrumental parts in cha-cha-cha or country-western rhythms, and the industry of pop music, with its studio sound and electronic keyboard work imitated throughout Indonesia. The exceptions are the lamentation tradition of *ende andung*—ever a singular, vocal-based tradition—and, of course, the sound of a congregation singing the *Buku Ende*, with one voice.

CONCLUSION

Toba Batak leaders assumed control over the HKBP in 1940 and approved a new confession in 1951, integrating elements of Lutheran and Reformed doctrine, an expression of theological autonomy that might have surprised those in Barmen. But the early decades of the twentieth century were not without struggles for self-governance. In 1909, fueled by nationalist ideas, a Toba Batak man who had trained at the RMG seminary, Sutan Panggabean, demanded autonomy from the missionaries and left the church with parishioners to found his own denomination, Hoeria Kristen Indonesia. After the internment of the German missionaries in 1940, the RMG *ephorus* (a title for bishop, derived from the Greek) was replaced with the Dutch *voorzitter*, and the question of whether German chorales should be removed from the hymnal was broached.[74] (They weren't, and the elected leader of the HKBP church is still called the ephorus.) However, it wasn't until 1968 that the strictures against the use of the *gondang* ensemble were lifted by the Batak-led HKBP, when their Order of Discipline allowed for the limited use of the ensemble in pre-funeral ceremonies.

In recent years, there has been a groundswell of popular support for "Ompu Nommensen" (Grandfather Nommensen) and the RMG mission. In 2004, nationally recognized Toba recording artists Viky Sianipar and Tongam Sirait released a single titled "Nommensen" that extolled the leader as *si boan dame* (peace bringer) to an alt-rock beat: its popularity has not waned. More recently, in 2015, ethnomusicologist Ritaony Hutajulu produced a stage performance called *The Story of Buku Ende*; although it ran only in Jakarta, it was fully sold out and inspired the then ephorus of the HKBP, Willem Simarmata, to write his thoughts about the Batak hymnbook in a newspaper article:

> The Buku Ende for Batak churches is like the Book of Psalms for Israel[ites] an element that is not divisible from religious life. For Israel[ites] the Psalms are like a river that flows, bring new life to living creatures. . . . The experience of the Psalmist becomes a part of the experiences of those who read the Bible. In this way, singing a psalm and understanding the context of its age can help us understand the meaning behind these songs. This is the marvel of singing a psalm: it can transfer the experiences of the faithful.[75]

At first, I found it remarkable that Simarmata said nothing about choirs, hymns, Luther, Nommensen, or the RMG. But in fact, he was exactly right to equate the old Toba Batak *ende* with the Hebrew psalms; in both genres, expression lives in the words, and singing is above all a way of experiencing their meaning. In fact, *The Story of Buku Ende* was replete with hymns of European origin and actually featured an operatic tenor singing "Ein feste Burg" in very good German. But the choristers were all Toba, as were the actors who played the missionaries. In Simarmata's formation, then, the work of the missionaries who brought Christianity to the Bataklands is accepted, to be sure. The true communion in this excerpt, though, is between the faithful of Israel and the faithful of Sumatra, connected to each other through human experience and divine revelation. Simarmata had the theological training to compose these thoughts and the authority to speak for the church he led, and the Toba audience watching the play had the requisite piety to recognize the intent of the songs and to integrate them deeply into their own, local lives. The European missionaries, then, were but the agents of the transfer—but they left as a legacy a corpus of song that could continue to work in their absence.

NOTES

1. Mauly Purba, "From Conflict to Reconciliation: The Case of the 'Gondang Sabangunan' in the Order of Discipline in the Toba Batak Protestant Church," *Journal of Southeast Asian Studies* 36, no. 2 (2004): 207–33, at 220.

2. Mauly Purba, "'Adat ni Gondang': Rules and Structure of the 'Gondang' Performance in Pre-Christian Toba Batak 'Adat' Practice," *Asian Music* 34, no. 1 (2002/03): 67–109.

3. Yoshiko Okazaki, "Music, Identity, and Religious Change among the Toba Batak People of North Sumatra" (PhD diss., University of California, Los Angeles, 1994); Purba, "From Conflict to Reconciliation."

4. Rita Smith Kipp, *The Early Years of a Dutch Colonial Mission: The Karo Field* (Ann Arbor: University of Michigan Press, 1990), 164.

5. Johannes Warneck, *Der Religion der Batak: Ein Paradigma für die animistischen Religionen des Indischen Archipels* (Gottingen: Vandenhoeck & Ruprecht, 1909), 47–48.

6. Julia Byl, "Harmonic Egalitarianism in Toba Liquor Stands and Studios," in *Sounding Out the State of Indonesian Music*, ed. Andrew McGraw and Christopher J. Miller, 19–39 (Ithaca, NY: Cornell University Press, 2022).

7. Julia Byl, "Music, Convert and Subject in the North Sumatran Mission Field," in *The Oxford Handbook of Music and World Christianities*, ed. Jonathan Dueck and Suzel Reily, 33–54 (New York: Oxford University Press, 2006). See this article for a discussion of missionary complicity in colonial projects, including the burning of villages during the Batak War of 1878.

8. Lothar Schreiner, "Nommensen in His Context: Aspects of a New Approach," in *Cultures and Societies of North Sumatra*, ed. Rainer Carle, 179–87 (Berlin: Deitrich Reimer Verlag, 1987), at 179.

9. Paul Pedersen, *Batak Blood and Protestant Soul: The Development of National Batak Churches in North Sumatra* (Grand Rapids, MI: William B. Eerdmans, 1970), 71.

10. Jubelando O. Tambunan, "Berteologi Melalui Nyanyian: Kajian Peran Buku Ende Membangun Spiritual Jemaat Geraja," *Clef: Jurnal Musik dan Pendidikan Musik* 2, no. 1 (2021): 11–18, at 15.

11. Huria Kristen Batak Protestan, *Buku Ende HKBP*.

12. Sandra Niessen, *Rangsa ni Tonun: A Film about the Sacred Batak Weaving Tradition, behind the Scenes* (Osterbeek and Jakarta: Bergoord, 2013).

13. Leiden University Special Collections: Or.3396: Collective volume with texts in Batak: Stories and other pieces copied in 1872 for Nommensen by Guru Sinangga from Sait ni Huta in Silindung; and other texts. Van der Tuuk's remarkable breadth is shown by his erudition in Batak manuscripts at the beginning of his life and work on Balinese manuscripts at its end, for which he assembled a tri-lingual dictionary (Kawi, Balinese, and Dutch). He is also the author of the definitive Toba Batak dictionary and two-volume grammar, published in 1861 and 1864/7, respectively.

14. Petrus Voorhoeve, *Codices Batacici* (Leiden: Universitaire Pers Leiden, 1977), 198.

15. Niessen, *Rangsa ni Tonun*, 8.

16. Groeneboer, *Een Vorst onder de Taalgeleerden*: Herman Neubronner van der Tuuk, Taalafgevaardigde voor Indië van het Nederlandsch Bijbelgenootschap 1847–1873 (Leiden: KITLV Uitgeverij, 2002), 2.

17. Jan Sihar Aritonang, "The Encounter of the Batak People with Rheinische Missions-Gesellschaft in the Field of Education" (PhD diss., University of Utrecht, 2000), 182n44.

18. Niessen, *Rangsa ni Tonun*.

19. Uli Kozok, "On Writing the Not-to-Be-Read: Literature and Literacy in a Precolonial 'Tribal' Society," *Bijdragen tot de Taal- Land- en Volkenkunde* 156, no. 1 (2000): 33–55.

20. Voorhoeve, *Codices Batacici*, 198.

21. Archive and Museum Foundation of the UEM, RMG 1.340, Estate Nommensen, Ingwer Ludwig, Folder 9.

22. Philip O. L. Tobing, *The Structure of the Toba-Batak Belief in the High God* (Amsterdam: Jacob van Campen, 1956), 81; Arthur Simon, "Gondang, Gods and Ancestors: Religious Implications of Batak Ceremonial Music," *Yearbook for Traditional Music* 25 (1993): 81–88, at 81.

23. C. M. Pleyte, "Singa Mangaradja de Heilige Koning der Bataks," in *Bijdragen tot de taal-, land- en volkenkunde* (January 1903): 34.

24. Robert W. Hefner, "Of Faith and Commitment: Christian Conversion in Muslim Java," in *Conversion to Christianity: Historical and Anthropological Perspectives on a Great Transformation*, edited by Robert W. Hefner, 99–125 (Berkeley: University of California Press, 1993), at 99.

25. Hefner, "Of Faith and Commitment," 104.

26. David Harnishand Anne Rasmussen, eds., *Divine Inspirations: Music and Islam in Indonesia* (New York: Oxford University Press, 2012), 23.

27. Purba, "'Adat ni Gondang,'" 209.

28. W. Robert Hodges, "'*Ganti Andung Gabe Ende*': The Changing Voice of Grief in the Pre-funeral Wakes of Toba Batak" (PhD diss. University of California, Santa Barbara, 2009), 150.

29. Aritonang, "The Encounter of the Batak People," 180.

30. Niessen, *Rangsa ni Tonun*, 7.

31. Pedersen, *Batak Blood and Protestant Soul*, 60.

32. Pedersen, *Batak Blood and Protestant Soul*, 52.

33. Purba, "'Adat ni Gondang,'" 73.

34. Purba, "From Conflict to Reconciliation," 217.

35. Georg Zimmer, "Erwünschte Nachricht aus Borneo," *Berichte der Rheinischen Missionsgesellschaft* 9 (1866): 275–277.

36. Zimmer, "Erwünschte Nachricht aus Borneo.", 276.

37. The article was published in 1941, after the German mission had been forcefully evicted by the Dutch in May 1940, and so had the sense of a summing up of a mission whose work was finished. J. Quentmeier, "Das Gesangbuch der Batakkirche," *Berichte der Rheinischen Missionsgesellschaft* 98 (1941): 52–56, at 52.

38. Quentmeier, "Das Gesangbuch der Batakkirche," 52.

39. Quentmeier, "Das Gesangbuch der Batakkirche," 53.

40. Published in Purba, "From Conflict to Reconciliation," 216.

41. Quentmeier, "Das Gesangbuch der Batakkirche," 54.

42. In the *Buku Ende*, "Innsbruck ich muss dich lassen" is an Easter hymn, "Hamu Saluhut Halak."

43. Quentmeier, "Das Gesangbuch der Batakkirche," 54.

44. Sommer, "Johann Matthäus Meyfart," 150.

45. Andrew Kloes, *The German Awakening: Protestant Renewal after the Enlightenment* (New York: Oxford University Press, 2019).

46. Jonathan Strom, *German Pietism and the Problem of Conversion* (University Park: University of Pennsylvania Press, 2017), 3.

47. Alfred Dürr, *The Cantatas of J. S. Bach* (New York: Oxford University Press, 2005), 692.

48. Jubelando Tambunan, "Berteologi Melalui Nyanyian: Kajian Peran Buku Ende Membangun Spiritual Jemaat Geraja," *Clef: Jurnal Musik dan Pendidikan Musik* 2, no. 1 (2021): 11–18, at 15.

49. Sita Thama van Bemmelen, "Good Customs, Bad Customs in North Sumatra," (PhD diss., Vrije Universiteit Amsterdam, 2012), 343.

50. Julia Byl, *Antiphonal Histories: Resonant Pasts in the Toba Batak Musical Present* (Middletown, CT: Wesleyan University Press, 2014), 198.

51. David Bebbington, *Victorian Religious Revivals: Culture and Piety in Local and Global Contexts* (New York: Oxford University Press, 2012).

52. Edith Blumhofer, "Fanny Crosby and Protestant Hymnody," in *Music in American Religious Experience*, ed. Philip V. Bohlman, Edith L. Blumhofer, and Maria M. Chow (New York: Oxford University Press, 2006), 215–32, at 236.

53. Anna Maira Busse Berger, *The Search for Medieval Music in Africa and Germany, 1891–1961: Scholars, Singers, Missionaries* (Chicago: University of Chicago Press, 2020), 157.

54. Quentmeier, "Das Gesangbuch der Batakkirche," 56.

55. Aritonang, "The Encounter of the Batak People," 370n88.

56. Zimmer, "Erwünschte Nachricht aus Borneo," 276.

57. Aritonang, "The Encounter of the Batak People," 269–71, 280.

58. Purba, "From Conflict to Reconciliation," 214.

59. Aritonang "The Encounter of the Batak People," 254n66.

60. Aritonang "The Encounter of the Batak People," 291.

61. Aritonang "The Encounter of the Batak People," 291n103.

62. Quentmeier, "Das Gesangbuch der Batakkirche," 56.

63. Busse Berger, *The Search for Medieval Music*, 132.

64. Philip V. Bohlman, "Prologue: Again, Herder," in *Song Loves the Masses: Herder on Music and Nationalism*, by Johann Gottfried Herder, trans. and ed. by Philip V. Bohlman (Berkeley: University of California Press, 2017), 1–18, at 13.

65. Quentmeier, "Das Gesangbuch der Batakkirche," 57.

66. Johannes Warneck states, about the *ende gasgas*, that the lyrics were a bit naughty as would be expected: "Die nicht gerade sauber sind." See Voorhoeve, *Codices Batacici*, 135.

67. Like the early hymnals printed in Laguboti, the readers were supposed to supply the hymn tune.

68. Mission Press di Si Antar, *Umpama Angka na Masa ni Habatahon* (Pematang Siantar: Rongkoman Rhein, 1903), 48.

69. Hodges, "'Ganti Andung Gabe Ende,'" 142.

70. Clara Brakel-Papenhuijzen, *Dairi Stories and Pakpak Storytelling: A Storytelling Tradition from the North Sumatran Rainforest* (Leiden: Brill, 2014).

71. Incidentally, the use of the word *logu*, clearly related to the Malay and Indonesian *lagu* but missing from precolonial Toba Batak writings, shows the growing proximity with the coastal areas and with the burgeoning discourse as the German mission developed.

72. Indeed, the work of professional itinerant musicians may be one exception for the *ende/* instrument division; many performers would travel with instrumentalists, particularly the *hasapi* or lute. Yet even in these genres, the focus is still on the single voice of the singer and the text that it interpreted.

73. Ritaony Hutajulu, "Analisis Struktural Musik Vokal pada Opera Batak: Dengan Pusat Perhatian pada Karya Tilhang Gultom" (bachelor's thesis: Universitas Sumatera Utara, Medan, Indonesia, 1988).

74. Aritonang, "The Encounter of the Batak People," 395.

75. Hotben Lingga, "Pentas 'The Story of Buku Ende: Hymns from the Bataklands' Sukses di Gelar di JCC, Jakarta," *GramediaPost*, September 7, 2015, www.gramediapost.com/2015/09/pentas-the-story-of-buku-ende-hymns-from-the-batakland-sukses-digelar-di-jcc-jakarta/.

7

___

A Missional Legacy

Musik Inkulturasi *and Printing Localized Catholic Hymnals in Indonesia*

Emilie Rook

Shortly after Easter, in April, 2018, I walked through a dusty cathedral parking lot in the city of Ende on the island of Flores (figure 7-1). Everywhere throughout this complex and the adjacent religious living quarters, the historic presence of the Societas Verbi Divini (SVD, Society of the divine word) missionaries met my eyes. I walked through the veranda where in the 1930s missionary priests had discussed philosophy with Sukarno, the then exiled leader of the nationalist movement against Dutch colonialism and future president of the republic. In the entry hallway, I passed a photo wall where largely European framed faces looked out at a now majority Indonesian-born religious community. Heading down the hill, I spotted a bumper sticker of the order's German founder on a bright yellow vespa in front of the oldest printing press in Indonesia.

The SVD founded Percetakan Arnoldus, which once printed the paraphernalia of a burgeoning independent Indonesian nation and still prints the material of church and state. This includes a handful of locally produced hymnals that musically support parishes on this majority-Catholic island. My walking companion, an Indonesian-born SVD brother, regaled me with stories of the order's history there, stories of the missionaries who built the buildings now slightly crumbling around us and the musicians who penned much of the music now frequently sung throughout the island. This was now his story, too, a story of missionary legacies reverberating through the religious lives and music of more than eight million Catholics throughout the Indonesian archipelago.

Indonesian Catholics exist in a power-filled web of identity politics, being simultaneously members of the Roman Catholic Church, the Indonesian nation-state, and local ethnic groups. This reality, coupled with a long and complicated

FIGURE 7-1. Kathedral Kristus Raja (Cathedral of Christ the King) in Ende, Flores. Photo by Emilie Rook.

missionary history, sounds through the music and hymnals produced by various centers throughout the country. Accordingly, this essay examines the music of Indonesian Catholics—in particular the genre of *musik inkulturasi* and the production of local Catholic hymn books—as musical reverberations of decades of missionary activity in what is now the Republic of Indonesia. By ethnographically examining the thought and processes behind this music material, this essay will highlight how local faith communities are using *musik inkulturasi* and localized hymnals in agentive and power-claiming ways. Ultimately, in this essay, I ask, How can emic understandings of *musik inkulturasi* and the printing of localized hymnals help us to remap the agency and power of contemporary Indonesian Catholic communities, beyond a history of missionary influence?

After a brief introduction to inculturation and *musik inkulturasi*, I will engage three ethnographic vignettes of liturgical music specialists in the work of re-understanding their definitions of *musik inkulturasi*, simultaneously implicating a re-understanding of the role of missionary activity therein. Following the work of Michael Herzfeld, I will then advocate for a postcolonial social poetic that sees in musical choices the agency of individual players and communities as themselves defining and musically enacting their identity as Indonesian Catholics.[1]

I then shift from theory to materiality, looking at the role of the missionary-founded printing press Percetakan Arnoldus in creating the tangible products of this missional legacy. Ultimately, I argue that ignoring these enculturated products because of associations with a missionary past would not only result in a failure to see and hear the contemporary musical practices of Indonesian Catholics but could effectively rob current communities of a music history and legacy now often considered, in the words attributed to the famous Archbishop Monsignor Albertus Soegijapranata, to be "100% Indonesian and 100% Catholic."[2]

INTRODUCING INCULTURATION/*INKULTURASI* AND *MUSIK INKULTURASI*

Inkulturasi is an Indonesian translation of the term inculturation, a particular kind of contextualization associated with the Roman Catholic Church and the ramifications of the Second Vatican Council.[3] As a highly theorized theological term, inculturation is also a localized and localizing practice, with histories, sights, and sounds both culturally contextualized and often site or country specific. Such is the case in Indonesia, where *musik inkulturasi* (inculturated music) has arguably become its own genre, which in my experience is typically associated with the people and practices of the Pusat Musik Liturgi (PML, Center for Liturgical Music) in Yogyakarta, founded in 1971 by the late German-born Jesuit priest Father Karl-Edmund Prier and the late Javanese choral conductor Pak Paul Widyawan. Here I am using the concept of genre not just as a category of work characterized by similarities but also to assert the idea of genre as a way of constituting self and other, as I believe is done through *musik inkulturasi*.[4]

According to PML-produced texts written by Romo Karl-Edmund Prier, *inkulturasi* is a process through which the gospel or word of God is "planted" into a local cultural context, often for use in the liturgy of the Mass and ultimately as a way to praise God.[5] Father, or Romo, Prier further defines *inkulturasi* in his *Kamus Musik* (Music dictionary), as follows: "The prefix, 'in-,' expresses an 'inward' process, for example to be included/to be planted in culture. That means, a value or information or message wants to be expressed in the form of a particular culture, wants to be transformed / to be improved through certain forms/expressions of culture."[6] While there are broader uses of *inculturation*—to denote an agentive localization of Christian belief before and beyond the Catholic Church and the mid-twentieth century—I use this term, and even more so *inkulturasi* or *musik inkulturasi*, to reference my interlocutors' language and a localized usage. Similarly, while it has import as a theoretical hermeneutic and Catholic theological concept, I employ it in this work chiefly because it was the term most consistently used by my interlocutors. Additionally, throughout my research, I noticed that *inkulturasi* was frequently employed to identify not just a process but also a product—specifically

PML-produced and/or PML-influenced *musik inkulturasi*—which transcends its theoretical implications in a very concrete and site/country-specific manner.[7]

At the same time, it is important to point out that while the implementation of inculturation did important work in not just localizing but also translating Catholic practice, the idea of inculturation was largely promulgated in the West for non-Western communities. Inherent in inculturation was a prescriptive othering of mission areas. Inculturation was not for the West, except in cases of Indigenous populations in the United States and Europe. As Néstor Medina points out in his work *Christianity, Empire and the Spirit: (Re)Configuring Faith and the Cultural*, since the beginning of the twentieth century and in particular during the Second Vatican Council, the Roman Catholic Church "was confronted with its own past and complicity with Western European colonial projects and the colonizing nature of missionary enterprise, [while at the same time realizing] that most Catholic Christians live(d) in the southern hemisphere, outside the centres of power in Western Europe and Euro North America."[8] Within this understanding, inculturation became an avenue through which a postcolonial Roman Catholic Church could reimagine or replant itself, despite what Medina articulates as the "colonial past and accompanying Eurocentrism" of the term itself.[9] In turn, I argue that a postcolonial reckoning with inculturation and its products is best comprehended emically, through the understandings of local practitioners. It is there that we begin, with an ethnographic exploration of how Indonesian Catholic musicians themselves define *musik inkulturasi*.[10]

MAPPING KEY INTERLOCUTORS IN THE CREATION OF *MUSIK INKULTURASI*

In order to examine the implications of inculturation among my interlocutors, I will present three ethnographic vignettes from key liturgical musical specialists. These conversations occurred in 2018 during my ten months of fieldwork with Indonesian Catholic communities on the islands of Flores, Java, and North Sumatra.[11] I will begin on the supposed margins in what has historically been the economically and politically disenfranchised island of Flores, which is also the island with the largest Catholic population in Indonesia. I will then travel to the Center for Liturgical Music in Yogyakarta, Indonesia, known for producing much of the *musik inkulturasi* now sung throughout the country. Finally, I will conclude in the political and economic center of Indonesia's capital of Jakarta, home to the Indonesian Bishop's Council (Konferensi Waligereja Indonesia, or KWI). Each vignette will begin with a brief contextualization of the island or city and the person's role in music and the Catholic Church there. Then I will present their definition of inculturation and give an example of how this "plays out" in the music they create. In this way, each interlocutor's experience of inculturation will be shown to be in dialogue with the music they produce while also resonating with issues of history, politics, and economics within their respective geographic locales.

Larantuka, Flores—Pak Yosef

Larantuka is a small coastal town on the eastern tip of the majority Catholic island of Flores, known for an enduring legacy of Portuguese Dominican missionization and its localized Good Friday candlelit processions to their patroness, Tuan Ma.[12] At the same time, Larantuka is also a linguistic and cultural outlier on an island that boasts great ethnic and biological diversity yet exists within the economic disenfranchisement of what is nationally considered *daerah terpencil* or a "remote area." I arrived there shortly before Easter in 2018 to participate in the renowned Larantukan Holy Week processions and to hear what Catholic liturgical music sounded like on their part of the island. Through contacts at the local cathedral, I was connected to Pak Yosef, a famed local liturgical music connoisseur, organist, choir director, and high school music teacher. He proudly identifies as a self-trained musician, conducts local church music workshops, and serves on the diocesan liturgical committee. When it came to inculturation, Pak Yosef's understanding invoked a historical perspective. After outlining the role of liturgical music before Vatican II, he explained:

> Then at that time [of the Second Vatican Council] the chance was given or space was opened for inculturated music, music that is born, is planted/grows, and develops in certain ethnic areas, that is what is called inculturation. And the church actually gives space for that to develop. We can include instruments for inculturated music, and here I usually use them, I usually use these instruments when there are large Mass celebrations. For that I always involve the drum, there is guitar, ukulele, there's flute, there's viola/violin, and that is what I always include.[13]

Pak Yosef went on to explain that certain traditional musical instruments—like locally produced bamboo flutes (often with local, non-tempered tunings)—are now becoming a rarity. While this kind of flute or traditional instrument is occasionally used for extra-special ecclesial celebrations, much more common renderings of *musik inkulturasi* travel to Flores through the PML's *Madah Bakti* hymnal and its accompanying four-part choral books, often disseminated to local choirs through photocopies.

Despite a decline in the production and teaching of traditional music in Larantuka, Pak Yosef is confidently sharing and producing local, inculturated music on behalf of himself and his community. He insists that even though he and his musical colleagues are self-trained, they as Larantukans are best fit to create "music that is born, is planted/grows, and develops in [their] ethnic areas."[14] At the same time, such self-sufficiency has its limits. Pak Yosef and others have inferred that most *musik inkulturasi* in Indonesia is sponsored and disseminated by Java-based groups, like the PML. Despite a desire to have PML training and workshops, the

Diocese of Larantuka does not have the funds for such endeavors. Inculturated music in Flores, according to Pak Yosef's definition, is thus both agentive and constricted. Here I understand *agentive* and, relatedly, *agency* as a quest for power, and I am using it to point to a person's or community's initiative through which they claim to shape how things are or at least should be. Caught between economic limitations and independent agency, the idea of inculturation has encouraged an important albeit imperfect process for the Catholic community in Larantuka.

Yogyakarta, Java—Pak Wahyudi

From Flores, we shift focus to the central Java city of Yogyakarta. Considered by some as the Rome of Indonesia, Yogyakarta boasts a high concentration of the island's Catholics.[15] Within this milieu, the Pusat Musik Liturgi has become a locus for the training of church musicians and the production of inculturated music.[16] Since the late 1970s, the PML has run *musik inkulturasi* workshops (known as *Lokakarya*) throughout the country and yearly hosts a training session for choral conductors and organists from "Sumatra to Papua," as one 2017 participant put it.[17] The PML's reach also extends through the publishing of media, much of which is dedicated to their particular understanding of *musik inkulturasi*, which aims to "propagate, renew and compose liturgical songs, especially according to the scales and rhythms of the local music traditions."[18]

Since 2017, I have gotten to know the PML's methods, staff, and products firsthand, including Pak Johannes Wahyudi. Catholic liturgical theologian by training and accomplished amateur traditional musician, Pak Wahyudi has a highly contextualized understanding of inculturated music. Ever since joining the PML team in the late 1990s (January 1997), he has developed a renowned ability to learn and then teach traditional instruments throughout Indonesia. To Pak Wahyudi, inculturation is

> all about identity. As a Javanese person, I pray in a Javanese way, to believe in Christ and understand with a Javanese mindset. Then to give expression to faith, with prayer and singing which I feel fit with my culture. So according to me, Javanese inculturated music, as an example within this one ethnicity, it helps me get closer . . . with God, yes, an expression of faith. . . . Yes, the process for me is that people must know their own culture, that's a process. Yes, if people don't know the culture, they cannot inculturate.[19]

This idea of inculturation requiring an understanding of one's own cultural identity is at the core of the PML's mission and process, in which the study of traditional musics in situ and from local experts is paramount. Pak Wahyudi went on to explain that inculturation is thus a process to help the faithful pray and meet God in such a way that cultural values harmonize with the values of the gospel. Even cultural and Christian (or Catholic) values were referenced here in an Indonesianized way, with the national rhetoric of *harmoni* (harmony) connecting cultural and Catholic, espousing a sense of national identity that the PML also professes in their promotional material.

While Pak Wahyudi speaks from his own experience as a Javanese theologian and amateur musician, it is important to point out that both his academic training and his over two decades of experience at the PML have been greatly informed by Father Karl-Edmund Prier, who was Pak Wahyudi's undergraduate thesis (*skripsi*) advisor before becoming Pak Wahyudi's boss and mentor at the PML. Romo Prier and the PML have had a great, I would even argue formative, role in establishing the sound and process of *musik inkulturasi* in Indonesia. However, not everyone in the Catholic liturgical music scene in Indonesia agrees with "inculturation as we do it every day here," a phrase Father Prier used in email correspondence to me to describe the work being done at the PML.[20]

Jakarta, Java—Romo Tanto

One such person is the late Father Antonius Soetanto, who at the time of my research worked as a parish priest, organ teacher, choir conductor, and composer in the economic and political capital of Jakarta. Romo Tanto, as he is locally called, was known for his role in creating the hymnbook *Puji Syukur*, produced under the auspices of the KWI.[21] For Romo Tanto, inculturation could not be explained without reference to Rome: "Inculturation—if it is according to original understandings, from Rome itself it was said that the purpose of inculturation was so that local people could understand the same theology. The same theology, in a more appropriate way. . . . So, [inculturation is] that which is of here, even though it often does not fit with the liturgical spirit."[22]

Romo Tanto went on to explain that many inculturated songs in Indonesia are predicated on what he referred to as a touristic understanding of traditional music and are more like cultural exhibitions than he thinks is liturgically or theologically appropriate.[23] Naming Romo Prier and the PML as some of those creating these unsound inculturated songs, Romo Tanto went so far as to cite colonialism and missionization as what these songs represent. Conversely, he considered the KWI's official liturgical book *Puji Syukur* "Indonesian" in process and product. Because of who created or produced it and the way the texts and tunes are theologically rendered, to Romo Tanto *Puji Syukur* has in some ways become an alternative to European missionary power in Indonesia. Interpersonal and interinstitutional tensions aside, these somewhat conflicting views of inculturation provide valuable insight into how *musik inkulturasi* is or is not living up to the postcolonial hopes of each interlocutor. An understanding of inculturation thus goes beyond the idea of simply localizing and instead implicates the agency of those who create it.

The ultimate irony is that there seem to be significant similarities in the musical environments out of which the national-level hymn books of *Madah Bakti* and

Puji Syukur were created. Both have songs rendered in Indonesian, with equal-tempered tuning and with the inclusion of at least some localized songs. Both were overseen by musicians and priests who received training in sacred music abroad. And both implicate a relationship with either missionaries or missionary influence in the musical and theological knowledge that served as the backbone for each hymnal. These observations would then suggest that the distinctions between the two books are in the meaningfully felt details, such as musical style and language, or the pre- and post-production methods of each organization.[24] Ultimately, it seems that the potential of Indonesian Catholics to feel represented and as owners over *musik inkulturasi* and related music material is relationally played out. As a result, despite somewhat similar musical roots, these feelings of representation are more connected to who created the hymnal or music, how they did so, and what it has been understood to represent as a result.

MUSIK INKULTURASI: FROM DEFINITIONS TO BROADER IMPLICATIONS

Accordingly, I argue that the process, more than the product, is key to understanding what is considered "postcolonial" inculturated music. According to Romo Tanto, *Puji Syukur*—often criticized as Javanized and Western-hymn centric—is a postcolonial Indonesian hymn book. In its capacity as a theologically sound official liturgical book, he understands it as standing from now until the end of time as a resource in line with the appropriate liturgical practice, encouraged by Rome and the KWI. At the same time, Romo Tanto considers *Puji Syukur* to be localized through national language and cipher notation but notes that it does not fall into the same traps as the *Madah Bakti* hymnal in being more touristic in its approach.[25] Romo Tanto's use of terms like *touristic* provides a playful example of Michael Herzfeld's social poetics, where the veneer of hegemony hides the strategic essentialism of social actors, here framed within an interpersonal ideological sparring match between Romo Tanto and Romo Prier, and relatedly the PML and KWI.[26]

Conversely, Pak Wahyudi, as a representative of the PML, has a definition of inculturation that centers around personal identity and knowing one's own cultural background. This context-oriented approach is reflected through the PML's *Madah Bakti*, which in its 2000 edition is purported to include roughly three hundred songs created in the style of local ethnic groups. The PML describes this process and their hymnal as trying to represent the "unity in diversity" of Indonesian Catholicism, a process that, again borrowing from national rhetoric, can also be seen to reify certain ethnic stereotypes while rendering locally produced songs in Indonesian and conforming them to twelve-tone equal-tempered tuning, playable on a keyboard or an organ.[27]

Finally, in Flores, inculturation has opened the door for greater independence and localization of liturgical music. At the same time, Pak Yosef acknowledges that money is what is preventing his diocese from having the training that would allow them to produce and disseminate *musik inkulturasi* on the level of national centers like the PML. The agency that allows local Catholic musicians throughout Flores to create and produce localized liturgical music is still understood against more monied national products, like *Madah Bakti/Puji Syukur*. As evident through these accounts, the articulation of inculturation connects issues of power, politics, money, and Euro-centrism to music production and performance that pervade every level of Catholic practice, from the provincial parish to those associated with the KWI itself.

Ultimately, the work that inculturation is being used to accomplish seems best determined through the words and works of the practitioners themselves. Examining the ways in which each of the above practitioners defines inculturation—within the constraints of their own context—presents alternative narratives to top-down, or in the case of Indonesia, Java-out, models of power and analysis. Instead, Pak Yosef's understanding and those of his colleges in Flores are held on par with those from the centers of power, particularly on Java and in places like the KWI and PML. In a similar sense, these narratives on *musik inkulturasi* are locally owned and shared, beyond the assumption or dismissal that can accompany reactions to music in missionary-influenced communities.

Accordingly, by ethnographically re-centering how we know about *musik inkulturasi*, we can come to a fuller understanding of the range of meanings and practices it represents. Returning to Michael Herzfeld's idea of cultural intimacy and social poetics, how one defines *musik inkulturasi* can provide insight into the often conflicting narratives and embarrassing essentialisms that can accompany this kind of contextualizing work, especially when a mission history is at play. As a result, *musik inkulturasi* can provide a glimpse into how formative social issues are inextricably intertwined with a person's positionality and affect both their conceptual understandings and musical-liturgical experiences. The tension of mission influence and postcolonial agency is further articulated in another concrete missional legacy central to the production of *musik inkulturasi*, namely, the machines that have printed much of this inculturated material.

Printing Presses, Local Hymnbooks, and a Missional Legacy

In his work on imagined communities, Benedict Anderson explains that one of the technological turning points in imagining nations was the advent of the printing press and the effect of affordable, mass-produced printing, which he terms "print-capitalism."[28] As a ready way to disseminate ideas, printing presses have been employed since the mid-fifteenth century for the sake of church and eventually state. In the case of the history of printing presses in Indonesia, the Roman Catholic Church served the state in a tangle of politics surrounding Indonesian independence, and no press did so more than the printing press we will focus on here: Percetakan Arnoldus on the island of Flores.[29]

Percetakan Arnoldus Press and Nusa Indah Publishing Company

The first and oldest printing press in Indonesia—the Arnoldus printing press (Percetakan Arnoldus)—was founded by Pater Petrus Noyen, SVD, in 1926 in Ende, south central Flores. With a machine imported from Germany, the press was first used to print a prayer book in Malay titled *Sende Aus*, or in Indonesian, *Utuslah* (Sent out).[30] Founded and supported by the SVD order—and thus aptly named after their founder, St. Arnold Janssen—the printing press, and Nusa Indah publishing company (Penerbit Nusa Indah) that sprung from it, "initially [printed] translated foreign books about spirituality to meet the needs of [Catholic] clergy and seminaries."[31] At the same time, the press has been used for more patriotic purposes, from printing the paraphernalia of a burgeoning nation—including Indonesia's first stamp—to turning out the highly regulated nationwide high school graduation exams. At the same time, Nusa Indah also publishes some of the oldest and most enduring Catholic hymnbooks in Indonesia, produced by and for communities (and ethnic groups) throughout Flores.

Localized Catholic Hymnals

An additional complicating factor to the narrative of *musik inkulturasi* is the handful of localized Catholic hymnals printed by Percetakan Arnoldus. Created by missionaries and/or missionary-trained musicians on the island of Flores throughout the twentieth century, songs from these hymnals—including "Dere Searni" (1947), "Syukur Kepada Bapa" (1976), "Yubliate" (1991), "Exultate" (1997)—are frequently sung in specific areas of Flores, and have become part of the institutional memory of many Catholics and Catholic Church communities throughout the island. At the same time, these locally produced hymnbooks were typically not included in the category of *musik inkulturasi* by my interlocutors but rather acknowledged as localized precursors to inculturation or simply as good-faith efforts.

One significant element connecting these arguably pre-inculturative missionary-made or missionary-influenced local hymnbooks to *musik inkulturasi* is the prevalence of "Western" musical principles, rife in these hymnals and taught to the Catholic school students throughout the country.[32] In Flores, this presence and perseverance of Western music pedagogical methods is due in large part to the roles Dutch and German SVD missionary priests played in Catholic and seminary music education. I attest to this not only through the continued prevalence of Western choral anthems I heard while traveling the length of Flores in 2018—especially, as it was Easter, a number of instances of various pieces from Handel's *Messiah*—but also by glimpsing instances of music education at the minor seminary in Mataloko, Central Flores. There, not only were the high school–aged seminarians practicing Gregorian chant tones on the stoop in front of the music classroom, but in the storage area behind the classroom space, the instruments being stored underscored an idea of music grounded in a Western paradigm. Guitars, marching band equipment, a drum kit, and a lack of any of the many local instruments suggested that at Seminari Menengah Berchmaninum the legacy of Western music education from foreign-born missionary priests was still strong and largely reflected in the two song books— *Yubilate* and *Syukur Kepada Bapa*— produced by priests there and printed by Percetakan Arnolds.[33]

TENSION WITHIN A MISSIONAL LEGACY

Given both their role in national history and the dissemination of localized Catholic hymnals, Nusa Indah and Percetakan Arnoldus stand as important sites for the production of local printed material for audiences throughout East Nusa Tenggara and beyond. In this way, Pater Noyen's initiative continues to support the changing needs of this local community nearly a century later. At the same time, the presence and production of Percetakan Arnoldus is complicated by its missional history. The press exists because of foreign missionary resources, at the behest of a foreign priest. Yet it persists in the tension of adoption and neglect. Percetakan Arnoldus is still in use for the service of church and state and yet serves as a reminder that the missionary funds that created and supported it are seemingly not sustaining the press and community as in years past. As I walked around the press and adjacent cathedral grounds in 2018, this contradiction was visible. From the peeling paint to the nostalgia surrounding the stories of how nice the compound was decades ago, the disparity between what the missionaries created and the legacy that a now largely Indonesian-born community has inherited is evident and necessary to acknowledge (figure 7-2). There are fewer foreign-born Catholic missionaries in Flores, and there are implicitly fewer foreign funds supporting contemporary needs. However, in my experience with Catholic parishes on the islands of Flores, Medan, and Java, there persists a degree of pride and ownership regarding local missionary history and its legacies in these Catholic communities. This repossession of faith and knowledge production took concrete form through the idea that these are our printing press, these are our buildings, our books, our music. Whatever hand the missionaries have or had in creating the scaffolding on which the music of Indonesian Catholics is built, these books and songs now belong to a people who consider themselves "100% Indonesian and 100% Catholic."[34]

In conclusion, this examination of *musik inkulturasi* and the people and presses that promulgate it show how formally missional practices can become powerfully understood and locally owned. Moving beyond complicated missionary histories, moving beyond interpersonal and interinstitutional conflicts and economic inequalities, Indonesian Catholics have become agents of their own religious identity, defining for themselves how that should look and sound. Ultimately,

FIGURE 7-2. Percetakan Arnoldus office entrance in Ende, Flores. Photo by Emilie Rook.

this ethnographic examination of *musik inkulturasi* and localized Catholic hymnals highlights the power of local communities in post-missional and supposedly peripheral places, making these places the centers that they are in terms of the creation, production, and consumption of inculturated musical products, despite and often because of the missional legacy they claim.

NOTES

1. Michael Herzfeld, *Cultural Intimacy: Social Poetics and the Nation-State*, 2nd ed. (New York: Routledge, 2005), 32.

2. This popular phrase of Archbishop Monsignor Albertus Soegijapranata is rooted in his 1954 speech at the All-Indonesia Catholic Congress where he argues the compatibility of Catholicism and patriotism.

3. While contextualization, in Indonesian *kontekstualisasi*, has been used in conjunction with inculturation among Christians (meaning for this instance both Protestants and Catholics) in Indonesia, I consider these terms as stemming from different theological traditions and ecclesiastical histories. See Marzana Poplawska, "Christian Music and Inculturation in Indonesian Music" (PhD diss., Wesleyan University, 2008), 17. In light of the fundamental differences in the denominational or sectarian distinction of each term—with inculturation generally referring to a Catholic context and contextualization to Protestant denominations, both in theological scholarship and specifically among my interlocutors in Indonesia—and the ways in which *inkulturasi* has become localized in an Indonesian Catholic context, I will use them as distinct terms. For more on contextualization, see Poplawska, "Christian Music," 22–24; and for a brief history of inculturation, see 18–22.

While many attribute inculturation to the actual documents of the Second Vatican council, and while there were theologians calling for a greater localization of liturgical and theological practices using this term during the early 1960s when the council was meeting (1962–65), it was not until the late 1970s that it first appeared in Vatican documents. During the meeting of Vatican II, however, cultural contextualization of liturgical and theological practices was tellingly referred to as *aggiornamento* or updating, underlining ideas of both relevance and process, while the idea of inculturation was still undergoing theological refinement. For more on the use of the term *aggiornamento* in the documents of the Second Vatican Council, see Dennis Doyle, "The Concept of Inculturation in Roman Catholicism: A Theological Consideration," in *U.S. Catholic Historian* 30, no. 1 (Winter 2012), 1–13. *Aggiornamento* in term, history, and context is dealt with on page 3 of Doyle's text. In a conversation about inculturation and the Second Vatican Council with Pastor Eman Sembiring, head of the liturgical committee for the Archdiocese of Medan, Pastor Eman explained, "A, *aggiornamento*, yes, [in] their language there [in Italy], but if it's in Indonesian, we try to translate [it to] 'adaptation.'" Personal communication with Pastor Emmanuel Sembiring, O. F. M. Cap., October 8, 2018, transcribed by Vini Alfarina. Unless otherwise noted, all translations from Indonesian to English for this article are done by E. Rook.

4. For more, see Fabian Holt, *Genre in Popular Music* (Chicago: University of Chicago Press, 2007), especially page 3; and Andrew Weintraub, "The Sound and Spectacle of Dangdut Koplo, Genre and Counter-Genre in East Java, Indonesia," *Asian Music* 44, no. 2 (Summer/Fall 2013): 160–94, especially 134.

5. Karl-Edmund Prier, "*Inkulturasi*," in *Kamus Musik* [Music dictionary] (Yogyakarta: *Pusat Musik Liturgi* [PML K-77], 2009), 71.

6. Prier, "*Inkulturasi*" in *Kamus Musik* [Music Dictionary], 71.

7. Another way to say this is that what inculturation looks/sounds like in one place may not be what it looks/sounds like, or how it is done, in another locale.

8. For more on both the problems with and promise of inculturation and the Roman Catholic Church, see Nestor Medina, *Christianity, Empire and the Spirit: (Re)Configuring Faith and the Cultural,*

Theology and Mission in World Christianity, vol. 11 (Leiden: Brill, 2018), 254. Especially pertinent to this article is chapter 7, "Inculturation, the Catholic Church and the Cultures of the World," 253–310.

9. Medina, *Christianity, Empire and the Spirit*, 255.

10. A similar approach was taken by ethnomusicologist Mazanna Poplawska in her book *Performing Faith: Christian Music, Identity and Inculturation in Indonesia*, where she details the different definitions of inculturation from other key clergy members on Flores and Java for the sake of explicating the term. In this essay, the practice of examining definitions is at the service of understanding the theoretical work this term or genre is being used for. See "Inculturation in the eyes of Indonesians," in Marzanna Poplawska, *Performing Faith: Christian Music, Identity and Inculturation in Indonesia* (New York: Routledge, 2020), 11–16.

11. In addition to concerns of safety and access, the choice of these specific locations highlights regions with either significant Catholic populations or a central role in the politics of both Church and state.

12. Pilgrims travel to Larantuka for its Good Friday processions—by foot and by sea/boat—following statues that arrived on the island in the sixteenth century, coinciding with the arrival of Portuguese Dominican missionaries.

13. Personal communication with Pak Yosef Uran, March 27, 2018.

14. Personal communication with Pak Yosef Uran, March 27, 2018.

15. Rome of Indonesia or "Roma di Indonesia" is from Karl-Edmund Prier, SJ, *Perjalanan Musik Gereja Katolik Indonesia Tahun 1957–2007* [The journey of Indonesian (Catholic) church music from years 1957–2007] (Yogyakarta: *Pusat Musik Liturgi*, PML A-79), 18, where Prier says, as an explanation for why the PML was begun in Yogyakarta and not Jakarta or Surakarta, "The city of Yogyakarta as a cultural city and the 'Rome of Indonesia' felt the best for it." Catholics on Java in Yogyakarta constitute 5–10 percent of Catholics in Java, which is significant considering that 19 percent of Indonesian Catholics live in Java. For more, see Poplawska, *Performing Faith*, 83 and "Christian Music and Inculturation in Indonesian Music."

16. The PML is loosely associated with the Jesuit Catholic University Sanata Dharma and housed in the University's building for catechetical training in Yogyakarta.

17. "From Sumatra to Papua" was a phrase used by one of the participants in the 2017 closing Mass and certificate presentation for PML penataran (training session) for organists and choir conductors on July 8, 2017, at the PML in Yogyakarta, Indonesia.

18. See *Pusat Musik Liturgi* website, "English Version," *Pusat Musik Liturg*, http://pml-yk.org /english-version. Accessed December 3, 2022.

19. Personal communication with Pak Yohannes Wahyudi, February 27, 2018.

20. Email correspondence with Father Karl-Edmund Prier on October 23, 2015.

21. In addition to composing numerous songs for *Puji Syukur*, Romo Tanto was highly active with the Indonesian Christian music publishing company YAMUGER and ran his own choir and organist training programs.

22. From personal communication with Romo Antonius Soetanto, SJ., August 8, 2018.

23. In Indonesian, *"kebanyakan pameran kultur, untuk turis"* ("the majority [of inculturated songs] are like cultural exhibits, for tourists"). Personal conversation with Romo Antonius Soetanto, SJ, August 8, 2018. Jakarta, Indonesia.

24. For more, see a discussion on "A Linguistic Comparison—Whose Indonesian?," in Emilie Rook, "Complex Centers and Powerful Peripheries: Catholicism, Music, and Identity Politics in Indonesia" (PhD diss., University of Pittsburgh, 2020), 153–59.

25. Another way of suggesting discontent with the supposed touristic spirit of *Madah Bakti* is expressed by former archbishop of Medan Mgr. Ancietus B. Sinaga in his article "*Madah Bakt,i*: An Experiment in the Inculturation of Liturgical Music," *East Asian Pastoral Review* 30, no. 2 (1993), 120–44, in which he refers to *Madah Bakti* as containing substandard melodies and local popular tunes instead of songs that hold a "'classical quality'" (144).

26. "The agents of powerful state entities and the humblest of local social actors engage in the strategy of essentialism to an equal degree, if not always with the same visibility or impact. Social poetics can be precisely defined as the analysis of essentialism in everyday life. The essentializing strategies of state legislators and ordinary citizens alike depend on a semiotic illusion: by making sure that all the outward signs of identity are as consistent as possible, they literally create, or constitute, homogeneity" (Herzfeld, *Cultural Intimacy*, 32).

27. Poplawska refers to *Madah Bakti* as containing "songs that are typical for Indonesia, being characteristic of different ethnic groups," resulting in a Mass that is considered to represent *bhinneka tunggal ika* (unity in diversity) (Poplawska, *Performing Faith*, 92–94; see also Poplawska, "Christian Music." Furthermore, *Bhinneka Tunggal Ika* itself is a phrase in Old Javanese that has become the country's national motto, mentioned in the Indonesian constitution and inscribed on its national symbol. Thus, using *musik inkulturasi* and *Madah Bakti* to create Mass music that could be considered to represent this unity in diversity is producing a musico-liturgical product that harmonizes with and ultimately reifies nationalistic rhetoric.

28. As Anderson explains in reference to fifteenth- and sixteenth-century Western Europe, "Print-capitalism . . . made it possible for rapidly growing numbers of people to think about themselves, and to relate themselves to others, in profoundly new ways" (Anderson, *Imagined Communities*, 36).

29. For an overview of the role of printing presses as a vehicle of Christian media in Indonesia, see Aritonang and Steenbrink, *A History of Christianity in Indonesia*, vol. 35. Particularly of interest here is chapter 21, "Christian Media" (951–76), including discussions in the subsections "The Catholic Press, Media and Magazines 1890–1942" (958–60), "Catholic Press, Media and Journals 1945–1990 (963–4), and "The Catholic *Kanisius*, the Protestant BPK *Gunung Mulia* and other publishers" (965–69).

30. For more on the Arnoldus printing press from Nusa Indah Publishing Company, see Nusa Indah's about us page ("Tentang Kami"), https://nusaindah.id/tentang-kami/. For more on the Arnoldus printing press as the oldest in Indonesia, see "Percetakan Tertua Itu Masih Menderu [The oldest printing press is still roaring]," *Kompas*, August 29, 2016, https://regional.kompas.com/read/2016/08/29/07331101/percetakan.tertua.itu.masih.menderu?page=all.

31. From "Tentang Kami" (about us), Nusa Indah Penerbit website, https://nusaindah.id/tentang-kami/.

32. It is important to note here that the norm for music education throughout Flores—and more generally in the Indonesian Catholic school and seminary education system—was, and I would argue largely still is, based in Western harmony and Western music ideas of choral music.

33. This legacy of music grounded in a Western paradigm persists in *musik inkulturasi*, which, though taking a much more localized and contextual or comparative approach, is still steeped in and stems from many of the tools of Western music theory (thinking here—especially with organ and choral music—of notation, understandings of tempo/meter, harmony, and form/use of counterpoint).

34. See note 2 for more on this quote from Archbishop Monsignor Albertus Soegijapranata.

8

———

Gaya X

An Ethnomusicological Look at Lagu Inkulturasi

Philip Yampolsky

In this chapter, I consider the inculturative songs (*lagu inkulturasi*) of the Roman Catholic Church in Indonesia. Although attempts at what would now be called musical inculturation began as early as the 1920s in Indonesia, for the past fifty years Catholic *lagu inkulturasi* have been created and promoted primarily through the efforts of the Pusat Musik Liturgi (Center for liturgical music, PML) in Yogyakarta, Java.[1] PML was founded in 1971 by the Jesuit priest Karl-Edmund Prier SJ as a response to the program for liturgical reform resulting from the Vatican II conference of 1962–65.[2] PML sought specifically to address the call for "adapting the Liturgy to the culture and traditions of peoples."[3] Incorporating into the liturgy elements of local language, music, ritual, and other traditional elements is called in Indonesian Catholic circles *inkulturasi*. In Indonesia, with over a thousand ethnolinguistic groups and subgroups, *inkulturasi* is a Herculean task.[4]

I must explain at the outset that I write as an ethnomusicologist, not a theologian. I call into question neither the spiritual benefits of *lagu inkulturasi* for Catholic worshippers nor the societal benefits of the Church's work in Indonesia. I am concerned here only with the impact of the inculturative program on the traditional music that it intends to harmonize with the liturgy of the Church.[5]

In explaining *inkulturasi*, PML begins with a statement from the High Council of Indonesian Bishops: "The aim of inculturation/indigenization [*pemribumian*] of the liturgy is the expression/celebration of the liturgy of the Church in a protocol [*tatacara*] that is wholly in keeping with the cultural tastes of the worshippers." PML (i.e., Rm. Prier) continues: "Or, to put it more simply: the aim of inculturation is to ensure that worshippers are deeply affected by the music, prayers, symbols, decorations, ritual—since these are all immediately understandable, they are all 'good' according to the standards of evaluation that obtain in the local culture."[6]

PML has been abundantly productive since its founding. Creating the repertoire of *lagu inkulturasi* has been one of its principal missions, but not the only one: it publishes books and a journal focusing both on Western music (history and theory) and on the theory and practice of *lagu inkulturasi* in Indonesia; it has published some fifty-five collections of the songs in cipher notation; it also publishes notated collections of Indonesian regional folk songs (*lagu daerah*) as well as cassettes, CDs, and DVDs of *lagu inkulturasi, lagu daerah,* and Western religious music; and it offers classes in music history and literature and training in performance (particularly for organists and choral directors).[7] Furthermore, it publishes one of the most widely used hymnbooks for Catholic worship, *Madah Bakti* (first issued in 1980 and revised and expanded in 2000).

Rm. Prier states that between 1977 and 2021, 1,657 *lagu inkulturasi* have been created in the PML program.[8] In *Madah Bakti 2000,* I count 396, which amounts to 53 percent of the 747 music items in that national hymnal. Nearly all of the 1,657 have been published in the smaller volumes issued for particular ethnic groups or geographical regions.

From 1977 until 2015, the crucial mechanism for the production of *lagu inkulturasi* was a string of fifty-seven *lokakarya komposisi musik liturgi* (workshops in composing liturgical music), conducted by PML in locations all across Indonesia, from Nias and Mentawai to Papua. The principal—and almost always the only—leaders of these workshops were Rm. Prier and his constant collaborator, the composer, arranger, and choral director Paul Widyawan.[9]

The first five *lokakarya,* from 1977 to 1979, followed an early model that PML came to consider too "centralistic": four of the five were held in Yogyakarta, with mostly Javanese participants. One was held elsewhere (in Flores, 1979), but, with this exception, the early workshops were only minimally concerned with the wide range of regional music that would become the focus of PML's work. (Rm. Prier later disparaged the early model as "bringing composers to Yogya to study music—and then forget the music of their own regions!"). In 1984, however, after a break of some years to promote the first *Madah Bakti,* PML initiated a new model in the belief that "the music of the Indonesian Church must develop from the 'grass roots,'"—or, in another phrasing, "Church music must be constructed from the bottom, not the top; in the remote areas [*pelosok-pelosok*] where traditional music lives." In the fifty-two *lokakarya* from 1984 to 2015, only four were held on Java and only two of those in Yogyakarta. The essence of the new model was an initial pattern of analytical engagement with local musical traditions, leading to new compositions incorporating features identified in that analysis.[10]

Each workshop invited participants from one or more of the ethnic groups in the region where the workshops were held. The participants in the first grass-roots *lokakarya* (Buntok, Central Kalimantan, June 1984) were primarily "farmers who knew traditional songs and dances but did not know notes." In the *lokakarya* held in Mataloko, Flores, in April 1997, six farmers, sixteen schoolteachers, one catechist, three office workers (*pegawai*), and three priests took part; two (one of the priests and one of the teachers) were already prominent composers of church music in Flores. According to Rm. Prier, writing in retrospect, a *lokakarya* needed three kinds of participants: local experts (*pakar*) in the musical traditions and culture of the region, catechists to monitor the religious content of the texts, and music teachers who understood the technical aspects of music and notation.[11]

The task of the participants was to create, under the leaders' guidance, *lagu inkulturasi* in the style (*gaya*) of the traditional music of their ethnic group or groups. (The crucial notion of *gaya* will come up frequently in this chapter.) Although these new *lagu* could be modelled on traditional melodies, they must be new creations, not simply *kontrafaktur* (traditional melodies given Catholic texts); they must have artistic qualities (*nilai seni*); and they must be singable by ordinary members of the congregation (*umat*). They should not remind worshippers either of secular (*profan*) melodies in their culture, such as those used for courtship, or melodies associated with practices contrary to Christian religion, such as animal sacrifice to call spirits, heal the sick, or appease the ancestors. ("*Inkulturasi* must be selective in the elements that are inculturated.") In short, the new liturgical *lagu* should be high (*tinggi*), exalted and noble (*luhur*), and pure (*suci*), because through them (just as through the standard, uninculturated liturgy) worshippers would meet God (*berjumpa dengan Tuhan*).[12]

That's a lot of work for a melody to do, but *lagu* here means the combination of melody and text, and in fact PML emphasized that the text had primacy, and the melody must "serve" it (*melodi harus mengabdi pada syair*). The text should be chosen first, and then the melody made to fit it. The sources of texts would ideally be biblical or liturgical, but PML recognized that biblical language could be stiff (*kaku*) and prosaic (*kurang puitis*), so rephrasing a text in more colloquial language, with optional reference to daily life, was permitted. A rule stated in workshop documents but not in the printed books, yet evident in all of the published collections of *lagu inkulturasi*, was that the language itself should be Indonesian, not the regional language of the *lokakarya*'s participants. (An exception was made for the language of Indonesia's largest ethnic group: the hymnbook *Kidung Adi*, published in 1983, just before the pivotal year of 1984, is in Javanese.)[13]

In fitting the melody to the text, there were rules to be observed. Melodic phrases should be coterminous with lines of text, and each line of text should have roughly the same number of syllables (seven or eight; not more than ten). Each section of the melody should have the same number of measures. The neutral vowel (schwa) should not fall on a strong beat; the vowel [i] (as in English *we*) should not fall on a high pitch. The most important words (God, love, peace) should fall on main beats. The character of the melody should suit the words; for example, the phrase *Kami cinta Kau* (we love You) should not be set to a descending melody, with the Deity arriving on the low tone. The solution for that particular problem would be to keep the descending melody but reverse the pronouns: *Kau cinta kami*.[14]

The participants were not expected to create new melodies out of thin air. Workshops began with demonstrations of local traditional music and dance performed by the workshop participants themselves or by local performers. (If no live demonstrations could be arranged, audiovisual documentation made beforehand was presented.) The first days of a workshop were devoted to analyzing the performances and asking performers about the meanings and functions of their songs and dances. Participants were led by Rm. Prier and Paul Widyawan to identify the scale or scales used, characteristic melodic and rhythmic motifs, and the format of performance (solo answered by chorus; solo picked up by a small group before the chorus comes in; alternating short and long choral refrains; recitative; melodic strophes; etc.). Traditional instrumental accompaniment, if present, was also analyzed.

The second part of each workshop was devoted to composition by the participants. First they were shown how to manipulate (*mengolah*) melodic motifs by means of augmentation, diminution, inversion, rhythmic displacement, sequences, ornamentation, and *fantasi* (i.e., elaboration).[15] Similar manipulations of rhythmic motifs were demonstrated. Then the participants were sorted into small groups of two to five members and assigned the task of composing melodies to suit specific liturgical functions (opening of the service, the sections of the Mass, songs to be sung during Communion, and so forth). First they had to choose or create a text, according to the guidelines given above; then the usual practice was to choose as a model one of the melodies analyzed earlier in the *lokakarya* and manipulate its motifs until they had a new melody that suited the chosen text. One rule the leaders laid down was that the new melody must not begin in the same way as the model.[16] Another possibility was to work directly with motifs that had been identified as typical of the music in question, without using a particular melody as a model. The new compositions produced by the small groups were reviewed by the workshop leaders and the other groups, and revisions were suggested. A *lagu* was considered finished when it had been accepted by the entire group. The one-line melodies were the goal of every *lokakarya*, and once they were completed, the participants went home and the PML team went back to Yogyakarta.

In due course, the one-line melodies would be published in *buku umat*, booklets for use by worshippers in church services. The pinnacle of acceptance for a *lagu* from a *lokakarya* was to be included in *Madah Bakti 2000*. Rm. Prier wrote that only "the very best" (*yang paling bagus*) of the *lokakarya* products were chosen for the national hymnal. In *Madah Bakti 2000*, *lagu lokakarya* are characterized in what I call the "*gaya X*" attribution: a headnote under the title, indicating that the lagu is in the *gaya* (style, musical idiom) of a particular ethnic group or region of Indonesia (or both): *gaya Sunda, gaya Nias, gaya Irian-Meybrat, gaya Flores-Ngada, gaya Jawa, gaya Batak Toba*, and so forth.[17]

Do the melodies accurately represent the *gaya* of the groups they are intended to reach? Since all or most of the participants in a *lokakarya* came from the source culture(s) and the melodies produced were all finally approved by the participants as a group, we must assume that the scales and motifs did not seem outlandish to the culture bearers; otherwise, they would presumably have objected.[18] My informal survey of the one-line melodies confirms that they tend to correspond to the scale analyses arrived at in the first part of a *lokakarya* and summarized in various PML publications.[19]

However, some features of *gaya* are disregarded in the PML melodies. Tuning, for all of the notations of *lagu inkulturasi*, presumes the Western diatonic tuning, which is enforced by keyboard accompaniment when it is available.[20] PML is also willing to override traditional compositional forms. *Lokakarya* participants were instructed to keep all lines the same length, and a symmetrical question-and-answer format was recommended, along with a melodic climax (*puncak*) supporting the essence (*hal pokok*) of the lyric.[21] Yoshiko Okazaki reports that in *lokakarya* in Pematang Siantar, North Sumatra, in the 1980s, the PML leaders suggested that Toba Batak melodic motifs be arranged in "Western simple song-forms" (her term) such as A, AB, AAB, ABA, ABC, or AABA. In contrast, she writes, "traditional folk songs consist of repetition of melodic formulas with or without small variations," as, for example: AAA'BAA'BCDC'DC'DEE'. She concludes:

> [PML's] composed hymns thus are something like Toba Batak ingredients marinated in Western principles. Some typical Batak elements are inevitably overlooked or changed. For example, an extended repetition of a single melodic phrase was criticized for being 'too monotonous, just repeating the same notes' and was altered in spite of the fact that repetition within a narrow two- or three-pitch range is quite natural in a Batak song.

And yet she also remarks that "Toba Bataks themselves prefer songs composed in Western elements. . . . Arranging indigenous Toba Batak materials using principles initially foreign to the culture in some ways corresponds to contemporary Toba Batak aesthetics. Contemporary Toba Batak people in general prefer songs with more varieties and contrast."[22] Her comments point to one of the paradoxes of *inkulturasi* that I will discuss at the end of the chapter: that Indonesians are moving away from precisely the traditional music that the Church wants to blend into the liturgy.

In addition to the *buku umat* resulting from a *lokakarya*, PML selected some of the one-line *lagu* from the *lokakarya* to be published in choral arrangements. Again, the arrangements have headnotes identifying the *gaya* of the melody and the *lokakarya* where the *lagu* was created; often they also indicate the *lagu dasar*, the melodic model it was based on. While the booklets for the *umat* were aimed at residents of specific regions or members of specific ethnic groups, the choral arrangements were more widely distributed, as PML encouraged church choirs to sing *lagu inkulturasi* from regions or ethnic groups other than their own. The *lokakarya* participants had no input in these choral arrangements; they were made single-handedly by Paul Widyawan. I argue that the arrangements deviate sharply from the traditions they claim, by the label *gaya X*, to represent.

Typically, the choral arrangements are for mixed choruses in four voices: soprano, alto, tenor, bass. As such, they are a radical departure from most of the musical traditions of Indonesia, in which group singing is normally monophonic (in unison or octaves, with no intentional harmony) or heterophonic (with several people singing together in loose approximations of a single melody, not striving for unison/octaves or tight rhythmic coordination, and again without intentional harmony). A few cultures have indigenous harmony, adding a second (and possibly a third) voice in parallel or mixed intervals with the main melody.[23] But in a striking statement, made during a *lokakarya* in Flores (where indigenous harmony is frequent), Paul Widyawan flatly dismissed this practice: "In traditional music [presumably he meant in Flores] there is a special feature where the music divides into parts [*bercabang*]. This seems to be an arrangement, but it is not an arrangement."[24] He reserves the term "arrangement" for what *he* does.

When the source tradition has a monophonic melody with a seven-tone scale, setting it into a four-voice arrangement wraps the melody in triadic, tonic-dominant-subdominant harmony. PML evidently regards this as unproblematic, routinely applying tonal harmony to heptatonic melodies. However, when a tradition uses only pentatonic scales, PML recognizes that tonal harmony will introduce tones foreign to the tradition. Rm. Prier has formulated instructions on how to avoid this:

> In pentatonic arrangements, polyphony should be prioritized. In finding [i.e., composing] the second voice (and third and so on), *imitation* of the main voice is what is hoped for, and the ideal is *canon*. . . . In pentatonic arrangements, manipulation of motives is very important. Moving a motif from one pitch level to another is a technique much used in polyphonic music, and it is the basis of imitative technique; it is the same in pentatonic music.[25]

Here we risk bogging down in terminology. *Polyphony* in its broadest sense refers to any plurilinear musical texture, that is, one with two or more simultaneous lines differing in some melodic or rhythmic respect.[26] The texture of many of the PML arrangements of heptatonic melodies—where each voice has its own melody, but the simultaneities (chords) are governed by the rules of tonal harmony, and all voices move together in much the same rhythm (not unlike Protestant hymns and chorales in the West)—may be more precisely termed *homorhythm*.[27]

Rm. Prier does not mean polyphony in the sense of homorhythm, or any of the other indigenous forms of plurilinearity in Indonesia. He means *counterpoint*, simultaneous and distinctive melodies contrasting in pitch and rhythm, and what he recommends for pentatonic arrangements is the specific type known as *imitative counterpoint* and its subtype *canonic imitation*. In these highly linear textures, characteristic of European art music of the Renaissance and Baroque eras, identical or similar melodic figures shift from one voice to another (usually with overlapping) and often from one pitch level to another. The conventions governing harmony in simultaneous intervals can be more relaxed in counterpoint than they are in homorhythm—that is why Rm. Prier recommends imitation, since there are not enough tones in a five-tone scale to allow conventional harmony. Any form of counterpoint is extremely rare in Indonesia—I know of only two examples—but imitative counterpoint and canonic imitation are, to my knowledge, quite unknown there.[28]

Rm. Prier has further guidelines (in the same article) for the arrangement of pentatonic melodies: avoid simultaneous thirds, V–I cadences, and other features suggesting tonal harmony; substitute fourths, fifths, and octaves for thirds; avoid simultaneous seconds on strong beats (but they add spice on weak beats).

The PML strategies have produced a consistent approach to arranging the one-line melodies of the *lagu lokakarya* and creating new compositions in *gaya X*. But we should not ignore how far the PML productions have traveled from the traditions they inculturate. They introduce harmony (whether triadic or quartal/quintal) where none exists traditionally, and they reject indigenous harmonic practices where they do exist. They further introduce the practice of imitative counterpoint, again with no traditional equivalent, and apply it to pentatonic melodies across the board. The various local practices of Indonesian music are thus homogenized into two generic classes: heptatonic homorhythm and pentatonic counterpoint. The melodic and rhythmic motifs manipulated in the *lokakarya* process presumably help to localize melodies for those who recognize the idioms, but the differences are, to my mind, overwhelmed by the sameness.

In PML's published recordings, *lagu inkulturasi* are performed by Paul Widyawan's choir Vocalista Sonora, almost always with some sort of instrumental accompaniment (whereas in traditional practice much group singing is unaccompanied).[29] In some cases, the accompaniment uses local instruments characteristic of the song's source culture. These accompaniments assert a song's *gaya* identity—more effectively, I believe, than do the melodies themselves—but few churches can make the assertion in services, since the traditional instruments are readily available only in their home regions. Churches elsewhere must make do with substitutes, or just with an organ or guitar. For them, *gaya* identity is asserted primarily by the song's "*gaya X*" headnote, while the music remains for the most part generic.[30] Other songs in the Vocalista Sonora albums are accompanied not by local instruments but by imitations of them—a random drum (or rhythm track) instead of the precise one; a melodica (if I'm not mistaken) instead of a Karo oboe—or just by organ. Rm. Prier advises that certain instruments (drum, bamboo flute, gong) may accompany *lagu* even if they are not used in the source tradition. Another versatile instrument he proposes is *angklung*, the tuned rattles played in sets, which are associated mainly with West Java. For a region that is "poor in melody instruments" (his example is Aru), *angklung* accompaniment could be used. "Although *angklung* come from West Java," he writes, "they don't have to be played as in Bandung. It is up to the inspiration of the person making the accompaniment to add nuances of art to the song."[31]

By the time a *lagu* has appeared in a *buku kor* and on a recording, with an Indonesian text, a generic arrangement, and, often, an unplaceable accompaniment, the attribution to *gaya X* comes to seem less an identification than a slogan. However, as I said at the start, I am not questioning the value of PML's providing worshippers with liturgical music that proclaims its link to them. Many in the congregation, I am sure, are thrilled to sing, or hear the choir sing, a song said to be in their own *gaya*.[32] What I question is the substance of that claim.

PML states unequivocally that it is not its responsibility to preserve traditional music. (That is the job of the culture bearers [*pemilik budaya*] and government culture officials, PML says.) Rather, PML maintains that *lagu inkulturasi* improve upon tradition. They "add nuances of art," as in the quotation about *angklung* above; similarly, the manipulation and variation of the initial motif in a *lagu gaya* Karo "add artistic value to this short *lagu*." Traditional music as it stands is unsatisfactory: "Traditional songs in their original form (for one voice only and untuned and defective instruments) of course cannot compete [*memang kalah bagusnya*] with the music we hear today," but "a dusty [*berdebu*] traditional song can become interesting [*menarik*] in the form of a *lagu inkulturasi*." The traditional songs of Kalimantan are usually short (*pendek-pendek saja*) and monophonic, but the 1985 *lokakarya* in East Kalimantan produced "good songs [*lagu-lagu yang bagus*] with developed melody, substantial lyrics, and interesting arrangements."[33] And, for a final example from Rm. Prier, echoing Paul Widyawan's dismissal of indigenous harmony: "Unlike the traditional practice of adding a second and third vocal line, Bapak Paul's effort is to make arrangements that are non-traditional [!], for the sake of variation and to keep the traditional music from becoming monotonous."[34]

The basic tenet in PML's program is that *lagu inkulturasi* transform traditional materials into new, liturgically effective music. One PML writer calls this process "purification" (*pemurnian*). In a startling 1993 formulation, Rm. Prier compared the analytical dissection and decontextualization of traditional music in the *lokakarya* and its reconstitution in the liturgy to Christ's death and resurrection: "Local culture [including music] must be ready to die in order to live again [in liturgy]." He later toned this down, saying (in 1999) only that both the "old culture" (i.e., local tradition) and the "new culture" (the Western traditions of the Church) are transformed in *inkulturasi*, resulting in a new creation (*kreasi baru*).[35]

The theology of *inkulturasi* has been carefully thought out. However, PML is caught in a sociological bind, for, as it points out repeatedly, Indonesians are abandoning their traditional music in favor of modern, Westernized forms. What people like now is secular popular music and, among Christian worshippers, the popular music on devotional themes called *pop rohani* (spiritual pop) and the upbeat, enthusiastic music of the Charismatic movement (*lagu karismatik*, musically very similar to *pop rohani*).[36] These popular forms are, in PML's view, too shallow in their theology and trivial in their music for *inkulturasi*, whereas in tradition, "we encounter the culture of the past, created by our ancestors and present in our genes."[37] The identity of a people is tied to its traditions, and if they lose their traditions, their identity is lost.[38] But, PML emphasizes, *inkulturasi* must focus on *living* tradition (*tradisi yang hidup*): "Inculturative music is rooted in traditional culture that is still alive. . . . There are places where traditional music has already disappeared. It is not the responsibility of the Church to preserve culture that is already dead. . . . The Church's target is people who are alive in the present era, to help young people in the future to understand the Good News in the cultural context they are familiar with."[39]

Here we see one of the paradoxes facing PML. If traditional music and culture are dying out, *inkulturasi* risks linking the liturgy to moribund symbols. If, on the other hand, what the younger generations know and prefer—the "cultural context they are familiar with"—is the popular culture that PML rejects, what can *inkulturasi* inculturate with?

Another paradox is that *inkulturasi* is meant to bring Catholic liturgy closer to "the culture and traditions of peoples" (to quote again from inculturation's founding document), but the language of *lagu inkulturasi* is Indonesian, not any of the local languages (other than Javanese).[40] The reason for this—never, to my mind, adequately acknowledged—is apparently strategic: the Church aspires to national scope. To tailor *lagu inkulturasi* to each of the source languages would fragment the *umat*. The same logic justifies the simplification of the music to common, generic idioms. To include the difficult or unusual features of some musics, such as nonstandard tunings, or the meters of five in Kalimantan and seven in Flores, or shifting meters, or the frequent simultaneous seconds of eastern Flores, or the long-held drones of Toraja, would be challenging to worshippers (and choirs) from other parts of the country.[41]

A third paradox, the one most distressing to an ethnomusicologist (at least to this one), is that *lagu inkulturasi* weaken the authority of traditional music in a community by "improving" it, particularly in the choral arrangements, but not only there. In 2002, a discussion was held at PML and summarized in *Warta Musik* on the question of whether Javanese gamelan music in church should be played in the classical style.[42] One speaker observed that the gamelan compositions (*gendhing*) created for use in church were different from gamelan music outside the church, and many of the classically trained musicians who were the keepers of the gamelan tradition found it difficult to play *gendhing inkulturasi*. To this, Rm. Prier replied that to play church *gendhing*, the skills of a classical musician were not needed, and the editor of the article agreed that simple accompaniment was preferable, since complicated—that is, classical—playing would disturb the concentration of the worshippers.

A second article in the same issue of *Warta Musik* is titled "Does Studying Gamelan = Getting Sleepy?" The author answers yes, if gamelan is played in the refined (*alus*) style, because that style is unsuited to the spirit of youth. If it's played in the loud style, they won't nod off. He recommends that gamelan performance be adjusted to the tastes of young people (*selera anak muda*).[43] (This logic—dispensing with the highly refined classical style of Javanese gamelan in favor of something more lively and exciting—is not far from the proposals, vehemently rejected by Rm. Prier, to use *pop rohani* and *lagu karismatic* in the liturgy.)

Similarly, PML's multipart choral arrangements "improve" on traditions of monophonic singing or indigenous harmonies. The choral arrangements claim to be in *gaya X*, but whatever indigenous elements there may be in the one-line *umat* versions are submerged in the harmonic and contrapuntal wash of the arrangements. Thus the dignity and coherence of the traditional idioms, developed over centuries to suit the needs, aesthetics, and social dynamics of local communities, are erased in favor of the theory and aesthetics of *inkulturasi*.

Rm. Prier reports that participants in PML *lokakarya* told him, after hearing songs they have worked on sung by a choir, that "I never thought our traditional music was so beautiful!"[44] I heard the same thing from a singer in a Kalimantan church in the 1990s. Rm. Prier offers this as evidence that PML is doing something right; I take it as evidence it is doing something wrong. Traditional music is indeed being abandoned in many parts of Indonesia, just as PML says. The reasons are societal and perhaps universal, and they cannot be blamed on PML. But what PML offers instead is pseudo-traditional music corresponding to none of the traditional musics of Indonesia, *gaya X*-es corresponding to no actual *gaya*. Theologically this is apparently acceptable—tradition dies to be reborn as liturgy—but culturally it is destructive. People accept with pride the Church's denatured simulacra of their traditions, even as the traditions themselves disappear.

ACKNOWLEDGMENTS

I want to thank Romo Karl-Edmund Prier, SJ, for friendly discussions and collegial assistance over many years, even though he knew that I am critical of aspects of his program. In particular, I am grateful to him for giving me photocopies of unpublished documentation for the several lokakarya held in Flores, 1990–2003. Sadly, as this book goes to press, I must note that Rm. Prier died on January 21, 2024, in Yogyakarta.

Other researchers have written incisively on the *lagu inkulturasi* program of the PML. Each has a particular focus, different from the others' and different from mine, but similar questions about the relation of PML's work to traditional music arise for all. Readers wanting further discussion of these issues should consult the dissertations of Thomas Manhart and Yoshiko Okazaki and Marzanna Poplawska's book *Performing Faith*, all cited in these notes, and also Emilie Rook's dissertation, cited in her chapter in this volume.

In this chapter, all translations from Indonesian (except in quotations from the authors just named) are my own.

NOTES

1. The earliest experiments are touched on briefly in a blog article by Karl-Edmund Prier SJ: "Inkulturasi Musik Liturgi Mas[a] Kini," posted September 12, 2021 (https://pml-yk.blogspot .com/2021/09/inkulturasimusik-liturgi-mas-kini-1.html). Unsystematic inculturative work in the period 1957–70, before the establishment of PML, is described in more detail in Rm. Prier, *Perjalanan Musik Gereja Katolik Indonesia tahun 1957–2007* (PML A-79; Yogyakarta: PML, 2008), 7–16.

2. Romo (Father; abbreviated Rm.) Prier was born in Weinheim, Germany, in 1937. He studied music and philosophy in Germany before coming to Indonesia as a Jesuit missionary in 1964. He lived in Java until his death in 2024. For his biography, see Rianti M. Pasaribu, *Mengembangkan Musik Liturgi Khas Indonesia: Perjalanan Hidup dan Karya-karya Karl-Edmund Prier* (Yogyakarta: Kanisius, 2015).

3. This phrase is the title of part 3, section D, of the constitution *Sacrosanctum Concilium*, promulgated by Pope Paul VI on December 4, 1963. (The official English translation is available online at www.vatican.va/archive/hist_councils/ii_vatican_council/documents/vat-ii_const_19631204_sac rosanctum-concilium_en.html.) Passages fundamental to the PML's program are found in articles 37–40 and 119–20.

4. In the 2000 census, the Indonesian government's Central Bureau of Statistics assigned codes to 1,072 ethnic and sub-ethnic groups; see Leo Suryadinata, Evi Nurvidya Arifin, and Aris Ananta, *Indonesia's Population: Ethnicity and Religion in a Changing Political Landscape* (Singapore: ISEAS, 2003), 10.

5. Since this is a chapter about music, I should clarify that *harmonize* is my word for this effort, not one of the metaphors used by the Church. And I should also clarify that in the context of this chapter, "the Church," capitalized, refers specifically to the Roman Catholic Church in Indonesia.

6. Both quotations in this paragraph are translated from Prier, *Inkulturasi Musik Liturgi I* (PML A-84, rev. ed., Yogyakarta: PML, 2014), 13, but the first is actually drawn by Prier from a 1984 document issued by the Majelis Agung Waligereja Indonesia, the High Council of Indonesian Bishops (since renamed the Konferensi Waligereja Indonesia).

7. Fifty-five is my unofficial count of *collections* so far. Most of the collections are published in two configurations: as *buku umat*, containing one-line melodies for the congregation to sing, and as *buku kor*, which present a selection of those melodies in choral arrangements for mixed chorus. The biggest collections (*Madah Bakti* [1980], *Madah Bakti 2000*, and the Javanese-language hymnbook *Kidung Adi* [1983]) require multiple volumes to contain all the mixed-chorus arrangements, more volumes of alternate arrangements for single-sex choirs, and still more volumes of *buku iringan* with written-out keyboard accompaniments, plus one-part gamelan accompaniments (*balungan*) for *Kidung Adi*. In all, PML has published nearly 150 books of *lagu inkulturasi*. In addition, there are eighteen collections of secular *lagu daerah*, published only in choral arrangements.

8. Prier, "Inkulturasi Musik Liturgi Mas[a] Kini."

9. Born in Yogyakarta, Java, Paul Widyawan (1945–2019) studied music in Java and later in Augsburg, Germany. In 1964 he formed the Paduan Suara (chorus) Vocalista Sonora, which is heard, under his direction, on nearly all of PML's recordings of *lagu inkulturasi* and *lagu daerah*. His fifty-year collaboration with Rm. Prier grew out of conversations beginning in 1967 (Prier, *Perjalanan*, 17). The march of *lokakarya* paused in 2015, with the illness of Paul Widyawan and Rm. Prier's advancing age, and it has so far not resumed.

10. The early *lokakarya* are described in Prier, *Perjalanan*, 33–37, and a list of all the *lokakarya* through 2007 is found at the end of that book. "Centralistic" and the "grass roots" sentence (which uses the English phrase) are from *Perjalanan*, 41. The sentences about bringing composers to Yogya and building Church music from the bottom up are from Prier, "Menemukan Spiritualitas Pelayanan

dalam Bermusik," *Warta Musik* [29], no. 6 (2004): 177–78. That article also contains a vivid description of the first grassroots *lokakarya*.

11. The farmers in Buntok are from Prier, "Menemukan Spiritualitas Pelayanan," 177. The Mataloko attendees are in "Hasil Lokakarya Komposisi Musik Liturgi III, tanggal 17 s/d 25 April 1997 di Mataloko, Flores" (unpublished workshop document), 10. Rm. Prier's statement is in *Perjalanan*, 46.

12. New creations: Prier, *Inkulturasi Musik Liturgi III* (PML A-86; Yogyakarta: PML, 2019), 16. Kontrafaktur: Prier, "Inkulturasi Musik Liturgi Mas[a] Kini." Artistic, singable, *tinggi, luhur, suci, berjumpa*: Prier, *Inkulturasi Musik Liturgi II* (PML A-82; Yogyakarta: PML, 2014), 9. Not secular or incompatible with Catholicism: Prier, *Inkulturasi Nyanyian Liturgi*, 3. The sentence about selectivity is quoted from Prier, *Inkulturasi Musik Liturgi II*, 60.

13. *Mengabdi pada syair*: Prier, "Kriteria Penilaian Nyanyian," *Warta Musik* [29], no. 1 (2004): 19; also Prier, "Lagu Anak yang Bercacat," *Warta Musik* [28], no. 2 (2003):49; also the blunt statement, "For liturgical music, the text is more important than the music," in Prier, *Inkulturasi Musik Liturgi II*, 8. Choose text first: "Hasil Lokakarya Komposisi Musik Liturgi, 26 Nop.–2 Des. 1990, di Mataloko, Flores" (unpublished workshop document), 29; also "Hasil Lokakarya Komposisi Musik Liturgi Gaya Rote-Ndao-Nagekeo, 15–22 Juni 2003 di Mataloko, Flores" (unpublished workshop document), 19. The June 2003 lokakarya, p. 19, is also the source of the statement that Biblical texts are *kaku* and may be revised to refer to daily life. Texts to be in Indonesian: "Himpunan Materi Lokakarya Komposisi Musik Liturgi . . . 20–27 Oktober 1996 di Rumah Retret Efata, Ruteng, Flores" (unpublished workshop document), 10, and other workshop documents.

14. Lines of text to match melodic phrases (*penggalan syair sinkron dengan penggalan lagu*): Prier, "Kriteria Penilaian Nyanyian," 19. Number of syllables: "Hasil Lokakarya Mataloko 1997," 24. Vowel placement: "Hasil Lokakarya Mataloko 2003," 19. Important words on strong beats: Wahyudi, "Inkulturasi Musik Liturgi Gaya Lio," *Warta Musik* [42] (2017): 154. *Kami cinta Kau*: "Hasil Lokakarya Mataloko 2003," 20.

15. Techniques for manipulating motifs are presented in three of the workshop books I have seen: "Hasil Lokakarya Komposisi Musik Liturgi 1–7 April 2000 di Kemah Tabor, Mataloko, Flores," 21; "Himpunan Materi Ruteng 1996," 21–22; and "Lokakarya Komposisi Musik Liturgi 27 Oktober–2 November 1998, Detusoko," 28 (this is the only one that mentions *fantasi*). But these techniques were surely taught in all the *lokakarya*. A demonstration of the derivation and use of motifs is found in Prier, *Inkulturasi Musik Liturgi IV* (PML A-93; Yogyakarta: PML, 2021), 39–49, in reference to *lokakarya* compositions in the *gaya* of the Karo people of North Sumatra.

16. Prier, *Inkulturasi Musik Liturgi IV*, 40.

17. *"Yang paling bagus"* is from Prier, "Madah Bakti—Edisi 2000 Terbit Akhir Oktober," *Warta Musik* 25, no. 6 (2000): 185. In *Madah Bakti 2000*, along with the headnote, there is a statement at the bottom of the musical notation identifying the *lokakarya* in which the *lagu* was created. The original *Madah Bakti* (1980) was published before the "grassroots" *lokakarya* began (1984), so none of the *lagu* from those workshops appear in it, but some from the 1977–79 *lokakarya* do. These also have the "*gaya X*" headnote but not the attribution to a specific *lokakarya*. Three hundred *lagu lokakarya* were included (with "*gaya X*" headnotes but not *lokakarya* sources) in the *Madah Bakti Suplemen* (1992), which was devoted wholly to *lagu inkulturasi*, and 181 of those were later selected for integration, along with 79 newer ones, into *Madah Bakti 2000*. In the 2000 volume, all the *lagu* from *lokakarya* (including those from 1977–79) show both kinds of identification. *Lagu* from *lokakarya* since 2000 have not yet been collected in a national-level hymnal.

18. On the other hand, Thomas Manhart, who observed a *lokakarya* in Nias in 2002, points out that the participants were all chosen by the Nias church authorities who hosted the *lokakarya*: "Only people are invited for the *Lokakarya* who are affiliated, . . . mostly in a highly engaged and active way, to the church. Thus, should any conflict arise between culture [i.e., actual cultural practice, including musical practice, in Nias] and the requirements of the church, participants are unlikely to challenge the opinion of the priest, who leads the discussion" (Thomas M. Manhart, "A Song for Lowalangi: The Interculturation of Catholic Mission and Nias Traditional Arts with Special Respect to Music" [Ph.D. diss., Southeast Asia Studies Programme, National University of Singapore, 2004]), 108).

19. Such as Prier, *Perjalanan*, the four volumes of his *Inkulturasi Musik Liturgi*, and the workshop documents.

20. Rm. Prier has written articles to explain how to accompany the pentatonic melodies that predominate in *lagu inkulturasi*, and PML has published several books of his keyboard accompaniments to the PML melodies. He stresses the importance, when accompanying a pentatonic *lagu*, of avoiding tones not present in the *lagu* (see, for example, Prier, "Mengiringi Lagu Batak Toba dengan Organ." *Warta Musik* 25, no. 5 [2000], 139-41). But there is no discussion of how vocal tuning might differ from the keyboard's equal temperament—because, it goes without saying, it should not.

21. Lines of same length: "Hasil Lokakarya Mataloko 1990," 30. Q & A, *puncak, hal pokok*: Prier, "Kriteria Penilaian Nyanyian," 19.

22. Simple vs. traditional song-forms: Yoshiko Okazaki, "Music, Identity and Religious Change among the Toba Batak People of North Sumatra" (Ph.D. diss., University of California at Los Angeles, 1994), 222; the melody diagrammed is *Andung ni Boru Sasada*, transcribed on page 284. Marinade: Okazaki, "Liturgical Music among the Toba Batak People of North Sumatra: The Creation of a New Tradition," *Crossroads* 12, no. 2 (1998), 64. Toba preferences: Okazaki, "Music, Identity," 222–23.

23. Examples of indigenous harmony can be heard in various recordings in Smithsonian Folkways' *Music of Indonesia* series: volume 8 (Flores: all selections), volume 9 (Flores: Ngada, Nage-Keo), volume 13 (Kalimantan: Kayan Mendalam and Kenyah tracks).

24. "*Dalam lagu tradisional ada kekhasan yang disebut musik bercabang. Bentuk ini nampaknya seperti aransemen, tetapi bukan aransemen.*" "Hasil Lokakarya Mataloko 1997," 14.

25. Prier, "Aransemen untuk Lagu Pentatonis," *Warta Musik* 24, no. 6 (1999): 172–73.

26. By that definition, heterophony is a form of polyphony; so is the drone polyphony heard in Toraja and in some parts of Flores, where a melody moves above or around a sustained pitch in another voice; and so also is the transient overlap that occurs when two soloists, or a soloist and chorus, superimpose the beginning of one phrase on the end of another, as happens in Nias and West Sumatra. For a clear catalogue of types of polyphony, see Simha Arom et al., "Typologie des techniques polyphoniques," in Jean-Jacques Nattiez, ed., *Musiques: Une encyclopédie pour le XXIe siècle, tome 5: L'Unité de la musique* (Paris: Actes Sud / Cité de la Musique, 2007), 1088–1109. For examples of drone polyphony: Dana Rappoport's CD *Indonésie, Toraja: funérailles et fêtes de fécondité* (Chant du Monde CNR 2741004). For overlapping, two examples in the Smithsonian series: Nias *hoho* (volume 4) and the opening of Minangkabau *selawat dulang* (volume 12).

27. The indigenous harmony that Paul Widyawan dismissed is also homorhythmic, but the pitches are not controlled by tonal harmony, as they are in Western hymnody or PML arrangements of heptatonic melodies.

28. In the Smithsonian series: *raego'* of the Uma in Sulawesi (volume 18) and *wera* of the Manggarai in Flores (volume 9).

29. The impression of sameness I just referred to is increased by Vocalista Sonora's extensive use of vibrato and bel canto vocal technique, neither of which occurs in Indonesian traditional singing.

30. In his keyboard accompaniments for *lagu inkulturasi*, Rm. Prier can sometimes incorporate musical allusions to the source tradition, as in the ostinato figures in the accompaniments to the Batak Toba Ordinarium. These ostinati resemble the four-gong *ogung* pattern that pervades the music of the Toba *gondang sabangunan* ensemble. (*Ordinarium Batak Toba: Buku Iringan Organ*, PML 200-I.)

31. Random drum: tracks 9 and 18 on the CD *Madah Bakti 2000 (1)*, PML 1021. Melodica: same CD, track 2. "Rm. Prier suggests": Prier, "Arena Dialog," PML blog, July 27, 2021 (https://pml-yk .blogspot.com/2021/07/arena-dialogpertanyaan-yang-belum.html). Angklung: "Arena Dialog." The two *gaya* Flores tracks on *Madah Bakti 2000 (1)*, tracks 1 and 13, have *angklung* accompaniment. There are no *angklung* in the traditional music of Flores.

32. Not always. Rm. Prier notes that in the first "grassroots" *lokakarya*, in Central Kalimantan, some participants were displeased that traditional melodies were transformed (*diolah*) to become new *lagu*. "This is no longer our music," they said (Prier, *Inkulturasi Musik Liturgi I*, 79). Thomas Manhart reports the same reaction when a Niassan member of Vocalista Sonora played the group's recording of

a Nias song for people back in Nias. "They appreciated the effort with a polite smile, yet declared their inability to recognize much of a Nias song; it is *bukan lagu Nias lagi*, 'no Nias song anymore'" (Manhart, "A Song for Lowalangi," 111–12). See also the comments by the Florenese priest and composer Pr. Pit Wani, quoted in Marzanna Poplawska, *Performing Faith: Christian Music, Identity and Inculturation in Indonesia* (Abingdon: Routledge, 2020), 184–85: "It [was] the arrangement [that] changed [that song]; no nuances, no idioms were preserved in it. . . . The name [i.e., the *gaya* attribution] [was] Nagekeo but in fact it was not at all. Even we, who are people from here, did not feel that. . . . [You] cannot [use] counterpoint, for them [indigenous people] it would be strange, for example." In a footnote (185), Poplawska cites a person from Manggarai saying that Manggarai songs, when given multipart arrangements and organ accompaniment, "are not considered indigenous anymore."

33. "Job of the culture bearers": See Tim Redaksi (editorial team), "Inkulturasi di Lio," *Warta Musik* 26, no. 2 (2001): 39. *Lagu gaya* Karo: Prier, "Lagu yang Tidak Bercacat," *Warta Musik* [28], no. 3 (2003): 82–83. "Traditional songs in their original form": Prier, album notes to the Vocalista Sonora CD *Ina Lou* (PML 1001), 1–2. (I thank Dieter Mack for bringing this statement to my attention.) "A dusty traditional song": Prier, "Lagu Inkulturasi Mas[a] Kini." "The traditional songs of Kalimantan": Prier, *Inkulturasi Nyanyian Liturgi*, 3.

34. Prier, foreword to "Hasil Lokakarya Mataloko 1990," 3. The exclamation point is my own insertion. Here is another statement from Rm. Prier, quoted by Marzanna Poplawska from an interview (*Performing Faith*, 52):

> Why Bach could have had written arrangements for single-part German songs, why Pak Paul cannot make [arrangement] for single-part songs of Alor? I think it is not appropriate if we say that in Indonesia it has to be original—one part [only]. Songs of the Reformation, at the beginning, also had one part, but arrangements were made, Bach created choir [parts]. Why we would have to say that this is not allowed here? I think if there is a desire to sing with a choir, it is also natural that we try to make an arrangement . . . [while] preserving the uniqueness; and the sound that we hear is grasped, processed to become an arrangement.

The question I raise in this chapter is whether it is possible to "preserve the uniqueness" when making arrangements on the PML models.

35. *Pemurnian*: Wahyudi, "Inkulturasi Musik Liturgi Gaya Lio," 154. Death and resurrection, 1993 version: "*kebudayaan setempat pun harus berani mati untuk dibangkitkan*" (Prier, *Inkulturasi Nyanyian Liturgi*, 4). Revised in 1999: Prier, *Inkulturasi Musik Liturgi* (PML A-66; Yogyakarta: PML, 1999), 7.

36. Prier, "Musik Gereja dalam Peralihan," *Warta Musik* [28], no. 6 (2003): 173.

37. Prier, *Inkulturasi Musik Liturgi IV*, 5.

38. "However proud we may be that the thousands of islands of Indonesia are united by satellite broadcasting, nevertheless this new 'culture' will eventually erase all forms of traditional music, because they will be felt to be inferior in quality and behind the times. This means that, willingly or not, the Dayak, the people of Maluku and Irian, etc., will lose their identity" (Prier, *Inkulturasi Musik Liturgi I*, 19).

39. Prier, *Inkulturasi Musik Liturgi I*, 12.

40. The *Sacrosanctum Concilium*. See note 3.

41. It is instructive to compare PML's procedures to those proposed by the Protestant missionary ethnomusicologists Vida Chenoweth and Darlene Bee for creating an "ethnic hymnody," different for every music culture, without seeking a musical lingua franca to bring cultures together. Taking linguistic analysis as their model, they developed a rigorous method:

> From the transcription of many songs the significance of musical components in various compositional styles is determined. Such components range from small units such as pitches, intervals, and nuances to the formal melodic and rhythmic plan of a composition. Determining these components parallels the phonemic analysis of a language. . . . By discovering the

rules of occurrence, co-occurrence, and progression of the musical elements, one can arrive at a description of the grammatical structure of any music system, and that description can be used as a basis for creative composition within the system. [Vida Chenoweth and Darlene Bee, "On Ethnic Music," *Practical Anthropology* 15, no. 5 (1968): 207–8]

In contrast, PML applies overarching standards of tuning, harmony, counterpoint, motivic variation, compositional structure, and aesthetics to the elements identified in its analyses of particular musics.

42. Tim Redaksi (editorial team), "Apakah gamelan harus klasik?" *Warta Musik* [28], no. 1 (2003): 5–6.

43. D. Danan Murdyantoro, "Belajar Gamelan=Bikin Ngantuk?," *Warta Musik* [28], no. 1 (2003): 11–12.

44. Prier, *Inkulturasi Musik Liturgi I*, 80.

PART IV

Missionaries and Anthropologists

9

Reconsidering the Place of Missionaries in Ethnomusicological History

Jaap Kunst and the Fathers of the Divine Word in Flores

Dustin Wiebe

In early July 1930, Jaap Kunst arrived in Flores to begin a seven-week tour of each of the island's five major regencies. Beginning in the far east, Kunst traveled westward, documenting the vocal and instrumental traditions he encountered along the way. Kunst published his findings in the landmark text *Music in Flores* (1942).[1] Throughout the book, Kunst acknowledges his indebtedness to the Fathers of the Society of the Divine Word (abbreviated SVD: Societas Verbi Divini) for their extensive assistance in facilitating his research. According to Kunst, during his trip he "came into almost daily contact with the [SVD] Fathers."[2] Kunst singles out one particular priest for his companionship and professional assistance: "More especially it was Father P. Heerkens who gave me the benefit of his great knowledge of Flores and its music, both during my sojourn in the island and afterwards, when, back in Holland, I was writing this book."[3] While *Music in Flores* remains an often-cited contribution to the history of music in Indonesia, its companion text—*Lieder der Florinesen* (1953)—today persists in relative obscurity.[4] Father Heerkens researched the book in the years he spent serving the SVD mission in Flores (1927–36) and wrote it at Kunst's suggestion in the years before his untimely death in 1944. Although both Kunst and Heerkens shared a deep admiration for indigenous songs of the East Indies, the former sought principally objective units of observation, while the latter became fixated on the "native psyche" with the ultimate objective of converting the "pagan" population of Flores.[5] The present state of relations between missionaries (and/or missionary scholars) and secular scholars, by contrast, is understandably fraught.[6] It is interesting, then, that Kunst—the widely recognized "father of ethnomusicology"—found himself in a fruitful working partnership with not only Father Heerkens but also several other missionaries from the SVD order. More recently, however, the general state of ethnomusicology since at least the 1970s is one where researchers and the missionaries are typically viewed as distinct and adversarial, not collaborative; and many accounts of late colonial-era ethnomusicological history (ca. 1885–1960) confine the contributions of missionaries to the periphery of disciplinary discourse. In other words, it is often suggested, missionaries (writ large) of the late nineteenth and early twentieth centuries were mere data collectors for those doing the heavy lifting of the budding comparative musicological enterprise. As I will show, however, a select handful of missionaries from this period made important contributions to ethnomusicological scholarship and research methodology, including the work of Heerkens, as *Lieder* most poignantly demonstrates.

Through this case study, I will show the role of the missionary-ethnographer in the history and development of ethnomusicology and also highlight the frequent historical inseparability of comparative musicologist from missionary and comparative musicology from missiology. From the outset, I should note that I am not interested in valorizing the work of missionaries but rather in illustrating their role in the historical and methodological development of ethnomusicology. Most of the primary source materials considered herein—letters, unpublished papers, photographs, and the like—are held in one of three archival collections located in the Netherlands, each of which I visited in March 2022: the Jaap Kunst collection at the University of Amsterdam; the Dutch Heritage Center of Monastic Life (Erfgoedcentrum Nederlands Kloosterleven, St. Agatha); and the St. Francis Xavier Mission House (Teteringen). This chapter proceeds in three main sections: "Father Petrus Heerkens: SVD Ethnographer and Missionary"; "Missionaries in Ethnomusicological History, Discourse, and Imagination"; and "Heerkens and Kunst: Contrasting Approaches to Field Research."

FATHER PETRUS HEERKENS: SVD ETHNOGRAPHER AND MISSIONARY

The Society of the Divine Word

Saint Arnold Janssen (1837–1909) founded the Society of the Divine Word (SVD) in the Dutch village of Steyl in 1875.[7] Janssen held formal education in high regard and established the study of science—especially geology, linguistics, and ethnography—as a central pillar of the new missionary order.[8] Father Wilhelm Schmidt, the prolific linguistic anthropologist, is the most well-known SVD priest to emerge from this scholarly tradition.[9] The SVD educated their seminarians in subjects "deemed useful for the future priest and missionary," including Hebrew, education, anthropology, geology, missiology, art, astronomy, and music.[10] Inspired by mission opportunities brought on by European colonization, the new Catholic order soon established field missions abroad, beginning in China in 1879. Several decades later, in 1913, the Society of Jesus handed control of missions to the entire Lesser Sunda Islands region—now the East Nusa Tenggara and Bali provinces of Indonesia—over to Divine Word missionaries, a region over which their Jesuit missionaries had held ecclesial jurisdiction for more than fifty years.[11]

In 1914, the SVD established their first missionary station in Flores, an island largely on the fringes of the Dutch colonial imagination but with a history of Euro-Catholic contact dating to the Portuguese colonial conquest of the region beginning in the sixteenth century.[12] During the first half of the twentieth century, SVD ethnologists and linguists in Flores both missionized and carried out research, including Fathers Paul Arndt, Herrmann Bader, Adolf Burger, and Jilis Verheyen, the latter of whom writes about the role of ethnology in missions in a brief article titled "Inheemse kerkzang in de Manggarai" (indigenous church singing in Manggarai) published in the SVD periodical *Pastoralia* (1938): "We must empathize with the thought world of pagans, not of high culture pagans, but of primitive, animistic pagans. It is impossible without some knowledge of ethnology."[13] The long history of Catholicism in Flores coupled with the efforts of SVD missionaries to convert the local "pagan" populations meant that by end of the colonial era (ca. 1945), Flores was already widely known as a "Catholic island."

Father Petrus Heerkens, SVD: Life and Works

Petrus (Piet) Martinus Heerkens (figure 9-1) was born on November 4, 1897, in the Dutch city of Tilburg. He began his seminary training in April 1914 at the SVD's St. Willibrordus mission house in Uden, the Netherlands. Thirteen years later, in 1927, he received the priestly ordination from the St. Francis Xavier Mission House in nearby Teteringen. From 1927 to 1936, Heerkens served the SVD mission in Flores, first as a teacher at the minor seminary in Toda-Belu and later as a pastor in the Sika region.[14] In 1930, the year of Kunst's visit to Flores, Heerkens published *Flores de Manggarai*, his first book on the peoples and customs of the island's western Manggarai region. The SVD stationed Heerkens in this western region, where the minor seminary was located, and the fact that the priest decided to focus his efforts on this one area indicates that unlike Kunst, Heerkens had relatively little time to travel throughout the island on ethnographic research trips and instead relied on doing fieldwork when and where he could. Most missionary ethnographers working during the late nineteenth and early twentieth centuries faced similar methodological constraint. In 1932, Heerkens published a collection of Florenese stories, *Sinjo, de slimme app* (Sinjo, the smart monkey).

Because of a digestive illness, Father Heerkens returned to the Netherlands permanently in 1936. Here he continued writing and began publishing more prolifically in both popular and scholarly idioms. This period, which concludes with Heerkens' death in 1944, begins with the publication of his Dutch translation of Thomas à Kempis's Latin devotional *The Imitation of Christ* (1937) followed by two

FIGURE 9-1. A headshot of Father Petrus Heerkens in his cassock. This photograph was likely taken shortly before he left the Netherlands in 1927 to join the SVD mission in Flores. Photo used by permission of the St. Francis Xavier Mission House, Teteringen, Netherlands.

Dutch-language novels, *Ria Rago* (1938) and *Ola Wolo* (1938).[15] Both novels are set in Flores and include significant musical content and insight into their respective narrative developments. I will discuss the content of these books further below. During his time in Flores, Heerkens also developed an interest in writing poetry in the Tilburg dialect, and upon his return to Europe, he published several collections of Tilburg poetry, including *Den Örgel* (1938) and *De Kinkenduut* (1940). Heerkens's brother Leo set dozens of these poems to music, which Piet sang regularly.[16]

An obituary from the *Nieuwe Tilburgsche Courant* describes Heerkens as "a finely tuned poet" and "the singer of the Tilburg dialect."[17] Kunst himself recalled Heerkens as "a lovely singer of Brabantian folk life."[18] In the years immediately before and after his passing, Heerkens published several other works, more scholarly in nature, including a Dutch translation of the epic Florenese poem "Wonga Wéa" (1943), the article "Het Lied van Saka Ladja" (1946), and, of course, *Lieder der Florinesen* (1953).

The Twin Volumes: Music in Flores *(Kunst 1942) and* Lieder der Florinesen *(Heerkens 1953)*

Let us now review the contents of the two texts under consideration a little more thoroughly, beginning with Kunst's work, *Music in Flores* (1942). The two-hundred-page manuscript contains hundreds of musical examples, six sketch maps, four tables, and sixty-seven illustrations. Kunst's 1930 expedition to Flores yielded considerable data, including "an abundant phonographic harvest of vocal and instrumental music (70 cylinders)" in addition to "as many as 90 musical instruments . . . [and] a series of photographs and films of players, dancers and instruments" (figure 9-2).[19] The recordings collected during this trip are among the earliest such sources in existence.[20] The transcriptions Kunst provides throughout the book are largely based on these recordings. With these materials, Kunst provides what he describes as "a condensed and regionally-ordered precipitate of what the [1930] trip has taught the author."[21] The text illustrates a general preoccupation with identifying and measuring regional scales and tunings and classifying musical instruments. Toward this end, Kunst organizes *Music in Flores* into two sections: chapters 1–5, a regionally oriented survey of vocal traditions, and chapter 6, a survey of musical instruments categorized according to the Hornbostel–Sachs system.[22] It is also worth noting that nearly a quarter of Kunst's cited academic sources are authored by SVD missionary priests, four by Heerkens and five by his senior colleague and noted anthropologist, Paul Arndt. Kunst leans on these published materials to help contextualize the data presented in *Music in Flores*, even revealing his admiration for Arndt's 1932 publication *Mythologie, Religion und Magie im Sikagebiet*, writing, "Perhaps I may permit myself another brief quotation from Father Arndt's rich and interesting study."[23] *Music in Flores*

FIGURE 9-2. Jaap Kunst (*far right*) pictured with members of a *labago* orchestra in the Ngada regency of west-central Flores. The image depicts the three instrument types in this ensemble: (1) hand-held gong (*go* or *gong*); (2) slender, single-headed drum (*laba wai*); and (3) double-headed roll drum (*lambo*). Kunst, *Music in Flores*, figures 37 and 55. Image used by permission of the Erfoedcentrum Nederlands Kloosterleven.

remains a landmark survey of Florenese music, perhaps rivaled only by Philip Yampolsky's similar survey during the mid-1990s.[24]

Lieder der Florinesen (1953) contains dozens of Florenese song transcriptions, complete with German translations of the original regional languages, which are also included in the monograph. Regarding the scope of his book, Heerkens notes, "I will mainly limit myself to the songs of the Lio area because circumstances have allowed me to devote more attention to them."[25] The book is therefore not as comprehensive as *Music in Flores*, which sets out specifically to include as many musical traditions as possible. Overall, Heerkens's data are more scattershot than that of Kunst, who progressed systematically across Flores, from east to west, gathering data at a rapid rate, as his SVD contacts and government budget allowed. Heerkens, on the other hand, was far more restricted in his travels throughout the island, gathering materials as time and budget allowed and, initially, without any intention to produce a scholarly work. He understood indigenous Florenese musics as a window into the native psyche, which he approached through the analysis of melody, text, and language. Heerkens completed the Dutch-language manuscript for *Lieder* in 1943, which Egbert Diederik Kunst, Jaap Kunst's father, translated into

German. Kunst Sr. completed the final edits to the text only days before passing on February 23, 1944, at the age of eighty-one.

MISSIONARIES IN ETHNOMUSICOLOGICAL HISTORY, DISCOURSE, AND IMAGINATION

Missionaries and Ethnomusicological Discourse: Now and Then

Over the past one hundred years, the perceived place of missionaries in (ethno) musicological practice and discourse has, generally speaking, shifted from accepted/acceptable collaborators to a position frequently characterized by suspicion and even disdain. Peter Pels outlines this progression, which begins in the second half of the nineteenth century. This "phase," he explains, is "one of compatibility of mission and anthropology," but this changes in the first decades of the twentieth century, when a more ambiguous relationship begins.[26] At this point, Pels argues that anthropology—and I would say comparative musicology as well—still "needed the missionaries" and that "the shift from the amateur ethnographer to the professional fieldworker . . . was not possible without the help of missionary ethnographers in the field."[27] Anthropologist Jean Michaud connects this past history to the common reality of more recent ethnographer–missionary relations:

> It is a telling symptom that open and frank debates between Western anthropologists and Christian missionaries took place only on a significant scale from the late 1970s onwards, after the colonial era was over. . . . The missionaries long considered the academic ethnographers as intruders and unconcerned intellectuals who they believed, spent just enough time with their subjects to produce a report or a thesis. . . . Academics, on the other hand, saw in the missionaries incompetent and moralistic hordes focused on normalizing the natives, causing their cultural and, often, material demise.[28]

That so many of the pioneers of ethnomusicology relied on ethnographic data collected by missionaries and that some of these missionaries were ethnographers—even comparative musicologists!—in their own right is a point not widely acknowledged in the contemporary discourse of ethnomusicological history.

As I have already alluded to, the common interests of early twentieth-century missionaries and comparative musicologists were frequently aligned, which led to various forms of professional collaboration. Kunst spoke openly about his indebtedness to the SVD missionaries in Flores and also worked with (and around) missionaries in other parts of Indonesia. He seems never to have encountered another equally fruitful partnership with any other religious organization. But why was his encounter with the SVD, and specifically Father Heerkens, so different? I believe it is because among the fathers of SVD order he encountered a familiar scholarly tradition of ethnography and linguistics.

Since the emergence of the academic field of ethnomusicology in the 1950s, the discipline as a whole has shown little interest in Christian subjects and has instead mirrored trends in anthropology, whereby engagement with Christianity tends to become either part of a normative colonial history or a mode of cultural erasure characterized by a loss of valued cultural knowledge (including language and arts).[29] Ethnomusicological methodology has also changed drastically since the mid-twentieth century, with perhaps no greater transformation than the shift away from a division of labor between field researcher and armchair scholar, a distinction most pronounced among adherents of the Berlin school of comparative musicology. During the second half of the twentieth century, ethnomusicology became nearly synonymous with the field-researcher/scholar, a single individual who both collects data (usually in situ) and publishes or otherwise presents on the findings. The collaborating missionary is now a relic of an earlier scholarly method. While there are known historical connections between missionaries and the development of ethnographic disciplines like ethnomusicology,[30] contemporary efforts to establish distinctions between missionaries and ethnographers are "more a part of present day . . . professional strategies than a studied assessment of the relationship between the two."[31]

Philip Bohlman, in his 1991 article "Representation and Cultural Critique in the History of Ethnomusicology," calls for ethnomusicologists to consider more seriously those sources from the colonial era that are often condemned as "naive." With specific reference to sixteenth-century descriptions of native South American music by Calvinist missionary Jean de Léry, Bohlman asks, "How have we dismissed [these descriptions] as simply naïve or ethnocentric, unworthy of rigorous objectivity of modern ethnomusicology? . . . How can such images belong to our ethnomusicology?"[32] Though Bohlman published these insightful challenges to practitioners more than thirty years ago, the influential, and often controversial, role of missionaries in the development of comparative musicology is still not widely understood.

I believe that the lacunae of knowledge that surrounds the history of ethnomusicology and the history of the contribution of missions and missionaries therein is, in part, a result of religion-based biases that distort our disciplinary history. As Cooley and Barz note in *Shadows in the Field*, more recent efforts to distinguish between contemporary scholars/scholarship and historical colonial agents (such as missionaries) "only serve to highlight our connection, for better or worse, with this legacy."[33] As the forthcoming pages illustrate, the contemporary reality of ethnographers at odds with missionaries is one that emerged only after World War II. This fissure in relations also informs how some prominent ethnomusicologists talk about Kunst in relation to missionaries.

Kunst and Missionaries: Distorting Disciplinary History

Contemporary accounts of Kunst provide misleading and over-generalized representations of the ethnomusicologist's varied encounters with individual mission societies and missionaries. In a review of Kunst's published—and now well-known—lecture to the Protestant mission school in Oegstgeest, Netherlands, ethnomusicologist Roger Vetter characterizes Kunst's thoughts on Christian missions as he speaks broadly about Kunst's negative perception of missions: "Kunst performs a tight-rope act throughout this lecture, trying not to overtly accuse the missionary cause of what elsewhere he has called the destruction of traditional musical cultures."[34] While Kunst undoubtedly held major reservations about particular mission societies (the Rheinische Mission in Nias, for example), he never made categorical claims about Christian missions as Vetter suggests. In his lecture to the missionary students, Kunst does speak disparagingly about the Protestant mission in Nias: "Statistically seen, the results for the Rheinische Mission could be called extremely satisfactory: the population of North and Central Nias is almost completely Christianized. But, at the same time, it has been uprooted and humiliated."[35] Despite such reservations, Kunst worked with the missionaries in Nias to complete his survey of that island's musical traditions. He even maintained a close relationship with the Protestant missionary Friedrich Dörmann, who assisted Kunst in translating song texts for his book *Music in Nias*.[36] Written communications between the two outline details of their professional collaboration and friendship. Kunst obviously viewed the Protestant mission in Nias as a cultural disaster, but he continued to assess individuals involved with that mission on a case-by-case basis, as his relationship with Dörmann and his family indicates.

Another review of the same lecture by ethnomusicologist Sarah Weiss offers similarly problematic and far-reaching characterizations of missions, this time in the form of an artificial dichotomy: "Knowing that missionary activity will proceed irrespective of what he might say, Kunst suggests that the best way to convert people is to be flexible and to encourage them to incorporate their own music and cultural traditions into Christian worship, thus fulfilling (however unsatisfactorily) the aims of both the missionaries and the cultural preservationists."[37] Weiss speaks in sweeping terms of "missionaries" and "cultural preservationists" as delineable categories, and in doing so imposes this perspective on Kunst. We know categorically that Kunst did not hold such an unnuanced conception of missionaries, as evidenced by his field collaborations with missionary ethnographers like Heerkens. Weiss's interpretation of Kunst's lecture also keeps the ethnomusicologist at arm's-length from missionaries, as he would presumably be considered a "cultural preservationist" and not a "missionary."

Still other accounts of Kunst and his work paint a picture of a somewhat isolated ethnomusicologist who conducted work in an intellectual vacuum. For example, Dana Rappoport provides a Columbian description of Kunst's 1930 Flores expedition: "In 1930, Jaap Kunst began his trip through Flores at the extreme eastern tip of the island. There he *discovered* [italics mine] the fascinating practice of two-part singing, to which he devoted a few pages in *Music in Flores*."[38] Besides the obvious point that this musical "discovery" was novel only to non-natives of

Flores, the two-part singing described by Rappoport was surely already known to the SVD missionary priests who assisted Kunst in his research. Furthermore, Philip Yampolsky reports that Kunst's *Music in Flores* remains "the only study on the island's music," a point that completely ignores Heerkens's contribution to this twin volume set.[39]

As we already know, Kunst recognized his missionary collaborators openly, speaking of the SVD fathers in particularly glowing terms in an unpublished 1938 book review: "I owe a lot to them in my research. By the nature of the matter, those who spent their whole lives on Flores . . . knew the country and people like no other. And they let me take advantage of that knowledge in a way that was not esteemed enough."[40] It is clear from these remarks that Kunst held the SVD fathers in high regard, recognizing also their significant contributions to the content of his research. More recent characterizations of Kunst himself and of his research trip to Flores by contemporary ethnomusicologists often minimize or ignore his professional connection with missionaries.

The "Native Psyche"

In a published review of *Music in Flores*, Heerkens describes his primary objective in writing *Lieder*: "My main task was to probe the psyche of the native [*psyche van den inboorling*] through their melodies and texts, as far as is possible for a European."[41] On May 28, 1943, Heerkens sent a copy of the abovementioned review along with a self-penned letter to a provincial superior in which he restates the intended purpose of his forthcoming book. He begins with a comment on *Music in Flores*: "Nothing is learned from that work [*Music in Flores*]—that is simply 'science'—but I suspect that this work [*Lieder*] will be welcome material for many missionaries on Flores to study and to penetrate deeper into the language and psyche of the native."[42] Of interest to the present discussion is Heerkens's seemingly contrasting use of the terms *science* and *psyche*. His use of quotation marks for the word "science" is not, I believe, an indication that he considers Kunst's work antithetical to science. Rather, Heerkens aims to draw a distinction between the empirical sciences (as espoused in Kunst's reliance on tuning, organology, etc.) and the emerging field of Jungian psychology, a concept well known throughout Europe by the early 1940s. In the preface to *Lieder*, Kunst himself underscores the psychological usefulness of Heerkens's work in rather emphatic terms: "May this last great work of Father Heerkens find the recognition it so fully deserves, not least on the part of the mission, because of its folk-psychological [*volkspsychologischen*] value."[43]

So how does Heerkens attempt to access the native psyche in the pages of *Lieder*? Precisely as he indicates: through (transcribed) melody, text, and language. And he uses these materials, combined with his own field observations, as the basis for the relatively brief analytical remarks he provides through the eight-chapter book. All but one of these chapters—the seventh—are arranged according to the aspects of social life that informed Heerkens's written remarks on the "native psyche": lullabies and other children's songs, work songs, gawi dance songs, satirical songs, love songs, lamentations, miscellaneous, and Portuguese songs in Sika.[44] Collectively, these songs cover topics of history, birth, life, sex, and death. In particular, Heerkens sees value in love songs: "Anyone who seeks to fathom the deepest and most specific nature of a people must turn to the heart of the people, to the love songs that are born of the people."[45] Heerkens's problematic conclusion regarding the love song "O Sara Kiré" is, however, one example of how his efforts to provide meaningful analysis of the native mind generally fell short: "That a text like this, which sings of lovemaking, should be married to such a solemnly sublime, even sacred, melody overflowing with religious feeling, is irreproachable proof of the truth of the thesis that the sexual development of primitive thought is of a religious nature."[46]

The implementation of Jung's ideas with colonial rule formed a sort of pseudoscience, which, in the Dutch East Indies, is traceable to the work of Dutch physicians who used the idea of a "normal indigenous psyche" to implement racist and repressive policies during the late colonial period.[47] Heerkens and Kunst both conducted their research at the peak of this period of psychological oppression. Historian Joost Coté rightly argues that "the 'native psyche' came to form a core element in the conservative interpretation of the inherent 'nature' of the colonial subject and was used to justify the correctness or failure of particular colonial policies."[48] A range of academic disciplines reflect this racist ideology, including the work of Dutch psychologist-turned-professor of ethnography, J. H. F. Kohlbrugge.[49] Heerkens conducted research within this intellectual milieu, and his works should be considered with this in mind. This point alone, however, ought not disqualify his work from consideration in the context of ethnomusicological history. Of particular interest here are his contributions to methodological development.

HEERKENS AND KUNST: CONTRASTING APPROACHES TO FIELD RESEARCH

The Phonograph

The rapid development of and increased interest in the intellectual subfield known as "comparative musicology" is closely linked to the invention of the phonograph in 1877.[50] For the armchair scholars of the Berlin school, phonograph recordings collected by Westerners living and traveling abroad (including missionaries) were the intellectual lifeblood of comparative musicologists, many of whom never traveled to the places where the recordings originated. In many ways, Kunst continued in this tradition (e.g., empirically oriented, emphasis on organology and scales); however, his reliance on his own field data and his long tenure of residency in the Dutch East Indies point ahead to methodological practices that became commonplace in the forthcoming decades. The wax cylinder recordings that Kunst made in Flores remained the most comprehensive collection of the island's music until well into the twentieth century.[51] The cylinders are presently held in the archives at the University of Amsterdam and remain one of the legacies of the 1930 voyage.

Heerkens, on the other hand, did not own a phonograph and did not commonly use one. The missionary describes his less technical approach: "My working method was quite simple. When I heard a song, I would try to get hold of the written lyrics and then notate the melody after hearing the song sung as a whole, lyrics in hand." Though Heerkens describes his method as "simple," he also describes the challenges of transcribing Florenese tunes onto the Western staff: "I couldn't get hold of the melody with my fountain pen. I couldn't lock it into the narrow cage of our grading system." Elsewhere, he describes difficulties involved with translating song texts: "They [Florenese song texts] are true picture galleries. However, one does not always make sense of them, because we [foreigners] do not always grasp the deeper meaning. A native explanation can help; but even that does not always bring the desired clarity."[52]

One wonders what Heerkens may have preserved if he had owned a phonograph, but as he describes, he intentionally decided to forgo using the innovative device. He states his apprehensions regarding audio technology:

> The phonographic recording can, like a snapshot in time, pinpoint an unfavorable moment. Only when recording multiple verses of the same song or the same song by different singers can one speak of a time recording or, more correctly, of a film recording with life and movement. The on-site recordings require a lot of time and effort; also, after all, many songs cannot be recorded in their entirety. . . . One often has to be satisfied with a result that would be comparable to a sketch, a drawing, and that is the main content of a song repeated ten to twenty times.[53]

Heerkens's phonographic hesitancy is rooted less in the technology itself than in his concern that the recordings will be essentialized and the richness of the living tradition(s) lost. Elsewhere in *Lieder*, Heerkens elaborates on this theme: "Regarding living song: a collection of songs such as this book offers, frankly, does not lead to a correct estimate of the wealth of songs in the Lio area, because only the very best from all sides has been selected and brought together."[54] He also notes the "time and effort" involved in making recordings, which likely underscores Heerkens's desire to experience musical activities in a given social context and, preferably, "in their entirety." To the best of my knowledge, the only time Heerkens worked with a phonograph was during Kunst's trip to Flores, so his published opinions about the technology were likely developed, in large part, during that time. Given this, it is reasonable to read these remarks as a response to the methods he learned from Kunst during the time they shared together in Flores.

The above quotation also indicates Heerkens's desire, perhaps both scientific and theological, to document Florenese vocal music as dynamic and variable.[55]

Though Heerkens does not mention Kunst by name, it is hard to read this as anything but a veiled criticism of the famed ethnomusicologist's relatively brief, yet expansive, survey of Flores. Elsewhere in *Lieder*, however, Heerkens offers more direct criticism of Kunst's methods: "The following little song was also written down by Mr. KUNST, but incompletely (No. 93); probably the singers were tired. . . . With my notes during the holidays, I always had the advantage of being able to devote a little time each day to my task; I was able to repeat a lot and give the singers time to prepare. The prospect of a reward, of some kind of clothing, after singing a few numbers inspired them to prepare thoroughly."[56] Heerkens notes his field advantage over Kunst, namely his ability to leverage time in a location and repeated visits to particular people to produce more accurate data.[57] Though phonographic recordings may have further bolstered his methodological approach, its use could have proven costly in other ways, for example by disrupting music and other social events. One wonders, Did Father Heerkens ever cringe at what he felt were socially inappropriate and slapdash measures employed by his esteemed colleague, Jaap Kunst? Did they ever discuss such matters of methodology openly, and if so, might Heerkens have shared his concerns? While we know that Heerkens often balked at criticizing Kunst directly, it is fun to imagine the conversations the two may have shared about how to best record—or not!—a survey of Flores's rich musical traditions!

Collaborative Methods

Mutual collaboration between Kunst and the SVD fathers aided the process of surveying musical tradition in Flores. The SVD alone did not have the time and financial resources to conduct such a review, and Kunst did not have the regional and linguistic knowledge, contacts, facilities, and transportation necessary to do it alone either. Kunst and the SVD fathers also collaborated with the many indigenous singers and other musicians who performed for recordings, posed for pictures, told their stories, or otherwise contributed to the Europeans' published research. Throughout their respective texts, Heerkens and Kunst name their main indigenous collaborators, including Petrus Ré, Alexander Kesu, Petrus Tonda, and A. Oka.[58]

In the foreword to *Music in Flores*, Kunst mentions his surprise when he found "the complete absence of any 'competitive' feelings toward the newcomer covering the same ground."[59] Heerkens elaborates on this point further in his published review of *Music in Flores*, noting that such a scholarly collaboration is well suited to the SVD's wider interests: "That he found a "complete absence" of those competitive feelings, on the contrary generous cooperation, is quite self-evident to a broad-sighted missionary; for when the Mission exhausts itself to advance the inhabitants of its territory in every way, it is to ennoble inner civilization, and if this understandably cannot happen except later, through study and in-depth research, then it is obvious that every ongoing study, by whomever, and in every field, should be most welcome to that Mission."[60] Given what we already know about the SVD's missiological approach, such openness to facilitating the field research of scholars outside the religious order comes as little surprise. A letter from Father Leven (SVD) to Kunst in October 1930 further demonstrates the interest of the order in Kunst's published research on Florenese music: "With glad anticipation we await your illustrated treatise on the flutes and polyphonic singing of Ngada and Nageh."[61]

Through personal letters and published articles, Kunst and Heerkens further describe the nature of their shared professional interests and ongoing interactions. In the *Music in Flores* foreword, for example, Kunst describes specific ways the SVD supported his research: "Now the Fathers put me into touch with well-known singers or mentioned songs and dances to be especially enquired after; now they offered me generous hospitality, repaired my film apparatus when it got out of order, . . . assisted in taking down or translating texts, or offered the use of the missionary motor lorry for free transport."[62] As Kunst indicates, the support of the SVD was wide-ranging and seemingly included aspects of support that would have been at some financial cost to the order, such as "free transport." The two film operators Kunst speaks of are undoubtedly Fathers Simon Buis and Piet Beltjens, who were in Flores at the time filming feature-length missionary propaganda films. I will return to these works below.

Heerkens carries on with more details of the collaboration, which was spurred by a rare mutual interest in the preservation and documentation of Florenese song:

> Mr. Kunst and the author of this article [Heerkens] are probably the only two people in the Netherlands and the Dutch East Indies who have studied the song on Flores; both, however, for quite different purposes: Mr. Kunst studied the chants as well as the instrumental music, while I confined myself to the living song alone [*levende lied alleen*]; Mr. Kunst studied the vocal and instrumental music on Flores purely as a musicologist, while my main task was to probe the psyche of the native through the melodies and texts, as much as a European can do. But we both were and remained, equally enthusiastic about the many discoveries in the field of indigenous song among this most musical of all inhabitants of the Dutch East Indies.[63]

From these remarks, it is clear that Heerkens understood their collaboration as simultaneously complementary and hierarchic. Complementary in the sense that Kunst applied a prescribed "musicological" (i.e., scientific) methodology while Heerkens focused on the more esoteric "native psyche." As he does elsewhere, Heerkens focuses on the living and dynamic aspects of Florenese music, a point that was generally of little concern to preservationist comparative-musicologists of this time. Regarding his own efforts, Heerkens notes that he is capable of them only "as much as a European can do," giving an air of superiority to Kunst's (scientific) work. Any postcolonial reading of *Music in Flores*, however, would surely reveal Kunst to be as much a European as Heerkens, and, therefore, subject to similar biases of perspective.

From Kunst's communications with Father Ehlert, we know he intended to carry on his collaboration with the SVD missionaries in Flores during a proposed

(1931) follow-up research trip: "I will probably return to Endeh on May 5, with the intention of moving east soon. The plan is to travel to the islands of Adonara, Solor, Lomblen, and Alor and to phonograph the song and film the various dances." The islands mentioned by Kunst lie to the immediate east of Flores and also had a strong SVD Catholic mission presence throughout the late colonial period. Kunst had previously performed music with Ehlert, and he hoped to do so again.[64] "I'll make sure to have some music for organ and violin with me" he wrote, "in the hope that either May 5th, or later, when I pass by Endeh again on the return journey, we will be able to play together again."[65] Kunst regularly performed his violin with and for the people he encountered in the field. This collaborative routine generally endeared people to him and it thus became an important part of his research methodology.

A review of his written communications show that the development and maintenance of working relationships with (mostly European) contacts throughout the Dutch East Indies was a common working methodology for Kunst, who was a master networker. Beyond Flores, Kunst also maintained working relationships with religious leaders in Europe (e.g., Father Wilhelm Schmidt) and missionaries elsewhere in the Dutch East Indies, including other SVD fathers like J. Pessers (Timor) and Protestant missionaries like F. Dörmann (Nias) and J. Verschueren (Papua).

In 1989, the well-known Austrian musicologist Gerald Florian Messner wrote about Kunst's trip to Flores. He provides sharp criticism of Kunst's methodology and, drawing from the work of anthropologist Edward T. Hall notes Kunst's inability to extricate himself from his strict, European sense of time (monochronic or "m-time").[66] What Kunst lacked, Messner argues, was a sense of polychronic time ("p-time"), or that highly flexible type of time employed by people of "East Florinese cultures." In a rather damning assessment of Kunst's work, Messner also notes, "Where one is not aware of these fundamental features [m- and p-time] there will be so-called 'cultural misunderstanding' which interferes severely with one's 'research' results."[67] While Messner's critique of Kunst's methodology is fair and even on point in many ways, it makes no mention of Heerkens or *Lieder* and completely ignores the influence of the SVD fathers on his field work. In many ways, the critiques levied by Messner against Kunst are evocative of those hinted at by Heerkens decades earlier—that recording p-time music in m-time will distort one's data. Heerkens timidly hints at this in his criticism of Kunst's use of the phonograph and again, somewhat unwittingly, in his characterization of Kunst as a "musicologist"—or, in other words, an m-time researcher. Heerkens's admittedly European efforts to observe and document a more indigenous perspective of Florenese music are more adept at responding to the variability of p-time. In this way, *Music in Flores* and *Lieder der Florinesen*, despite their many flaws, are deeply complementary and the result of a mutually informative collaboration. That Messner overlooks the influence of the SVD on Kunst's field research and the published findings—a point clearly stated in *Music in Flores* —is another example of how ethnomusicological discourse tends to dismiss, even erase, the disciplinary contributions of missionaries.

*Heerkens and Kunst: Respective Representatives
of the "Popular" and the "Scientific"?*

Though much of this chapter focuses on Heerkens's scholarly and methodological contributions to (ethno)musicology, he was better known in his own time for his more "popular" efforts to draw attention to both SVD missions and Florenese music. He mentions this approach to Kunst in reference to an upcoming radio lecture:

> I may also inform you that on the Friday before Easter I will give a lecture for the K.R.O. [Katholieke Radio Omroep, Catholic radio broadcasting] about the Cross procession in Sika [a regency in central Flores]. . . . I will also sing a few songs to it, restored chorale songs from the Portuguese time. You will probably be interested in that, although by nature I will focus more on the popular and less on the scientific side.[68]

Heerkens was often deferential to Kunst, and the priest's efforts to establish his own "popular" approach was likely his way of deferring to his "scientific" colleague. Of course, Heerkens was a missionary, and he wanted to spread the word about what he regarded as the good work of the SVD in Flores. Because of the evangelical bent to Heerkens's scholarly work, he, and others like him, were inclined to get their message out by more popular means. In 1938, when Heerkens penned the above letter, the terms "popular" and "scientific" were hierarchic in their academic prestige—'scientific' at the top and 'popular' somewhere (far) below. In contemporary discourse, however, there is a much more acceptable place for the popular within academia, especially those media that can appeal to a broad, public audience. Certainly, "popular music studies" have enjoyed increasing visibility in the last few decades.

Heerkens's efforts to popularize SVD missions in general and Florenese music in particular are best exemplified in his two historical fiction novels, *Ria Rago* and *Ola Wolo*, each of which contains considerable musical content.[69] Heerkens intertwines several Florenese songs with the story of *Ola Wolo*, the "brown slave" who must do the bidding of his immoral chieftain, Rani Noemba. The songs are transcribed in numeric cipher notation and could have been easily sung by the novel's readers.[70] Kunst wholeheartedly endorses Heerkens's efforts, noting that "each page speaks of a rich knowledge of land and people, acquired over years of interaction through intelligent observation: the writer was thus able, as it were, to get under the skin of his figures."[71]

Heerkens's second novel employs music as a central motif to tell the story of *Ria Rago*, a teenaged girl who defiantly resists the efforts of her "pagan" parents to marry her to a wealthy and much older Muslim man. Ria is forbidden to visit the nearby Catholic mission; however, she is initially drawn to the church by the sound of singing: "Strange singing! It sounds very nice from afar, as if there's a celebration! Would they dance, too? Ria would like to dance and sing with them. . . . She loves singing and music! Her mother and father don't want her to join, but if she is only going to listen, she can, father didn't forbid that."[72] As this excerpt alludes to, Ria eventually becomes involved with music in the Catholic Church, a point that causes conflict with her family. The story contains several scenes involving Florenese music and dance, including descriptions of culturally situated performances in Ria's village.[73] *Ria Rago* concludes with the title character's tragic death at the hands of her abusive parents. With reference to Ria's life and death, Heerkens describes the didactic nature of his text: "On reading the manuscript, the objection was raised that the discourse of the bride is something distasteful. Yes, it is, and it wants to be in this book, which depicts abuses as well as the possible, because this novel is not written for pleasure, but for learning."[74] Music is clearly, and not at all surprisingly, among the primary themes of *Ria Rago* and *Ola Wolo*.

Father Simon Buis: The SVD Goes to Hollywood

While Father Heerkens focuses on music more than his other SVD-scholar colleagues, he was not the only SVD priest to utilize popular media to promulgate knowledge and ideas about Florenese culture (including music) and the mission in Flores. Father Simon Buis (1892–1960) is the most prominent such example. He worked in Flores as an SVD missionary and educator beginning in 1919 (he was not yet an ordained priest). He returned home to the Netherlands in 1924 and shortly thereafter came across several reels of unedited film footage from German videographer Willey Rach's 1923–24 voyage to visit the SVD mission in Flores. Buis edited the footage and added some additional scenes, in which he plays a recurring role as SVD missionary, to create the widely popular narrative documentary *Flores Film* (1924). Based on the same footage, Buis also created the more strictly documentary style film *Bali-Floti* (1925). The films, and especially *Flores Film*, were commercially successful and critically acclaimed.[75] Both also contain many extended scenes of music and dance in Flores, and given the scarcity of film footage from Flores during this period, make such images unique in the visual history of music in Flores.

In 1928, Buis secured approval from his SVD superiors in the Netherlands to travel to the United States, where he completed his studies and training at the SVD seminary in Techny, Illinois. While in the United States, Buis and his fellow SVD filmmaker, Beltjens, also took courses in filmmaking in New York City at the Institute of Photography. In 1929, they traveled cross-country to California, where they spent time at studio sets in Hollywood to learn cutting-edge film and lighting techniques before boarding a passenger ship out of San Francisco to begin their long journey to Flores, where they planned to film their three new feature-length films: *Ria Rago* (1930), *Amor Ira* (1932), and *Anak Woda* (1932). Heerkens's novel, published eight years after the release of the Buis film of the same title, describes a similar, though not identical, plot to the one outlined in the earlier Buis film. This point leaves one to question whether Heerkens mirrored the story and copied the title in the hope of gaining from the success of Buis's earlier, well-known movie.

The priests filmed throughout much of 1930, and their stay overlapped with that of Kunst's seven-week trek across Flores. We already know from the letter cited above that Kunst encountered Buis, at least by reputation. He was clearly surprised by the missionary's lofty training, even mentioning it in the foreword to *Music in Flores*: "there were two film operators, both trained in Hollywood, among the missionaries!"[76] Kunst's connection to Buis extends beyond whatever brief encounter they had in Flores, as the ethnomusicologist is listed as the official music advisor for *Ria Rago* in an official typeset script preserved at the Heritage Center archive in Sint Agatha, the Netherlands.[77] Interestingly, Kunst's name does not appear in the film credits, and as such, his involvement with "THE great mission film of the 1930s" has been largely forgotten.[78] The point is made more acute since the music arranged and composed for *Ria Rago* and *Amorira* is now lost. Three written accounts confirm Kunst's involvement in the musical accompaniment to *Ria Rago*; the account of Dutch archivist Ine van Dooren is the most comprehensive, not only discussing Buis and Kunst's involvement, but also mentioning Buis's own musical talents:[79]

> Father Buis knew the impact that the right choice of music can have on presenting a film. He provided accompaniment for violin and piano and thus managed to touch the hearts of many.[80] With the film RIA RAGO, his interest in sound had another purpose. The songs and music of the Ndona tribes were so intrinsically linked to the ancient Indian culture that the recording of the voices and instruments served an ethnological purpose. While the images are dominated by a "Western Catholic perspective," the native music provides an "Eastern commentary," as it were. Buis received advice from the anthropologist Dr. Jaap Kunst, who was just on the island to research the music of the Florenese. The recordings, recorded on wax rolls, were later transferred to gramophone records in Berlin. These melodies were edited into a special composition [by the German composer Frits Pohl] for the film and so sound was added to the footage.[81]

Church historian Eddy Apples reports that Beltjen was tasked with delivering the above wax rolls to the Berlin phonograph archive. Furthermore, he notes that the Orchestra of the German Opera recorded Pohl's composition but that there are no known surviving copies of the recording or the orchestral scores.[82] The only surviving component of the original *Ria Rago* music appears to be the recordings collected by Kunst and his SVD collaborators in Flores. At present, we can only hope that in the future more information might come to light regarding the use of the 1930 Flores recordings in Pohl's composition for *Ria Rago*. What is clear, however, is that Kunst had significant involvement in the development of the film's musical soundtrack and that he was not hesitant to involve himself with highly public aspects of the SVD's missiological interests.

CONCLUSION

A common conceptualization of ethnomusicological history begins with the likes of comparative musicologists like Adler, Hornbostel, Sachs, Ellis, and Schneider, each firmly rooted in the scholarly traditions and institutions of Western academia. Armchair scholarship was a very acceptable research method at the time and it was common for ethnologists in Europe, like the above-mentioned, to employ missionaries in their service as data collectors to support their intellectual enter-prises in Europe. Some of these missionaries were ethnographers and scholars in their own right who were known within their respective fields, including com-parative musicology. In short, there was no neat division of labor between musi-cologists and missionaries, as many more contemporary accounts of this history often reflect. The twin volumes *Music in Flores* and *Lieder der Florinesen* reflect the interface that the fields of comparative musicology and missiology once shared.[83]

Heerkens made important observations about the state of musicological field methods and spoke of the potential pitfalls of phonographic technology. In par-ticular, Heerkens's criticism of recording technology and his commitment to phonograph-free field research made him an outlier and in ways a pioneer in ethnomusicological research. His concern for the natural integrity of "living" musi-cal events within the rhythms of local life would surely find greater acceptance in today's ethnomusicology methods seminar than it did among many of the leading comparative musicologists of the early twentieth century, who were most concerned with the type of "objective" data that the phonograph could provide. Heerkens, on the other hand, sought to recognize the variability of Florenese music and felt that the phonograph would distort such dynamism. Together with Father Simon Buis, Heerkens also helped popularize Florenese music in the Netherlands, especially among Catholics, through propagandist films and books, which often included music-related themes and content.

NOTES

1. Jaap Kunst, *Music in Flores: A Study of the Vocal and Instrumental Music among the Tribes Living in Flores*, (Leiden: Brill, 1942).

2. Jaap Kunst, "Ola Wolo, de Buine Slaaf. Roman uit de Timor-Archipel, Door P. Heerkens" (University of Amsterdam, Jaap Kunst Collection, 1938), 1.

3. Kunst, *Music in Flore*, ix.

4. The full title of Lieder: *Lieder der Florinesen: sammlung 140 Florinesischer lieder und 162 texte mit übersetzung aus dem sprachebiete der Lionesen, Sikanesen, Ngada's und Manggaraier* [Songs of the

Florenese: A collection of 140 Florenese songs and 162 texts with translation from the language areas of the Lionese, Sikanese, Ngada's and Manggarai].

5. The SVD fathers stationed in Flores felt compelled to compete with the island's existing Muslim population for the souls of those who did not belong to either religion. Such peoples—whom SVD missionaries commonly referred to as "pagans"—typically lived in Flores's highland regions, away from the more regionally connected villages and cities along the coast.

6. John Bellarmine Vallier, "Ethnomusicology as Tool for the Christian Missionary," *European Meetings in Ethnomusicology* 10 (2003): 85–97. Brian Schrag and Neil R. Coulter, "Response to 'Ethnomusicology as Tool for the Christian Missionary,'" *European Meetings in Ethnomusicology* 10 (2003): 98–108; Brian Fairley, "Vessels of Song: Ethnodoxy and the Enduring Legacy of Missionary Work," *SEM Student News* 14, no. 2 (2018): 37–40. Accounts of missionary contributions to these disciplines from this period are commonly dismissive, as, for example, "haphazard" (Ernst Heins, "The Netherlands," in *Ethnomusicology: Historical and Regional Studies*, ed. Helen Myers [New York: W. W. Norton], 101–10, at 102) and "unreliable" (Mervyn McLean, "Oceania," in *Ethnomusicology: Historical and Regional Studies*, ed. Helen Myers [New York: W. W. Norton 1993], 392-400).

7. See the history page of the Divine Word Missions website, www.svdvocations.org/about-divine-word/history.

8. An Vandenberghe, "Entre Mission et Science: La Recherche Ethnologique du Pére Wilhelm Schmidt SVD et Le Vatican (1900–1939)," *Missions et Sciences Sociales* 19 (December, 2006): 15–36. SVD historian Ernest Brandewie notes Janssen's vision for higher education within the SVD order: "[Janssen] envisioned a cadre of well-educated priests within the Society dedicated to the study of science. . . . [He] remained firm on this and always supported higher studies for those who had the ability and interest" (Ernest Brandewie, *In the Light of the Word: Divine Word Missionaries of North America* [Maryknoll, NY: Orbis, 2000], 131).

9. With Janssen's encouragement, Father Wilhelm Schmidt earned a PhD at the University of Berlin in 1895. Schmidt never travelled to Asia but nonetheless became a pioneer of linguistic anthropology of East and Southeast Asia. He relied primarily on his contacts to foreign missions and missionaries in these regions for much of the primary source material used in his hundreds of academic publications.

10. Brandewie, *In the Light of the World*, 149.

11. Jan Sihar Aritonang and Karel Steenbrink, *A History of Christianity in Indonesia* (Leiden: Brill, 2008), 141.

12. Aritonang and Steenbrink, *A History of Christianity in Indonesia*, 244.

13. Verheyen continues:

Not as if ethnology were already able to give a sufficient and satisfactory explanation of many facts and phenomena, but in addition to the knowledge of the facts, that is, the knowledge of what people think and do on all possible occasions, it is for a fruitful education, in my view, we still need to know or feel to some extent where the solution should be sought. We gain this insight through ethnology. Do not expect any systematic analysis or great synthesis from me. I only intend to show in a few articles, on the basis of some worked examples, what practical use we can have in the care of the soul of our acquired adat ["customary"] knowledge (P. Verheyen, SVD periodical *Pastoralia* (1938), 118. N.B. Published as "P. Verheyen").

It is likely the "P." stands for *Pater*—Dutch for "Father"—and that Jilis penned this short article, which also overlaps with his known period of residence in Flores beginning in 1935 (Marie-Antoine Willemsem, "In Memoriam Jilis A. J. Verheijen, SVD: A Collector's Life," *Bijdragen tot de Taal-, Land- en Volkenkunde* 154, no. 1 (1998): 1–12, at 3).

14. A minor seminary is a secondary school for young boys interested in perusing vocations within the Catholic Church, especially the priesthood. Following graduation, those still committed to a priestly life were encouraged to attend a major seminary to obtain the requisite tertiary credentials.

Rolf Janssen, *We hebben gezongen en niks gehad: Muzikanten en liederen uit Midden Brabant* (Tilburg: Boekhandel Gianotten B.V., 1984), www.cubra.nl/pietheerkens/pietheerkensleoheerkens.htm.

15. In January 1944, Heerkens underwent major surgery for a chronic stomach illness. He died shortly thereafter on January 28, 1944.

16. Janssen, *We hebben gezongen en niks gehad.*

17. "Pater P. Heerkens, SVD Overleden: Een Fijnbesnaard Dichter van Het Tilburgsche Dialect," January 29, 1944, *Nieuwe Tilburgsche Courant,* www.cubra.nl/pietheerkens/pietheerkensinmemo riam1944.htm.

18. Kunst, preface to *Lieder der Florinesen.*

19. Kunst, *Music in Flores,* ix.

20. In addition to his Flores research materials, Kunst also collected similar "samples" in other research he conducted during the years he lived in the Dutch East Indies (1919–36). All these materials are held in the archival collections of the University of Amsterdam. They are also among the featured materials of the "Decolonizing South East Asia Sound Archives" project, a multi-institution consortium focused on the digital preservation and dissemination of rare and previously inaccessible sources. The project is led by the musicologist Professor Barbara Titus, University of Amsterdam.

21. Kunst, *Music in Flores,* ix.

22. Eric M. von Hornbostel and Curt Sachs, "Systematik Der Musikinstrumente. Ein Versuch," *Zeitschrift für Ethnologie* 46, no. 4/5 (1914): 553–90.

23. Kunst, *Music in Flores,* 111.

24. Philip Yampolsky, comp., "Vocal and Instrumental Music from East and Central Flores," *Vocal and Instrumental Music from East and Central Flores.* Music of Indonesia Series, no. 8, CD, Smithsonian Folkways Recordings, SF40424, Washington, DC, 1995. Like Kunst before him, Yampolsky speaks of SVD hospitality: "We are very grateful also to P. Leo Kleden, SVD and P. Daniel Kiti, SVD, of the Sekolah Tinggi Filsafat Katolik [Catholic college of philosophy] in Ledalero, who helped us to find our feet in Flores" (23).

25. Piet Heerkens, personal communication with "High Rev. Father Provincial," "Hoog Eerw. Pater Provinciaal," May 28, 1943, Erfgoedcentrum Nederlands Kloosterleven, 138.

26. Pels, "Anthropology and Mission," 81–83.

27. Pels, "Anthropology and Mission," 83.

28. Jean Michaud, *"Incidental" Ethnographers: French Catholic Missions on the Tonkin-Yunnan Frontier, 1880–1930* (Leiden: Brill, 2007), 7.

29. Suzel Ana Reily and Jonathan Dueck, eds., *The Oxford Handbook of Music and World Christianities* (Oxford: Oxford University Press, 2016), 3.

30. Philip V. Bohlman, "Representation and Cultural Critique in the History of Ethnomusicology," in *Comparative Musicology and Anthropology of Music: Essays on the History of Ethnomusicology* (Chicago: University of Chicago Press, 1991), 131–51. See especially Anna Maria Busse Berger, *The Search for Medieval Music in Africa and Germany, 1891–1961: Scholars, Singers, Missionaries,* New Material Histories of Music (Chicago: University of Chicago Press, 2020). Busse Berger notes that during the early twentieth-century, prominent scholars like Erich von Hornbostel and Marius Schneider "were aware of the fact that missionaries were doing important ethnographic and linguistic work in Africa" (123). Such missionary ethnographers include the German Moravians Traugott Bauchmann (1865–1948) and Franz Gerdinand Rietzsch (1902–?); the latter studied comparative musicology with the phonetician Wilhelm Heinitz (144).

31. Pels, "Anthropology and Mission," 92.

32. Bohlman, "Representation and Cultural Critique,"132.

33. Recent efforts include Fairley, "Vessels of Song"; and Timothy J. Cooley and Gregory Barz, eds., *Shadows in the Field: New Perspectives for Fieldwork in Ethnomusicology,* 2nd ed. (New York: Oxford University Press, 2008), 5.

34. Roger Vetter, "Reviewed Work: Indonesian Music, and Dance—Traditional Music and Its Interaction with the West: A Compilation of Articles (1934–1952)," *Asian Music* 29, no. 1 (1997): 125–28, at 127.

35. Kunst, *De Inheemsche muziek en de zending*, 62.

36. Kunst, *Music in Flores* (Leiden: Brill, 1939).

37. Sarah Weiss, "Review of: Indonesian Music and Dance—Traditional Music and Its Interaction with the West—A Compilation of Articles (1935–1952), by Jaap Kunst," *Yearbook for Traditional Music* 31 (1999): 130-31, at 131.

38. Dana Rappoport, "The Long Journey of the Rice Maiden from Li'o to Tanjung Bunga: A Lamaholot Sung Narrative (Flores, Eastern Indonesia)," in *Austronesian Paths and Journeys*, ed. James J. Fox (Canberra: ANU Press, 2021), 161–92, at 131.

39. Yampolsky, "Vocal and Instrumental Music from East and Central Flores," 12.

40. Kunst ca. 1938, *Ola Wolo* review, unpublished.

41. P. Heerkens, "Boekbespreking: J. Kunst, Music in Flores. Leiden 1942," *Cultureel Indië* 5 (1943): 138–41, at 138, personal communication with "High Rev. Father Provincial."

42. Heerkens (May 28, 1943), personal communication with "High Rev. Father Provincial."

43. Kunst 1945—preface to *Lieder*. Here Kunst references the *Völkerpsychologie* tradition that emerged in Germany in the mid-nineteenth century (Busse Berger, *The Search for Medieval Music in Africa and Germany*, 23).

44. Chapter 7 is simply titled "Miscellaneous," which, unlike the other titles, does not describe any particular aspect of the "native psyche" under consideration.

45. Heerkens, *Lieder der Florinesen*, 97.

46. Heerkens, *Lieder der Florinesen*, 99.

47. Hans Pols, "Psychological Knowledge in a Colonial Context: Theories on the Nature of the 'Native Mind' in the Former Dutch East Indies," *History of Psychology* 10, no. 2 (2007): 111–31.

48. Joost Coté, "Thomas Karsten's Indonesia: Modernity and the End of Europe, 1914-1945," *Bijdragen Tot de Taal-, En Volkenkunde* 170 (2014): 66–98, at 85.

49. Coté, "Thomas Karsten's Indonesia," 85, 66–98.

50. Guido Adler, "Umfang, Methode und Ziel der Musikwissenschaft," *Vierteljahresschrift für Musikwissenschaft* 1 (1885): 5–20.

51. Yampolsky, "Vocal and Instrumental Music from East and Central Flores."

52. Heerkens, *Lieder der Florinesen*, 2, 28, 4.

53. Heerkens, *Lieder der Florinesen*, 2.

54. Heerkens, *Lieder der Florinesen*, 88.

55. Elsewhere, Heerkens describes such musical dynamism further: "The Florenese are true natural singers who sing like the birds in the trees, always varying, and at the same time proving that the song in the country is very much a living song; different in different places, never uniform . . . [and] the same song, written a few years later or earlier, also varies from the same singer, both in text and in melody" (*Lieder der Florinesen*, 138).

56. Heerkens, *Lieder der Florinesen*, 48.

57. Heerkens speaks of the Sikanese effort to reestablish lost hymn traditions as a result of his protracted efforts to write down the texts and tunes: "As I began to write down these hymns, old hymns still surfaced from the recesses of older memories, hymns that had long since ceased to be sung, and the Sikanese took the opportunity to completely restore the old precession to theirs under my direction, to revive its original form" (*Lieder der Florinesen*, 186).

58. Petrus Ré (*Lieder der Florinesen*, 72), Alexander Kesu (*Lieder der Florinesen*, 10), Petrus Tonda (*Lieder der Florinesen*, 92), and A. Oka (*Lieder der Florinesen*, 47).

59. Kunst, *Music in Flores*, ix.

60. Heerkens, *Lieder der Florinesen*, 138.

61. Kunst, letter to Leven, November 7, 1930. In 1934, the SVD fathers in Ndona-Endeh write to Kunst, mentioning their ongoing appreciation for his scholarship: "With one of the last postal

shipments we received your gifted copy of *Oude westersche liederen uit oostersche landen*, collected and edited by you. We have read it with great interest and have no doubt that His High Excellency Monsignor H. Leven, to whom you sent the copy, will read it with the same interest" (Kunst, letter to Leven, March 19, 1934).

62. Kunst, *Music in Flores*, ix.

63. Heerkens, *Lieder der Florinesen*, 138.

64. In an unpublished review of Heerkens's novel *Ola Wolo*, Kunst speaks of his encounter with Ehlert in 1930: "As a musicologist, of course, I first came into contact with the Fathers, who, because of their talent, were more occupied with music than the others.... Thus I will never forget how one morning old Father Ehlert and I sang Gregorian chant, and those evenings we performed a kaleidoscope of compositions for seraphine and violin for a breathlessly listening school population" (Kunst, *Ola Wolo* unpublished review, c. 1938, 1–2).

65. Kunst, letter to Ehlert, 1931.

66. Edward T. Hall, *The Dance of Life: The Other Dimension of Time* (New York: Anchor, 1984).

67. Gerald Florian Messner, "Jaap Kunst Revisited; Multipart Singing in Three East Florenese Villages Fifty Years Later: A Preliminary Investigation," *The World of Music* 31, no. 2 (1989): 12.

68. Heerkens, letter to Kunst, March 8, 1938.

69. Heerkens describes his approach to historical fiction: "This novel [*Ria Rago*] is written according to historical data, like my other Indies novel, *Ola Wolo*. Is Ria Rago still alive? A novel is not history, nor a historical novel a history book! I paint situations, figures, and events. A painter is not a photographer, he is a painter! That is why it does not matter whether Ria Rago is still alive, because there are many Ria Rago's on the beautiful islands of the Timor archipelago" (Heerkens *Ria Rago*, 200).

70. Heerkens describes his disappointment that the songs were printed in cipher and not on the Western staff, as Heerkens presumably wanted: "This month my first novel will be released: 'Ola Wolo: the brown slave.' There are even Lio songs in it!!! Too bad the melodies had to be given in ciphers!" (Heerkens, letter to Kunst, January 13, 1938).

71. Kunst, unpublished 1938 *Ola Wolo* review.

72. Heerkens, *Ria Rago*, 28, 30.

73. Heerkens, *Ria Rago*, 81–86, 107, 174–76. In one of these accounts, Heerkens describes Ria in an ecstatic state, inspired by the sounds of music in the village: "The gongs and drums called out a very old, peculiarly rhythmic melody. . . . She worked herself into the melody. This soon brought her to ecstasy as she danced, expressing her joy in a way that was entirely her own" (Heerkens, *Ria Rago*, 83–84).

74. Heerkens, *Ria Rago*, 200.

75. Many Dutch serials printed positive reviews of *Flores Film* and *Bali Flotti*. The accompanying printed program to *Flores Film* shows several, including a review from the periodical *Tijd* (Time): "Rarely have we seen a film that showed mission work in all its wonderful versatility in such a clear, captivating and often touching way." The *Maasbode* (Messanger) also speaks glowingly of the film: "A rare film. A work of art of great ethnological value and immediately deeply moving content. This magnificent mission film is the most beautiful and richest ever made" (SVD 1925:18).

76. Kunst, *Music in Flores*, ix.

77. Simon P. Buis and Piet L. Beltjens, "Ria Rago," film script, Erfgoedcentrum Nederlands Kloosterleven (1930).

78. "The film [*Ria Rago*] became a huge success [and] even became THE great mission film of the 1930s." Eddy Apples, "Missie Naar Flores: Pater Simon Buis SVD En Zijn Flores-Films, 1925–1934," *Audiovisuel Archief, Jaarboek* (1996), 7–31, at 23.

79. Henk de Beer, "Kort historisch overzicht van de film-activiteit, unpublished document, Erfgoedcentrum Nederlands Kloosterleven (1992); Ine van Dooren, "De Missiefilm Ria Rago: Een Gedramatiseerd Document," *GBG Nieuws* 33 (summer 1995): 8–16. Apples, "Missie Naar Flores."

80. A typed screenplay of Buis's film *Amorira* includes extensive handwritten musical parts/ideas/ motifs. There is no indication who wrote these materials down but, given de Beer's account of the missionary-priest's musical prowess, it is reasonable to think the hand may be Buis's own (Buis n.d. [ca. 1930]). Further work should be done to identify a more complete picture of the musical content of this document, which is held in the archival collections of the Erfgoedcentrum Nederlands Kloosterleven (Sint Agatha).

81. van Dooren, "De Missiefilm Ria Rago," 14.

82. Apples, "Missie Naar Flores," 18.

83. Kunst, *Music in Flores*; Heerkens, *Lieder der Florinesen*.

10

Jaap Kunst and the German Missionaries in Nias

Anna Maria Busse Berger

Jaap Kunst's strong criticism of the behavior of German Protestant missionaries during his 1930 visit to Nias is legendary, reprinted many times, most prominently in the *Garland Library of Readings in Ethnomusicology*:

> The entire population has been converted to the Christian religion and the missionaries of the [Rheinische Mission] had seen fit to make the exclusion of the Holy Communion the penalty for singing old songs and dancing the ancient dances. [He continues in a footnote:] It furthermore appeared that walking and bicycling on Sunday were forbidden and they were seriously considering the advantage of forbidding playing football on that day as well. . . . In turning against the old native art, the Rhineland Mission has strayed far indeed from the standpoint, once adopted by the missionary Fries and laid down in his treatise "Niassische Gesänge."[1]

There are a number of reasons why it makes sense to investigate whether Kunst's account of missionary activities is correct. First, he seems to believe that they started to introduce these rules only after one of their missionaries, Eduard Fries, whom he obviously admired, left the island in 1920.[2] Second, he never raised similar concerns about Rheinische missionaries in numerous other Indonesian Islands, for example in Mentawai and Sumatra. After all, these other missionaries came from the same background, had the same education, and were guided by the same mission directors. And third, there is a fascinating correspondence with one of the Nias missionaries, Friedrich Dörmann, whom he met in 1930, that shows clearly that they collaborated in ethnomusicological research and became friends.[3] In short, there is ample reason to look into the activities of the Nias missionaries. We want to know first, what kind of music they introduced into the service, and second, if they were interested in music that was not associated with the service and if they did indeed forbid the performance of other music.

195

Missionary activities in Nias began in 1865, and the first generation of missionaries were all under the influence of Gustav Warneck (1834–1910), who founded the field of missiology as well as the first missionary journal, *Allgemeine Missionszeitung*.[4] He served from 1871 to 1874 as a theology teacher at the Rheinische Mission. Under his guidance, the ideas of Johann Gottfried Herder became the most important guide for missionary activities. Missionaries were taught to preserve as much as possible of local traditions when converting the Indigenous population. But we should not for a moment assume that they would have preserved and transferred whatever they found when introducing Christianity. On the one hand, there is no doubt that missionaries did remarkable work with local languages and ethnography. The linguist Wilhelm von Humboldt, for example, was in close contact with missionaries from all over the world who made grammars for him; he would not have been able to do his linguistic studies without their help.[5] Generally, missionaries would first make a grammar, then translate the Bible and try to find local metaphors. Then they would record local myths and epics, describe rituals in fascinating detail; some would even try to transform them into Christian rituals. They would collect local art and make drawings. But on the other hand, when it came to music, it didn't even occur to them until the 1920s to adapt local music for the Christian service.[6] Even for the most progressive missionaries, the Christian service was invariably connected with Western hymns until at least the 1930s. But we have to remember that this does not necessarily mean that they would not try to describe local music, often with admiration.

When the first missionary Ernst Ludwig Denninger (1815–76) arrived in Nias in 1865, he had already worked several years earlier on the translation of the New Testament into the Nias language while living in Padang among more than three thousand people from Nias.[7] Similarly, Heinrich Lagemann (1851–1933) is responsible for the 1920 hymnbook and an important 1909 article titled "Ein Heldensang der Niasser. Gesang der Gäste beim Feste eines Häuptlings, als er sich den Titel, 'Balugu' beilegte" (A heroic song of the Niasser: Song of the guests at the feast of a chieftain, when he attached the title 'Balugu' to himself).[8] The article gives the original text with a German translation and explains in detail how it was recited. It is written with great respect for the local ritual.

These missionaries were followed by the much-admired Eduard Fries (1877–1923), who was without a doubt a special case.[9] His upbringing might provide a clue as to why he was so receptive to art and ethnography in Nias. He grew up in the August Hermann Francke Foundation in Halle, which housed the oldest ethnographic showcase in Germany, a place that Fries frequented during his youth. He did important linguistic studies, explored the entire island, and documented what he found with aquarelles and drawings. In particular, Fries provided fascinating accounts of the headhunting rituals.[10] Last but not least, he assembled a small ethnographic collection that he brought with him to Germany. The collection was the focus of an important recent exhibition in 2006 in the Dresden and Herrnhut

Museum of Anthropology in Germany.[11] Many of the items he brought back from Nias are extremely rare. More about this later.

As I mentioned earlier, it did not occur to any missionary to use local music in the service. They translated and adapted German, Dutch, and English hymns and folk songs into the local languages, trying hard to find images that the local population would understand. The first Nias hymnbook is from 1898, followed by others from 1905, 1920, 1923, and 1931.[12]

The translation of European hymns was to be expected in the early years. But things changed in the 1920s, and in my opinion here lies one possible reason for Kunst's criticism of the Nias missionaries. In 1926, the African comparative musicologist Nicholas Ballanta gave a talk in LeZoute at the International Missionary Conference, a meeting certainly attended by the Rheinische Mission directors, strongly advising missionaries to introduce local music into the service.[13] Two years later, Erich Moritz von Hornbostel published his important article on African music, encouraging missionaries to use local music in the service.[14] Both events cannot have passed unnoticed. And Kunst was certainly aware of Hornbostel's article and argued similarly in later publications.[15]

From the late 1920s on, several German mission societies tried to introduce local music into the service. Not so the leaders of the Rheinische Mission (and I think we have to distinguish them from the missionaries in Nias). Kunst came in 1930 to Nias, and his trip coincided with fundamental changes in the administration of the Rheinische Mission. When mission inspector Eberhard Delius (1903–45) joined the top administration of the Rheinische Mission in Wuppertal in 1930, local music was no longer admired. Delius was a well-educated theologian with a particular interest in music (he wrote his dissertation on the Psalms). He was hired as a teacher at the seminary of the Rheinische Mission from 1930 on and took over responsibility for all publications of the mission in 1935.[16] Remarkable is that Delius was never active as a missionary himself. On the one hand, he showed great courage in opposing the Nazi government and was a vocal member of the Confessing Church, the Lutheran Church group that did not support Hitler, this despite the fact that in the early 1930s, many at the Rheinische Mission were members of the Nazi paramilitary group Sturmabteilung. On the other hand, he wrote a number of articles in the late 1930s about local music in Nias, Sumatra, and Mentawai that show a complete lack of understanding for non-Western music. I believe that Kunst must have read these articles and that they greatly contributed to Kunst's statements about local missionaries in Nias.

In 1939, mission inspector Eberhard Delius wrote the following about church music in Sumatra to the Heidelberg theology professor Gerhard Rosenkranz: "In our hymnal there is not a single hymn composed by a Batak. . . . Our Batak Christians are not yet ready to compose useful songs. I have read many songs by natives. . . . They are still too crude. As a rule, they contain only general phrases with the thought process: God is great, may he bless us."[17] A survey of hymns sung in the German Lutheran church leaves little doubt that Delius seems to have an exaggerated opinion of many texts, which also often simply praise the Lord.

In a 1939 article, he similarly writes, "Batak music is not useful for the native church. Artistically it has no or only moderate value, it is too monotonous. Our Batak also feel this, especially the educated ones."[18] He even goes so far as to say that the Rheinische missionaries taught the local population to learn how to sing. A service will easily include four hundred to six hundred singers. He asks why the Christians in these islands love to sing so much. His answer is obvious: because the Germans taught them so well, they have finally introduced them to proper music, and they turn out to be very musical. He concludes that he has never heard such pure singing as he heard here.

Delius's most important article on church music appeared in 1939 in the flagship journal of Rheinische Mission, *Berichte der Rheinischen Missionsgesellschaft*. He repeatedly stresses that in all areas where the Rheinische Mission was active, that is, Indonesia, present-day Namibia, China, and Papua New Guinea, there is no music worth preserving. He writes about music in present-day Namibia, "In Southwest Africa it is said: 'One cannot really speak of a music of one's own among our people, if one does not want to call the monotonous hooting, with which certain deeds of their great ones are sung, singing or music. The Christians gladly accept the new ways of singing, whereby it is to be noted that the easily movable English melodies often find more approval than the carried German chorale melody.'"[19] The next statement about Nias and Sumatra shows clearly how defensive he is toward scholars and missionaries who try to introduce local music in Indonesia:

> From Nias and Sumatra it is similarly written: "Since there is no native church music on Nias yet, there is little sense and value in discussing the question of the usefulness of native music in the service of gospel preaching. That must be left to development." Our care belongs to the church music that is most popular among our people today, and that is European music. The people of Nias will never be grateful to us if we take away from them the treasures they have received through our German music. Therefore, there are no indigenous melodies in the hymnal at all.[20]

The hymns were obviously used as a missionary tool. Missionary Johannes Warneck wrote in an article titled "The Gift of German Christianity to All Nations" from 1936:

> Alongside the oral invitation and instruction, everywhere in the mission comes the song, the sung word, which exults joy and thanksgiving for salvation, which sings the great deeds and gifts of God into the hearts, and brings the preached word close to the hearts. Paganism and Islam do not know singing in their services. They may have recited formulas that are recited in a monotonous manner by the priests. But this is not singing that lifts up the hearts. The celebrating crowd does not sing. The mission has a strong ally in the song. The song and its melody take hold of the listeners and imprint the heard word on the hearts. Of the power of song, mission history has much to say.[21]

The local population in Nias, Sumatra, and Mentawai took to German hymns with a vengeance. When a church in Dahana in Nias was consecrated on November 6, 1921, a missionary wrote:

> All the nearby congregations were well represented. There was almost a small singing competition, since all the individual choirs had rehearsed several songs and now also tried to perform them as well as they could. The celebration itself lasted four hours, and if I had not shortened it by force, it would have been at least five. The people would have liked it if it had lasted through the evening. One is always amazed at the perseverance of the people, both in rehearsing and in performing the songs. They do not get tired. It is no longer true what used to be said that the Niassians could not sing and did not want to sing; today, at least, I would say the opposite. People like to sing, and many choirs can be heard. When a festival is coming up, their perseverance in rehearsing knows no bounds. Often they start right after church at noon and finish in the evening without a break.[22]

Most of these statements were published in journals that Kunst could have easily accessed before he wrote his book. It is no wonder that he might not have approved of them. But the singing of hymns is not enough to explain Kunst's criticism. Hymns were sung all over Indonesia, and he does not criticize missionary activities elsewhere.

This brings me to the second point, his claim that local music was prohibited by the missionaries. It is clear that nineteenth- and early twentieth-century missionaries were highly critical of wooden and stone figures because they were associated with ancestor worship. A missionary writes in 1901, "We started with chants, recitation of the Ten Commandments and prayers. With hatchets and knives, bigger and smaller idols were chopped off. Then I threw the first idol down the deep slope in front of the house with the words: 'The Lord is God and not the idols.' And then others followed, numberless, more than thousand pieces followed."[23]

Missionary Heinrich Sundermann would perform baptisms in front of wooden sculptures that would then be burned. Similarly, missionary Johannes Bieger personally felled a sacred tree in Central Nias associated with the origin of the Nias people in the early years of the twentieth century. He was convinced that this action would get rid of superstitions and fear of spirits.[24]

Eduard Fries, so much admired by Kunst, was both full of admiration for local art and music and of the belief, as a deeply religious person, that destruction or removal of wooden figures was necessary for Christianity to take over. But because he also understood their value and had a passionate interest in ethnography, he tried to take as many as possible with him to Germany. He left in 1920 to become director of Rheinische Mission only to die shortly thereafter from blood poisoning. He was much admired in Germany and Nias throughout the 1920s and 30s. As far as I can determine, the missionaries who followed him shared his views.

The question now is, What did these missionaries whom Kunst encountered in 1930 think of local music? I found a letter by missionary Friedrich Möller written in the 1930s describing in enthusiastic prose the music in a wedding ceremony in Nias: he loves the big orchestra with the large drums and gongs that played throughout the night. According to Möller, some Westerners might think this is exhausting, but Möller writes that "these people have fortunately not been touched by civilization," even though they are Christian.[25]

Some missionaries were cautiously trying to adapt earlier customs to Christian ones and admired local music. However, whenever this topic comes up, the missionaries refer to local evangelists called panditas, who would never allow any use of local music. Nias missionary Friedrich Dörmann (1901–83), a close friend and collaborator of Kunst's, certainly did not object to local music. It is clear from their correspondence, which begins on February 14, 1930, that Kunst could not have done his research without Dörmann.[26] Dörmann translated all the texts, which Kunst then sent to Hornbostel.[27] He gave him information on the photographs. And Kunst constantly mentions the good times they had together. In fact, Dörmann tried to convince the mission administrators to buy a phonograph so that he could record their music. Kunst told him which one to buy and how much it would cost.[28] Then Kunst asked Dörmann to find *adzus*, also called *adu* (carved figures representing ancestors) for Kunst, which Dörmann did.[29] Theses *adzus* can vary in size; some are as small as twenty centimeters tall, and some as tall as two meters.[30] There is a collection of them in the Ethnographic Museum of Vereinigte Evangelische Mission in Wuppertal. During Kunst's 1930 visit to Nias, Dörmann brought up in a conversation with the local church elders or evangelists the possibility of using gongs, which were associated with Indigenous musical traditions, to call the congregation to church. Again, we have here a missionary who tried to preserve a local instrument. The *panditas* did not approve:

> We shall never give our consent to put the gongs in the place of our sounding-bell . . . . The sound of the gongs reminded them too much of the paganism; it revived in their hearts the fear of evil spirits, and perhaps in their secret souls they still felt the seductive charm of the, after all, very recent past; and so the idea of having this heathenish, though beautiful, music intruding in their Christian ceremonies, seemed intolerable to them.[31]

This is further evidence that not only did some of the missionaries try to preserve local music; they were also prevented not only by the mission administration in Germany but also by the newly converted panditas.

Read, for example, missionary Johannes Warneck, who explains in 1936 why it is impossible to transfer local music into the service:

> The natives of Africa, Sumatra, and Nias do not want to hear even these old melodies in their worship. They say that their songs are far too immersed in the mood and nature of the old pagan cults to recommend them for the new world of thought. *It is with them as with many an old folk custom that the missionaries would like to see used in building up the life of the congregation; the young Christians, however, warn against*

it, because it is connected with moods and mental processes that unintentionally put the young Christians back into the pagan bondage, thus achieving the opposite of what is intended [emphasis added]. Again and again, missionaries have tried to have native Christians compose songs in their own way and to find a folkloric garment for them. They rarely succeeded.[32]

We can observe here what is common in all recently converted congregations, whether in Africa or Indonesia: the church elders are completely opposed to any performance of tribal music, whether in the service or in general. It reminds them too much of their previous beliefs. But in Nias, the situation was more extreme because of mass conversions. The missionaries referred to these events as *die grosse Reue* (the great penitence). The conversions began in Helefanikha village near Gunungsitoli and then quickly spread throughout the island. Two points are noteworthy about what happened in Nias. First, mass conversions are normally led by missionaries, but in Nias, these mass conversions, which began in 1916, when Fries was still in Nias, and continued through the 1930s, did not originate with the missionaries but with the local evangelists or panditas. And second, these conversions overtook the entire island. To give you an idea of the dimensions of these mass events, in 1916, there were some 18,000 Christians in Nias, and by 1924, there were 580,000, and only about 25,000 "heathens."[33] Usually, the panditas would address crowds in a church built close to an ancestral place of worship and threaten those in attendance with hell and damnation. Then, hundreds would come forward and confess to "murders, whoring, thefts, in addition to idolatry" before they were baptized.[34] Then, the panditas would forbid things like the raising of megaliths and the carving of wooden statues. In addition, the ancestral figures would be destroyed by the newly converted Christians, often with the help of the missionaries. The missionaries faced a dilemma: on the one hand, they wanted the local population to become Christians, and they participated in the destruction of these objects also because they wanted to prove to the Nias people that no harm would come to them when they are burned; on the other hand, they had often learned to appreciate the art that was now being destroyed.[35] The missionaries fully realized the artistic and cultural value of these artifacts, so they encouraged collecting them and bringing them to Europe. In other words, even though the missionaries participated in the destruction of these artifacts, ironically, they are also the ones who conserved them—hence Fries's ethnographic collection and Kunst asking Dörmann for an *adzu* (figure 10-1).[36] And this story also shows that the issue of looted art is quite complex. While conversion to Christianity by the missionaries resulted in the destruction of these artifacts, without these missionaries, there would be little left. It is noteworthy that when the missionaries describe these conversions in their letters, the majority voiced misgivings. And they were also very much aware that often the converts did not remain converted for long.[37]

Let me sum up. Kunst was certainly right in criticizing the Rheinische Mission for their prohibition of local music. But as usual, the picture is more complicated.

FIGURE 10-1. Adzus from Museum Rietberg. *Wikimedia Commons*, https://commons.wikimedia
.org/wiki/File:Nias_Ahnenfiguren_Museum_Rietberg_RIN_403.jpg.

In the first years, missionaries tried to document local ritual and culture, though there was no one with music training. But after the appointment of Eberhard Delius, things changed. He surely must go down in music history as one of the most Eurocentric mission administrators in existence, and this was at a time when much serious research was being undertaken by missionaries of other societies. The local missionaries present a more complex picture, with many showing cautious admiration and respect for local music and dance. And finally, let us not forget the converted local population, who rejected anything that reminded them of their religious past. As a result of the mass conversions, the panditas introduced many rigid rules and a strong hostility toward local music and art. While the missionaries certainly played along, they were not solely responsible for this attitude. It seems likely that they did not dare to contradict the panditas, who wanted to get rid of anything that reminded them of their old beliefs.

AUTHOR'S NOTE

For an overview of earlier discussions of music in Nias, see Thomas M. Manhart's PhD dissertation "A Song for Lowalangi: The Inculturation of Catholic Mission and Nias Traditional Arts with Special Respect to Music" (National University of Singapore, 2004). The dissertation also includes a detailed discussion of inculturation in the Catholic Church in Nias. See also the many important publications by the

Catholic missionary Johannes Hämmerle; a list can be found in Dominik Bonatz, "'Nicht von Gestern': Megalithismus auf Nias/Indonesien," *Antike Welt* 1 (2002): 25–32. See also Johannes Hämmerle, *Nias—Eine eigene Welt. Sagen, Mythen, Überlieferungen*, vol. 43 of *Collectianea Instituti Anthropos* (St. Augustin: Anthropos Institut und Academia Verlag, 1999). For recordings, see Philip Yampolski, "Music of Nias and North Sumatra," booklet accompanying *Music of Nias and North Sumatra*, Smithsonian Folkways Recordings, Music of Indonesia Series no. 4, SF40420, 1992. I am very grateful to Christian Froese and Julia Besten of the Archive of Vereinigte Evangelische Mission in Wuppertal for help and advice during my work at the archive.

NOTES

1. Jaap Kunst, *Music in Nias*, trans. Mrs. Carrière-Lagay (Leiden: Brill, 1939), 2. See also Shelemay, *The Garland Library of Readings in Ethnomusicology: Ethnomusicological Theory and Method* (New York: Garland, 1990), 102.

2. Jaap Kunst, "Indigenous Music and the Christian Mission," lecture presented to the missionary school in Oegstgeest, Netherlands, in 1946.

3. I would like to thank Dustin Wiebe for sharing with me copies of the Kunst-Dörmann correspondence. The correspondence is housed in the Jaap Kunst Collection, University of Amsterdam.

4. Hans Kasdorf, *Gustav Warnecks missiologisches Erbe: Eine biographische-historische Untersuchungen* (Basel: Brunnen, 1990).

5. See Anna Maria Busse Berger, *The Search for Medieval Music in Africa and Germany, 1891–1961: Scholars, Singers, Missionaries* (Chicago: University of Chicago Press, 2020), 20–23.

6. Busse Berger, *The Search for Medieval Music in Africa and Germany*, part 3.

7. Gustav Menzel, *Die Rheinische Mission* (Wuppertal: Verlag der Vereinigten Evangelischen Mission, 1978), 83.

8. H. Lagemann, *Missionar auf Nias. Tijdschrift voor Indische taal-, land- en volkenkunde*, Teil 48 (Koninklijk Bataviaasch Genootschap van Kunsten en Wetenschappen, 1906), 341–407.

9. For a recent excellent evaluation of Fries, see Martin Humburg, Domonik Bonatz, and Claus Veltmann, *Im "Land der Menschen": Der Missionar und Maler Eduard Fries und die Insel Nias* (Bielefeld: Regionalgeschichte Verlag, 2003).

10. On headhunting, see his "Das 'Koppensnellen' auf Nias," *Allgemeine Missionszeitschrift* 35 (1908): 73–88. Fries's papers at the archive of Vereinigte Evangelische Mission, Wuppertal, show a translation of a wedding ritual, a death song, and a parable, all very carefully annotated.

11. See the Herrnhut Ethnological Museum exhibit description at https://voelkerkunde-herrnhut .skd.museum/en/ausstellungen/im-land-der-menschen-eduard-fries-missionar-auf-der-insel-nias/.

12. The 1931 hymnbook was published by the distinguished German publishing house Bertelsmann in Gütersloh, a close supporter of the Rheinische Mission. It was published under the title *Niassa, Soera zinoenö ba Niha Niassisches Gesangbuch*; see also Gerhard Rosenkranz, *Das Lied der Kirche in der Welt* (Berlin: Verlag Haus und Schule, 1951), 49.

13. See my "Nicholas Ballanta," in *The Search for Medieval Music in Africa*, 74–88.

14. Erich M. von Hornbostel, "African Negro Music," *Africa: Journal of the International African Institute* 1 (1928): 30–62.

15. Kunst, "Indigenous Music and the Christian Mission"; see note 2.

16. Menzel, *Die Rheinische Mission*, 328–30.

17. Eberhard Delius, "Singende Kirche auf dem Missionsfeld," *Berichte der Rheinischen Missionsgesellschaft*, 96 (1939): 12. Rosenkranz surveyed all German mission societies to find out how much local music was sung in the mission stations as compared to German hymns.

18. Delius, "Die Batakkirche in der Feuerprobe," Wuppertal, Ms. 1944, p. 2.

19. Delius, "Singende Kirche auf dem Missionsfeld," 13.

20. Delius, "Singende Kirche auf dem Missionsfeld," 13.

21. Johannes Warneck, "Eine Gabe der deutschen Christenheit an die Völker," *Berichte der Rheinischen Missionsgesellschaft* 93 (1936): 215.

22. "Das Jahr 1921 in der Niasmission," *Berichte der Rheinischen Missionsgesellschaft* 79 (1922): 110.

23. Excerpt is from the untitled contribution of O. Rudersdorf in *Berichte der Rheinischen Missionsgesellschaft* 59, no. 5 (1902): 139–40.

24. Mai Lin Tjoa-Bonatz, "Idols and Art: Missionary Attitudes toward Indigenous Worship and Material Culture on Nias, Indonesia, 1904–1920," in *Casting Faiths: Imperialism and the Transformation of Religion in East and Southeast Asia*, ed. Thomas David Dubois (Basingstoke: Palgrave Macmillan, 2009), 105–28, at 112–14.

25. Archive in Wuppertal, Möller, Ble 59, 1907–1982.

26. Thanks to Dustin Wiebe for sending me a copy of Dörmann's correspondence with Kunst. Jaap Kunst Collection, University of Amsterdam, 231. NR 2.

27. Jaap Kunst Collection, 231. NR 3.

28. Jaap Kunst Collection, NR 3.2.

29. Jaap Kunst Collection, NR 6.

30. See, for example, Florina H. Capistrano-Baker, ed., *Art of Island Southeast Asia: The Fred and Rita Richman Collection* (New York: Metropolitan Museum, 1994), 78.

31. Kunst, "*Indigenous Music and the Christian Mission*," 63.

32. Warneck, "Eine Gabe der deutschen Christenheit an die Völker," 216.

33. "Nachwirkungen der Erweckung in Nias," *Berichte der Rheinischen Missionsgesellschaft* 8 (1924): 126.

34. Johannes Noll, "Die falsche Götzen machen zu Spott," *Berichte der Rheinischen Missionsgesellschaft* 85 (1928): 98–99, at 99.

35. Tjoa-Bonatz, "Missionare und Kunst." The stone sculptures were not destroyed; missionaries would add religious symbols and use them as gravestones. Needless to say, the local population did not consider the *adzus* art. There is a vast literature on the subject. For a beginning, see Robert Layton, "Anthropology and Art," *Oxford Art Online*, www.oxfordartonline.com/groveart/display/10.1093/gao/9781884446054.001.0001/oao-9781884446054-e-7000003169?rskey=n6755z&result=4.

36. The Wuppertal Museum auf der Hardt is owned jointly by the churches in Africa, Indonesia, and Germany, and the artifacts are shown in all three continents. www.vemission.org/museum/archive. It is not clear how the missionaries acquired the artifacts. Most likely they were simply discarded by the local population.

37. See "Nachwirkungen der Erweckung in Nias," in *Berichte der Rheinischen Missionsgesellschaft* 8 (1924): 126.

PART V

Technologies of Indoctrination

11

History and Mythology in Javanese Performing Arts

Sumarsam

In one of the scenes of *The Empire Strikes Back* (1980) of the film series Star Wars, Luke Skywalker is learning to use the Force (a state of mind that can do anything telepathically, including move things). One day, Luke crashes his X-Wing fighter jet into a swamp. He tries to lift the starfighter by applying the Force but has a hard time. Discouraged, he tells an ancient Jedi master, Yoda, that he is trying his best:

YODA: No! Try not. Do. Or do not. There is no try.

LUKE: I can't. It's too big.

YODA: Size matters not. Look at me. Judge me by my size, do you? Hm? Mmmm. And well you should not. For my ally is the Force. And a powerful ally it is. Life creates it, makes it grow. Its energy surrounds us and binds us. Luminous beings are we . . . not this crude matter. You must feel the Force around you. Here, between you . . . me . . . the tree . . . the rock . . . everywhere! Yes, even between this land and that ship!

LUKE: You want the impossible.

Then Yoda turns toward the X-Wing fighter. With his eyes closed and his head bowed, he raises his arm and points at the ship. The fighter rises above the water and moves forward as their faithful droid, Artoo-Detoo, beeps in terror and scoots away. The X-Wing moves majestically, surely, toward the shore.

I preface my essay with this excerpt as a response to comments I have often received (explicitly or implicitly) from my American colleagues that I, as an Indonesian ethnomusicologist with distinctive training, have a special status as an arbiter between Javanese and Western ideas.[1] My American colleagues sometimes treat me as if I am a Yoda, brimming with Javanese wisdom. Most often, however, I feel more like Luke—I carry too much baggage to fulfill their expectations— "You want the impossible!" Nevertheless, I will try my best to be the middleman.

My essay focuses on the *canthang balung*, a unique ritual specialist with apparent origins in Buddhist Tantrism who appears throughout Javanese history and often inserts a seemingly dissonant element into the refinement of Javanese court ceremonies.[2] The *canthang balung*, I argue, manifests a sacred-profane paradox, expressed by the Javanese term *manunggaling kawula lan gusti* (a perfect union between the commoner and the lord), a Javanese approach to a perfect democratic ideal. I trace the *canthang balung* in a variety of historical and mythological sources and draw upon my observations as both an insider and an outsider to Javanese culture to illuminate its significance.

Regarding insider and outsider voices, I have come to realize that the issue of emic/etic voices (as the "insider/outsider" distinction is sometimes characterized) is not limited to a Westerner looking at Javanese culture versus a Javanese looking at his own culture.[3] It is important to realize that, even within Javanese society, insider and outsider voices exist. I will expand my discussion of this point later; for now, however, suffice it to say that the subject of this essay is cultural tradition in the Javanese royal court. And the perspective of the members of the royal family, or of individuals who embrace the practice of the court tradition (insiders), often, but not always, contrast with the perspectives of non-royal members of society.

On what did George Lucas base Yoda's cosmological ideas? Apparently, he was familiar with the work of Joseph Campbell, a scholar of mythology/religion. In an interview with TV personality Bill Moyers in 1999, Lucas acknowledged having learned a lot about questions of cosmology from "Joe" (as he calls Campbell).[4] The interview makes it sound as if Lucas personally met Joe before he produced the film. But another source tells us that "George Lucas was an avid admirer of Campbell's writings, and used them as a direct reference in his creation of Star Wars. The two didn't meet face to face until after Lucas had already finished his original trilogy of films."[5]

Beginning with an excerpt from a Star Wars scene is one of my small contributions toward becoming an arbiter between Java and the West. I draw a connection between Yoda's idea of power and Javanese ideas of power in *wayang* performance by following Benedict Anderson's (1965) explication of the concept of power; in the West, Anderson contends, power is abstract, based on relationships, but in Java, power is concrete, emanating from nature, odd things, and art objects.[6] Hence, wayang puppets and gamelan might be a source of power. Many great characters in the wayang stories, such as knights (e.g., Arjuna) or gods (e.g., Kresna, an incarnation of Wisnu), are already doing what Yoda was doing. My larger point is to demonstrate how the creation and performance of myth are infused and inspired by history and that history is infused and inspired by myth.

ECCENTRIC *CANTHANG BALUNG*

Bedhaya and *serimpi* are two of the most refined dances among Javanese court dance genres in the Kasunanan court of Surakarta. The dancers perform graceful and highly stylized movements, with choreographed shifting positions in orderly, well-designed configurations. A *serimpi* dance is accompanied by refined gamelan pieces, with smooth transitions between sections. Yet in the middle part of the performance, the audience will hear a loud, peculiar, stylized vocal interjection—*Ééééé, yooooooook, hayu tå, yå tå*—performed by a pair of male singers. This auditorily conspicuous vocal interjection, almost covering the sound of the whole ensemble, is called *senggakan* or *alok*. When I was a student at the conservatory and academy of gamelan in Surakarta (1962–70), I learned to play pieces for this *serimpi* dance, but I did not learn to sing *senggakan*. So when I first heard these vocalizations while performing, I was surprised. I had no idea of the significance of this intense vocal interjection. In retrospect, I question why neither I nor my friends ever asked our teachers, many of whom were court musicians, about these vocalizations and why they did not explain them to us. Perhaps, due to our belief that the *kraton* were the center of Javanese culture, producing *alus* (refined) cultural performances, we just accepted what we were told.

Two decades later, in the late 1980s, while writing my dissertation that eventually became my first book, the source of these vocalizations—individuals known as *canthang balung* (figure 11-1)—was one of the subjects I encountered while researching performances in the context of Javanese court culture during the colonial period.[7] I examined the *canthang balung*'s roles both in court ritual and outside the court, relying on Stutterheim's 1935 description and secondary sources.[8]

According to Stutterheim, "The task of the canthang balung included guard duty, performing senggak or alok (short vocal interjection) and keplok (clapping) with the gamelan to accompany serimpi dances, and to dance at the garebeg festival when the king departs to inner court."[9] In addition, once a year, they had special duty:

> to play the clown in a procession of the garebeg mulud festival to celebrate the birth of the Prophet Muhammad. In the procession, when the canthang balung arrived at the outer hall of the court (pagelaran), they clown in as funny a way as they could, including imitating dogs mating. This was because if the prime minister laughed at the clowning of the canthang balung, he had to pay them. This was no longer done at the time of the writing of Soewandi's report in the late nineteenth- or early twentieth-century (1938). According to Stutterheim, "this custom was abolished probably for the sake of decency because many European of the Resident's (later the Governor's) retinue were present at the garebeg ceremony."[10]

FIGURE 11-1. *Canthang balung* performing "Vlegen" (Flying), "Gresservanderij" (Clowning), and "Gadjah Ngombe" (Drinking elephant). Adapted from Brandts Buys, "Uit de pers."

Outside the court ritual context, I was surprised to learn that historically, *canthang balung* were employed as the supervisors of the dancer/singer/prostitutes called *talèdhèk*; the *canthang balung*'s duties include issuing identification cards (*serat pikekah*) to be purchased by the *talèdhèk* to show their dancers' legal status. The *canthang balung* would also make sure that *talèdhèk* were always ready whenever court officials demanded that the dancers to perform in a court celebration. For this reason, the *canthang balung* (also called *lurah badhut*) had their own *talèdhèk* living in their houses, which also served as brothels.

The practice of prostitution had negative impacts on society, such as the exploitation of the *talèdhèk* by *canthang balung*, fighting between the clients of their brothels, and the breakup of marriages. Eventually such negative impacts led the abolishment of the authority of the *lurah badhut* over *talèdhèk* and of the court assuming the direct administration of *talèdhèk*.[11] I was surprised to discover that these sexually promiscuous cultural practices were embedded in this aspect of court cultural production. How, I wondered, could it be that this eccentric behavior existed within the courtly, aesthetically deep, refined performing arts, characterized by *adiluhung* (super beauty, the product of high civilization)? How to explain this paradox?

HADIWIDJOJO ON *CANTHANG BALUNG*

In thinking about this question, I searched for literature containing information about *canthang balung*. In so doing, I stumbled upon a speech delivered by Gusti Pangeran Harjo Hadiwidjojo (a son of King Paku Buwana X), who was educated at Leiden University in the Netherlands. In 1953, in his capacity as the head of Radyapustaka Museum, he delivered a lecture that described in depth the peculiarities of *canthang balung* performances at the court of Surakarta and their unusual lifestyle. At first, he was not sure if talking about *canthang balung* and their lascivious work was necessary, since he and his audience lived in a different era and might not be interested in them and their practices. It was at this juncture that his position as a Dutch-educated intellectual took over his intentionality. With the encouragement of his colleagues, he meticulously listed the definitions of *canthang balung* from dictionaries and oral information from both Dutch and Javanese sources. He concluded that *canthang balung* were extraordinary personnel—not clowns, not musicians, not common beings, but rather a sacred phenomenon whose performances were at times tied to a religious procession. He insisted that although they performed clownish dancing, the context of their performance was religiously significant. For example, they performed in conjunction with the Islamic Muludan religious procession. They danced to the sound of the gamelan composition (*gendhing*) "Rambu," an opening piece of the performance of the sacred gamelan Sekatèn. Hadiwidjojo describes the task of *canthang balung* at length:

> Therefore, if I am not mistaken, originally canthang balung was the head of procession whose task was to lead a presentation of the offering to pay homage to our ancestors, forebears, pioneers, etc. In today's context, they [*canthang balung*] are chief religious personnel (kaum or pengulu). In the context of Buddhist era, they were priests, brahmans. Therefore, the pengulu performs ritual in the mosque = [the equivalent of] the temple. [the pengulu do not perform ritual] before the king, as commonly how nowadays wilujengan ritual is done in the house. The [Islamic]

> Mulud Nabi ritual = [the equivalent of] when the ritual was carried out by [*canthang balung*] in the temple. I assume you all know that mulud in Arabic means the celebration of birth (*weton*). Hence the celebration of the "birth of temple" = in the Buddhist tradition in Bali, it is called *odalan*—this [odalan] might be an old tradition. Subsequently, the ritual was Islamized by *wali* (Islamic saints). Because the strong influence of the [Islamic] power, it continues to be practiced in the form we see it today. Subsequently, people don't know the original practices of canthang balung. Their status as priests is degraded to clowns.[12]

Hadiwidjojo's speech enriches our discussion of *canthang balung* by including in our discourse an "insider" perspective (from a court intellectual), layered on my "outsider" work (as a non–court intellectual studying court culture). Hadiwidjojo positioned himself as an unbiased learned member of the aristocracy. Had he presented his speech as a member of the royal family from an insider's *adiluhung* perspective, he would have most likely skipped discussion of this especially peculiar court cultural practice. He claimed to have received much of his information from insider informants, including his father, King Paku Buwana X, and the leader of the court musicians, R. T. Warsadiningrat. Apparently, Hadiwidjojo had observed *canthang balung* for roughly two decades before he gave this speech at the Radyapustaka Museum in 1953.

W. F. Stutterheim was clearly an outsider. His article, titled "A Thousand Years Old Profession in the Princely Courts on Java," however, relies on insiders' notes.[13] "As early as 1932," Stutterheim writes, "through the kindness of prince Kusumayuda and Hadiwidjojo, I obtained a few accurate notes concerning the nature of the activities of these canthang balung; these notes I reproduce here in extension."[14]

One of Stutterheim's main theses is the connection between the image carved on the wall of the ninth-century Central Javanese Mahayana Buddhist monument, Borobudur—which depicts a dancer or dancers dancing with man or men in brahman dress—and its possible link to contemporary *canthang balung* and their practice at the court of Surakarta (figure 11-2). In this regard, he concludes that the official relationship of *canthang balung* "to the dancing-girls, their function at the serimpi-dance and finally the wearing of beard, which usage is preserved in Surakarta, are sufficient indication that we are dealing with the present holders of the same profession or a profession most closely related to that which the Borobudur-reliefs represent."[15]

To strengthen his argument, Stutterheim references a practice of Buddhism in the twelfth-century East Javanese kingdom of Singhasari among a particular sect that practiced a ritual called *pancamakara*, which involved the enjoyment of the "Five Ms" (*mada*, drinking liquor; *maithusa*, sexual intercourse; *mudra*, meditation; *matsya*, eating fish; and *mamsa*, eating meat), which according to Stutterheim's source can still be found in the so-called chaṇṭang balung, two bearded "buffoons" with the upper part of their body naked and with yellow strips, whose duty is it to become fuddled in public with gin or *arak* and to dance in an intoxicated state. These court functionaries not so very long ago received their

FIGURE 11-2. An image of a man or two in brahman dress facing a dancing girl, depicted at the wall of the ninth-century Buddhist monument Borobudur.

official income by keeping dancing girls and prostitutes. Their name, probably a nick-name, is probably due to the fact that originally they performed their "dance" on the *kṣétra* [cemetery], "rattling with bones" (nyanṭang balung).[16]

DUL BIRAHI, SERAT TJENṬINI, ZOETMULDER

The fascinating descriptions of *canthang balung* by Hadiwidjojo and Stutterheim and their possible historical links to Buddhist Tantrism and the *pancamakara* ritual inspired me to want to know more about any other traditions like the practice of *canthang balung*. What came to my mind was a description of an Islamic tradition called Dul Birahi, as described by the authors of the nineteenth-century literary work *Serat Tjenṭini*, namely Ranggasutrasna, Sastranagara, and Sastradipura. The authors describe the opening of a mass whirling *dhikir*, in which participants, with eyes covered by batik cloth or paper, formed a circle, held their breath intermittently, and cried unconscious with shaking heads, the male and female devotees acting out various behaviors:

> They were everywhere, one on the top of the other,
> Like banana trees that had been cut down
> Men and women mixed together
> Those who were on the top of the other did not mind.
> The ones who were naked were not concerned
> There was no punishment.
> That was the way of the people of Dul Birahi,
> Whoever achieved superiority, no questions were asked
> About their behavior.

> Those santri whose èlmu was inferior
> Surrendered their wives' bodies and soul,
> Presenting them [to the superior ones] for whatever purposes.[17]

At this juncture, I begin to wonder if by presenting behavior that exposes sexual relationships, I will be labelled as someone looking to sensationalize discussion based on controversial topics. The answer is yes and no. In the first place, my point of view does not represent the view of the *kraton* insider. I base my writing on other scholars' writing and description from literary work such as *Serat Tjentini*. For the latter, the issue is whether what's said in literary work or religious language is literal in its intentionality.[18] However, speaking about Tantric practice, White asserts that the tendency to literalize symbolic statements or practice is a hallmark of these "hard core" Tantric movements. As I am quoting White, a scholar studying Indian Tantrism, it reminds me of Zoetmulder's discussion of Dul Birahi.[19] He suggests that Dul Birahi's practices are similar to Pasupata, Kapalikas, and other Buddhist Tantric sects in India. In both traditions, sexual intercourse and promiscuity are integral parts of their rituals. Furthermore, Zoetmulder asserts that the term *birai* is "a bastardisation of bhirawa, birawa, or birawi," which is a word that implies getting oneself into a state of ecstasy, hence pointing to the primary sexualized meaning of *bhairawa*.[20] To strengthen his point, Zoetmulder quotes passages from *Suluk Lonthang*, which explicitly describes *ambirawa*, the act of *bhirawa*.

Here again, by investigating *Serat Tjentini* and *Suluk Lonthang*, we rely on the language of literary work. But there is a nineteenth-century Dutch report on Islamic ritual in Madiun called *dulguyer*, which is somewhat similar to the *bhairawa* practice. And dancing and music were integral parts of the ritual:

> Their ritual consisted of beating on the drum and singing continuously "Ha-Illa-Lah, Ha-Illah-Lah" while moving their bodies back and forth or sideways, until they got into a trance and became unconscious. Men and women and old invalid people who could not even walk ordinarily then began to dance [*tandakken*]. The unconscious followers were believed to be in the happiest of states since they were in communion with God. Yellow water [*boreh*?] would be smeared on them and they then became conscious again while everybody was offered yellow water to drink.[21]

The mention of *boreh* (yellow unguent or lotion) reminds us of *canthang balung*, whose naked bodies were stained by stripes of yellow unguent or lotion.

RAMAYANA KAKAWIN

The mention of *boreh*, dancing, music in the context of *canthang balung*, and Dulguyer or Dulbirahi Islamic tradition has reminded me of passages from the ninth-century *Ramayana Kakawin*. The passage in question was written in a form of allegory, in which birds were used to satirically represent ascetic and political characters:[22]

Once upon a time, the *kuvoṅ-bird* and starling (*jalak*-bird) had a lively conversation. They were despising each other. Kuvoṅ-bird accused starling encamping near the weaver-bird. Starling enraged, comparing kuvoṅ to an unworthy *vidu* (wayang-player). Ironically, kuvoṅ was also an official.

> [Starling:] You are *taṇḍa* [official]! You have a very mean "palace," living in holes in the ground. You are stained, *kuvoṅ!* Homeless, unattached, while leading the life of a vagabond performer, a vidu (wayang-player), but you are endowed with manifold abilities, having magical powers![23]

According to the starling, the *kuvoṅ*-bird and the *vidu*, which the bird represents, are enigmatic figures. Why was the *vidu* (wayang performer), who was endowed with many abilities and magical power, was also homeless and unattached to his community? This description of *vidu* reminds me of the practice of *canthang balung*, and to a certain extent, the Dulguyer or Dul Birahi tradition, of being someone with questionable status but religiously potent and which, as Becker mentioned above, can be linked to the Tantric sect called Pasupata. Agreeing with Becker, Acri suggests that *canthang balung* was the remnant of an even more extreme Tantric tradition, Kapalika.[24] Acri details the descriptive practice of Kapalika, which is similar to the practice of *canthang balung*:

> Those practitioners were scornfully depicted as supernaturally endowed, yet evil, sorcerers who often posed as false Brahmans or ascetics; they sang, danced and played in theatrical performances; they encouraged the practice of drinking alcohol and engaging in sex with female attendants, whom they admitted into their order; and their attire included ornaments and musical instruments made of [allegedly human] bones, as well as human skulls or parts thereof. The etymology of the [nick]name *canthang balungs* would perfectly make sense in a Kāpālika milieu, for the "rattling bones" may be nothing else than a local variant of the rattle-drums [*ḍamaru*] made of bones that constituted one of the most characteristic marks of the Śaiva Kāpālikas. Also indicative of a Kāpālika origin may be the strings of flowers adorning their naked bodies, which is reminiscent of the garland of flowers offered to the gods [*nirmālya*] worn by Atimārga ascetics, and the emphasis on laughter, which is reminiscent of the observance of aṭṭahāsa or vehement laughter prescribed by the Pāśupata observance [*pāśupatavrata*].[25]

Acri also finds that the practice of smearing a yellow ointment over the body or hairs and beard of *canthang balung* can be found in certain Sanskrit texts of the practitioners of the Bhairavamarga. The characters they play and the tall cap (fez) they wore are strongly reminiscent of the Pāśupata and Kāpālika and other Indian ascetic practices.[26]

LIVED RELIGION VERSUS FORMAL RELIGION

What has emerged from the preceding discussion is the practice of searching for spiritual experiences. Our common conventional understanding of achieving spiritual enlightenment of oneself and/or collectively is through formally institutionalized process, such as the Friday gathering of Muslims for prayer or Sunday services for Christians. However, the discussion above reveals another means of achieving spiritual experience, namely through events in the public sphere that involve theatrical acts, processions, and music performances associated with community activities. This is what some scholars called "lived religion," that is, those practices and rituals carried out by religious laity in their everyday lives, which consist of a range of activities that may have religious significance or contain spiritual potency.[27]

For example, music and theatrical performances can be presented in the activity of a preacher and in religious festival. It is not uncommon in this preaching context to see gamelan and wayang presented side by side with religious songs, displays of magic, and religious prayer. Another example of the practice of lived religion is a court festival to commemorate the birth of Prophet Muhammad, the Sekatèn week, which Hadiwidjojo mentions in connection with the presence of *canthang balung* in the processional event and dancing in the accompaniment of *gendhing* "Rambu" performed by a sacred gamelan Sekatèn. It is not only that the Sekatèn festival is an important religious event, but all kinds of court *pusaka* (magically charged heirloom relics), including the performance of gamelan Sekatèn and the parade of sacred court weapon, bring about spiritual potency to those Javanese who believe in courtly traditional culture. It should be mentioned, however, that the Sekatèn festival is held in the context of a worldly mundane occasion, an event no different from a market fair. There, during the Sekatèn week, one finds in the courtyard in front of the mosque all sorts of vendors selling food, souvenirs, and clothes. Aside from gamelan Sekatèn performed in the immediate compound in front of the mosque, all types of performances are also presented in temporary stages or an improvised circular stage on the ground of the courtyard.

The point I would like to make is that obtaining spiritual enlightenment can be achieved not only through a formally institutionalized religious gathering but also through informal community gatherings such as in community festivals. An event such as Sekatèn festival is no different from what Meredith McGuire describes regarding a ritual by Latinos in the United States in blurring the boundary between the sacred the profane. They engage in concrete religious practice that can enable them to experience a sense of the sacred, but they do so in the domestic sphere and in their neighborhood communities. She goes on to say,

> Today, as in medieval times, much popular religious practice is devoted to getting in touch with sacred power and somehow tapping it for one's needs. Pilgrimages, processions, and performances are among the most important popular religious tradition by which U.S. Latinos gain access to sacred space and divine powers. Because such public practices blur the boundaries between sacred and profane, they also challenge the boundaries between religious and political ritual.[28]

SEMAR

Despite the above elucidation, a question lingers regarding religious potency one can obtain by the presence of jokester *canthang balung* in the court dance performance

FIGURE 11-3. Semar, a contradictory character represented in a paradoxical iconography, juxtaposing sacred and profane, power and powerless.

and the procession during the Sekatèn festival. Does humor or levity have any place in religious ritual? Certainly, from the perspective of formal theology, religion is a most serious business, not a laughing matter. In other words, humor is incongruent with religion. However, if we define religion as a lived popular religion or community-oriented system of belief, humor tends to always appear as part of the practices and rituals designed to facilitate closeness to God.[29] Humor in this popular religious event evokes playfulness or lightheartedness, but it can be serious or even subversive. The point is that humor facilitates people's obtaining spiritual experience. In connection to this point, I cannot resist mentioning the clown figure named Semar in wayang performances, since he signifies the same figure as *canthang balung* in terms of representing sacred-profane trajectory (figure 11-3).

Semar represents a contradictory character and paradoxical iconography (an interpretation of the meaning of the content of images). The Semar puppet looks like he is sitting down, yet he is standing up. Standing up, he looks like he is sitting down. "He is ornamented like a woman, his clothes are those of man, yet his face is that of neither man nor woman. About his character, Semar 'though a humble and comical retainer,' is yet the most powerful of Gods. . . . He is the repository of the highest wisdom, yet this flashes from in between his gentle jokes, his clowning, and even his persistent uncontrollable farting."[30] The esteemed wayang expert and author, Mulyono says more about Semar:

> What manner of creation is this, who stands leaning on his belly? or is it,
>   who sits rocking on his buttocks?
>
> The mid-day sun is sallow beside the radiance of his face.
> How can such brilliance emanate from one as pallorous as a corpse?
>
> No parent, no children has he. His smile misted in tears.
> Bleak perils of humanity, softened in the gentle rain of his compassion.
>
> Goodness itself, this god made man, who
> Dominates the *satria* with servitude.
>
> Kings grovel before him; gods honour him;
> Even the Most-High does his bidding.
>
> Invincible through non-deeds, omnipotence in inertia.
> Here lies the source of his *sakti* [divine might].
>
> Dawn at dusk, sunset at daybreak.
> The perfect being: Ismaya.[31]

The paradoxical nature of Semar epitomizes a perfect democratic ideal, namely that the highest status is in perfect unity with the lowest status; *manunggaling kawula lan gusti* (a perfect union between the commoner and the lord) is a philosophical expression in Javanese that captures well the meaning of this concept. But for the purpose of our discussion, clearly Semar, as in the case of *canthang balung*, also captures the sacred-profane paradox.

CONCLUSION

In 1965, there was a mass crackdown against followers of the Indonesian Communist Party (Partai Komunis Indonesia [PKI]) during which more than one million people were killed, and Indonesia's first president, Sukarno, was deposed. In her 2019 novel *Manjali dan Cakrabirawa* (Manjali and Cakrabirawa), Ayu Utami, who lived through the political upheavals and violence of 1965, writes:

> Jati had finished observing all he could with his fingers. People are waiting for news from his mouth. "There is a dog, a skull. And a trident." He describes what his fingers see. "He is a Shiva Bhairawa statue" he said. "Such a statue is also called Chakra Chakras." Marja felt a strange thing flowing in her body. . . . The subtle tension that rose from inside his stomach, strengthened, then spread to the direction of her neck. . . .

She felt as if it is coming from contact with an invisible presence. The unknown. Now the vibration became acute on the back of her neck, before disappearing, evaporating out of romantic love. . . . Now Marja is back to normal. She swallowed saliva and shook her head a bit, convincing herself that she was conscious. "Shiva Bhairawa? Chakra, Chakra? What has it got to do with Cakrabirawa, Jati?" [ask Marja].[32]

The novel goes on to describe a related massacre of the residents of the village where the Shiva Bhairawa statue was found, whose citizens were accused of hiding an officer of Cakrabirawa (President Sukarno's bodyguards) who was believed to have been involved in the killing of the six army generals as a part of the coup d'etat against Sukarno. Founded in 1962, Cakrabirawa was a military regiment whose special duty was guarding President Sukarno. Most likely, the name Cakrabirawa was chosen by Sukarno himself, who was very keen in his allegorical use of wayang stories in his political discourse. By combining the name of Kresna's powerful weapon (Cakra) and *birawa* (i.e., a fierce manifestation of god Shiva, an image of horrible power), Sukarno mobilized age-old mythological concepts to create a code name—Cakrabirawa—that endowed his powerful bodyguard with almost mystical powers. Given the suffering that ensued from the 1965 coup in Indonesia, juxtaposing Sukarno's recycling of myth and history to George Lucas's exploitation of Joseph Campbell's universal "monomyth" may seem facile.[33] However, my essay demonstrates how the *canthang balung*, along with wayang stories, sociopolitical protocols, Indian religion, and Indonesian history, are interconnected and inextricably intertwined. For the Javanese, whose tradition emphasizes oral transmission but also acknowledges the greatness of written materiality, their lives and beliefs are shaped by two most powerful cultural sources and forces: history and mythology. The figure of the *canthang balung* hearkens back to multiple historical and mythological sources, and *canthang balung* characteristics continue to resonate in different forms in the present as well. On the one hand, the creation and performance of myth are not only the product of imagined world but are also infused and inspired by history. On the other hand, history might be infused and inspired by myth.

NOTES

1. My ethnomusicological training is unlike most ethnomusicologists. In the first place, the ethnomusicology program at Cornell University, my alma mater, is under the umbrella of musicology. Under the supervision of my advisor, Professor Martin Hatch, the program allowed me to design my course of study, such as what classes I should take. I took only three classes in the Music Department: Seminar in Ethnomusicology, Bibliography, and a rudimentary class on Western music. The rest of my classes were in Southeast Asian studies: the history of Southeast Asia, an anthropology course on the mainland of Southeast Asia, and a course on political science and culture of Indonesia.

2. Hadiwidjojo, "Sesorahipun Pangarsa Paheman Radyapustaka 'G.P.H. Hadiwidjojo' wonten ing Walidyasana" [A speech by the head of Radyapustaka Museum 'G.P.H. Hadiwidjojo' in the Walidyasana Hall]. Typed manuscript, 1953; W. F. Stutterheim, "A Thousand Years Old Profession in the Princely Courts of Java," in *Studies in Indonesian Archaeology* (The Hague: Nijhoff, 1956 [1935]).

3. See K. L. Pike, *Language in Relation to a Unified Theory of the Structures of Human Behavior*, 2nd ed. (The Hague: Mouton, 1967); M. Harris, "History and Significance of the Emic/Etic Distinction,"

Annual Review of Anthropology 5 (1976): 329–50, www.jstor.org/stable/2949316.

4. See Moyers & Company, "George Lucas Tells Bill Moyers About the Mentors in His Career," YouTube, May 4, 2017, video, 2:39, www.youtube.com/watch?v=dNs7c41JbTI, 1999.

5. Lucas Seastrom, "Mythic Discovery within the Inner reaches of Outer Space: Joseph Campbell meets George Lucas, Part 1," Starwars.com, October 22, 2015, www.starwars.com.

6. Benedict Anderson, *Mythology and the Tolerance of the Javanese* (Ithaca: Southeast Asia Program Cornell University, 1996 [1965]).

7. Sumarsam, *Gamelan: Cultural Interaction and Musical Development in Central Java* (Chicago: University of Chicago Press, 1995); Brandts Buys, "Uit de pers. De tjaṇṭang baloeng's.—Javaansche en Balische kleppers.—Bedåjå ketawang.—Édan-édanan," *Djåwå* 13 (1933): 258–62; Andrea Acri, "Birds, Bards, Buffoons and Brahman: (Re-)Tracing the Indic Roots of Some Ancient and Modern Performing Characters from Java and Bali," *Archipel* 88 (2014).

8. W. F. Stutterheim, "A Thousand Years Old Profession in the Princely Courts of Java," in *Studies in Indonesian Archaeology* (The Hague: Martinus Nijhoff, 1956 [1935]), 91–103; Soewandi, R. M. *Djedjèrèngan bab: Beksa Tajoeb, Bondhan, Tuwin Wirèng* [The description of Tayuban, Bondhan, and Wiring dance] (Yogyakarta, 1938, typed manuscript).

9. Stutterheim, "A Thousand Years Old Profession," 95.

10. Stutterheim, "A Thousand Years Old Profession," 96; Sumarsam, *Gamelan*, 121.

11. Sumarsam, *Gamelan*, 121–22.

12. Hadiwidjojo, "Sesorahipun Pangarsa Paheman Radyapustaka," 4. My translation.

13. Stutterheim, "A Thousand Years Old Profession."

14. Stutterheim, "A Thousand Years Old Profession," 94.

15. Stutterheim, "A Thousand Years Old Profession," 98.

16. Stutterheim, "A Thousand Years Old Profession," 99.

17. Ki Ngabehi Ranggasutrasna et al., *Serat Tjenṭini* (Betawi: Firma Ruygrok, 1915), 5–6, 92.

18. David Gordon White, *Kiss of the Yoginï: "Tantric Sex" in Its South Asian Contexts* (Chicago: University of Chicago Press, 2003).

19. P. J. Zoetmulder, *Pantheism and Monism in Javanese Suluk Literature: Islamic and Indian Mysticism in an Indonesian Setting* (Leiden: KITLV Press, 1994). First published in Dutch in 1935.

20. Zoetmulder, *Pantheism and Monism*, 237–38.

21. Onghokham, "The Residency of Madiun Pryayi: Priyayi and Peasant in the Nineteenth Century" (PhD diss., Yale University, 1975), 71.

22. Andrea Acri, "On Birds, Ascetics, and Kings in Central Java: 'Ramayana' Kakawin, 24.95–126 and 26," *Bijdragen tot de Taal-, Land- en Volkenkunde* 166 (2010): 475–506.

23. *Kakawin Ramayana*, translated by Acri in "On Birds, Ascetics, and Kings in Central Java," 62.

24. Acri, "On Birds, Ascetics, and Kings."

25. Acri, "Birds, Bards, Buffoons and Brahman," 37.

26. Acri, "Birds, Bards, Buffoons and Brahman," 37–38.

27. Rinallo et al., *Consumption and Spirituality* (New York: Routledge, 2013); Soewandi, *Djedjèrèngan bab*.

28. Meredith B.McGuire, *Lived Religion: Faith and Practice in Everyday Life* (New York: Oxford University Press, 2008), 50.

29. Rinallo et al., *Consumption and Spirituality*, 3.

30. Benedict Anderson, *Mythology and the Tolerance of the Javanese* (Ithaca, NY: Cornell University Press, Studies in Southeast Asia 37, 1965), 22–23.

31. Mulyono (1975), as translated by E. G. Koentjoro in Paschalis Maria Laksono, *Tradition in Javanese Social Structure*, trans. E. G. Koentjoro (Yogyakarta: Gadjah Mada University Press, 1986), 25.

32. Ayu Utami, *Manjali dan Cakrabirawa* (Jakarta: Kepustakaan Populer Gramedia, 2019). My translation.

33. Joseph Campbell, *The Hero with a Thousand Faces* (Princeton, NJ: Princeton University Press, 1949).

12

Dakwah, Missionizing, and Wayang

Hindu, Islamic, Christian, Buddhist

Kathy Foley

The Abrahamic religions (Judaism, Islam, and Christianity) have sometimes had a vexed relationship with theatrical performance. Visualizations and representations of the sacred and enactments can cause puritanical rejections. The aniconic bent may come from a focus on the divine as incomparable in perfection and radically separated from creation. In this line of thinking, by separation of self from everyday experience of the senses and the embrace of stillness, the embodied subject has the best possibility of encounter with the absolute.

Disembodied principles—written text and God-given laws/commandments—become the binding covenants that attach us to the eternal. Of course, such traditions use the arts but with some ambivalence, often awarding higher marks to less immediately sensorial manifestations. Writing, music, and church/mosque architecture, which can give a sense of distance and our smallness, may have pride of place. Visual arts representing the sacred may be considered more appropriate if they move toward the calligraphic and abstract, as in Islam and Judaism. Christianity, due to the embodiment of the godhead in Jesus, grants dispensation to bodily representation of the divine, but arguably the still visuals and sonic arts trump the mimetic. Embodied arts—dance and theater—rank lower since the body is regarded with some suspicion, needing to be disciplined in life and sloughed off in eternity to meet a divine, which has no tangible face.[1]

Hindu-Buddhist traditions, especially those with tantric leanings, operate differently. Manifestations of the divine are potential sources of destruction (Siwa/ Shiva-Uma/Durga) as well as of creation and the divine and the material often are seen as having permeable borders (for example, avatars). Trance can sometimes allow human bodies to manifest the divine. This encourages a different hierarchy of the arts. Tangibility enhances, so sacred dance and theater, as the fuller representations of how the divine suffuses the mundane, receive high valuation. Visual representations (yantra, mandala, sculptures, paintings) flourish, since the physical can manifest divinity in creation. The body in Tantrism is the sine qua non for human ascent toward the divine. Writing and music remain valued but do not seem to dominate in Mahayana (large vehicle, popular Buddhism) or yogic tantric cults, especially for lay people.

These very broad generalizations serve as background for spiritual practice in Javanized Southeast Asia, where preexisting spirituality related to ancestors, place spirits, and shamanic belief was a foundation. However, Austronesian religious strains will not be dealt with here but rather the persistent spiritual valuation of wayang, a music-dance-puppet theater of Indonesia and the Malay areas around the Gulf of Thailand.[2] Wayang serves historically as part of life-cycle ceremonies on Java for weddings and circumcisions as well as village purifications (*bersih desa*, literally "cleansing the village" of malign influences), and individual *ruwatan* (purification) ceremonies. This essay will point out Javanese/Sundanese wayang's traces of Hindu-Buddhism of the eighth to the fourteenth centuries, in its lore of Indian culture bringer Aji Saka, which set the precedent for embodiment in spirituality; share legends of Islamization in the fifteenth to seventeenth centuries by the Nine Saints (Wali Songo) showing spiritual valuation persisted in Indonesian Islam; and, finally note postcolonial experiments highlighting spiritualty. The latter forms include Christian *wayang wahyu* ("revelation" wayang) from 1957; contemporary Buddhist *wayang buddha* beginning in 1975 and other experiments developed more recently; and neo-Islamic *wayang sadat*, promoting *dakwah* ("invitation"/ proselytization) from 1985. Wayang in ritual first evolved in Hindu-Buddhist praxis. Puppetry for Islamic *dakwah* may be more legend than documented history, but the Islamic spiritual intents of the repertoire remained clear, if Sufi, in orientation. The postcolonial reinventions, if dimmed by secular modern urban culture, show puppetry with spiritual dimension continues across religious boundaries.

Spiritual mission is avowed by *dalangs* (puppet masters), who see wayang as both aesthetic entertainment and vehicle of spiritual communication. For example, in the 2021 International Wayang Day, Institute Seni Indonesia (Indonesian institute of the arts, ISI)-Surakarta sponsored a *ruwatan* (purification) performance for twenty-five individuals. Meanwhile, in a conference at ISI-Denpasar, faculty members—Balinese *dalang* I Ketut Kodi of ISI-Denpasar and Javanese *dalang* Bagong Pujiono from ISI Surakarta—emphasized spiritual-philosophical impacts of being a *dalang* in talks.[3] The spiritual intents of *tuntunan* (advisement, teaching) are central, these *dalangs* said, while social aspects of *tontonan* (spectacle, entertainment) allow audiences to receive teachings, Hindu, Muslim, or other.

HINDU-BUDDHIST CONVERSION: AJI SAKA

Aji Saka (*saka*—"pillar, core") is the mythical Indic Hindu-Buddhist culture bringer who is credited with importing the Indian Hindu-Buddhist calendar to Java. No dates are given for his arrival, but aspects of Indian culture have been present in the archipelago since the fifth century CE. Aji Saka is said to have ruled in "Medang Kemulan" (Old Mataram). By the ninth century, we encounter Javanese inscriptions with clear references to wayang-like puppetry and masking (*topeng*)—both of which now fall under the broader term wayang. The major repertoire from the ninth century to the present is adaptions of Indian epics (*Mahabharata* and *Ramayana*), reworked to local needs. By the eleventh century, literature gives recognizable description of wayang performances, and thirteenth-century temple bas reliefs, such as those at Penataran in East Java, show iconography similar to current puppet figures of Bali. The Indian-influenced religion philosophically posits an unseen/unseeable power from which the universe was generated, which does not always clearly separate the divine from the negative as Middle Eastern religions do. Hence, there is significant concern in Hinduism with appeasing the demonic, probably contributing to wayang's plenitude of demonic characters.

Aji Saka as cultural bringer remains significant in wayang, however shadowy. This hero from Bumi Majeti (India) comes to Medang Kemulan (Kingdom of origin) where he defeats Prabu Dewata Cengkar (Barren spirit), a cannibalistic spirit king, pushing him into the southern ocean where Cengkar becomes Bajul Putih (White crocodile). Aji Saka sends word to his two servants, Doro and Sembada, to bring his *kris pusaka* (heirloom dagger) to him. Each suspects the other of malfeasance. They fight and kill one another. To commemorate their deaths, Aji Saka wrote the pangram/poem inventing Java's Indic-based alphabet (*hanacaraka*) and linked to word magic of old Javanese culture. The phrases are associated with cardinal points.

> Ha-na ca-ra-ka. (There is a story, or, there was a ruler. East)
> Da-ta sa-wa-la. (Two were sent. South)
> Pa-dha Ja-ya-nya. (Equal in power. West)
> Ma-ga ba-tha-nga. (Both win death, or, carry the dead. North)

In addition to inventing writing, Aji Saka fathers a *naga* snake-child when Aji Saka ejaculates at the sight of a beautiful village girl while on a hunting excursion. His spilt seed results in a miraculous, outside-the-womb conception, as his semen along with the maid's female flow are swallowed by a chicken that lays an egg, which becomes the *naga*/snake Jaka Linglung (Stupid youth). This unruly child is tended by his mother and lives in her rice storage shed.

Jaka Linglung seeks his father, who tests the *naga*/snake, sending him to finish off to crocodile Dewata Cengkar in the southern ocean. In the 1814 *Serat Centhini* version of the story, Jaka Linglung kills the white crocodile, then marries Nyi Blorong, a manifestation of /or the chief follower of Lara Kidul, the chthonic goddess of the southern sea who can bring wealth and worldly power. Jaka Linglung abandons Nyi Blorong for a home in volcanic mud (becoming a traditional deity of the Grobogan-area salt workers), where he eats children who enter his open mouth, which they mistake for a cave.

I will not unpack fully this imagery—out-of-womb conception, rice houses as the "womb" of life, cannibalism, snake men, sea women, animistic dangers of the southern sea (full of vulcanism and tsunamis)—but merely note the following two parallels with other wayang lore.

1. Directional thinking. Civilization and religious truth comes from maritime arrivals on the north coast, establish on the central plain (Medang Kemulan) east to west, and push demons—representing both fertility and danger—to the South Sea. This directional mandala is related to an Indic worldview and establishes the geography of the central plain of Java as core of life.
2. Spiritual figures deal with, but also generate, the demonic (as Aji Saka fathers Jaka Linglung). Thus, our Hindu missionizing source (Aji Saka) and the chaotic natural (Dewata Cengkar, Jaka Linglung, Nyi Blorong) are balanced rather than simply suppressed. Purification, not elimination, is the pattern of Indic thinking.

The story of Aji Saka is only rarely played in wayang. Yet Aji Saka remains part of wayang's mindscape. In the *murwa*, the opening narration of Sundanese and north coast puppeteers, Aji Saka, and his alphabet are referenced.

Asta gangga wira tanu patra. Asta? Asta is hand. *Gangga* is water. *Wira* is poet, high minded person. *Tanu* is ink. *Patra* means pen. Ink is transformed into the alphabets *wilanjana-wilanjani.* The *wilanjana* are *aksara alip* [Arabic alphabet]. The *wilanjani* [Javanese alphabet] are the *aksara ha.*

The *wilanjana* fall to the west [Arabia] becoming the thirty letters: *alip, ba, ta, tsa . . . .*

Pause with the Arabic alphabet, tell of the Javanese alphabet. These letters are thrown to the east, arriving in the island of Java, becoming the alphabet *kalih dasa* [twenty letters]. *Kalih* is two, *dasa* is ten. They are split to the four directions. . . . *Hana cara-ka* "the one who sends." *Data sawala* "those who are sent." *Pada jayanya*, "equal in struggle." *Magaba tanga* [carrying the corpse], not to be said. The letters fall, dead in the north.

Leave the twenty letters, return again to the *wilanjana-wilanjani.*

Wilanjana is the semen of the Father. *Wilanjani* is the flow of the mother. The Father's semen meets the mother's flow in the *kenya puri* [palace meeting hall/rice storage barn/womb].

Kenya? Kenya is the container/mother. And *puri* is the palace.

In what kingdom do we open? The palace of Astina is the scene. Open the story *eka adi dasa purwa* [oneness, nobility, tenfold-ness, origins]. Who is the king who rules here? Guru Nata [Siwa/Shiva]. *Guru* means teacher. *Nata* means king.

The one who becomes the *dalang* [puppeteer] is Dora Sembada. Dora is liar. Sembada is truth-teller. What is the proof? There is evidence. What evidence? The *wayang purwa* of origins.[4]

Thus, in opening, a traditional Sundanese wayang summons up palm leaf manuscripts as its origin: "Asta ganga wira tanu lan patra" ("Hand, water, writer, ink/soot, pen"—how one inscribes palm leaf), thereby referencing Aji Saka and all the literati (*pujangga*) who wrote with dampened soot on palm leaves (*lontar*). These civilizers gave us wayang's textual base. Their tales, transmitted through writing (*hanacaraka*), are now in performance orally delivered in improvised language, providing access to Hindu-Buddhist knowledge. The passage praises the two alphabets, the Arabic (*wilanjana/aksara alip,* generating the Quran) and the Javanese (*wilanjani/aksara ha[nacaraka],* generating the Indian-based stories). The *murwa* tells us the poet (*wira,* i.e., Aji Saka) splits the letters to the four directions, moving from east ("hana caraka," beginnings and birth) to north ("maga bathanga," endings and death). The two messengers (Doro and Sembada, "those sent") represent the twoness experienced in the material world (right-left, male-female, day-night, heaven-earth, life-death, good-bad), which must be reconciled in oneness (ruler/divinity), both in the microcosm and the macrocosm. The twoness is echoed again in discussing performance as "lie" (Dora, associated with the left hand that usually holds the ogre character) and "truth" (Sembada, associated with right hand that grasps the hero). Wayang points us back to beginnings—*purwa* (origin). The ruler (*nata*) as the "one who sends," linked with mind/poet/ruler/teacher/Aji Saka/divine. Stories, like society and the cosmos have positivity countered by the negative, but both come from the same source, the divine teacher [Siwa]. The twoness (servants) must be reconciled in the oneness (Aji Saka/guru/divinity/mindfulness) that precedes them.

The two alphabets in the *murwa* are further identified with the male and female principles. "The Father's semen meets the mother's flow in the *kenya puri,*" the womb. The *murwa* then continues, in a section not included above, to discuss the arrival of the nine Islamic saints (Wali Songo, who will be discussed later), as a second wave of culture bringers. Then it advises the hearer to *golek* (search for the meaning) of/in the wayang, since understanding our being is the task each human is sent into life to accomplish. Language and ideas of the *murwa* are admittedly obscure—most *dalangs* when interviewed give only approximations of what it all means—but it was traditionally intoned at the beginning of each story to remind, in a mantric way, of both Aji Saka and the Wali Songo as bringers of truth and give performances spiritual weight.

The Hindu-Buddhist legacy is widespread in the openings of puppet shows in Southeast Asia. The fight of two servants is just words in Sundanese wayang but is echoed in the played-out battle of two Hanumans (black vs. white) at the beginning of Thai *nang* (leather puppet traditions), as well as the two *dewa panah* (spirits, called "male" and "female") in Kelantanese wayang. The Thai and Malay fights do not end with death, as with the Doro-Sembada fight, but instead with a scene of their reconciliation by the guru (*reusi*/the sacred teacher) who is an equivalent of Aji Saka—the guru is the divine (Siwa/Shiva as Batara Guru). This concept—two in opposition, leading back to the one who controls knowledge—is set at the beginning of most Southeast Asian puppet genres and tied to a common Hindu-Buddhist puppet heritage.[5]

Another echo of Hindu-Buddhist patterning is tales of split seed generating a demonic child who eats people. The Jaka Linglung episode has similarity to the wayang purification story of the demon Kala (Time), the son of Batara Guru/Siwa. Kala, as with Jaka Linglung, is conceived outside the womb from an ejaculation when Batara Guru tries to rape his wife (Goddess Uma/Durga). Batara Guru's seed falls into the ocean, creating Kala and havoc. As Jaka Linglung seeks out Aji Saka, Kala searches for his father Batara Guru. Both gain acknowledgment from the missing parent and then eat people. In Kala's case, Wisnu as *dalang* assuages Kala's demonic tendencies by reading syllables/mantra that were written by Siwa on Kala's limbs. This rite seems inspired by *nyasa*, a Hindu-Buddhist purification, by imaginatively placing syllables, gods, and other visualization on different parts of an adept's body; by moving from the lower regions, up the spine and head, one can trace his/her return to the divine source.[6]

I will not here cite particulars of the exorcism (*ruwatan*) but note that song and mantra magic provide purification by placing powers at directional points.[7] In both the *ruwatan* and in the Aji Saka legend, the refined rulers give rise to the demonic by their bad behavior (spilt seed), behavior that also exists in ordinary people. To subdue our external/eternal threats and internal/finite failings, we must work back from our demonic impulses to find everything's origin in the divine. The writing on Kala's limbs, which he cannot understand/read himself (and so the *dalang* must read/sing to him), and the *hanacaraka* (assigned by Aji Saka's poem to the directional points) make up a cycle of birth, life, and death that underlies all human stories, each of us being this cycle's center. The *ruwatan* are tales and the *murwa* are prompts toward human self-knowledge of divine origins and demonic potentials of being in the material world. The *murwa* and aspects of Aji Saka's legend acknowledge our place at the center of our mini-world, yet also are enmeshed in cosmic processes. The Aji Saka tale, like the story of Kala, is about how misbegotten humans, fallen from some divine source and encountering demonic challenges, can reformulate themselves via mantric practice. Life comes from and goes back to higher principles. Sounding/performing causes one (or at least *dalang*) to *golek* (search for) the meaning of these obscure mantras and odd stories that haunt the genre.

Nor are memories of Aji Saka forgotten in contemporary Javanese arts practices. Recent digitalization of the Javanese *aksara* was supported by the cultural department of Yogyakarta and led by Sultan Hamengku Bowono X (born Herjuno Darpito, 1946–) and was celebrated with the Sultan's 2020 choreography of "Beksan Aji Saka," an all-male, strong character-type dance performed by ten dancers and inspired by *Serat Ajisaka* (Book of Ajisaka). The dance was choreographed to communicate the "essential meaning behind the Javanese script (Ha Na Ca Ra Ka, etc.). The Javanese script, which is full of meaning on noble teachings, and then is used in education in human identity as the most perfect creation."[8] A 2017 animated film version of Aji Saka's tale was also done with wayang-style animation.[9] Aji Saka's letter magic and directional thinking persists in contemporary Java, and performances show how the demonic is calmed by higher potential via dance, music, and story. This spiritual insight has been translated across religions in Java and was recycled in the Islamic period in Sufistic thought.

WALI SONGO

The Nine Saints or Wali Songo are the next wave of culture bringers and credited with the Islamic proselytization of Java. Wayang and the other arts are seen as their tools of conversion. The most prominent performer-saints are Sunan Kalijaga (1460–1513), credited with *wayang kulit purwa, topeng* mask dance, *ronggeng* (female/male cross-dresser song-dance), and *pencak silat* (martial arts); Sunan Giri I (1442–1506), Saint of the Mountain, credited with *wayang gedog* (telling Panji and Damar Wulan tales); Sunan Kudus (d. 1550), creator of *wayang golek*, said to be modeled on *wayang kulit* shadow puppetry; and Sunan Bonang (1465–1525), creator of gamelan whose musical expertise provided the score.[10] They, along with other saints, are said to have contributed to wayang. In reality, there are, of course, more than nine *walis*. When one died, he was replaced by a son or close associate, who often took the same name/title, confusing genealogical tracing.

Some *walis*, such as Siti Jenar (1426?–1517?), one of the original nine, were ousted as heretics for teaching mystical gnosis (not sharia) as the path to perfection.[11] The other Wali Songo are said to have agreed that Siti Jenar's interpretation was literally true but bad for social order, so lore says they executed him in the mosque at Demak. A similar saint-heretic is Sunan Panggung (Saint of the Stage, d. 1613), a son (or some say follower) of Sunan Kalijaga who also studied with Siti Jenar. Sunan Panggung was supposedly condemned to the stake for bringing his dogs, scandalously named Iman (Faith) and Tawhid (Oneness of God), into the mosque. "Suluk Maling Sumirang," a poem attributed to Sunan Panggung and supposedly written amid the flames, includes the following: "If a person does not understand heretical teachings, he is certainly not yet perfect, his knowledge is still immature. He should choose to become a heretic, for heresy is indeed the final perfection. This heresy is faith, the witness and ritual prayer; it is also worship, feeling and life, and also the essence of peace."[12] The strict constructionists condemn such antinomian teachings as un-Islamic. Lore says the flames did not harm Sunan Panggung (or his dogs) and he either retreated to a forest hermitage or ascended into heaven at the time of his burning. One can, however, visit his grave in Tegal, a site where some puppeteers may spend the night in contemplation (*ziarah*) to accumulate performance power.

For tales of saints and heretics founding Javanese Islam using the arts, consider stories of the Wali Songo.[13] For the purposes of this essay, I merely note that these saints are seen as those who converted Java and the wider area around the Gulf of Thailand to Islam via performances, reworking puppetry, music, and dance. The terminology of *orang putih* (white ones, those who hold to strict sharia and condemn the use of arts in religion) and the *abangan* (red ones, those who take an ecumenical approach to Islam) may have crystalized only in the late colonial period.[14] However, the idea of Islamic artist-missionizers is old and was deeply ingrained in the thinking of my wayang teachers in the 1970s. *Dalangs* Abeng Sunarya and Otong Rasta, whose families originated in the north coast Cirebon area, saw themselves as both literal and metaphorical "descendants of the Saints" (*keturunan para wali*), since wayang passes down in family lines. Puppeteers believed that their stories that came from the *Mahabharata* or *Ramayana* were remolded by the Wali Songo to teach Islamic religious truths.

Java's conversion (*dakwah* or "invitation") saw Islam as the completion of pre-existing spiritual knowledge. Sunan Kalijaga is said to have taught, "Between Buddhism and Islam there is no difference. They are two in form but one in name."[15] The mythos says that Kalijaga (also known as Seh Melaya, Raden Said, and Ki Lokajaya) first created *wayang kulit purwa* (leather puppetry telling Hindu derived tales) and soon inspired other saints to create their own permutations of wayang. Conversion of Java and, sometimes, Malaya is credited to Kalijaga. While we know that wayang preexisted Islamization, there were changes in the narratives, music, and other features to better fit with Islam (Pandita heroes like Dorna were denigrated, Drupadi's five husbands in India were reduced to one Pandawa hero, Yudistira, as spouse, etc.). But the extensive use of theater and dance to communicate spiritual ideas shows that the strain of Islam imported to Java was not imitative of Hijaz culture. There, theater has always been sparse.

Arguments continue as to the bloodlines (and hence Islamic brand) of these *wali* figures. Champa, a Hinduized Muslim kingdom now part of Vietnam is the source of a central figure Malauna Malik Ibrahim (d. 1419), who is said to have been born in Samarkand or may have had Chinese blood, perhaps a link to Indo-Iranian Islam.[16] Maulana Malik established a school for teaching Islam in Surabaya/Gresik, and his son Sunan Ampel (1401–81) was teacher of Sunan Kalijaga (*wayang kulit purwa*) and Sunan Giri I (1442–1506), whose *wayang gedog* told Panji and Damar Wulan tales. Sunan Kalijaga is said to have married Sunan Giri's sister—wayang was in the family. Sunan Prapen (1510–1605), either a son, grandson, or great-grandson of Sunan Giri I, is said to have converted parts of Bali, Lombok, Sumbawa, and Bima, performing *wayang sasak*, which tells tales of Amir Hamzah (the uncle of Mohammed and a hero of Islam before the Prophet's revelation).[17] This leather shadow form in Lombak uses figures approximating the iconography of the *wayang gedog* characters (hence its assignment to the lineage of Sunan Giri). Amir Hamzah's feats of Islamizing the world (before the birth of the Prophet) became popular on Java and Lombok in the seventeenth century.

Though tales say Sunan Prapen's missionary zeal created the community of *waktu telu* ("three times" a day praying Muslims), who long predominated in

FIGURE 12-1. Figures from the Muslim story of Amir Hamzah (uncle of the Prophet). *Left to right*: Minister Bestak, Raja Nursiwan of Persia, his ally Raja Jobin, Raja Amir Hamzah (uncle of Mohammed), Minister Umar Maya, and the clown servants Lam Si Jang and Sabda Palon. Photo by Kathy Foley.

Lombok, this *waktu telu* religion now wanes.[18] The post-1980s Muslim revival with strict Sunni leaders (*tuan guru*), demands *waktu lima* ("five times" a day observance) and generally attacks *wayang sasak*. Hence, stories of Amir Hamzah that came to Indonesia via Shi'a lines from the Indo-Iranian area are now attacked on Lombok as un-Islamic by Sunni religious teachers.

On Java, other Indo-Iranian links appear. Sunan Kudus (Sayyid Ja'far Shadiq Azmatkhan d. 1550), yet another of the Nine Saints, it is said to have created *wayang golek*, wooden doll rod puppetry, presenting Panji, Amir Hamzah, and local histories (*babad*), chronicles that may even present the stories of the Wali Songo's conversion of Java (figure 12-1). Sunan Kudus' personal name, "Ja'far Shadiq," is the same as that of the sixth Shi'a imam who lived 732–65 CE. Sunan Kudus' grave is refurbished on the tenth of Muharram, the day Shi'a commemorate the Prophet's grandson Hussain's death at Karbala. These links, pointing to Persia and Shi'a lines as a possible source of Javanese Islam, prove distressing to Indonesia's contemporary Sunni cohorts who advocate Wahabi orthodoxy.

A story told by my teachers is that as the Nine Saints were discussing how to convert people to Islam, Sunan Gunung Jati, the ruler-saint of Cirebon, outlined a figure of a wayang shadow figure in the sand, and Sunan Kalijaga used that design for the first *wayang kulit purwa* (leather shadow puppet for the Hindu-based epics). He played in the Cirebon and Demak mosques. To enter a performance "payment" was recitation of the confession of faith, the Kalimat Sahadhat ("There is no God but Allah, Mohamed is his Prophet"). In another well-known episode, Sunan Kalijaga meets Yudistira, the hero of the *Mahabharata*, now living on the Dieng Plateau in Java. Yudistira, though already many centuries old, cannot die until he understands the meaning of his heirloom treasure the Kalimasada. Sunan Kalijaga recognizes that the writing is Arabic and the Islamic Kalimat Sahadat, the avowal of faith. Yudistira enters Islam, and Dalang Sunan Kalijaga does a *ruwatan* performance to release Yudistira's soul into eternity.

Of course, Hindu-Buddhist temple friezes and pre-Islamic literature document that wayang was alive and well long before the *walis*. But figure design, narrative structures, musical features, and dance aesthetics of wayang were, indeed, remolded post-Islam to fit the new religion.[19] The features were, from the fifteenth century, reinterpreted by puppeteers to teach Islamic wisdom with Sufi inclinations, and they also presented Muslim stories, especially tales of the local Islamization. Although the Islamic bone fides of wayang are being questioned by contemporary fundamentalist Islamic teachers (as I noted with *wayang sasak* and will discuss later with *wayang purwa* in Java), the traditional association of wayang with Islamic teaching remains the credo of performers and the moderate Islamic community.

POSTCOLONIAL WAYANG AND MISSIONIZATIONS

Postcolonial Indonesian experiments have attempted to use wayang to promote Christianity, Buddhism, and the post-1979 Islamic revival. As with earlier wayang repertories—Panji, Amir Hamzah, and history chronicles—new genres generally look to the *wayang purwa* models for characterizations, story patterns, music, and so on. Arguably, the mystical leanings of the *purwa* repertoire have made mission-izers of Christianity, Buddhism, and revivalist Islam value wayang as a tool.

The late colonial period further developed narratives on spiritual-civic moral-ity supporting nationalist ambitions at time when more formal education of pup-peteers solidified. Palace *dalang* schools and post-independence, national high schools and universities of the preforming arts highlighted stories that emphasized spiritual values. Suratno notes that story lists from the late nineteenth century include only eleven *wahyu* (divine power) *lakon* (plot narratives), but by the 1980s the common repertoire in Central Java included over forty well-known stories with this "vision/quest" pattern.[20] While *wahyu* stories are generally set in the *Mahabharata* locus, the pattern would be adapted to concepts of Catholic "grace" and contemporary Buddhist enlightenment.

Wahyu stories concern acquisition of a mystical power—sometimes envisioned as a radiance, other times as a secret teaching, supernatural weapon, or idealized princess (who is in reality a manifestation of divine power)—needed by a righteous hero to save the polity. Normally, a righteous Pandawa and greedy Kurawa (the *Mahabharata*'s two sets of cousins and their offspring) are candidates pursuing the same blessing. The Pandawa's moral compass brings success; the worldly Kurawa fail. Factors that encouraged the proliferation of *wahyu* stories include the political situation moving from colonial dependency to post-independence self-governance and the use of such stories in formal education of puppeteers, supplementing the previously family lineage training.

In the 1920s through 1940s, the Central Javanese palaces created training programs with curricula that continue today. *Dalang* training in Solo began at the Museum Radyapustaka in the Kesunan Palace under monarch Pakubuwana X (1866–1939) in 1923. The Habirandha School in Yogyakarta was established by Sultan Hamangku Buwono VIII (1880–1939) in 1925. Solo's Prince Mangkunegoro VII (1885–1944) created a training program at PDAAN at his palace in 1931. Lessons were thought to improve the village *dalangs* by exposing them to the palace models. The more elite concerns of palaces meant that often, *wahyu* (spiritual power) stories were chosen as training devices, making performances more *alus* (refined) and steering learners away from simple stories of kidnapped ladies, marriage contests, and petty fights between Pandawa and Kurawa. Stories like *Wahyu Cakraningrat* (Divine power of kings) were preferred; in this tale, Lesmana (the coarse son of the Kurawa King Duryodana), Samba (the overly proud son of Kresna), and Abimanyu (the refined son of the Pandawa Arjuna) vie for a spiritual power descending into the world.[21] Such stories inculcated socio–religious values that underscored Javanese ideals of a just ruler (*ratu adil*), helping lay the groundwork for lofty home rule.[22]

Even in 1978 when I was studying in West Java, the Central Javanese palace model of *wahyu* stories was clearly impacting the curriculum at the government High School of the Arts in Bandung (SMKI, Sekolah Menengah Karwitan Indonesia). Rather than learning a story from the active Sundanese *wayang golek* repertoire, our year-long wayang course was *Wahyu Makuta Rama* (Power of Rama's crown), an adaptation of a wahyu story from Central Java. The mystical power of the *Ramayana* heroes, King Rama (avatar of the preserver god Wisnu/Vishnu) and Laksmana (Rama's brother), reincarnate in *Mahabharata* heroes Kresna and Arjuna, respectively. Suratno notes that *wahyu* tales were popular in the 1950s as the new republic emerged from the colonial shadow, faded in the 1960s as fierce political rivalries of communist verses capitalist exploded, but returned by the 1980s as critique to Suharto's corrupt New Order regime.[23] In this same era, new forms of wayang were innovated by Christians, Buddhists, and revivalist Muslims, and the *wahyu* concept, spiritual and moral, promoted the borrowing.

Wayang Wahyu

Postcolonial changes in Western religions' missionization made *wahyu* an apt hook for indigenizing the "good news" of the Bible.[24] *Wahyu Cakraningrat* was adapted to become the first Christian wayang performance, with the Bible's King David replacing the Pandawa hero who attains the spiritual-religious grace. In postcolonial era, indigenization was replacing the enforcement of earlier Eurocentric religious models of music and liturgy in churches. Valorizing agency of precolonial ancestors was good cultural politics in newly independent Africa, South America, and Asia. The Latin mass, Gregorian chants, classic European hymns, and passion plays with a white Jesus and Mary were passé. Inculturation (using elements of local culture) was embraced.[25] Liberation theology attention to the local, already at work in the 1950s, was fully affirmed by Catholics at the Second Vatican Council (1962–65), freeing clerics' choices for the mass and other liturgies.[26] In Java, European missionaries were being replaced by indigenous priests and bishops. European priests who stayed were ones attuned to local culture, for example, the Jesuit Petrus Josephus Zoetmulder (1906–95), who devoted himself to training a new generation of Indonesian scholars in the wonders of Javanese spiritual thought as expressed in Kawi and Middle Javanese literature.

Catholic missionaries introduced local music and theater for teaching and liturgy. Brother Timotheus L. Wignyosoebroto (FIC, Brothers of the Immaculate Conception), the Jesuit head of Pangudi Luhur (High seeker) Catholic School in Solo was instrumental in Catholic wayang. On October 13, 1957, Dalang M. M. Atmowijoyo presented the adaptation *Wahyu Cakraningrat*, but now adapted to the Bible as *Daud Medapat Wahyu Keraton* (David receives the divine power of kingship). This performance used standard *wayang kulit purwa* figures for Bible characters; refined knight Bambang Wijanarka (a son of Arjuna) was David and *Ramayana* giant Kumbakara became Goliath. The success of this first effort led Brother Timotheus to commission an actual set of puppets portraying Bible figures (made from cardboard by R. Roesradi Wijayasawarno). Dalang Atmowijoyo presented this further developed form in *Malaikat Mbalelo* (Rebellion of the angels) on February 2, 1962. Soon, leather puppets were made; a full set contains 200–250 figures. Working in committee, Catholic educators-priests and wayang and gamelan experts (both Christians and Muslims) innovated and designed. Jesuit Mgr. A. Soegijapranoto named the form *wayang wahyu* ("revelation *wayang*") and soon the form was presented nationally in 1969 and 1974 during the important Pekan Wayang (Wayang festivals) that occur every five years.[27]

Poplawska notes, "Wayang Wahyu was conceived first of all as an alternative communication medium to spread God's revelation as recounted by the Bible. It forms a unique synthesis between art and religious communication [*pewataan*]."[28] Clergy oversaw the accuracy of the Bible narratives, with special attention to New Testament stories, but *dalangs* (sometimes Muslims like Atmowijoyo) collaborated creatively to see how tales could be "fit" into wayang narrative structure. In time, a number of priests and lay Catholics became *dalangs*. Popular stories include Genesis, Samson and Delilah, David and Goliath, Joseph, Esther, Noah, Isaac, Daniel, Moses, John the Baptist, Maria Magdalen, the Nativity (figure 12-2), Flight into Egypt, the Passion, and the Resurrection.

FIGURE 12-2. *Wayang wahyu* Nativity scene of Joseph (*left*) and Mary holding baby Jesus. Photo by Kathy Foley.

Music was originally the traditional wayang repertoire of Solo with the role of the *pesindhen* (female singer) deemphasized in favor of group choral singing.[29] Song texts for *suluk* (mood songs) were drawn from Psalms rather than the old Javanese poetry used in *wayang purwa*. Major church holidays (Christmas and Easter) were prime times for shows in parishes. The form had a strong presence in the 1980s in performances Ngajab Rahayu (Blessings foundation) troupe. The genre lapsed in the 1990s but was revived in the 2000s. Radio Republic Indonesia, where a female *wayang wahyu dalang*, Lucia Siti Aminah Subanto (1955–), is affiliated, broadcasts stories for Christian holidays.[30] Catholic Schools commission performances, and church bursaries and private donors pay the considerable costs for such events. Celebrations of rites of passage for individual families might also include a show.

Wayang wahyu was also taught at what is now Institut Seni Indonesia (ISI, Indonesian institute of the arts) in Surakarta/Solo, where the Christian Dalang Blacius Subono (1954-2024) was on the faculty of *padalangan* (puppetry).[31] Subono was the son of Dalang Yusuf Kiyatdiharjo, a famous Solo *dalang* who mentored top Javanese *dalangs* like Ki Anom Suroto and Ki Manteb Soedarsono. Subono's mother was a female singer.[32] Subono's students included local Christians and even some foreigners. American *dalang* Matthew Isaac Cohen in a blog post discussed Subono's 2009 performance:

> *Purwaning Dadi* (Genesis) was by Blacius Subono, one of my teachers at ISI Solo between 1988 and 1990. It was a three hour performance about Lucifer's revolt against the Almighty and the temptation of Adam. Paguyuban Wayang Wahyu [troupe name] and all the musicians (an ensemble of some 30 players and singers) were teachers at Pangudi Luhur [Solo Catholic School] or associated schools. . . . Performing 5 times over the last couple of years with three different puppeteers. . . . [They] bring an obvious passion for the work.[33]

Pop and *keroncong* songs as well as standard wayang music are included, especially for the prelude and clown scenes—*limbukan* (female servant clown scene) and *goro-goro* (clown scene with Semar). Puppeteers may normalize non-Biblical material; for example, Limbuk's joking was explained as a "dream" of Adam in the performance above. The important clowns (the god-clown Semar and his three sons) in *wayang purwa* make the ideas of the narrative accessible to and comically applicable for audiences. In *wayang wahyu*, they became Jesus's disciples: Gareng becomes Marcus (Mark); Petruk, Matius (Matthew); Bagong, Yohanes (John), and so on.

Blacius Subono, along with Brother Savio, FIC, helped with further development in the 2000s. Subono was the major composer of new music for the form, giving it a specific opening composition ("Talu Wayang Wahyu"), closing tune ("Panutup Pra Sadulur"), and other compositions. The style of *pakeliran padat* (heavily rehearsed, short performances with tight cues, a form developed by Subono and others in the 1980s at ASKI/ISI) has become the style.[34] Innovations like dubbing voices (provided by students of St. Joseph High School [SMA St. Yusep]) was done for a story of Samuel developed by Bambang Suwarno, Subono's colleague at ASKI/ISI. Frank Fosdahl, a Protestant missionary from Colorado, is one of Subono's students. I observed Fosdahl's manipulation in a 2003 class in Surakarta, and it was clear that Fosdahl, who has written a number of *lakon* (puppet plays/scenarios performed by Subono and others), had mastered puppet movement. Some of Fosdahl's performances have used the large screen with multiple manipulators casting shadows at the same time, another innovation of the national schools.[35] Pangudi Luhur School, where *wayang wahyu* first emerged, now includes regular training in the form in its curriculum. Dalang Indra Suroinggeno, another student Subono trained, founded Bhuana Alit (Microcosm) Workshop, which trains young Javanese Catholic students in *wayang wahyu,* and he performs regularly. Ernest Udayana and Father F. X. Wiyono are other *wayang wahyu* puppet masters. There have even been festivals of *wayang wahyu* with various child puppeteers.[36]

Surakarta is not the only site. Yogyakarta activities developed at Duta Wacana Christian University, a Protestant private institution, under Ki Johanes Yulius. Fr. Agustinus Handi Setyanto, a Catholic priest in the Diocese of Purwokerto and rector of a seminary in Tegal, has performed over fifty-one times since 2009. In a 2022 interview, Fr. Agustinus noted, "As far as I'm concerned, the *wayang wahyu* is important because I can spread Catholic teachings through the nation's most popular and entertaining puppet show."[37]

Presentations are truncated (two to four hours). Puppets are generally more realistic than traditional *wayang kulit purwa* figures (and so do not always move perfectly in fight scenes due to different balance). Bambang Suwarno made figures closer to traditional wayang in style and therefore better suited to manipulation. The logic of adaption of *purwa* figures makes sense to those who know *purwa* stories; the image of Jesus for the Passion, for example, is modeled on Abhimanyu, the son of Arjuna who is brutally slain by his Kurawa uncles. The puppet of Abimanyu in his suffering *wanda* (manifestation), when pierced by multiple Kurawa's arrows, is apt for Jesus with his crown of thorns when carrying the cross.

Other Christian groups have followed the Catholic model but sometimes give the form a different name. Protestant *wayang prajanjian* (Biblical/"promise" wayang) uses both *wayang kulit* shadows and *wayang golek* (wooden rod puppet) forms.[38] In Klatan Protestant wayang is called *wayang warta* ("[good] news" *wayang*). Sundanese teachers at a Christian university in West Java spoke to me in 2009 of their use of Sundanese-style *wayang golek* for Bible tales. Comic book versions of *Alkitab Wayang* (*Wayang* Bible) are advertised with the invitation, "Let's read Bible stories and get acquainted with *wayang orang* through *the Wayang Bible*."[39] Illustrations show characters in wayang dress, influenced by *wayang purwa* models. Dance dramas using wayang style have also been presented. Choreographer Bagong Kussudiarjo (1928–2004) created *wayang wong* (human wayang, dance drama), such as *Kebangkitan dan Kelahiran Isa Almasih* (The ascension and the birth of Jesus, 1968) with movement and characterization for Mary modeled on Sumbadra (refined wife of Arjuna in the *Mahabharata*), Herod on Rawana (ogre king and antagonist in the *Ramayana*), and the adult Jesus on Bima (strong hero and second of the Pandawa brothers in the *Mahabharata*). Music for Bagong's performance was by noted maestro Wasitodipuro (1909–2007), who chose *pelog* tuning, appropriate given that non-*purwa* stories (i.e., Panji, Amir Hamzah, Damar Wulan, and now the Bible) traditionally used *pelog* accompaniment.[40]

Christian *wayang wahyu* and dance dramas have continued to evolve but are still sometimes limited by Eurocentric thinking regarding church arts, as some parishioners call for European church hymns over gamelan accompaniment. This can limit freedom to exploit the well-defined tools (figures, music, story patterns) that traditional wayang affords. Still, liberation theology encouraged Christian clerics to explore local art resources. Modern Javanese priests, lay persons, and Muslim collaborators in molding *wayang wahyu* have followed the example of the Wali Songo. They have reworked preexisting wayang, recognizing its potential for spiritual teaching and harnessed puppetry to guide the faithful while attracting converts. As *dalang* Fr. Agustinus Setyanto responded when queried about a 2022 attack of fundamentalist Muslim cleric Ustadz Khalid Basalamah on the idea of using wayang: "The (Second) Vatican Council told us that every form of knowledge and culture should be respected and preserved. . . . As stated in *Gaudium et Spes* n. 58, the Catholic Church should cement her union with all local cultures so that both parties can enrich each other."[41]

Wayang Buddha

Recent Buddhist revivals, while less widespread than *wayang wahyu*, also exist. *Wayang buda/buddha* was first developed by visual artist Hajar Satoto at Akademi Seni Rupa Indonesia (ASRI, Indonesian academy of art) in Yogyakarta in 1975 and presented as *wayang arca* ("statue/sculpture" wayang) at Sasana Mulya Cultural Center.[42] In 1976, Satoto did a performance with new music composed by R. L. Martopangrawit (1914–86) and executed with Rahayu Suppangah (1949–2020) leading the gamelan, Dalang Bambang Suwarno (b. 1955) narrating, and movement by Agus Tasman. Hajar's puppets were inspired by the *nang yai/nang sbek* (large leather puppetry of Thailand and Cambodia, respectively) wherein a single dancer presents a large panel puppet, which may either be a single figure or a scene in which multiple characters interact. The dancer-manipulator's lower body executes the customary gaits of dance (according to the character type of the figure/scene); meanwhile, the figure is held above the mover's head. A long white screen is used. The original puppets were made of thin metal but proved unwieldy, so large leather figures soon replaced them.

Suprapto Suryodarmo (1945–2019), a Surakarta dancer, meditation practitioner, and ASKI[/ISI]-Surakarta faculty member, was intrigued. Suprapto advanced the form in the 1970s and 1980s. He collaborated with artists and students of ASKI-Surakarta in his version. Narration was by Dalang Blacius Subono, the exponent of *wayang wahyu*. Making puppets and contributing additional narration were Subono's fellow faculty members in the puppetry division, Dalang Bambang Suwarno and Dalang Sumanto. Suprapto, a Surakarta style classical Javanese dancer, combined *sumarah* (Javanese meditation, a form of *kebatinan*) learned from his father with contemporary Vipassana Buddhist meditation (based on Burmese traditions and popularized in a transnational spirituality movement). Suprapto has been affected by and himself influenced international somatic movement and meditation models. Over time, Suprapto became an internationally known teacher of modern Javanese spiritualism and eco-improvisation, teaching what he dubbed Joged Amirta (Amirta movement training) at his Padepokan Lemah Putih (White earth workshop), founded in 1986, an international arts training center currently run by his son. *Amirta* is the elixir of life/enlightenment churned out of the Sea of Milk in Hindu myth; movement was Suprapto's way of accessing oneness, nature consciousness, and *amirta*. *Wayang buddha* evolved in this context.[43]

Suprapto's *wayang buddha* was initially accompanied with Buddhist chant by Sukemi Darmosurjo, a Buddhist monk, and was presented first in 1975 for a Wesak (Buddha's birth and enlightenment day) performance at Mendut Temple, a ninth-century Buddhist monument. Mendut along with Borobudur is part of a Buddhist pilgrimage each Wesak. Suprapto's initial version involved improvised movement using leaves as puppets (adhering to Suprapto's eco-somatics technique). But soon he developed the actual puppets and a more formal, full-scale narrative based on the Buddhist old Javanese *Kekawin Sutasoma*, a fourteenth-century Kawi manuscript by Mpu Tantalur.[44] Born as a prince, Sutasoma converts an elephant-headed demon, a *naga*/snake, and a tigress as he offers each attacker his body for food—each animal instead decides to become Sutasoma's disciple. Finally, Sutasoma offers himself to the demon Kala to spare the lives of a hundred kings. Sutasoma's is a tale of self-sacrificing Buddhahood. Short episodes from *Kunjarakarna*, another old Javanese Buddhist *kakawin*, and *Digahayu* (Longevity) have been additional *wayang buddha* themes presented by Suprapto's group.

Suprapto worked with both international and national artists, including Solonese master choreographer Sardono Kusumo. Suprapto's group performed at the National Wayang Festival (1978), where traditional *dalangs* I knew puzzled over this large ensemble from the Surakarta academy with comparatively static scenes and slow narrative. Plié poses, multiple large figures in formations, and momentary freezes were reminiscent of Thai-Khmer art rather than emulating Java's solo *dalang*'s delivering sharp action of *wayang kulit* performance scenes. However, it was clear to all that Suprapto and cocreators were forging a new style.

Spiritual transformation through movement was always Suprapto's goal, rather than theater qua spectacle. Suprapto noted, "The essence of movement is not expression but a form of transformation. The form could be a movement from the state of being unaware to being aware, existence to non-existence."[45] Though the initial experiment lapsed from the 1980s, *wayang buddha* was revived in the 2000s as a performance-meditative form for Buddhist holidays using the leather puppets. Rather than "dance drama" with a tight narrative, Suprapto's work focused on embodiment and non-anthropocentric recognition of being through movement. His dancers presented outdoors at ancient Buddhist temple sites, including for the Borobudur International Festival (2013), which used new figures crafted by Bibit Jrabang Waluyo Wibowo. Other Buddhist groups in Indonesia have also explored presenting Jataka (tales of Buddha's previous incarnations) with wayang. Performances are usually connected with Buddhist temples, part of the Buddhist school education, and for holidays like Wesak. Performances often borrow heavily from normative *wayang kulit purwa* music, staging conventions, and so on, with figures from standard *purwa* shadow puppet sets rather than purpose made figures.[46]

Islamic Revival and Wayang Survivals

In light of the post–1979 Islamic revival, Indonesian Muslims revisited the concept of wayang as a tool of religious thought to renew or deflect attacks by fundamentalists on the practice of wayang as "un-Islamic" due to its depiction of humans. *Wayang sadat*—short for "Sarana dakwah dan tabligh" (Means of proselytizing Islamic teachings)—was created in 1985–86 by Suryadi WS (Warnosuhardjo) a *dalang* and math teacher of Mireng Village, Trucuk District, Klaten, who trained at the Muhammadiyah Klaten School of Teacher Education (SPG).[47] Inspired by *wayang wahyu* performances, Suryadi sought to "clean up" *wayang kulit*, which he saw as the legacy of the *walis* but which his *santri* (observant) family felt was now polluted by "un-Islamic" elements—humor, sexual innuendo, and Hindu-based characters. His puppets featured the conservative Middle Eastern style dress that in the 1980s was a growing style in Java. His male figures wear turbans and the females wear the hijab (veil). Stories of the Wali Songo's Islamization of Java—the founding of the Demak Mosque, the story of Sunan Kalijaga, and so on—are the repertoire. His clowns (Semar and his sons) are named Kyai Imam, Ki Salim, and Ki Kasan, and they are students at Sunan Ampel's religious school. Shows open with singing "Assalaamualaikum" and close with "Hamdalah." Songs during the performance are mostly created by Suryadi's Sanggar Sadat and include, "Basmalah," "Istighfar," "Robbana," "Pengawal Islam," and "Arkanul Ima."[48]

Drums initially replaced the gamelan (though current performances may use gamelan), and Muslim prayer in Arabic replaced *suluk* (mood songs). Performers, like puppets, wear Middle Eastern styles rather than normal Javanese formal dress. Though Suryadi's efforts achieved only modest attention in the 1980s, *wayang sadat* has widened its audience as the Islamic revival progressed and has been performed at Islamic boarding schools (*pesantren*), for the Office of the Ministry of Religion, TVRI, RRI, the Muslim Istiqlal Festival, universities, and the Jakarta Wayang Museum for the Muharram Festival. One of Suyadi's *kayon* (tree of life) figures was inscribed with Arabic calligraphy, and another features the mosque at Demak (founded by the *walis*), the latter inspired no doubt by the *wayang wahyu kayon* that features St. Peter Basilica in Rome.

Since the 1990s, ordinary *dalangs* have seen some of their business at weddings and circumcisions co-opted by Muslim *ustadzs* (teachers, speakers) who give sermons instead of performing wayang. They of course generally frown on traditional community performances such as *bersih desa* (purification of village). A son of my teacher Abeng Sunarya, Agus Sunarya, pivoted from being a *dalang* to giving these Islamic speeches at these life cycle events. (It was useful to have both kinds of "performers" in one family, and the advice *dalangs* supply at life cycle events is not unlike what the *ustadz* sermonizer does.) Groups of fundamentalists in the 2000s have broken up performances of wayang or torn down statues representing the traditional figures of wayang, finding them *syirik* (worshipping another god than Allah). Top *dalangs* have responded by becoming more overtly observant and incorporating more Arabic prayers and concepts into performances.[49] For example, Dalang Enthus Susmono (1966–2018) created *wayang santri* to make it easier for observant Muslims to hire performances. His troupe wore white "Islamic garb" and used more Arabic phrases throughout. Saskia Boonstra described Susmono's mix of prayers and coarse humor:

> There was also a puppet whose head was not fastened to its body and therefore could kiss his own genitals. And then there was Enthus Susmono's famous drunken puppet. This puppet peed in his bottle of grog, then promptly forgot that he had done so and took another sip. The crowd screamed with laughter, took pictures and recorded the action on their phones. But then, the dalang closed the lively show with a prayer.
>
> I was struck to see Enthus Susmono perform his usual crude—to some perhaps vulgar—jokes in a most obviously Islamic wayang show. The alternation of these jokes with Islamic songs appeared contradictory, but nobody in the audience seemed to care. The crowd couldn't get enough of the spectacle.[50]

What Enthus was doing with *wayang santri* was what *dalangs* always do: they move with and reflect the values of the audience, combining *tuntunan* and *tontonan*, advisement and entertainment. Enthus' blend of spirituality and raw humor reflects the mixture of high and low in Javanese culture (see Sumarsam's essay in this volume).

Some overtly "Islamic" forms of the past, *wayang menak* and *wayang sasak*, both presenting Amir Hamzah stories featuring the uncle of the Prophet, have lost popularity and have pulled back to the relative sanctuary of "intangible cultural heritage," hoping for life support from local departments of culture. Today, defining *menak* repertoires as "Islamic epics" brings fundamentalist ire from the Sunni fanatics. Even *wayang kulit purwa*, despite its venerable place in society and its declaration as a Masterpiece of World Heritage (2003) and Intangible Cultural Heritage of Humanity (2008) by UNESCO, has suffered these attacks as un-Islamic. Rituals that once opened the show are often cut. The village purifications that once had been annual events in rural areas are becoming more infrequent as the country grows more observant along Middle Eastern lines. In a 2022 posting of a video of Makassar-born Ustadz Khalid Basalamah, this popular Islamic teacher advised a follower, "If he has [a puppet], then it is better to destroy it, in the sense of the word, it's better to get rid of it" and if "in Islam it [*wayang*/image making] is forbidden, we should leave it."[51]

Dalangs protested vociferously. On February 18, 2022, Dalang Ki Warseno (Hardiodarsono) Slenk did a performance at Ora Aji, an Islamic school in Yogyakarta led by the moderate ulama Gus Miftah. A puppet resembling Ustadz Khalid was beaten up by the *Mahabharata* character Baladewa and other figures in Warseno's show called *Puppet Haram, Dalang Ngamuk, Wayang Basalamah Dikepruki Dalang* (Puppets banned, dalangs outraged, Basalamah beaten up by the *dalang*). On February 20, the video was uploaded on Adara NH's YouTube. Fundamentalists then filled social media with attacks on Dalang Warseno and Ustadz Gus Miftah.

The *dalang* organizations of Banyumas and Bandung gave more measured responses than Warseno yet expressed outrage. The moderate Nahdlatul Ulama (NU) intellectual Syafiq Hasyim argued, "Ustaz Khalid Basalamah's controversial lecture on the destruction of *wayang* to his congregation was similar to the actions of the Talib[an] ruler, ISIS in Afghanistan, who destroyed historical heritage statues from non-Muslim groups."[52] Dalang Purbo Asmoro of Solo at the same time created a new story in which a bigoted ulama (again resembling Khalid Basalamah) obstructed the marriage of two young lovers. Meanwhile, Dalang Kanda Buwana (using the *dalang's* story name during the *ruwatan* purification when he is seen as the living power of Wisnu) intervened.[53] Purbo's story *Wayang Ilang, Dhalang Nantang* (Wayang tested, *dalang* protested) ended with the puppet of an *ustadz* (made of cardboard for the event) burning as the *padalangan* (puppetry) students from ISI-Surakarta cheered. Ki Purbo's version clarified that it was the spirit of Kala (the demon son of Siwa that necessitates the *ruwatan*) that infused the meddling *ustadz* causing attacks on wayang, heritage, and true religion. In the same period, the Hindu Balinese *dalangs* discussed freedom of speech at ISI-Denpasar. Professor I Nyoman Sedana wrote:

> Article 32 paragraph (1) of the 1945 Constitution of the Republic of Indonesia mandates that "The State shall advance the Indonesian national culture [WAYANG] in the midst of world civilization."
>
> The fact [is] that Indonesia is the home of Wayang since Ancient Mataram kingdom as recorded in Matyasih inscription Saka year 825.
>
> Arab Saudi is the home of Ustadz. Please kindly go back to your own home and do whatsoever you like in your own home.[54]

To cool the inflamed social media, Ustadz Khalid Basalamah made a tempered apology, as did Ustadz Gus Miftah and Ki Warseno. But the disagreements have not dissipated. Attacks make it clear that a puppet form that started with Hindu teaching, was adapted for Islamic *dakwah,* and has accommodated Christianity, modern Buddhism, and neo-Islam spiritual messages is caught in an ongoing battle in contemporary Southeast Asia.

CONCLUSION

Traditional wayang on Java represents a spirituality that uses a multi-sensorial embodied approach to the divine. Mimesis, dance, comedy, and narrative encourage us to consider our lowest and highest impulses, recognizing that the demonic and the divine are interrelated; Siwa or Aji Saka is parent and demon Kala or Jaka Linglung is child. Hinduism, Sufi thought, Javanized Christianity, and contemporary Buddhism can accept and celebrate this message. Wayang teaches that human limitations and greed can be surpassed if we learn to explore our body-mind and that this can be done imaginatively, via performance. Ajisaka's noble letters give us tools of *nyasa* that allow us to experience our inner demonic and climb our spine, to return to our divine best—Siwa/Batara Guru. Understanding this range and speaking openly of this spiritual grounding may prove problematical for the free-thinking saints (Siti Jenar, Sunan Panggung) but remain a spiritual praxis in wayang that has persisted in local thinking. *Wayang wahyu*'s Christianity and *wayang sadat*'s reformed Islam may allow a more limited range for the human in relation to the cosmic (we can never fully be divine in Christianity or Islam), yet all religions find the spiritual aura, the *wahyu* in wayang, useful in affirming that the embodied, the danced, the sounded, and the visualized can launch us into the disembodied, the still, the silent, the unseen that is the encounter with eternity. Thus, these diverse religious communities borrow wayang as a space to meet and explore the unseeable, unknowable, and beyond-ness and, as with Suprapto's *wayang buddha*, aver that art is the best chance in life to enlarge ourselves to power here and yet ever "out there" beyond our ken.

NOTES

1. Granted that Jesus, prophets, saints, and imams were and are represented and evoked great devotion in lay people, especially women and children to promote religiosity, but for the male elites, this may be seen as lower-order thinking.

2. Puppetry and mask performance of Thailand, Cambodia, and Burma have some related features, but will be excluded here.

3. PEPADI Bali, Seminar Nasional Dalam Rangka Perayaan Hari Wayang Nasional 2021 [National seminar celebrating national wayang day 2021], November 7, 2021, via Zoom.

4. See Lembaga Kebudayaan Betawi "Kekawin" for this version at www.kebudayaanbetawi .com/4002/kekawin/. Compare with Ki Harsono Siswocarito's "Kekawin," for a second approach to the Sundanese opening passage (in English translation), http://englishlakonet.blogspot.com/2007/11/.

5. Kathy Foley, "First Things: Opening Passages in Southeast Asian Puppet Theatre," in *Puppet Theater in Contemporary Indonesia,* ed. Jan Mrazek (Ann Arbor: Centers for South and Southeast Asian Studies, University of Michigan, 2002), 271–83.

6. Yogic ideas of the chakra points, *ida* and *pinggala* channels weaving around a central channel, are related to microcosm-macrocosm equivalencies in wayang and are represented in the *kayon* (tree of life) puppet with demons at the bottom and lotus at the top. The Kala figure and snake are found on this puppet figure. The iconography is a summary for those trained in *wayang* for the different energies that make up the individual, social order, and cosmos. On the possible sources of the clowns and other Indic features, see Andrea Acri, "Birds, Bards, Buffoons and Brahmans: (Re-)Tracing the Indic Roots of Some Ancient and Modern Performing Characters from Java and Bali," *Archipel* 82 (2014): 13–70.

7. Kathy Foley, "The Origin of Kala: A Sundanese *Wayang Golek Purwa* Play by Abah Sunarya and Gamelan Giri Harja I," *Asian Theatre Journal* 18, no. 1 (2001): 1–58, doi:10.1353/atj.2001.0002.

8. See Karaton Ngyogyakarta Hadiningrat's videos: "Beksan Ajisaka"; and "Beksan Ajisaka Uyon-uyon Hadiluhung Jumadilakir 1954 Jimakir/1 Februari 2021," www.youtube.com/watch?v=oe3lQR3JOwc.

9. See "Animasi 2D Indonesia // Ajisaka [Trailer]," MSV Studios (Mataram Surya Visi Ltd.), directed by Aryanto Yuniawan, YouTube video, www.youtube.com/watch?v=rEOeZcz32L8; and Mataram Surya Visi Ltd and Universitas Amikom, "Hikayat Ajisaka di Flickfair Los Angeles," http://msvstudio.co.id.

10. Dates of the *walis* are impossible to verify; multiple generations in a family used the same title, complicating identifications. The Wali Songo are legendary in the same way as St. Patrick, the fourth-century Catholic culture bringer of Ireland, or Padmasambhava, the eighth-century Tibetan Buddhist saint. Dates here reflect Indonesian Wikipedia's versions. Sunan Kalijaga (literally, "Lord who meditated at the stream"), a prince of north coast city of Tuban, is credited as the first *dalang* and has a pilgrimage/gravesite in Kadilangu in the city of Demak; other saints have their own shrines along the north coast.

11. *Manunggaling Kawula Gusti* (union of individual and divine) is associated with figures like the martyred mystic Mansur al-Hallaj (858–March 26, 922) and Sufi lineages. Some suggest that stories of Siti Jenar and other Javanese Islamic heretics are merely borrowings of the Mansur's story to a Javanese setting.

12. R. N. Yasadipura, *The Book of Cabolèk*, trans. and ed. S. Soebardi (The Hague: Nijhoff, 1975), 151.

13. See Solichin Salam, *Sekitar Wali Songo* [Regarding the Nine Wali] (Yogyakarta: Menara Kudus, 1960); Yasadipura, *The Book of Cabolèk*; Nancy Florida, *Writing the Past, Inscribing the Future: History as Prophecy in Colonial Java* (Durham, NC: Duke University Press, 1995); D. A. Rinkes, *Nine Saints of Java*, trans. H. M. Froger, ed. A. Gorden (Kuala Lumpur: Malaysian Sociological Research Institute, 1996); R. Michael Feener, "A Re-examination of the Place of al-Hallaj in the Development of Southeast Asian Islam," *Bijdragen tot de Taal-, Land- en Volkenkunde* 154, no. 4 (1998): 571–92; George Quinn, *Bandit Saints of Java* (Melton Mowbray: Monsoon, 2019); Rinkes, *Nine Saints of Java*; Kathy Foley, "The *Ronggeng*, the *Wayang*, the *Wali*, and Islam: Female or Transvestite Male Dancers-Singers-Performers and Evolving Islam in West Java," *Asian Theatre Journal* 32, no. 2 (2015): 356–86, www.jstor.org/stable/24737037; Foley, "Les Wali reduit au silence" (Silencing the Walis), in *Marionettes et Pouvoir*, ed. R. Fleury and J. Sermon (Montpellier: Deuxieme Epoque, 2019), 150–70; and Foley, "Saintly Puppet Masters and Sacred Clowning: Antinomian Religion and Patterns in Islamic Puppetry," in *Puppets and the Spirit*, ed. Claudia Orenstein and Tim Cusack (NY: Routledge, 2022), 184–96, among other sources.

14. Geertz in his *Religion in Java* (1960) uses the terms *santri* for the purists and *abangan* (from *abang*, red) for the Javanized Muslims. While Feener ("A Re-examination of the Place of al-Hallaj") may be right that the terms are from the nineteenth century, I believe that the association of loose constructionists with red may come prior to the late colonial era since an alternate name of Siti Jenar is "Seh Lemah Abang" (Saint of the Red Earth) and areas where crafts persons often live are often called Lemah Abang, though of course, it is possible the areas are just named after red clay in places where artisans settled. Red is also the color associated with the Sufi singer mystics, animal trainers, and

wandering followers of South Asia's Lal ("ruby color") Shabaz Qalandar (1177–1274). It may again point toward Islamic roots that come not from Arab merchants but from Indo-Iranian Islam.

15. K. van Dijk and P. Nas, "Dakwah and Indigenous Culture: The Dissemination of Islam," *Bijdragen tot de Taal-, Land- en Volkenkunde* 154, no. 2 (1998): 218–35, at 226.

16. Such contentions of Chinese or Persian connections are distressing to Javanese Muslims given the anti-Sinitic and anti-Persian/Shi'a bent of Sunni orthodoxy in postcolonial Indonesia.

17. Credit for *wayang sasak* is also sometimes given to Pangeran Sangupati Urip sent by the Wali Songo to cure disease (David Harnish, *Change and Identity in the Music Cultures of Lombok, Indonesia* [Leiden: Brill, 2021], 118), or a wandering religious figure who cures a famine by a wayang performance, or Wali Nyatok who as a child magically spent a night in Java learning wayang and returned to demonstrate it in Lombok the following day. For some different stories, see Abdul Latief Apriaman, "Wayang Sasak Tumbuh di Bawah Bayang Kecurigaan" [Wayang Sasak growing under the shadow of suspicion], *Tempo*, July 23, 2019, https://travel.tempo.co.

18. See Judith Ecklund, "Paradoxes and Realities of Wayang among the Sasak of Lombok," in *Puppet Theater in Contemporary Indonesia: New Approaches to Performance Events*, ed. Jan Mrázek (Ann Arbor: Centers for South and Southeast Asian Studies, University of Michigan, 2002), 205–21. David Harnish, "The Worlds of Wayang Sasak: Music, Performance, and Negotiations with Religion and Modernity," *Asian Music* 34, no. 2 (2003): 91–120, www.jstor.org/stable/4098458.

19. Comparison of post-*wali* puppet figures with Hindu-Buddhist East Java temple friezes in wayang style shows greater stylization of puppets, different musical instruments, and so on.

20. Suratno, "Studi Tentang Lakon Wahyu Dalam Pakeuran Wayang Kultt [*sic*] Purwa Di Surakarta" [A Study of Wahyu plays in the Surakarta style puppetry in the last decade], *Harmonia: Journal of Arts Research and Education* 5, no. 1 (2004).

21. This story remains popular in Java and beyond, for example Sumarsam, performed it in 2023 to celebrate fifty years of the Wesleyan University World Hall of Music. See www.youtube.com /watch?v=6_DzgGsrObk.

22. This model continues. For example, concerning a performance of Dalang Danang Suseno for the 2018 election, editor Danar Widiyanto wrote, "Wahyu Cakraningrat will only penetrate into the knights who are clean and spiritual, intelligent and resistant to temptation, virtuous, and high social sensitivity," and Widyanto then quoted Hidayat Nur Wahid, the deputy speaker of the Majelis Permusyawaratan Rakyat (People's Consultative Assembly) on the event: "In this political year, it is very fitting to take *Wahyu Cakraningrat*'s philosophy. There, the struggle for power is fully carried out ethically, humanely and with an awareness of prioritizing togetherness in behavior. It's not unjust an unscrupulous behavior"; see "Wahyu Cakraningrat, Sebuah Filosofis untuk Merebut Kekuasaan," *Krjogjan.com*, www.krjogja.com.

23. Suratno, *"Studi Tentang Lakon Wahyu."*

24. For in-depth discussion of *wayang wahyu*, see A. Handi Setyanto, Dr. Wisma Nugraha, Ch. R, M. Hum, and. Prof. Dr. Soetarno, DE. "Sajian Ki Blacius Subono: Mediasi Kisah Alkitab," Wayang Wahyu Lakon Hana Caraka Nabi Elia (Ki Blacius Subono's Presentation: Mediation of Bible Stories "Wayang Wahyu Play Hana Caraka"), S2 (M.A.), University Gajah Mada, 2016. Agus Handi Setyanto, *Wayang Katholik: Cara Cerdas Berkatese* (Catholic Wayang: A Smart Mode of Catechism) (Yogyakarta: Pt. Kanisius, 2017); Marzanna Poplawska, "Wayang Wahyu as an Example of Christian Forms of Shadow Theatre" *Asian Theatre Journal* 21, no. 2 (2004): 194–202, www.jstor.org/stable/4145461; Poplawska, *Performing Faith: Christian Music, Identity and Inculturation in Indonesia* (NY: Routledge, 2020).

25. Setyanto, *Wayang Katholik*, 27–38; Poplawska, "Wayang Wahyu as an Example of Christian Forms of Shadow Theatre."

26. Setyanto, *Wayang Katholik*, 28–29.

27. Syahrul Munir Ungaran, "Wayang Wahyu, Kisah Alkitab yang Disajikan dalam Bentuk Wayang," *Kompas* (2017). Ungaran discusses recent developments in Semarang. The most detailed history with discussion of the art analyzed in five periods is Setyanto, *Wayang Katholik*, 40–55.

28. Marzanna Poplawska, at 196.

29. This practice alleviated accusations of sexy female singers stealing the show and kept decorum. Current performances may feature female singers.

30. She was very active, performing up to the death of her drummer husband in 1993.

31. Schools mentioned in this essay have all changed their names multiple times over the years as they have added higher degrees, and all are branches of national colleges/universities of the arts. In the 1980s, this school was called ASKI (Akademi Seni Karawitan Indonesia, Indonesian academy of music), later STSI (Sekolah Tinggi Seni Indonesia, Indonesian college of the arts), and is now ISI-Surakarta.

32. See Ganug Nugroho Adi, "Blacius Subono: An Outlandish Dalang and Musician," *Jakarta Post*, December 30, 2013.

33. Matthew Isaac Cohen, "Wayang Wayu," *Indonesian Performance* (blog), February 15, 2009, http://indonesianperformance.blogspot.com.

34. See Benjamin Brinner, "Performer Interaction in a New Form of Javanese *Wayang*," in *Essays on Southeast Asian Performing Arts: Local Manifestations and Cross-Cultural Implications*, ed. Kathy Foley (Berkeley: Centers for South and Southeast Asia Studies, University of California, Berkeley, 1992), 96–114, for more on *pakeliran padat*. For Subono's innovations, see Setyanto, *Wayang Katholik*, 48–49.

35. For a sample of Fosdahl's play for Pangudi Luhur School in April 2013, which uses a wide screen, multiple *dalangs*, Indonesian dialogue, and more, see "Wayang Wahyu Lakon *Wahyu Manunggal Sejati* Karya Frank Fosdahl," www.youtube.com/watch?v=8ayxsml9C3c.

36. Setyanto, *Wayang Katholik*, 54.

37. See Mathias Hariyadi, "Muslim Scholar against 'Wayang,' Indonesia's Traditional Theatre," *Asia News*, February 18, 2022, www.asianews.it/news-en/Muslim-scholar-against-%27wayang%27, -Indonesia's-traditional-theatre-55181.html.

38. Poplawska, *Performing Faith*, 145.

39. See Boen Boen, *Alkitab Wayang=The Wayang Bible: Perjanjian Baru=The New Testament* [Illustrations by Ammar Fauzi] (Jakarta: BPK Gunung Mulia, 2018), comic book.

40. Poplawska, *Performing Faith*, 149–50.

41. Hariyadi, "Muslim Scholar against 'Wayang.'" The reference is to Paul IV (1998), "Pastoral Constitution on the Church in the Modern World *Gaudium Et Spes*," promulgated December 7, 1965, which notes, "Efforts must be made so that those who foster these arts feel that the Church recognizes their activity and so that, enjoying orderly liberty, they may initiate more friendly relations with the Christian community. The Church acknowledges also new forms of art which are adapted to our age and are in keeping with the characteristics of various nations and regions. They may be brought into the sanctuary since they raise the mind to God, once the manner of expression is adapted and they are conformed to liturgical requirements." www.vatican.va.

42. See Senawangi, "Wayang Budha," https://senawangi.org.

43. See Katya Bloom, Margit Galanter, and Sandra Reeve, *Embodied Lives: Touched by the Art of Amerta Movement with Suprapto Suryodarmo* (London: Karnac Books, 2014); and Lise Lavelle, "Amerta Movement of Java 1986–1997: An Asian Movement Improvisation" (PhD diss., Lund University, Centre for Languages and Literature, 2006). Also see images at the Routledge Performance Archive, www.routledgeperformancearchive.com/multimedia/video/human-nature-spirit, for sense of his eco-somatic workshops.

44. On Suprapto, see Mathew Isaac Cohen, "Contemporary 'Wayang' in Global Contexts," *Asian Theatre Journal*, 24, no. 2 (2007): 338–69, www.jstor.org/stable/27568418. On Sutasoma, see Soewito Santoso, *Sutasoma: A Study in Javanese Wajrayana* (New Delhi: International Academy of Indian Culture, 1975).

45. Suprapto's life is detailed in "Obituary, Suprapto Suryodarmo 'Free Movement' Guru for Hundreds of Dancers," *Jakarta Post*, December 30, 2019. www.thejakartapost.com.

46. For other Buddhist-related experiments, see Anugrah, "Wayang Jataka Berbasis Sastra," (Jataka Wayang based on Literature), *Berita Magelang* (Magelang news), December 6, 2021, http://beritamagelang.id, on wayang inspired by Boroboudur panels. Another experiment using new puppets and projections was an intercultural production by Christopher Romero, I Gusti Putu Sudarta, and Andy McGraw in Bali; see Christopher Romero, "Wayang Machinima Jataka Preview," 2007, www.youtube.com/watch?v=rbNqN8vz1gk.

47. See Sutarjo, "*Wayang Sadat* in Javanese Culture." For a recent version of *wayang sadat,* see a scene that features Sunan Bonang converting Lokajaya (Sunan Kalijaga) presented at a 2016 Mystic Music Festival/Konya at "Wayang Sadat—6" (2017), at www.facebook.com/watch/?v=1353691058005070. Note the ending with Islamic call to prayer at 8:31.

48. Sutarjo, "*Wayang Sadat* in Javanese Culture," 198.

49. Foley, "The *Ronggeng,* the *Wayang,* the *Wali,* and Islam"; and Foley, "Les Wali reduit au silence."

50. Boonstra, "Performing Islam."

51. Reported in "Banuyas Dalang Will Police Khalid Basalamah about Haram Puppet Lecture," *World Today News,* 2022, www.world-today-news.com.

52. "NU Intellectuals Are Surprised There Are Still People Like Ustaz Khalid Basalamah, Destroying Puppets Similar to the Taliban," VOI, February 21, 2022, https://voi.id/en/news/137260/nu-intellectuals-are-surprised-there-are-still-people-like-ustaz-khalid-basalamah-destroying-puppets-similar-to-the-taliban.

53. See Purbo Asmoro, *Wayang Ilang, Dhalang Nantang* (Wayang disappears, dalangs protest), trans. Katheryn Emerson, February 18, 2022, www.youtube.com/watch?v=-4lIH1jIlug.

54. Sedana, email to author, February 26, 2022.

PART VI

Technologies of Preservation: Archives

13

Has "God" Made the Apparatus?

Missionaries as Phonographic Mediators in New Guinea and Melanesia

Sebastian Klotz

Missionaries played a key role during the colonial expansion, affecting the social structure, religion, and cultural expressions of local cultures, fostering their own economic enterprises, and contributing to ethnological and anthropological research. But their main aim was to spread the word of God and implement the Christian liturgy, and it is through this missionary practice that they forged intense interactions and alterations of local rites, education, the structure of local communities. Oceania had become a laboratory for Western concepts of race early in the eighteenth century, and for missionary activities in particular.[1] Yet missionary work was identical neither with the colonial effort of colonial states nor with ethnological research undertaken in the academy, to the effect that structural tensions and irritations informed missionary practices. It is through the lens of these tensions, which were an effect of their interventionist practices in the field of education and their economic activities regarded as competitive by other commercial actors, that we can gain some understanding of their role within the network of ethnic and colonial actors.

It will be argued that their ambivalent stance to local languages and the role of German in their pedagogical work, to academic anthropologists and ethnologists, and to semiofficial colonial institutions such as the Neuguinea Companie affected their phonographic recording practices.[2] Missionary recording activities need to be placed against the wider mobilities of people, phonographs, biological specimen, ethnographic objects, scientific data, and the plants and fruits grown on New Guinean plantations that led to the multidimensional entanglements that were enabled by colonialism and that actively nourished it. Whereas existing research that reconstructs ethnographic activity in the early twentieth century tends to choose a primarily regional perspective and thus canonizes a geography of knowledge construction established at the time, my aim here is to carve out the contradictory motivations, the multiethnic experiences and contexts, and the agencies of actors and institutions involved.[3] This critical review of phonographic activities may stimulate a postcolonial assessment of the material heritage assembled in the form of phonographic recordings and the hidden power asymmetries they represent. From this angle, procedures that may take shape from the contours of narratives not delivered, of recordings not taken, of "meanings," biographies, and cultural experiences that resisted easy integration into Western knowledge are a prerequisite for a dialogue with the former cultures of origin and local communities.

COMMERCIAL, ACADEMIC, AND MISSIONARY PHONOGRAPHIC RECORDING PROJECTS AFTER 1900

Phonographic recordings for documentation and research purposes do not happen in passing but are carefully orchestrated ethnic and cultural encounters that take place within a specific technical setting. As there is no systematic survey on the attitudes missionaries were entertaining toward the phonograph, it makes sense to turn to a well-researched area in which missionaries were active. New Guinea and Melanesia fall well into this category, and although geographically they represent an outlier viewed from Indonesia, some relevant insights may be gained that might radiate across the Indonesian realm.

Phonographic activity may have been a novelty in the small villages and colonial stations on the coastline. With respect to Asia in general, the recording business had been thriving, leading to considerable recording campaigns and to large imports of phonographs and cylinders into the region.[4] The record industry targeted the larger commercial ports as transcultural hubs in which marketable new genres emerged.[5] Colonial officers, missionaries, and a mobile workforce traveling from Europe to the large transcontinental ports and then farther to Indonesia and Papua New Guinea would most likely have taken notice of these developments as they transformed the soundscape of port cities and marked the arrival of phonographs in the households of the local elites.

This commercial endeavor of record companies unfolded parallel to the academic recording campaigns that, in contrast, focused on seemingly untouched rural and isolated musical practices. As a third party, we have missionaries whose attitude to the recording of language and music was ambivalent. Given the high number of missionaries active in the area, only a very small share did recordings, while considerable numbers of anthropologists, naval officers, and physicians were involved in recording campaigns.

A CONTEXTUALIZING APPROACH TO PHONOGRAPHIC RECORDING PRACTICES

New Guinea, divided among Germany, Britain, and the Netherlands, provides a case in point, as it attracted a plethora of ethnographic and recording activities that has been fairly well documented.[6] While the role of missionaries for these recordings has been acknowledged, we have no detailed idea of the role that recordings played for them, with respect to both their professional career (i.e., in the context of their religious order) and their interaction with local communities. Moreover, how did missionaries come in contact with phonographic activities? Under which conditions were they implicated in such activities? How did they position their phonographic activities vis-à-vis other actors in the field and other institutions who also made recordings? How did their presence affect phonographic activities by other actors? And how were phonographic activities of missionaries transformed into "results" and "knowledge" that could be circulated in the Western academy?

Recording expertise and ethnomusicological methods, fields that had just been emerging around 1900, were not part of the curriculum of German missionaries. Furthermore, as interventionist actors immediately affected local practices and language, the proactive stance of missionaries could not be brought in line with the research goal of comparative musicology, which very early on was concerned about the loss of Indigenous musical practices and thus pleaded for a salvage ethnography. In a way, missionaries undermined the conviction of ethnologists and comparative musicologists that ethnic actors should be studied and their culture documented in their "original state." Furthermore, it is safe to assume that the pioneering recordings of early ethnologists in the United States and by anthropologist Franz Boas were not widely known among missionaries. Even if a phonograph was at hand, it remained unclear to what end it should be applied. Record-based didactics of foreign languages did not take shape after 1910, primarily stimulated by Wilhelm Doegen in Berlin.[7] Again, we cannot establish any link between Doegen's recordings and writings and the training of missionaries. So what evidence do we have of missionary recording practices in New Guinea?

It is from this angle of the cultural situatedness of phonographic recordings and recording ideologies that I would like to present some material and insights primarily relating to New Guinea and Melanesia. In the early twentieth century, this region saw astounding phonographic and anthropological activity, mainly by British, German, and Austrian biologists, anthropologists, ethnologists, naval officers, marine physicians, and linguists. Inspired by Anna Maria Busse Berger's penetrating monograph *The Search for Medieval Music in Africa and Germany, 1891 to 1961*, by the extensively commented on CD edition of early Austrian recordings in New Guinea, and by research contextualizing British research in the Torres Straits, I hope to offer some initial thoughts on the understudied topic of the relationship between missionaries and phonography that may be of use to further engage the research and recording contexts in Indonesia as well.[8]

PERSONAL AND INSTITUTIONAL INTERACTIONS
IN THE LIGHT OF DIFFERENT RESEARCH PARADIGMS

Special attention will be paid to the close interaction of the missionary Franz Vormann and the Austrian physician Rudolf Pöch. The latter wrote ample reports that were published by the Royal Austrian Academy of Sciences. He also made extensive documentation of the recordings and their performance contexts, and the recordings have survived and have been edited by Gerda Lechleitner and commented on by Don Niles in a project that could serve as a model for such editions.[9] Furthermore, missionary Vormann coauthored a grammar of the Monumbo language that implicated phonographic recordings.[10] These written documents and recordings allow us to reconstruct the interaction between these two men and the local population, whose songs, dances, and oral statements are captured on wax. As we have no complete picture of all recording projects and additional potential missionaries involved, it is hard to say if this collaboration was exceptional.

A second important source to understand the role of mission stations in phonographic activities are the diaries of Alfred Haddon, the biologist and zoologist who did research in the Torres Straits and New Guinea in the last decade of the nineteenth century, preceding the Austrian and German campaigns. Complementing his monograph *Head-Hunters: Black, White, and Brown*, which was published in 1901, and the multivolume documentation of the Cambridge Anthropological Expedition to Torres Strait, which he directed and whose first volume was published in the same year, we are able to reconstruct the complexity of interactions with local actors and British missionaries, and its relevance to Haddon's phonographic activities.[11]

Hypothetically, missionaries can be conceived of as having played an ambivalent role, poised between the observing, analytical stance of ethnologists and the ethnological aspiration to supply ethnographic objects and data and the expectation of their missionary orders to become transformative agents by converting an ethnic population to Christianity. Unlike ethnologists and early comparative musicologists, missionaries lacked a protocol for phonographic practice and a coherent workflow as laid out by Carl Stumpf, Felix van Luschan, and Erich von Hornbostel for early comparative musicology in Berlin. For this reason, only a fraction of the large number of missionaries active in New Guinea and Melanesia ever got in touch with a phonograph. While anthropologists were used to hands-on measurements and to collecting data and specimens and psychologists were accustomed to using measuring devices and could easily familiarize themselves with the phonograph, as did materially oriented ethnologists, missionaries, with their concern about language and liturgy, had few points of contact with technology. Also, none of the German and Dutch missionary societies active in New Guinea and Melanesia—the Herz-Jesu-Mission, the Steyler Mission (Societas Verbi Divini, SVD), the Neuendettelsauer Mission—had their bases in Berlin, so that apparently no missionary reported to the Ethnological Museum there to pick up a phonograph that was held in store for travelers.[12] This is not to say that individual missionaries did not actively collaborate with ethnologists.[13] But it took a couple of years before leading figures such as Pater Wilhelm Schmidt promoted the case of the missionary-ethnographer-anthropologist, equipped with a phonograph for the documentation of local musical cultures so as to lend them more authority vis-à-vis the academy, especially in ethnology and anthropology.[14]

The institutional interaction between missionary societies, German colonialism, and academic anthropological and ethnographic research was complex. Usually, missionaries were active in regions in which their orders anticipated that a missionary project could be successfully realized. Academic research followed a different agenda, influenced by existing research, competition with other Western nations, and the prospect of collecting anthropological data and ethnographic objects. Colonialism was not untouched by these factors but unfolded against the background of national interests, economic competition, and profit-driven expansion. Colonial discourse would exploit discursive figures familiar from the missionary project, such as the conceived pacifying and culturally elevating impact of Western colonial rule on "primitive cultures," but the relationship had been marked by tensions ever since the rise of the German colonial project.[15] Similarly, ethnography and anthropology, as well as comparative musicology, could not be subsumed as colonial sciences or disciplines in the service of colonial politics.[16] Likewise, missions had to adapt to unfolding economic and administrative structures brought about by colonialism. Trade-based colonialism had effects on the ground very different from a plantation-based model. As missions were seeking to establish long-term impacts on the cultures they were converting, they were immediately affected by the different dynamics of economic, administrative, and political processes that colonial rule brought to the areas in which missions were active. The situation in New Guinea and Melanesia was unique, as the colonial powers were unable to persuade settlers to come to the region to run plantations and businesses and to establish Western-style ports and cities. Missionaries were thus acting as fairly isolated outposts, depending on the local colonial administration.

The wider research questions of anthropologists who came to the region help clarify the role and self-conception of missionaries. The large expeditions, such as the Torres Strait project and the German Marine expeditions, did cross-disciplinary research, studied the spread of disease, undertook the collection of ethnographic objects and human remains, performed psychological tests, did phonograph recordings, and systematically processed and published on these activities and interventions. Richard Thurnwald studied the social structure of local societies, Pöch did extensive documentations of language and performance practices. Both took phonographic recordings that were analyzed in the Berlin and Vienna archives. The wider research issues of human evolution, of the features that constituted the cultural level of a local culture, and of scientific racism were discussed in a frame in which conceptual concerns of missionaries did not rank very prominently. Common ground could be found in the context of diffusionism, but the academic networks of university and museum experts and the division of labor among academic institutions that processed the objects and findings of expeditions to foreign cultures were initially completely separate from the networks operated by missionary orders.[17]

Missions were valuable for establishing contact with local communities so that German colonial actors did not have to start from scratch. At the same time, missions became competitors of colonial companies and entrepreneurs when they set up their own plantations, securing an influx of labor from the villages in which they were active, thus establishing a self-sufficient educational and economic system motivating the young to acquire a good education to be able to find work on the plantation as local teachers in missionary schools or even with the colonial administration and local police force led by German officers.

Missionaries were valuable for similar reasons to ethnologists and anthropologists. Some mission stations ran hospitals that were of extreme importance in the tropical climate and with its constant threat of malaria and other diseases. Through their educational activities, they had access to large groups of ethnic actors, were familiar with their customs and rites (which they tried to replace violently by Christian rites), could identify potential informants, and could recommend travel routes, and although ethnologists followed the ideal of subjects without previous intercourse with Western foreigners, they were mostly grateful to have missionaries in the area. Comparative musicologists who were eager to gather musical expressions from as many cultures as possible did accept recordings from missionaries, especially as they were intimately linked to the ethnic groups with whom they interacted and could supply reliable documentation. A fair share of the wax cylinder recordings of the Berlin Phonogram Archive was thus supplied by missionaries.

THE RECORDINGS MADE BY FRANZ VORMANN AND RUDOLF PÖCH

The Vormann-Pöch collaboration in Potsdamhafen (present day Monumbo Bay), which has been covered in great detail by Don Niles, was initiated in 1904.[18] Vormann had been active since 1896 when his order, the Societas Verbi Divini (SVD), began its activities in German New Guinea.[19] The German Neuguinea Companie had conquered the area in the mid-1880s, equipped with a warrant from the Kaiser, so they considered this land to be German.

Vormann had studied the Monumbo people since 1899, so Pöch could rely on his ample insights into the culture, psychology, religion, and language of the Monumbo.[20] Startled by the wealth of cultural expressions in music and dance, Pöch, who was of Austrian origin but based in Berlin at the time, undertook an extensive recording campaign. It is safe to assume that Vormann's familiarity with local ethnic actors stimulated this campaign and established trust among the Monumbo population and Pöch. Ideally, a recording was undertaken under the supervision of a language specialist, as in the case of the recordings for the Lautarchiv made by Wilhelm Doegen, who appointed linguists for the respective languages of his campaign during World War I. Pöch, by the mere luck of having found Vormann, anticipated this model. Pöch fell short of an informed musical and cultural, let alone comparative, analysis of the recorded music and dance, but his campaign represents an important reference point for current New Guineans in the search for their own history. From his extensive reports we learn about the performance conditions and contexts.[21] It is here that the template developed by the Vienna Phonogram Archive became relevant as it assured that detailed recording protocols and transcriptions were being made.

As a result of these protocols (figures 13-1 and 13-2), we are able to identify singers, musicians, dancers, and speakers, genres, titles, occasions of their cultural production, and, with the help of Vormann, the texts they used for music and dance.[22] From Vormann's point of view, the situation must have been ambivalent. The study of language was an intermediary stage on the way to conversion. Missionaries had to learn local languages to access local populations but at the same time disrupted linguistic and cultural practices through their implementation of Christian rite and faith. Why would a recording matter to Vormann? One could argue that it helped him penetrate the complex linguistic structures, pronunciation, and use of language in the context of music and dance. Western linguists had soon suggested that colleagues recording foreign languages should urge speakers to use standard texts read out in front of the phonograph from a text sheet so that recordings could be compared. These comprised passages from the Bible as well as elementary grammatical structures, the alphabet, and numbers. And indeed, among the Vormann-Pöch recordings, we find sequences of words apparently read from a grammatical table by George Amambura, who was about fourteen years of age.[23] I was able to identify the very same conjugation in the Monumbo grammar published by Fr. Vormann and P. Wilh. Scharfenberger in 1914, though in a slightly different transcription.

In informal language instruction, it is unlikely that one would read out the whole sequence of a conjugation or declination of verbs and nouns. As Vormann makes no reference to phonographic practices in his Monumbo grammar (nor in other publications), we cannot gauge the function of these standardized recorded exercises.[24] Did they enhance language instruction of "his" Monumbo pupils, or were they a method that would allow him to grasp the grammatical structures of the language in a manner

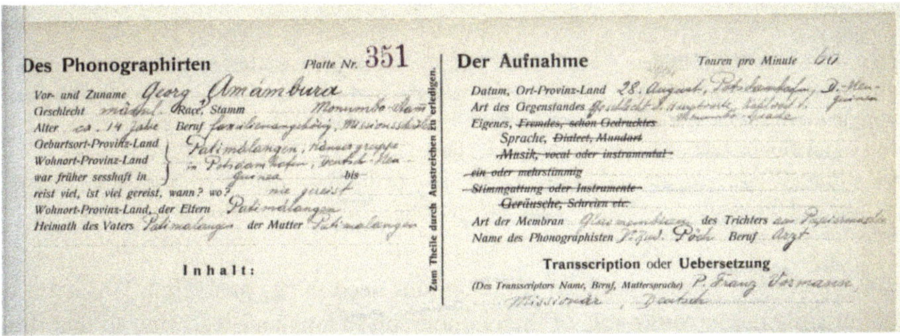

FIGURE 13-1. The top section of the questionnaire of the recording protocol (the template of the Vienna Phonogram Archive) for PhA (call no.) 351, which gives the personal core data of the recorded person. From the CD-ROM supplied with the CD edition (Niles, "Comments").

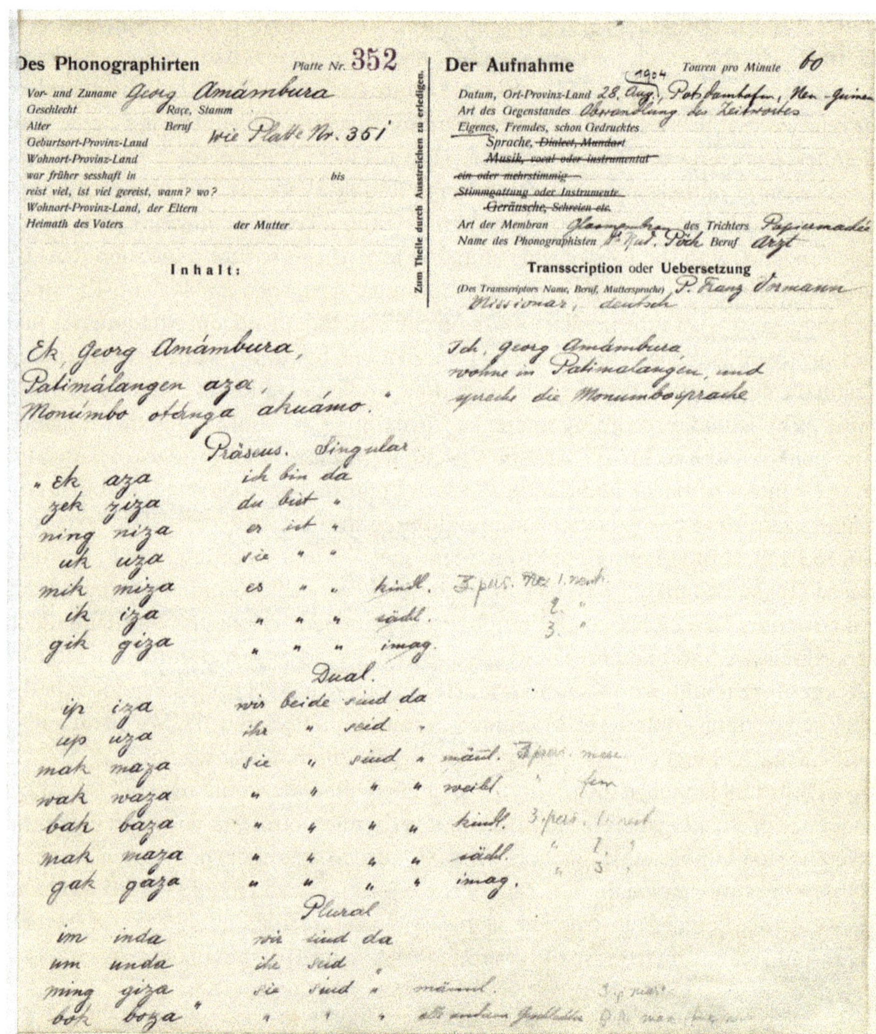

FIGURE 13-2. The complete questionnaire and sheet for PhA 352. The top section refers us to PhA 351 (pictured in figure 13-1) for the personal data. In the lower section, we find the conjugation of a verb and its translation into German. The role of Fr. Vormann in the transcription and translation is acknowledged in the top section. From the CD-ROM supplied with the CD edition (Niles, "Comments"). Readers can listen to this recording by visiting the UC Press website and the companion SoundCloud website: https://soundcloud.com/uc-press/sets /missionaries-anthropologists-and-music.

not practised by native speakers? More options need to be considered. Was it a way of initiating pupils to the role of the phonograph in language teaching, so that they would listen to German grammatical exercises in a similar way? Was he using recordings of German at all? Were there structures in the Monumbo language that he—and foremost, Pöch—could penetrate only by repeatedly listening to the phonograph?

The ambivalence may have run even deeper, given the conviction of missionaries that their word was representing and evoking and performing the word of God. Could such linguistic and religious authority be shared with a machine, side by side with a missionary being the medium of God? In this configuration, the role of recording media was unclear, poised between the mimetic, the potentially magical, and the transcendent, between orality and the mechanistic, quasi-primitive scripturality of the groove.[25] Can the phonograph evoke the four senses of scripture? Can the phonograph pray?

Wilhelm Schmidt had shown active interest in linguistic matters and in the notation of the *laute*, the concrete sounds and articulations of spoken language, implementing his *Anthropos* notation after a systematic survey of existing notation methods that he considered unsuitable and worth improving.[26] But he did not relate the notation of *laute* by way of transcription to the "notation" of the phonograph.[27]

THE COMPLEXITY OF CULTURAL INTERACTIONS DURING THE PÖCH RECORDINGS

Pöch encouraged local actors to play the phonograph as well. Further complicating the conceived notion of appointed subjects in front of the phonograph being their sole form of interaction is the fact that the local population accepted the machine and apparently integrated it into their festivities, enjoying listening to what had been recorded from them. Pöch provided sets of listening tubes to enhance the quality of rehearsals so that locals could check their own recordings, but in most cases, the wide display funnel was used to guarantee broad diffusion of sounds to some fifty to eighty people present.[28] These are clearly interactions not anticipated by Erich von Hornbostel's instructions on the use of the phonograph that he issued in the form of a typescript.[29] Von Hornbostel was extremely anxious to ensure that Western researchers get representative recordings, that only reliable subjects should be chosen, that recordings of songs should be double checked the next day to avoid being misled about their reputation in the local population or their performance details.

Furthermore, we learn from the reports by Pöch that he used various recording equipment, including a Wiener Archivphonograph and an Edison phonograph, depending on purpose of recording; that he undertook rehearsals to stimulate a sense of acceptable/non-acceptable recordings among the group he was interacting with; that he displayed European songs; that the locals were dealing easily with phonographic presentations, and finally that a local actor asked missionary Vormann in the presence of Pöch, if "'God' had made the apparatus."[30]

Recording sessions and dialogues leading to such complex and apparently informal and confidential interactions were made possible by missionaries who spoke the language. A second direct effect can be gathered from Pöch's detailed documentation and the inclusion of young students from missionary schools in the recording sample.[31] Again, Vormann's presence is crucial here. Missionaries aimed at children in their effort for conversion, and this substantially expands the age range of recorded local actors in the recording campaign by Pöch.[32]

A study of the circumstances of Pöch's recordings yields additional insights. His travel to Cape Nelson in British New Guinea put him in contact with the head of the Methodist Mission, George Brown, and with British Colonial administrators.[33] In Oro Province, he relied on the assistance of a member of the Motu by the name of Támotu, in the service of the government, when recording the Baifa.[34] In Pöch's report covering this leg of his trip, there is a photograph accompanying the recording with the call no. Ph 524 for the Vienna Phonogram Archive so that we can synchronize an image of the actors with the recording.[35] (Readers can listen to this recording by visiting the UC Press website and the companion SoundCloud website: https://soundcloud.com/uc-press/sets/missionaries-anthropologists-and -music.) We learn that the recorded ensemble from the Baifa ethnic group had traveled far and had rehearsed specifically for this recording, giving us a rare instance of an inter-ethnic recording situation and a photograph from which the Western researcher is absent, adding to the paradoxical absence of Western voices (figure 13-3).[36]

FIGURE 13-3. Pöch's photograph of the Baifa recording group. The original caption reads, "Baifa people sing into the Archiv-Phonograph" (Pöch, "Zweiter Bericht über meine phonographischen Aufnahmen in Neu-Guinea," 818).

RECORDING DISPLACED VOICES FROM NEW GUINEA

The obsessive interest in children and young adults is also evident from the fact that the missionaries brought two young boys from New Guinea to Europe, where systematic phonographic recordings of one of them were made. The first boy was Bonifaz (Tamatai) Pritak-Mawi from Karesau.[37] He was trained at an SVD missionary school and learned to sing German tunes. On his en route stop in Sydney, he tried to escape but was found and taken to Europe in 1906, as was Joseph Apo from Tumleo Island. Forty-two recordings of Tamatai were taken by Pater Wilhelm Schmidt himself with the assistance of Wenzel Vobornik in Vienna in 1907, adding to the complex mobilities of local and Western actors, as Vienna had become a recording site of Guinean musical practices, embodied by this young boy at age fifteen.[38] We can assume that this encounter and the recording experience persuaded Pater Schmidt to encourage missionaries of his order to use phonographic equipment in their work.[39]

In a similarly surprising extension of recording sites, linguist Otto Dempwolff, who served in the German Neuguinea Companie and later as a medical officer of the German Schutztruppen in both New Guinea and Africa, recorded sailors from the German South Sea in Daressalam, Africa, in 1906.[40] As German administrators in New Guinea recruited sailors primarily from mission stations, where some familiarity with the German language could be expected, we can tentatively assume that they were indirectly involved in this recording project as well, which forms part of the wider picture of recordings taken from actors from New Guinea outside their home territory. World War I led to an unprecedented displacement of soldiers from their home territory. This resulted in the foundation of a secret Prussian Phonographic Commission to study representatives of all the ethnic groups held captive in German POW camps. After World War I, a series of recordings of songs and poems in Malay were recorded in Berlin.[41] They were overseen by the linguist Walter Trittel.

GLOBALIZATION AND MULTI-SITE EXPERIENCES OF WESTERN RESEARCHERS AND OF LOCAL ACTORS

These facts underline the impact of modern globalization. It could be felt in the composition of ship crews who came to New Guinea, in the ethnic composition of workers on the New Guinean plantations, many of them with Malay and Chinese origins, in the hiring of New Guineans to work in Queensland/Australia and Samoa, in the deployment of soldiers from Oceania in Europe during World War I, and in the multi-site experiences of ethnologists and physicians who performed fieldwork and did recordings in New Guinea, many of whom had gathered professional experience in other regions of the world:[42]

Otto Dempwolff, physician and linguist: German East Africa, New Guinea
Richard Thurnwald, anthropologist: Italy, Egypt, New Guinea
Rudolf Pöch, ethnologist: India, Africa, New Guinea
Augustin Krämer, Navy physician and ethnologist: South America, Oceania
Emil Stephan, Navy physician: China, Oceania

Likewise, local populations had experienced a long history of interethnic commerce and mobility across the Melanesian archipelago and should not be considered as actors tied to one place. The Berlin Kolonialausstellung of 1897 featured a "Südseedorf," the Munich Oktoberfest of 1910 a "Samoan village." World fairs implemented anthropological laboratories to study a cross section of the world's populations and to perform hearing tests. Brokers, impresarios, and travel agents ensured that people from Oceania were regularly brought to these occasions. And they were soldiers from Oceania in the "enemy armies" of France and Britain, exposed to anthropometric measurements and recording campaigns in German POW camps during World War I. The meticulously filled questionnaires by German linguists and musicologists in the German camps of the prisoners chosen for a linguistic or musical recording provide a glimpse of war-ridden biographies and global displacements affecting so many people.[43]

TWO COMPETING GERMAN
ETHNOLOGICAL INSTRUCTIONS

Returning to Pater Schmidt's ambition in ethnographical documentation, with the founding of his journal *Anthropos* in 1906 and the publication of the *Anleitung zu ethnographischen Beobachtungen*, he entered into direct competition with academic ethnographic and anthropological research and with the emerging comparative musicology.[44]

The Berlin *Anleitung für ethnographische Beobachtungen und Sammlungen in Afrika und Oceanien* are essentially instructions on how to collect and to research in German Africa and Oceania, the two key regions where Germany held colonies.[45] It became mandatory for travelers to collect a phonograph from the Berlin museum, and for this purpose, von Hornbostel compiled detailed instructions on how to use the phonograph in the field, which circulated as a typescript.[46] The printed *Anleitung* by von Luschan included specific paragraphs for the documentation of music, most likely following the advice by von Hornbostel, who oversaw the Berlin Phonogram Archive (figure 13-4).[47] A comparison with Pater Schmidt's instructions specifically designed for missionaries and published as a supplement to the journal *Anthropos* reveals extensive overlap and almost identical phrases in the musical section.

In a strategic magazine article from 1908 that sought to confirm to the German public and to colonial science and potential sponsors the relevance of his Phonogram Archive, which he had founded at the Psychological Institute of

3. Jeder Reisende in einem noch wenig erforschtem Gebiete sollte mit einem phonographischen Apparate ausgerüstet sein und möglichst viele typische Musikstücke (Einzelgesang, Orchester usw.) aufnehmen. Dabei ist nach der folgenden Anweisung zu verfahren.

A. Ausrüstung.

a) Phonograph oder Grammophon mit Aufnahme- und Wiedergabemembran, Schalltrichter, Schlüssel.
b) Reservemembranen oder Reparaturausrüstung.
c) Ölkanne, Staubpinsel, Lederlappen, Schraubenzieher.
d) Walzen, tunlichst vor Erschütterung, grosser Hitze, Nässe zu schützen.
e) Stimmpfeife (Normal-a = 435).

B. Aufnahme.

a) Uhrwerk vor jeder Aufnahme ganz aufziehen.
b) Uhrwerk gewöhnlich mit mittlerer Geschwindigkeit laufen lassen; bei sehr hoher, sehr leiser oder sehr schneller Musik grosse Geschwindigkeit.
c) Der Apparat ist festzustellen und während der Aufnahme nicht zu verrücken.
d) Jede Aufnahme hat damit zu beginnen, dass das a des Stimmpfeifchens in den Apparat hineingeblasen, dann die Journalnummer und der Titel der Aufnahme hineingesprochen wird.
e) Schallkörper des Instrumentes, Mund des Sprechers oder Sängers möglichst dicht an den Schalltrichter bringen, ohne diesen zu berühren.
f) Der Spieler (Sänger) möge, wenn angängig, den Takt durch Händeklatschen markieren (möglichst nahe der Schallöffnung des Trichters).
g) Nach Gesangsaufnahmen ist der tiefste und höchste Stimmton des Sängers aufzunehmen (Stimmumfang).
Instrumentalmusiker mögen die vollständige Skala ihres Instrumentes in der bei ihnen üblichen Reihenfolge in den Phonographen hineinspielen; bei Saiteninstrumenten sind die leeren Saiten besonders aufzunehmen.
h) Jede Aufnahme ist sofort probeweise ganz zu reproduzieren.
i) Notierung der Journalnummer des Orts und Titels der Aufnahme auf der Walzenschachtel.
k) Möglichst sorgfältiges Ausfüllen des Journals.
l) Es empfiehlt sich, gelegentlich von einem Musikstück zwei Aufnahmen zu machen (auch von verschiedenen Musikern).

C. Journal.

a) Fortlaufende Nummer der Aufnahme:
b) Datum und Ort der Aufnahme:
c) Person des Sprechers oder Musikers:
   a) Volksstamm:
   b) Name:
   c) Alter:
   d) Geschlecht:
   e) Beruf:

FIGURE 13-4. A section from Felix von Luschan's *Anleitung für ethnographische Beobachtungen und Sammlungen in Afrika und Oceanien* (61), covering the documentation of musical practices and the use of the phonograph.

Friedrich-Wilhelms-Universität in Berlin, Stumpf praises "researchers" and their key role in making and supplying recordings. Among the important collections received by the archive, he makes sure to include recordings made by missionaries, thereby counting them among the "travelling researchers."[48]

Haddon's journal shows similar almost informal applications of the phonograph during his research and during the Torres Strait Expedition. While the surviving recordings follow the scientific aim to document local customs, dance, and performance practices, this was by far not the only use of the phonograph. It was used to display Western marches to both missionary and local audiences, to replay recordings made from local actors to themselves for repeated listening, as if the phonograph had become a constant companion and a tool to initiate dialogue, to provide demonstrations and amusement, and to provide a break from anthropometric measurements that were taken.[49] In many cases, missionaries provided the context, established contact, and invited Haddon and his team as well as locals to their school premises. He acknowledges their help and assistance, including the provision of boats.[50] And he advocates the training of missionaries in anthropology.[51]

The interaction of the British researchers with missionaries appears to have been more friendly than between Richard Thurnwald and the German missions. The anthropologist, who did extensive research and recordings in German New Guinea, harshly criticized missionaries for the miserable working conditions on their plantations and the manipulation of local communities by seizing their fear of evil powers to make them amenable to the missionary project.[52] Other missionaries provided valuable information on local language and customs, as in the case of Josef Winthuis, a Sacred Heart Priest (MSC) who was active in New Guinea for almost twelve years.[53] Winthuis systematically collected music and dance on phonographic recordings and learned the Tolai language.[54] The total quantity of his several dozen recordings is unknown.[55] From the protocols included in the CD edition of his recordings, we learn that he called local actors by a Christian first name followed by their name ("Andreas Tamana," "Barbara laLuka," "Carolina laTaraka" etc.), a practice we also encounter in Pöch (see "George" Amambura and "Bonifaz" Tamatai as discussed above).[56] Winthuis published extensively on their culture, but to my knowledge, he did not reflect on the use of the phonograph. It is notable that language exercises and language (as in the case of Vormann and Pöch, see above) were apparently not recorded by him on the phonograph, suggesting that the use of the phonograph even among missionaries was fairly diverse.

THE BERLIN SCHOOL OF COMPARATIVE
MUSICOLOGY AND THEIR RELATIONS
TO MISSIONARY RECORDINGS

The German Kolonialkongresse underlined the interdependencies of missionary work, ethnographic research and colonial administration in the composition of their committees, the topics discussed, and the active participation of missionaries.[57] In a rare explicit attempt to actively place comparative musicology and the Berlin Phonogram Archive within the German colonial effort, Stumpf argued in a magazine article as follows: "The new Reich is proud of its colonies and does everything in its power to exploit them materially. It is our duty to combine this with scientific exploitation, i.e., the research into nature and the native culture of the new territories."[58] While for the Berlin school of comparative musicology the recordings were paramount to creating a disciplinary paradigm and to the development of sophisticated methodologies, missionary coordinators such as Pater Wilhelm Schmidt sensed that phonographic recordings should be included in missionary research and brought in relation to wider concepts such as evolutionism and diffusionism and linguistic research. Yet the outcome fell short of the centralized academic recording campaigns overseen by the phonogram archives and the museums in Vienna and Berlin and by the rise of comparative musicology as a new field of research that followed. This is not to say individual missionaries were not active suppliers to the Berlin Phonogram Archive and important correspondents of von Hornbostel. He included recordings made by missionaries in the representative Demonstrations-Sammlung, the compilation of 120 Edison cylinders with recordings across all continents that aimed at schools and the general public and was available in the early 1920s, though in the somewhat outdated format of Edison wax cylinders. Reflecting the geography of Germany's colonies, the collection features many African and Asian recordings. For the region under review here, von Hornbostel included two recordings from the island of Lenggano near Sumatra made in 1909 by the collector and missionary August Lett of the Rhenish Mission.[59] Lett recorded, among others, a "Vaterunser" and other Christian songs, which were of course not included in the Demonstrations-Sammlung, as it ideally comprised only genuine local musical expressions.[60]

From a missionary perspective, the situation was ambivalent: Would a Christian hymn sung by a local class be proof of educational progress, or would the phonograph simply be used to drill the pupils with the promise of hearing their voices on a recording? Were they used for rehearsals, or to instill competition among classes or mission schools? Did missionaries play genuine Western commercial recordings to local schools?[61] Would missionary authorities measure the missionary success on the basis of recordings? The complete catalogue of the wax cylinders in the Berlin Phonogram Archive carries many entries on "hybrid" musical recordings, that is, recordings of Western and/or Christian tunes sung by non-Western actors in either a Western or a local language, some of them recorded by missionaries. And in most cases, the recorded singers were trained in missionary schools.[62]

Recordings in Indonesia made for the Berlin Phonogram Archive have not been met with a surge of research similar to those in New Guinea and Melanesia. Apart from missionary Lett mentioned above, the following German travelers were active in the region, some of whose recordings were selected for the Demonstrations-Sammlung:

Odo Deodatus Tauern, ethnologist, recorded in Sawai on the
island of Seram, Moluku province of Indonesia (included in the
Demonstrations-Sammlung)

Max Moszkowski, physician, traveler, and explorer: Sumatra

Dr. Eugen Rudel, physician and explorer: Java (included in the
Demonstrations-Sammlung)

Hermann Schoede, surveyor: Sumatra (included in the Demonstrations-
Sammlung)

Bernhard Hagen, physician and ethnologist: Sumatra (Demonstrations-
Sammlung)

It would be vital to study the recording and performance contexts and the
involvement of missionaries for these recording projects as well.[63]

TRUE ECHOES

Similarly, the *True Echoes* project on early wax cylinder recordings that has
recently been undertaken by British researchers and researchers and communities
in Oceania stimulates additional questions.[64] How were the British recordings in
British New Guinea organized? What interaction with the local populations did
they entail? Did missionaries play a role here as well? And, on a conceptual level,
what kind of "echo" speaks to us and to local communities from these recordings? Is the echo a biological trace of ethnic actors, as part of a wider extraction of
human remains, ethnographic objects, plants, insects, hair samples, bones? Or is
it a mere rendering of the performance situation, captured on wax? Is it echoing a
specific conception of doing science, of collecting, observing, extracting? Or do the
recordings echo the complex entanglements, such as in the case of Tok Pisin,
the local pidgin that was first captured on record by Pöch in East New Britain
Province, and of having different ethnic groups present during a recording (Motu/
Baifa, see the Pöch example above), of having recorded Oceanic actors in Africa
and Vienna, and of having New Guinean congregations sing Christian hymns?[65]

The echo surely also constitutes a way of doing science, as it was conceived
in the early twentieth century, foremost an orientation toward an "experimental-
ization of life."[66] This dispositive informed physiology, anthropology, and experimental research during the nineteenth century. It set out to analyze, with the
help of technological apparatuses and devices measuring reaction times, blood
pressure, and perceptual thresholds, the physiological manifestations of the living in the process of making, speaking, and performing. Phonographic recording practices can be placed within these new discursive systems, becoming a part
of experimental designs that appear to capture the "natural" or "the primitive"
but that were actually complicating these conceptions. We should seek to expose
these complications so that they become visible as a component of ethnological

and anthropological ideologies. Whose "life" has been captured here, and to what avail? Could this asymmetrical power relation ever be broken up and considered as a shared history?

We should complement the exclusively Western perspective of a history of science and research ideologies through pluri-versal questions that address the resonances these practices have found in the researched communities. Did the phonographic campaigns leave a trace in the local imagination, storytelling, crafts, and memory? Do we find instances of a mimetic alterity as observed by Michael Taussig in the Cuna mola that absorb, modify, and transgress the talking dog, the brand image of Victor Company?[67] When we consider the several hundred recordings made by the Torres Strait Expedition, the German expeditions, and Pöch and Thurnwald in the region, we can safely assume that a fair share of the population was exposed to the apparatus. To do justice to the recordings, we must first acknowledge that the recordings are always in excess to any preconceived meanings or functions ascribed to them and that local actors and groups were genuine coproducers of them.

Following the path opened by Julie To'Liman-Turalir on the relevance of early Tolai recordings for the Tolai people today, Don Niles and his collaboration with the Vienna Phonogram Archive and local actors, and the coordinated effort of the *True Echoes* project, which includes institutions from Oceania, we should continue to reflect with local communities, community-based researchers, and global academic audiences about how exactly these recordings relate to traditions of music-making and linguistic practices, while avoiding any thinning of the experience and any strategic ethnic essentialism.[68]

. . .

In summarizing, a small number of missionaries in New Guinea and Oceania made use of the phonograph. It appears to have been a tool in the study of language and for the documentation of local dance and musical practices, but phonographic activity as such is not methodologically reflected in missionary writings. While Pater Schmidt advised Catholic missionaries to use a phonograph, this was not met with the same response as among ethnologists, anthropologists, and navy physicians who supplied large recording collections to the Berlin and Vienna Phonogram Archives, who had set up systematic recording campaigns, followed by systematic transcriptions and comparative analyses of musical practices and the tonal systems and instruments used. On a second look, however, it becomes evident that missionaries were implicated in these projects, too, as enablers of contact with local communities, providers of infrastructures such as school rooms and boats, or direct interlocutors during recording sessions.[69] In contrast to the academic research undertaken for ethnological museums and phonogram archives, however, missionaries lacked a clear working protocol to compile, process, collect, and compare phonographic recordings.

The present discussion has yielded insights into the complexity of phonographic situations and the recording ideologies of missionaries and ethnologists, as well as anthropologists. By carving out their diverse range of interests and the conditions that led to multi-site experiences of both researchers and members of local populations, the latter forced to travel to Africa and Europe as an effect of World War I, we can widen our understanding of cultural encounters and of power relations during the era of colonial globalization. The informal use of the phonograph by researchers and the open-mindedness of local populations to the apparatus and its acoustic representations can lead to a more profound discussion of the agency of local actors, their role of coproducers of recordings, and of the cultural encounters of which phonographic campaigns were a part.

. . .

As we reconstruct the role of missionaries as phonographic mediators in an increasingly collaborative fashion, powerful contemporary voices from Oceania emerge. This time, they are not "invited" or exposed by Western ethnologists or missionaries. In her proud and reflexive, highly empathetic narrative "Tell Them" (2011), Kathy Jetnil-Kijiner from the Marshall Islands evokes the power of nature, local traditions, myth, religion, the appeal of local handicraft circulating globally, and the skills of her community in her own words, not under the gaze and analyzing ears of Western collectors. In a move countering easy self-exoticization, she advocates human universality in the face of climate change:

> tell them we are sweet harmonies
> of grandmothers mothers aunties and sisters
> songs late into night
> tell them we are whispered prayers
> the breath of God
> a crown of fushia flowers encircling
> aunty mary's white sea foam hair
> [. . .]
> tell them that some of us
> are old fishermen who believe that God
> made us a promise
> some of us
> are more skeptical of God
> but most importantly tell them
> we don't want to leave
> we've never wanted to leave
> and that we
> are nothing without our islands.[70]

In "Tell Them," the missionary and colonial age are not addressed directly. Yet "Tell Them" opens a rich space in which the wax cylinder campaigns and the ambitions they represent to convert the world to Christianity and to document local languages and musical practices in order to understand how they evolved and relate to Western "high culture" and *Tonkunst* may keep resonating, though in a manner not anticipated one hundred years ago.

NOTES

1. Douglas Bronwen and Chris Ballard, eds., *Foreign Bodies: Oceania and the Science of Race 1750–1940* (Canberra: Australian National University Press, 2008); Helen Gardner, "The 'Faculty of Faith: Evangelical Missionaries, Social Anthropologists, and the Claim for Human Unity in the Nineteenth Century," in *Foreign Bodies: Oceania and the Science of Race 1750–1940*, ed. Douglas Bronwen and Chris Ballard (Canberra: Australian National University Press, 2008), 259–82.

2. Among the New Guinea missions, there was no consistent language policy concerning the German language. See Peter Mühlhäusler, "Die deutsche Sprache im Pazifik," in *Die Deutsche Südsee 1884–1914: Ein Handbuch*, ed. Hermann Joseph Hiery (Paderborn: Verlag Ferdinand Schöningh 2001), 239–62, especially 243; see also S. Werkmeister, "Die verhinderte Weltsprache. 16. Dezember 1915: Adalbert Baumann präsentiert 'Das neue, leichte Weltdeutsch,'" in *Mit Deutschland um die Welt: Eine Kulturgeschichte des Fremden in der Kolonialzeit*, ed. Alexander Honold and Klaus R. Scherpe (Stuttgart: J. B. Metzler, 2004), 464–72.

3. I will thus not offer an ethnomusicological analysis of the recorded music, dances, poems, linguistic samples per se.

4. Pekka Gronow, "The Record Industry Comes to the Orient," *Ethnomusicology*, 25, no. 2 (May 1981): 251–84.

5. Michael Denning, *Noise Uprising: The Audiopolitics of a World Musical Revolution* (London: Verso, 2015).

6. The western part of New Guinea, which was under Dutch rule, was part of the wider Dutch dominion of Indonesia. The best survey of early twentieth-century recording activities in New Guinea is the one provided by Don Niles, who includes maps that show where researchers were active and supplies the quantity of recordings taken for each collection. The survey focuses on the activities for the Berlin Phonogram Archive but includes Austrian, British, and other European academic recording campaigns as well. Don Niles, "The Contribution of the Berlin Phonogramm-Archiv to the Study of Papua New Guinea Musics," in *Music Archiving in the World: Papers Presented at the Conference on the Occasion of the 100th Anniversary of the Berlin Phonogramm-Archiv*, ed. Gabriele Berlin and Artur Simon (Berlin: Verlag für Wissenschaft und Bildung, 2002), 189–200.

7. Viktoria Tkaczyk, *Thinking with Sound: A New Program in the Sciences and Humanities around 1900* (Chicago: University of Chicago Press, 2023), 188–98.

8. Anna Maria Busse Berger, *The Search for Medieval Music in Africa and Germany, 1891–1961: Scholars, Singers, Missionaries* (Chicago: University of Chicago Press, 2020). Don Niles, "Comments," *Papua New Guinea (1904–1909): The Collections of Rudolf Pöch, Wilhelm Schmidt, and Josef Winthuis*, OEAW PHA, CD 9 (Tondokumente aus dem Phonogrammarchiv der Österreichischen Akademie der Wissenschaften, Gesamtausgabe der Historischen Bestände 1899–1950, 2000), CD booklet, 17–142. See Anita Herle and Sandra Rouse, eds., *Cambridge and the Torres Strait. Centenary Essays on the 1898 Anthropological Expedition* (Cambridge, UK: Cambridge University Press 2008); Sebastian Klotz, "Murray Island versus Aberdeenshire: Contextualizing the Cross-Cultural Hearing Tests of the Cambridge Anthropological Expedition to Torres Straits, 1898–1899," in *Testing Hearing: The Making of Modern Aurality*, ed. Viktoria Tkaczyk, Mara Mills, and Alexandra Hui (Oxford: Oxford University Press 2020), 77–108.

9. Niles, "Comments."

10. Franz Vormann, SVD, and P. Wilh. Scharfenberger, SVD. *Die Monumbo-Sprache*, vol. 1, *Grammatik und Wörterverzeichnis*, with introduction and appendix by P. Ferd. Hestermann, SVD (Vienna: Mechitharisten-Buchdruckerei, 1914 [*Anthropos*, Linguistische Bibliothek, Internationale Sammlung linguistischer Monographien]).

11. Alfred C. Haddon, *Head-Hunters: Black, White, and Brown* (London: Methuen, 1901); Haddon, *Reports of the Cambridge Anthropological Expedition to Torres Straits*, 6 vols. (Cambridge, UK: Cambridge University Press, 1901–35).

12. The situation for missionaries in Africa seems to have been a lot more favorable and the museum's plea to have them travel with a phonograph more successful. See Busse Berger, *The Search for Medieval Music*, 29.

13. Potentially existing documents for contacts between missionaries in New Guinea and Berlin's comparative musicologists, such as those found by Anna Maria Busse Berger for Africa (Busse Berger, *The Search for Medieval Music*, 147) have not yet been studied from a systematic angle.

14. Don Niles found evidence that Pater Schmidt, from 1907 onward, was anxious that Catholic missionaries in all regions of the world were equipped with a phonograph "for the purpose of recording the traditional music in the areas in which they worked" (Niles, "Comments," 94). This would clearly mean Pater Schmidt had expanded his linguistic agenda to musical practices.

15. Markus Joch, "Der Katechismus zur Kolonialfrage. Februar 1879: Friedrich Fabri fragt: 'Bedarf Deutschland der Colonien?,'" in *Mit Deutschland um die Welt: Eine Kulturgeschichte des Fremden in der Kolonialzeit*, ed. Alexander Honold and Klaus R. Scherpe (Stuttgart: J. B. Metzler, 2004), 51–58.

16. Stephan Besser, "Die Organisation des kolonialen Wissens. 10. Oktober 1902: In Berlin tagt der erste Deutsche Kolonialkongreß," in Honold and Scherpe, *Mit Deutschland um die Welt*, 271–78.

17. Suzanne Marchand contextualizes Schmidt's missionary ideology within ethnology; see Suzanne Marchand, "Priests among the Pygmies: Wilhelm Schmidt and the Counter-Reformation in Austrian Ethnology," in *Worldly Provincialism: German Anthropology in the Age of Empire*, ed. H. Glenn Penny and Matti Bunzl (Ann Arbor: University of Michigan Press, 2003), 283–316.

18. Niles, "Comments."

19. Niles, "Comments," 27.

20. Niles, "Comments," 27.

21. Pöch regularly submitted research reports from his expeditions to the Imperial Academy of Sciences in Vienna, which published them in their proceedings. Rudolf Pöch, "Bericht über Aufnahmen mit einem Archivphonographen der kais. Akademie der Wissenschaften in Wien, unter den Monumbo auf Neu-Guinea vom 28. Juli bis 24. November 1904," in *Sitzungsberichte der mathematisch-naturwissenschaftlichen Classe der Kaiserlichen Akademie der Wissenschaften, Wien*, 2Abt-a-114. Rudolf Pöch, "Zweiter Bericht über meine phonographischen Aufnahmen in Neu-Guinea (Britisch Neu-Guinea vom 7. Oktober 1905 bis zum 1. Februar 1906)," in: *Sitzungsberichte der Mathematisch-Naturwissenschaftlichen Classe der Kaiserlichen Akademie der Wissenschaften Sitzungsberichte der mathematisch-naturwissenschaftlichen Classe der Kaiserlichen Akademie der Wissenschaften, Wien*, 2.Abt-a-116. Band (1907): 801–817(=Nr. X der Mitteilungen der Phonogramm-Archivs-Kommission der kaiserlichen Akademie der Wissenschaften in Wien).

22. I acknowledge that ethnic names, terms, and geographic places used by Vormann and Pöch and their Western colleagues represent their perspective and need to be critically contextualized.

23. Niles, "Comments," 54.

24. Franz Vormann, "Tänze und Tanzfestlichkeiten der Monumbo-Papua (Deutsch-Neuguinea)," *Anthropos* 6, no. 2. (1911): 411–27, www.jstor.org/stable/pdf/40443727.pdf, 202.

25. See Sven Werkmeister's brilliant analysis of primitivism as a discursive figure in Western ethnology, and as a feature of recording technology of the mechanical age. Evoking the tattoos of indigenous actors, the stylus of the phonograph in the form of a co-movement (*Mitbewegung*) literally notates the frequency fluctuations initiated by musical and vocal articulations during a recording session, evading any symbolic dimension that stands at the heart of most scriptural systems; see

Werkmeister, "*Die verhinderte Weltsprache*," 383–87, for a résumé of his findings.

26. Utz Maas, "Schmidt, Pater Wilhelm," in *Verfolgung und Auswanderung deutschsprachiger Sprachforscher 1933–1945*, last updated in 2018, available online at the website of the Center for Literary and Cultural Research Berlin (ZfL), https://zflprojekte.de/sprachforscher-im-exil/index.php/catalog/s/415-schmidt-pater-wilhelm.

27. See Pater Wilhelm Schmidt, P. G. Schmidt, and P. J. Hermes, "Die Sprachlaute und ihre Darstellung in einem allgemeinen linguistischen Alphabet / Les sons du langage et leur représentation dans un alphabet linguistique général," *Anthropos* 2, no. 2. (1907), 282–329, available online at www.jstor.org/stable/pdf/40442189.pdf?refreqid=excelsior%3A4915bd1619893e4b84fb5495f2885c38&ab_segments=&origin=&initiator=&acceptTC=1. In a parallel endeavor, early comparative musicology reflected on the transcription of exotic melodies, seeking a reliable systematic protocol. Otto Abraham and Erich von Hornbostel, "Vorschläge für die Transkription exotischer Melodien," *Sammelbände der Internationalen Musikgesellschaft* 11, no. 1 (October–December, 1909): 1–25.

28. Pöch, "Bericht über Aufnahmen mit einem Archivphonographen," 801–17.

29. See the section "Two Competing German Ethnological Instructions" in this chapter.

30. Pöch, "Bericht über Aufnahmen mit einem Archivphonographen," 901.

31. Phonographic recordings were primarily taken from adult male voices and musicians, certainly curtailing their conceived representative character with respect to the age, range, and sex.

32. Educational statistics compiled by Hermann Joseph Hiery show that some twenty-seven thousand pupils were going to elementary school in the "German Südsee." Schools were run primarily by missionaries. Government schools played a minor part (Hermann Joseph Hiery, "Schule und Ausbildung in der deutschen Südsee," in *Die Deutsche Südsee 1884–1914. Ein Handbuch*, ed. Hermann Joseph Hiery (Paderborn: Verlag Ferdinand Schöningh 2001), 198–238, at 212.

33. Niles, "Comments," 55.

34. Pöch, "Zweiter Bericht über meine phonographischen Aufnahmen," 806.

35. Niles, "Comments," 63.

36. Pöch, "Zweiter Bericht über meine phonographischen Aufnahmen," 808. This visual absence adds to the acoustic absence: none of the researchers' voices have been captured on recordings.

37. Niles, "Comments," 83–93. I rely entirely on Don Niles's comments here.

38. Niles, "Comments," 84.

39. Schmidt himself mentions this use only in passing, focusing on linguistic rather than musical analysis, reserving a musical transcription of these recordings for a later stage. See Niles, "Comments," 84.

40. Susanne Ziegler, *Die Wachszylinder des Berliner Phonogramm-Archivs* (Berlin: Staatliche Museen zu Berlin, Preußischer Kulturbesitz, 2006) (Veröffentlichungen des Ethnologischen Museums Berlin, Neue Folge 73, Abt. Musikethnologie, Medien-Technik und Berliner Phonogramm Archiv XII), 121, 336.

41. Information on these holdings can be accessed online at www.sammlungen.hu-berlin.de. Recordings from prisoners during World War I carry PK (Phonographische Kommission) as call number heading. After World War I, the recordings of this secret commission comprising over 1,600 items (language and music recordings) in more than 250 dialects were split up between the Berlin Phonogram Archive and Doegen's Lautabteilung (the present-day Lautarchiv of Humboldt University in Berlin; see Reinhard Meyer-Kalkus, "'Bizarres Philologentum' und Repräsentation akustischer Weltkulturen. Phonographische Sprachaufnahmen aus deutschen Kriegsgefangenenlagern im Ersten Weltkrieg im Berliner Lautarchiv," in *Wege zur Weltliteratur*, ed. Gesa Dane et al. (*Komparatistische Perspektiven der Editionswissenschaft*, 15), (Berlin: Weidler, 2015), 43–70. On the website given at the beginning of this note, regional search queries under "Ozeanien" or "Indonesien" or a search for persons such as "Dempwolff" lead to the metadata of the items recorded. Call no. LA 570 features a camera technician of Malay origin named Tando Oemar Saetan Mansoer—who spoke Malay, Dutch, German, English, and French, could write in Arabic, and played the zither and flute—documented in a recording session on December 22, 1925, in Berlin. Readers can listen to this recording by visiting the UC Press

website and the companion SoundCloud website: https://soundcloud.com/uc-press/sets/missionaries
-anthropologists-and-music.

42. Niles, "Comments," 52.

43. A further cross-sectional observation underlines the entanglements of researchers, a multiplicity of recording sites and contexts; some ethnologists researching in German New Guinea before 1910 were also taking recordings from prisoners during World War I. They are Pöch, Paul Hambruch, who was on the Hamburger Südsee-Expedition (Ziegler, *Die Wachszylinder*, 142–44, especially 344; and the "Hambruch" entries on the website www.sammlungen.hu-berlin.de; see note 42), and Otto Reche, who participated in the same Hamburger Expedition and who did research on POWs in Germany, though without phonographic recordings. On Reche, see Andrew D. Evans, "Anthropology at War: Racial Studies of POWs during World War I," in *Worldly Provincialism: German Anthropology in the Age of Empire*, ed. H. Glenn Penny and Matti Bunzl (Ann Arbor: University of Michigan Press, 2003), 214.

44. The founding document of *Anthropos* in which Schmidt positions Catholic missionary work in the context of linguistics and ethnology is available online at www.anthropos.eu/media/anthropos/docs/PWSAufruf.pdf. Today's editors of *Anthropos* consider the questionnaire as part of the founding documents. It is available online at www.anthropos.eu/media/anthropos/docs/PWSFragebogen.pdf.

45. Felix von Luschan, "Anleitung für ethnographische Beobachtungen und Sammlungen in Afrika und Oceanien," in *Zeitschrift für Ethnologie* (Sonderabdruck) 36 (1904), available online at https://echo.mpiwg-berlin.mpg.de/ECHOdocuView?url=/permanent/vlp/lit39587/&pn=3.

46. Lars-Christian Koch, "Images of Sound: Erich M. von Hornbostel and the Berlin Phonogram Archive," in *The Cambridge History of World Music*, ed. Philip V. Bohlman (Cambridge, UK: Cambridge University Press 2013), 475–97.

47. Luschan, "Anleitung für ethnographische Beobachtungen und Sammlungen in Afrika und Oceanien," 58–65.

48. Carl Stumpf, "Das Berliner Phonogrammarchiv," *Internationale Wochenschrift für Wissenschaft, Kunst und Technik* 22 (February 1908), 225–46. Quoted from Artur Simon, *Das Berliner Phonogramm-Archiv 1900–2000: Sammlungen der traditionellen Musik der Welt* [The Berlin Phonogramm-Archiv 1900–2000] (Berlin: Verlag für Wissenschaft und Bildung, 2000), 70.

49. See numerous references in Anita Herle and Jude Philp, eds., *Recording Kastom: Alfred Haddon's Journals from the Torres Trait and New Guinea, 1888 and 1898* (Sydney: Sydney University Press 2020).

50. Haddon, *Head-Hunters*, xi.

51. Sandra Rouse, "Haddon, Missionaries and 'Men of Affairs,'" *Cambridge Anthropology* 21, no. 1 (1999): 9–27.

52. Marion Melk-Koch, *Auf der Suche nach der menschlichen Gesellschaft: Richard Thurnwald* (Berlin: Staatliche Museen Preußischer Kulturbesitz 1989), 98.

53. Niles, "Comments," 94.

54. Niles, "Comments," 94.

55. Ziegler, *Die Wachszylinder*, 312.

56. Niles, "Comments," 99–100.

57. The bulky proceedings of the 1902 Kolonialkongress are available at https://brema.suub.uni-bremen.de/dsdk/periodical/titleinfo/2009560. See also Besser, "Die Organisation des kolonialen Wissens."

58. Stumpf, "Das Berliner Phonogrammarchiv," 83.

59. Erich M. von Hornbostel, "Phonogramm-Archiv des Psychologischen Instituts der Universität, Berlin C.2, Schloss(sz), Demonstrations-Sammlung," unpublished typescript, ca. 1920, Quoted from Artur Simon, *Das Berliner Phonogramm-Archiv 1900–2000: Sammlungen der traditionellen Musik der Welt* [The Berlin Phonogramm-Archiv 1900–2000] (Berlin: Verlag für Wissenschaft und Bildung, 2000), 100; Ziegler, *Die Wachszylinder*, 214, 359.

60. Ziegler, *Die Wachszylinder*, 214; and the CD-ROM of Ziegler's catalogue.

61. Anna Maria Busse Berger provides evidence of Leipzig missionaries playing recordings of Lutheran chorales by the Thomaner Choir to the Maasai in the 1920s and 1930s from a phonograph. Busse Berger, *The Search for Medieval Music*, 172.

62. To my knowledge, there is no systematic survey of this repertoire and of the function of these hybrid recordings cutting across the regional logic.

63. The publication by Jan Sihar Aritonang and Karel Steenbrink would provide a suitable starting point; see Jan Sihar Aritonang and Karel Steenbrink, *A History of Christianity in Indonesia* (Leiden: Brill, 2008).

64. For further information, please visit the True Echoes website, www.true-echoes.com.

65. Niles, "Comments," 52.

66. Hans-Jörg Rheinberger and Michael Hagner, eds., *Die Experimentalisierung des Lebens: Experimentalsysteme in den biologischen Wissenschaften, 1850/1950* (Berlin: Akademie Verlag, 1993).

67. Michael Taussig, *Mimesis and Alterity: A Particular History of the Senses* (London: Routledge, 1993), 223–35.

68. See Julie To'Liman-Turalir,. "Why Historic Recordings Are of Value to the Tolai People Today." In *Music Archiving in the World: Papers Presented at the conference on the Occasion of the 100th Anniversary of the Berlin Phonogramm-Archiv*, 55–58. Berlin: Verlag für Wissenschaft und Bildung, 2002; Niles, "Comments."

69. Pöch, "Bericht über Aufnahmen mit einem Archivphonographen."

70. Excerpts from the lyrics (middle section and closing lines) of "Tell Them" by Kathy Jetnil-Kijiner. The full text can be found at https://jkijiner.wordpress.com/2011/04/13/tell-them/.

Epistemic Shifts and Ideological Persistence

Ethnographic, Archival, and Historiographical Practices in the Legacy of Jaap Kunst

Barbara Titus

In his essay *Cultural Relations between the Balkans and Indonesia*, published in 1954, Jaap Kunst shared the following profound experience:

> In September 1951 I had the privilege of attending the great National Yugoslav Folk-dance Festival at Opatija (previously Abbazzia) as the representative of the Netherlands Government. During those unforgettable days we made the acquaintance of a flourishing folk-culture which was enchanting because of the wealth and variety of what was displayed before us, the great musical talent of which it bear [*sic*] witness of, the inborn feeling for rhythm, and the feast of colour presented bij [*sic*] the beautiful regional costumes. Whatever the performance happened to be at the moment—whether it was the singing of weaving Serbian matrons. . ., or the *kolo* with its emotional scale of hardly restrained energy flaming up brightly into joy of life; the coquettish harem dances of the Bosnian women; the grand epic hymns of the *guslars*, the inspired performance of the Macedonian *tapan* and *zurla* players; the metallic-sounding two-part songs of the Dinaric mountain dwellers; the exciting and fascinating sound-complexes of the *sopele* duo from the island of Krk—the audience breathlessly gazed and listened without a moment's slackening of attention.
>
> But this pleasure in what one heard and saw was not all that this experience held: a great and quite unexpected discovery awaited me and I think it is sufficiently important to deserve your attention for a few moments.
>
> As I sat in the great hall at the Kvarner Hotel with all this beauty sweeping over me, I closed my eyes for an instant and suddenly I felt as if I were back in East Flores near the remote Bélèng Lake, and some moments later I seemed to be in the land of the Nagé in West Flores. It was the same music to which I was listening here, in the most literal sense of the word: it seemed to me that in several cases it was not only a matter of a certain similarity or parallelism but now and then of complete identity.[1]

Kunst's experience deserves to be quoted at length since it constitutes a powerful aural transportation to different times and places. This incites him to explore these musical resemblances in his ten-page essay. He outlines the aural resemblance he experiences between the Croatian *ojkanje* singing and the two-part singing in East Flores and between the Bosnian "gurgling laryngeal trills" and similar guttural trills in West Flores.[2] He notes that both the Albanian people in the Balkans and the Nageh people on West Flores happen to denote these trills with the guttural name "*grko.*" He states unreservedly that on this basis, these musical expressions *must have* a common origin.[3] The rest of the essay is devoted to proving this common origin.

Such a search was not out of place within the scholarly norms and practices of the mid-twentieth century. Kunst also published an article about the cultural relationship between Indonesia and Central Africa.[4] Better known is his almost lifelong search—proceeding from Erich von Hornbostel's blown-fifth theory—for an all-encompassing Eastern music theory that was supposed to have originated in China as a counterpart to the Western Pythagorean tuning.[5] In southern Africa, Kunst's contemporaries such as Percival Kirby (1887–1970), the first professor of music at the University of the Witwatersrand, and Hugh Tracey (1903–77), the English scholar of African music, made similarly sweeping claims with regard to "Bantu" music and musical instruments, even if they did not argue for a theoretical foundation of these alleged common origins.[6]

In this chapter, I engage myself with Kunst's 1954 essay about the alleged cultural relations between the Balkans and Indonesia to outline some of his scholarly practices that became normative when political decolonization and increased mobility of people and sounds reconfigured academic engagements with music. Being one of Kunst's successors at the University of Amsterdam in the Netherlands and the curator of his legacy that is held there, I scrutinize my own position vis-à-vis the grand narrative Kunst poses in his 1954 essay, contemplating whether and to what extent his historicist, ethnocentric, and comparative paradigms still shape my own historiographical and ethnographic practices, consciously as well as subconsciously.

Trained as a lawyer, Jaap Kunst (1891–1960) lived and worked in the Dutch East Indies between 1919 and 1934 as a colonial administrative officer. He worked in the office from 7 a.m. to 2 p.m. and devoted all his spare time, including late evenings and early mornings, to his research of musics of the Indonesian archipelago that he regarded to be at the brink of extinction. In 1930 and 1931, he occupied the unique post of government musicologist, a job he had lobbied into existence by himself, with the help of historian Johan Huizinga.[7] His many letters speak of his urge, obsession almost, to capture, collect, and safeguard as much music as he could before it would stop being practiced. To a large extent, he paid for his research—recording equipment, expeditions, musical instruments, archiving tools—from his own private resources.[8]

During his expeditions on the islands of Java, Bali, Sumatra, Celebes (Sulawesi), Nias, Sumba, Flores, Timor, the Kai Islands, Banda, and Waigeo, he and his wife, Katy Kunst-Van Wely (1897–1992), recorded music on wax cylinders, collected musical instruments, took photographs, and shot silent films. They also recorded music at events in Java with music from Kalimantan and the Moluccas. Missionaries and colleagues, such as Father Jan Verschueren and C. C. F. M. le Roux in West Papua and pastor Pieter Middelkoop in Timor, recorded material on Kunst's request or sent their recordings to him to be galvanized and copied.[9] Kunst's wax cylinder collection encompasses more than three hundred indexed items recorded by Kunst and Kunst-Van Wely, about twenty-five indexed items from Father Verschueren, and around fifty indexed items recorded by le Roux.[10] The continuous stream of publications, initially in Dutch and later also in English, that resulted from these recordings presented Indonesian music to a Northern Hemisphere readership—often based in colonial metropoles—and it established Kunst's reputation (his, not hers) as the foremost expert on Indonesian music and as one of the founding fathers of ethnomusicology, a term he has been credited with coining in the 1950s.[11]

Kunst sent his sound recordings directly from Batavia to Berlin, where his friend and mentor Erich Moritz von Hornbostel (1877–1935) galvanized and copied them at the Berlin Phonogramm-Archiv. The Phonogramm-Archiv sent copies to the Colonial Institute in Amsterdam (later, the Royal Tropical Institute), where Kunst worked as a curator from the late 1930s onward, after his return to the Netherlands. He was succeeded there by Felix van Lamsweerde, who made an inventory of Kunst's sound material in this Institute.[12] In the early 2000s, the Phonogramm-Archiv digitized and systematically described all wax cylinders.[13] Not surprisingly, Van Lamsweerde's inventory and Ziegler's Berlin description of Kunst's sound recordings largely overlap.

Kunst was a very active and successful networker and devoted special attention to maintaining his social and professional relations, to a large extent through written correspondence. Not only did he keep the letters he received; he also kept copies of the letters he sent out. Thus, the Jaap Kunst Collection holds some ten thousand letters, including scholarly correspondence, from the period 1920–60, encompassing forty thousand pages. These letters include scholarly correspondence to colleagues in the Dutch East Indies, Germany, the Netherlands, and Britain, and to members of the Javanese nobility, government officials, universities, museums, and professional societies, among others.

The collection also encompasses research reports; about 6,000 projection slides for teaching purposes with images of musicians, musical instruments, music transcriptions, and dance forms; 1,600 glass plates (copies of those held at the National Museum in Jakarta); 6,500 photographs of musical instruments, dance and theater performances, and numerous musical activities from the entire archipelago; travel diaries from trips to Australia and the United States in the 1950s; a library; and around two meters of publication manuscripts.

When Kunst passed away from cancer in 1960, Katy Kunst-Van Wely sold the Collection to the University of Amsterdam (UvA), where Kunst had been teaching since 1942, on the condition that the material would be kept together. Kunst's assistants and successors Ernst Heins and Felix van Lamsweerde maintained and enlarged Kunst's collection with material from their own collections and those of their students and colleagues. Heins founded the Ethnomusicologisch Centrum Jaap Kunst (ECJK) at the UvA that was dismantled in the early 2000s. Thus, against Heins's wish, the university violated the agreement with Katy Kunst-Van Wely to keep the collection together. Kunst's written archive (correspondence, reports, photographs, teaching material, manuscripts) is currently stored at the UvA's Special Collections division at the university's Allard Pierson Museum. Kunst's library was usurped in the university library's general collection. The sound archive of the ECJK (with recordings from many parts of the world, recorded by Kunst's students and successors on a range of sound carriers) is still part of the musicology department and is currently in the process of being digitized. In 2021 and 2024, Kunst's granddaughter Clara Brinkgreve donated newly discovered letters and photographs by and of Jaap Kunst to the University of Amsterdam.

The diversity of information carriers (sound recordings, transcriptions, music analyses, silent film, photographs, written reports, annotated manuscripts and books, correspondence) with detailed accounts and reflections of Kunst's research practices makes the collection one of the foundational ethnomusicological collections of the world. The collection is well known among ethnomusicologists worldwide, but it is not particularly accessible, because it is being kept in multiple locations and has been digitized only to a limited extent. In May 2024, most of the sound files were made accessible online via the jaapkunst.org and the pratinada.net websites, initiated by the Decolonizing Southeast Asian Sound Archives consortium (DeCoSEAS). The written and visual material of the Jaap Kunst Collection remains to be digitized.

Kunst's collection is also an emblematic colonial collection. As a civil servant of the Dutch East Indies government, he adhered to the terms on which colonizer and colonized were supposed to encounter each other and interact. At the same time, he was an early fieldworker in direct contact with the people he recorded; this led him to acknowledge that music from outside Europe should be studied and judged on the basis of the aesthetic, technical, and formal starting points of those participating in the community or "ethnos" in which the music was created and enjoyed and not on the basis of European aesthetic premises.[14] Thus, his approach interrogated the supremacist aesthetic values of comparative musicology that identified European music as the unquestioned pinnacle of human civilization. Nevertheless, Kunst's "salvage ethnology" (capturing the music before it becomes extinct), his archiving practices, and his often racialist (if not racist) ethnographic and historiographical descriptions of the many musics of the Indonesian archipelago feature one of the most widespread paradoxes of colonial thought: Kunst explicitly vindicated the "civilizing" mission of colonial rule, but he also regretted and condemned the uprootedness and denouncement of allegedly precolonial music practices.[15] The notion of "ethnos" and the practice of "ethnography" are crucial in allowing this paradox to exist. Kunst's collection is meant to reflect the Dutch Empire in all its systematic colonial categorization and taxonomy. Through his sound recordings, film footage, photographs, and reports, he could conceive of distinct, homogeneous, and static cultures as abstracted entities (the "ethnos") that were supposed to be intrinsically different from European cultural practices, the latter remaining unquestioned normativities. To such a distinct "ethnos," singers and instrumentalists (who regularly remained nameless) contributed with their voices, their sounds, and their bodies as *specimens* of this ethnos in the empire. Kunst indeed used the word *specimens* to indicate the people and the practices he documented.[16]

As one of Kunst's successors in his post at the University of Amsterdam, after Ernst Heins and Wim van der Meer, I am implicated in this legacy, not only in disciplinary respect (am I an ethnomusicologist?), but also in institutional, and even personal, respects. I was raised in an academic family with an expertise on Indonesia, where Jaap Kunst had always been a ringing name: a humanist, a man of reason, a scientist, and a protector of fragile Indigenous cultures against a voracious globalized mass culture. Large parts of my childhood in the 1970s and 1980s were spent in Yogyakarta, since my father was affiliated with the Universitas Gadjah Mada for three months each year. It was here that Kunst, after hearing Javanese gamelan played at Yogyakarta's Paku Alaman court in 1919, decided to stay in Indonesia. When I was appointed as an associate professor at the University of Amsterdam in 2013, the curatorship of his legacy came with the job. This legacy encompasses not only his archived material but also the ideological stances, disciplinary constellations, and contributions and agencies of many actors that have remained subservient or nameless in his collection. Engaging with this legacy meant coming full circle for me, not in the least since I increasingly recognized that critical engagement with Kunst's collection is long overdue, possibly because of his status as a founding father of ethnomusicology, a reputation based on the emblematic status of his collection during his lifetime and beyond.

Since my appointment as curator of the Jaap Kunst Collection, I have been trying out modes of engagement with Kunst's work in oral presentations and publications, through meLê yamomo's project *Sonic Entanglements: Listening to Modernities in Sound Recordings of Southeast Asia, 1890–1950*, and through the project *Decolonizing Southeast Asian Sound Archives (DeCoSEAS)* that I coordinated from 2021–24, together with meLê yamomo, and that remains to be active as a consortium.[17] The publications (including the present one) display my search for a mode of engagement with Kunst's legacy, which changes its tint all the time, since I continue to find new dimensions in my investment in this material that complicate my earlier stances. I cherish the unfinalized status of this search, which means that I recapitulate material from my earlier publications about Kunst mentioned above in order to demonstrate how my current thought builds on and diverges from my earlier findings. Thus, my engagement with Kunst's legacy is a work in progress with regard not only to research findings but also to research methods. Readers are invited to consult my earlier publications side by side with the present one to get an idea of the overlaps as well as the shifts in approach.

When I started reading Kunst's essay *Cultural Relations between the Balkans and Indonesia*, I was amused by the grand sweeping claim that the title page already conveys. However, I cannot deny that I gradually got hooked by Kunst's attempts to substantiate his rather implausible hypothesis. Each new argument to establish these relations made the hypothesis less unlikely in my eyes and ears. "What is going on here?" I wondered. It is in any case a powerful illustration of Ana María Ochoa's observation that "archives contribute to the reorganization of the senses and the redistribution of the sensitive."[18] It also supports Foucault's dictum that scientific discourse is a locus where objects are recreated or even invented.[19]

Apparently, the historiographic and ethnographic techniques, as well as the archival material that Kunst employs to support his unlikely hypothesis, constitute a normativity for me that I seem to have internalized. Even if I distance myself consciously and unequivocally from the essentialism, positivism, and universalism that featured mid-twentieth-century scholarly *paradigms*, my willingness to become convinced by his argument suggests that his scholarly *practices* persist. What do we do with this persistence of practices in a scholarly environment that aims to distance itself from their positivist paradigms? I have no unequivocal answers to this question, but raising it might help us discuss critically the premises of historiography and ethnography as exertions of power on a global epistemic scale, practices that I think all of us engage in and—speaking for myself—not only with skepticism but also with passion.

My autoethnographic study of my willingness to become convinced by Kunst's unlikely argument led me to observe three manifestations in Kunst's essay of an epistemic shift that continues to feature practices of ethnography, archiving, and historiography in equal degree. This shift is closely intertwined with the most widely used technology of knowledge formation in the humanities, namely the production of texts, which is one of the reasons I "shifted along" while reading. I argue here that it is this shift that enables the feasibility of the colonial paradox of Kunst's proudly presenting the Dutch Empire with its civilizing mission while regretting its uprooting consequences.

The first manifestation of this shift has been identified by Miguel García in his seminal article "Sound Archives under Suspicion" from 2017, a shift featuring ethnographic practices of archiving sound throughout the twentieth century

1. Yugoslav Folk-song. Note the two-part seconds and the end on such a second, the slow gurgling laryngeal trill and the final cry (After L. KUBA)

FIGURE 14-1. Yugoslav folk song (Kunst, *Cultural Relations between the Balkans and Indonesia*).

2. Phrases of two-part singing from East Flores, with seconds, and ending with such a second (1st phrase) and a cry (2nd phrase)

FIGURE 14-2. Phrases of two-part singing from East Flores (Kunst, *Cultural Relations between the Balkans and Indonesia*).

while often remaining unacknowledged and even unnoticed by those who did the archiving. Sound that is being collected, García points out, can be removed from its context, alienated from its creator, and lodged in containers such as files, discs, wax cylinders, diaries, shelves, and cases, and yet despite all these interventions by a range of people, these sounds-that-turned-into-things are supposed to be free of the collector's influence, and they can keep the qualities they had before the collector's intervention: "the recording of the song" becomes "the song."[20]

While listening to the Croatian *ojkanje* singing in the Kvarner Hotel's great hall, Kunst memorized the recordings he had made in East Flores some twenty-

3. Final cadences of a Serbian and an Indonesian melody respectively

FIGURE 14-3. Final cadences of a Serbian and an Indonesian melody, respectively (Kunst, *Cultural Relations between the Balkans and Indonesia*).

five years earlier. The subsequent substantiation of his experience of resemblance revolves around "the recorded thing" he had repeatedly played back for the sake of transcription and comparison.[21] He presents notated samples of "Yugoslav Folksong" and "two-part singing from East Flores," pointing at the harmonies in seconds and the "slow gurgling laryngeal trill and final cry" in both samples (figures 14-1 and 14-2).[22] He continues to compare final cadences of melodies from Serbia and Eastern Indonesia (the island of Babar; figure 14-3). He directly projects the analytical descriptions of the Yugoslav musicologist Vinko Žganeć about Croatian people's songs and dances (*Hrvatske narodne pjesme i plesovi*) to recorded songs of East Flores, pointing out organ points, singing registers, and prominent intervals in the music.[23] His aural and conceptual establishment of resemblance is based on his archived recordings of songs as repeatable and material objects.

A second manifestation of a similar epistemic shift occurs in Kunst's attempts to historicize the resemblances he heard by securing possible cultural relations through a timeline. Leo Treitler's critique of this historicist method, reaching back to the 1960s, is directed at the same kind of shift that is subject to García's critique of archiving practices: in the act of history writing "what might have happened in the past" shifts into "what happened in the past," just like in the act of sound archiving "the recording of the song" shifts into "the song."[24]

In proper historicist fashion, Kunst assembles data as "historical evidence" to prove "what happened in the past." In addition to the visual representation of music-structural resemblances on the basis of his archival recordings, Kunst points out organological and choreographical similarities between the musical instruments and dances, not only of various Yugoslav and Indonesian peoples but also of musical practices in southern Russia, "Asia Minor," and the "Far East," including South China and "Further India." He bolsters these observations with excursions into resemblances in weaving, sculpture, and metal forging in all these regions.[25]

All these data serve his aim to raise two hypotheses that should clarify these resemblances, relying on work by musicologists, archaeologists, and "Balkanologists." His first hypothesis is his own, claiming that an "ancient Neolithic-megalithic culture" with its cradle in the eastern Mediterranean spread eastward over thousands of years. This huge (pre)historical category of the New Stone Age lies 12,000 to 6,500 years behind us. The second hypothesis has been offered to him by the Austrian ethnologist Robert von Heine-Geldern (1885–1968), who assumes a "Pontian Migration" around 800 BCE, when "nomadic Scythians" settled in south Russian plains and pressed out other peoples farther eastward, including "perhaps Germanic elements." Kunst continues to argue that "an offshoot of this movement reached East Indonesia."[26] Please note that both hypotheses (the Stone-Age migration 10,000 years BCE and the "Pontian Migration" 800 years BCE) proceed from a migration from West to East. No mention is made of a possible migration from East to West, or of more messy multiple migrations in both directions. I will further unpack this assumption below.

Surely, in the early twenty-first century, we have amply theorized the dangers of historicism conflating messy multiple pasts into neat and linear historiographies. However, the strength of Treitler's critique of historicism is that he also outlines the narrative plot structure of histories that remain tempting to use as a mode of argumentation, even if historicism is debunked. Treitler points at what I count as a third manifestation of the same epistemic shift that remains mostly unnoticed and unacknowledged, also in our own work: an implicit intersection of the plausible and the inevitable.

> We seek explanations when we are puzzled about things, and we feel we have got them when our minds are more or less at rest about them. Having reached that stage, we say that we *understand*. Note that nothing has been said about how we shall know when we have reached that stage, or about the form that satisfactory explanations must take under this criterion.
>
> [. . .]
>
> It is left in the end for the questioner to judge whether a sufficient explanation has been given. And he will judge on this basis: whether the explanation makes the outcome appear, not *inevitable*, but *plausible* in the light of the circumstances. Now it must be the case that only one explanation for any event can satisfy the inevitability criterion, whereas several explanations may be tenable from the viewpoint of plausibility.[27]

Whereas Treitler consciously distinguishes between the inevitable and the plausible, in Kunst's argument we see how the plausible gradually shifts into the inevitable, not only argumentatively, but also experientially, because without this inevitability, the implausible cannot be made plausible. Both ethnography and historiography rely on the tight intersection of the plausible and the inevitable to manage and control the implausible. James Clifford and Tim Rice have outlined how ethnographers extract experiences from their environment (like archivists extract sounds) and turn them into texts.[28] In a similar vein, historiographers, also the anti-historicist ones like me, in Treitler's words, "isolate a central thread of events and . . . separate off from this those details that are . . . not essentially contributory to *the final outcome*."[29]

While reading Kunst's essay, I was shifting along in these three epistemic shifts: from the sound archived thing to the sound itself, from messy pasts to linear history and from the plausible to the inevitable.[30] All these epistemic shifts have been exposed by my peers, some more than fifty years ago, but apparently they have not been dispelled, even if Treitler's critique has received powerful postcolonial updates in the work of, for instance, Dipesh Chakrabarty and Olivia Bloechl.[31] Apparently, these shifts are functional to what historians, ethnographers, and archivists do in fundamental ways. Such shifts enable the sharing of experiences with those who were not necessarily physically present at the experienced event, which is an extremely effective mode of knowledge dissemination and formation. Sometimes consciously and at other times unnoticed, account and event become interchangeable through a manipulation of the ontological status of what is experienced. In shifting from event to enunciation (and back), we objectify.

In Kunst's narrative, the functionality of these epistemic shifts is relatively easy to point out. Kunst's profound and mind-blowing experience of aural resemblance between sonic expressions in the Balkans and Indonesia is both problem and proof for the existence of their common origin. The circular argumentation is closed; the narrative is nevertheless directional toward a goal (or as Treitler says, *a final outcome*). The goal is so obvious that it does not need articulation, and, moreover, should not be articulated, because it is not supposed to become subject to interrogation. This is the lure of narrative plots: what keeps us engaged as readers is the road toward a goal that we have known all along and hence does not need to be explicated.

In fact, Kunst's essay bolsters *two* larger narrative goals that are not explicated and should not become subject to interrogation, since they provide the intellectual, ideological, and experiential foundation and legitimization for infrastructures and distributions of power that were under intense critical scrutiny after the political independence of Indonesia from the Netherlands with a devastating War of Independence between 1945 and 1949. As we have seen in the description of Kunst's foundational ethnomusicological collection, these infrastructures and distributions of power were preconditions for the existence of such a collection in the first place.

In the Netherlands, this Indonesian War of Independence has only in the last few years become denoted as such. Until very recently, the Indonesian War of

Independence was euphemistically referred to, in both Dutch journalistic and academic discourses, as "police actions" to restore order after the Japanese occupation (1942–45). The results of the first thorough investigation into this war were presented by the Royal Netherlands Institute of Southeast Asian and Caribbean Studies (KITLV), the Netherlands Institute for Military History (NIMH), and the NIOD Institute for War, Holocaust, and Genocide Studies on February 17, 2022. From this investigation, it emerged that "the Dutch government and military leadership deliberately condoned the systematic and widespread use of extreme violence by the Dutch armed forces in the war against the Republic of Indonesia."[32]

Dutch engagement with the colonial pasts of the Netherlands, not only in Indonesia but also in Sri Lanka, South Africa, the Caribbean, and Suriname, is only now gaining momentum. Gradually, a generation of Dutch and Indonesian journalists, scholars, opinionators, and policy makers who have not personally experienced and shaped the politics and policies of Dutch colonial rule find themselves in a position to speak. Moreover, many of the veterans who fought in this war—often badly trained and with limited means, barely recovered from five years of German occupation during World War II—have passed on. The Dutch King Willem-Alexander apologized in March 2020 for the "excessive violence" inflicted on Indonesia during his country's colonial rule. Nevertheless, the Dutch government still to this day refuses to acknowledge the founding of the Republic of Indonesia on August 17, 1945, when Sukarno declared independence, sticking instead to the Dutch transfer of sovereignty on December 27, 1949, after at least forty-six thousand and possibly one hundred thousand Indonesians and six thousand "Europeans, Indo-Europeans, Moluccans, Minahasans, Timorese and other Indonesians on the Dutch side" had been killed.[33]

I dwell on these geopolitical facts because they were very much part of Indonesian and Dutch lives in the mid-twentieth century, even if many dimensions of them remained unarticulated up to 2022. Thus, I am also interested in what is not said in Kunst's essay but is nevertheless presupposed. Like many of his Dutch contemporaries, Kunst was plainly unable to acknowledge the sovereignty of the Republic of Indonesia. He consistently portrayed Indonesia's first President Sukarno (1901–70) and his administration as "a bunch of thugs."[34] Kunst's son, Jaap Jr., had fought on the Dutch side in the Indonesian War of Independence and never physically and mentally recovered from this experience.[35] Only months after the publication of Kunst's essay, the Asian–African Conference in the West Javanese city of Bandung was held in April 1955. This was Sukarno's successful attempt at initiating a South-to-South dialogue, establishing an international political economic network without the involvement of former colonizing powers from the North Atlantic. The knee-jerk reactions of these (former) colonizing powers, imposing bans and preventing representatives of liberation movements and civil rights movements from attending, indicate the importance of this Bandung Conference with demonstrable impact on liberation movements in various colonized African countries and on the civil rights movement in the United States.[36]

Hence, I argue that in Kunst's essay, many of the colonial orderings that had shaped his world and that of his associates as not-to-be-questioned realities are implicitly bolstered, because they became increasingly questionable through the Indonesian War of Independence and the Bandung Conference, among many other geopolitical events. These not-to-be-questioned realities constitute the essay's two narrative plots. One of these narrative plots is the suggestion that mankind's cultures have a common origin, from which they developed into the distinct purities of their own ethnos(es). Such a suggestion requires a hard cut between the past (the common origin) and the present (the distinct purity). The second of these implicit narrative plots is the cultural self-containment and self-sufficiency of Europe. World civilization emerged in the cradle of European civilization (namely ancient Greece) and spread from there over the rest of the world. At no point in his narrative does Kunst allow for the option that cultural influences from elsewhere may have impacted Europe; surely the Balkans cannot be an offshoot from East Flores. This assumption requires another hard cut, namely between here (Europe) and there (the rest of the world). Kunst's collection, like many archives and museums of the time, has been set up to secure these borders between then and now and between here and there and to present each ethnos from the Indonesian archipelago in its distinctiveness and uniqueness, untouched by the current "Western contaminations" (*Westersche smetten*) of European missionization and burgeoning global mass culture.[37]

The deconstruction of what Dipesh Chakrabarty calls such "master narratives" is in full swing, suggesting historiographical modes of diversification and decentering. I mention Julia Byl's book *Antiphonal Histories* and David Irving's work *How the World Made European Music*.[38] History itself is increasingly acknowledged as, in Chakrabarty's words, an "imperious code that accompanied the civilizing process that the European Enlightenment inaugurated in the eighteenth century as a world-historical task."[39] Olivia Bloechl calls this "the disingenuousness of historicism's continuous times and spaces." She also notes, however, that "the ideological preference of one origin story over another always leaves traces." Acknowledging and following these traces, according to Bloechl, requires "a tolerance for the 'uncanny,' [out-of-joint], haunted time of diachrony, because only this allows an experiment of the subaltern as subject of her own history." "Subaltern signification" she continues in the footsteps of Chakrabarty, "indicates cultural memory that is barred from being plausible knowledge," but that, precisely thanks to this exclusion, "also ensures the impossibility of secure memory." Subaltern signification, "in short, [is] any aspect of . . . histories or other forms of memory that makes it impossible to really know who we are and where we come from, because we have always already come from somewhere else in a time other than now."[40]

Bloechl's observation compels me to look for the subaltern traces left by Kunst's origin story. Kunst's powerful experience in the Grand Hall of the Kvarner Hotel in 1951 Opatija, Yugoslavia (now Croatia), is an outright uncanny one. It transports him back to 1930s East Flores, more than 10,000 km down the road, within a matter of seconds. The experience is so powerful because it is so out of joint; it messes with his and our historicized memory and our cartographic notions of space. Kunst manages to control and integrate this uncanniness through a re-historicizing of this experience, and visual and cartographical representations of this history. He is making the implausible plausible within the existing intellectual, ideological, and experiential infrastructures and distributions of power.

The result is a coherent narrative with plot structure. The unsettling experience of diachronous time is made consecutive and linear through such historical narratization. It is up to us, as peer readers, whether, in Treitler's words, "sufficient explanation has been given" to clarify this uncanny experience, whether "the outcome appear[s] . . . plausible in the light of the circumstances." We like to assume that these circumstances have changed since 1954. While Kunst is trying to make the implausible plausible, Bloechl and Chakrabarty, by contrast, invite us to reach beyond the realm of the plausible. They urge us to "learn to practice history in ways that disturb the operation of a universalizing translation by which history forgets what is subaltern as the basis for its own memory."[41]

Although I find illustrious examples of such disturbances in the work of my colleagues, I also think the disturbance of history's imperious code is easier said than done.[42] The fact that I felt so attracted by Kunst's narrative, despite my obvious skepticism, may have been fostered by my wish to forget the essentialist, purist, universalist, and even racist aspects of his thought. It may also have been sparked by my own historicized memory being so securely embedded in notions of a "civilizing process that the European Enlightenment inaugurated in the eighteenth century as a world-historical task."[43] This is the teaching I was brought up in; I have internalized it. This eighteenth-century civilizing process is also what the archive under my curation has been assembled for.

Such internalization is particularly prominent in aural experiences and acts of hearing. Wax cylinder nr. 185 from Kunst's collection contains the peculiar two-part singing from East Flores that Kunst was reminded of in the Kvarner Hotel. Readers can listen to this recording by visiting the UC Press website and the companion SoundCloud website: https://soundcloud.com/uc-press/sets/missionaries-anthropologists-and-music. Two male singers, Merien and Raja, sing the Lamaholot walking songs "Be'odong" and "Barassi hama" that Kunst recorded in July or August 1930 in the village Riangkroko in northeastern Flores. The sustained second intervals between the voices (see figure 14-2), at times in even tighter distance than one would aurally expect from a second interval within European tuning systems, was a sonic marker of difference from internalized European musical norms that caught Kunst's ear.[44] For me, it remains a sonic marker of difference in this respect. Moreover, I am also able to hear the resemblance of this vocal practice with records of a Croatian "Gigetanje" responsorial song recorded in the late 1960s (an odd fifteen years after Kunst heard Croatian *ojkanje* in the Kravner Hotel) that can be found in the ECJK Archive at the University of Amsterdam.[45] Readers can listen to this recording by visiting the UC Press website / the companion SoundCloud website: https://soundcloud.com/uc-press/sets/missionaries-anthropologists-and-music. The sustained vocal seconds, the vocal glides and the glottal stops that feature both the Croatian "Gigetanje" song and the Florinesian "Barassi hama" song can easily be aurally related to each other.

Yet what do these experiences of aural relation mean? Rather than ascertaining whether Jaap Kunst's establishment of cultural relations between the Balkans and Indonesia is plausible or implausible, I am interested in how Kunst and his consociates (including myself) attribute meaning to hearing such resemblance, for instance by writing historiographies as origin stories that leave subaltern traces. Bloechl and Chakrabarty note that "subaltern pasts represent moments or points at which the archive that the historian mines develops a degree of intractability with respect to the aims of professional history" exactly because, in García's words, the archive is discursive, based on specific ideological, aesthetic and scientific paradigms.[46]

As project leaders and principal investigators of the project Decolonizing Southeast Asian Sound Archives (DeCoSEAS), meLê yamomo and I intend to disclose the Jaap Kunst Collection (among others) to inheritors of the communities from whom Kunst recorded, collected, and moved the music. Such disclosure is not an aim in itself but rather a means to rethink practices of (sound) archive curation. The archive's (historiographical) intractability is important to consider in such rethinking, since it points us at the implications of historiographical "mining" of resources per se. There is a tension within the DeCoSEAS project between the need for archive's disclosure on the one hand and respect for its intractability on the other. Our own historicized and cartographied memories are cases in point to deal with this tension.

One way of dealing with this tension is to build a network of archive users with divergent sensory and discursive historicized memories (as archives in themselves). This allows for the manifestation of various forms and instances of intractability and accessibility or compatibility; what is implausible or unthinkable for one user might be obvious for another, and what is easily mined for historiographical, linguistic, or political aims according to one user should be left in peace according to another. Realizing such diversification of experience and use of the archive is one of the main aims of the DeCoSEAS consortium. I would like to illustrate this with another item from the Jaap Kunst Collection that DeCoSEAS has digitally disclosed.

Wax cylinder nr. 83 of the Jaap Kunst Collection contains the invocation of an *éré* (sorcerer-priest) from the village Balôdano in the region of Ma'u on the island of Nias. He is accompanied in all likelihood by *koko-koko* (or *kato-kato*) wooden percussion, indicated by Kunst as "kôlekôle." This recording cannot be consulted on the UC Press website / the companion SoundCloud website, since we are unsure if it is supposed to be heard by those it does not concern. Kunst notes that the invocation is meant to reanimate dying individuals (*"om stervende menschen tot het leven terug te roepen"*).[47] This record begs all kinds of questions: In what circumstances was it recorded? Was it staged or was Kunst actually present at a session retrieving a dying person from the dead? What would the *éré* have thought about his invocation being captured, moved, stored, replicated, and repeated? How is this record a remnant of a scholarly culture (*Wissenschaftskultur*) rather than of a distinct ethnos on Nias?

Apart from these historiographical questions, there are more uncanny questions pointing at the archival record's intractability from a historiographical perspective, questions that touch on "cultural memory that is barred from being plausible knowledge" and hence, thanks to this exclusion "ensures the impossibility of secure memory."[48] That makes these questions inescapable: Does the invocation keep or lose its power once it has been recorded? Can "the recording of the invocation" ever become "the invocation," or do they both have the agency and the power to disrupt such an epistemic shift? Can they prevent, reverse, or undo acts of objectification? Thus, can this record be played at all, and if so, under what conditions? Whose conditions?

Raising and attending to such questions unsettles notions of plausibility and inevitability that constitute aural, sensory, and discursive hegemonies comparable to the unthinkability of Indonesian people ruling themselves, as expressed by those in the mid-twentieth century who previously benefited from Dutch colonial rule in the Dutch East Indies. Within the DeCoSEAS consortium, we demonstrate that many such epistemic hegemonies remain to be unsettled by considering plausibilities that were previously unthinkable. We see this unsettling taking place in various branches of scholarship, such as the acknowledgment in zoomusicology of the presence of animal languages and musics and the acknowledgment in anthropology of the sociability and consciousness of plants.[49]

Moreover, attending to such questions might uncover subaltern traces and voices in the archive. In that way, developing a tolerance for the uncanny and training a susceptibility to forms of cultural memory that do not find themselves immediately in the realm of humanities scholarship might be employed as a viable method for scholarly investigation. A number of (music) anthropologists already turn to such methods. Think, for instance, of Eduardo Viveiros de Castro's engagement with Amerindian notions of perspectivism and the multiverse, David Graeber's proposal of radical alterity, and Bernd Brabec de Mori's conceptualization of the "sonicoid."[50] All these engagements carry the risk of epistemic appropriation but also the potential for becoming susceptible to hitherto unheard voices. It is important to note that despite the universalism and essentialism of his master narratives, Jaap Kunst consciously developed a similar susceptibility, even in quite different circumstances.

Kunst's execution of "a universalizing translation" in his 1954 essay, "by which history forgets what is subaltern as the basis for its own memory" leaves subaltern traces in his origin story.[51] They concern the absence of the possibility of an East to West migration (with Europe having been formed and influenced by Asia) and the absence of the notion that hearing and listening are culturally situated. This latter absence is temporary, since Kunst acknowledged on other occasions that his European ear was culturally situated. Here, however, his experience of resemblance is so powerful that universalist truth claims need to be employed for the sake of plausibility as inevitability. These absences allow for the belief in and (re)installment of a way of hearing and analyzing sound, European in origin but now universal, that was so typical of twentieth-century modernism but that has not become any less tempting for the skilled listeners that we are.

Seen from this perspective, Kunst's origin story can be compared with the *éré*'s chanting from Nias that Kunst recorded on cylinder 83. Both are epistemic practices, different in aim and content but comparable in structure and operation. Kunst's origin story functions within normative and globally hegemonic practices of knowledge formation, the anonymous *éré*'s recitation represents cultural memory that is barred from being plausible knowledge in mid-twentieth-century and current constellations of epistemic practice. Yet both are invocations. Through regular, repetitive, and formulaic utterances, they invoke a soothing predictability that manages the uncanny, signifies what is out of joint, and distracts from what is unthinkable. What is thinkable and unthinkable for the *éré* remains intractable for me so far, even if the aim of the DeCoSEAS consortium is to include actors like him. However, being part of Jaap Kunst's *Wissenschaftskultur*, I am able to observe that his search for cultural relations between the Balkans and Indonesia was also an attempt at dispelling what could no longer be denied: past and present cannot easily be separated and Europe is not culturally and epistemically self-sufficient but dependent on the rest of the world, just like humans turn out to be dependent on forests and fungi.[52]

As indicated earlier, what is being dispelled in Kunst's origin story—implicitly or explicitly—is not only what is unthinkable (such as Indonesians running their own sovereign state) but also what is part of everyone's lives, yet unspeakable (such as the atrocities committed by the Dutch army in the Indonesian War of Independence). Hearing takes place on a crossroads of invocation, conceptualization, objectification, and narrativization. Hearing facilitates epistemic shifts from recorded sound to sound, from experience to text, from past to history, and from the plausible to the inevitable: "I hear it, so it must be true!" Hearing also facilitates the disruption of such practices of objectification and textualization in allowing for the existence of experiences that are audible yet unspeakable and unconceptualized. What we cannot or do not dare to think can be heard nevertheless, enabling us to transgress borders between here and there, then and now, self and other, scholarship and art. However, the options to transgress are no guarantee for a more inclusive, democratic, and less extractivist scholarly practice. Not only do the grand narratives that clearly feature Kunst's thinking and his archive still linger in my own scholarly mind, but also the unsettling and dispelling of existing grand narratives might lead to the erection of new grand narratives with concomitant regimes of inclusion and exclusion.

It is this insight that features Caroline Bithell's praise song to our ancestors in ethnomusicology and anthropology.[53] She adopts a broad and inclusive notion of exorcization that I have adopted in earlier publications to indicate my relationship with Jaap Kunst.[54] This adds a third layer of invocation to my argument here: my own dispelling of Jaap Kunst's legacy that exists side by side with the recorded invocation from the *éré* from Nias and with Jaap Kunst's invocation in revitalizing the fading societal and epistemic structures of the Dutch East Indies in the 1950s through his origin story about the Balkans and Indonesia. To exorcize someone, Bithell argues, is not only and not primarily to drive someone out; it also means to communicate with someone, make peace with someone and set them free.[55] There is no point in "throw[ing] out the grandfathers with the bathwater"; they are part of the family tree, so we always communicate with them, whether we want to or not.[56] Since my appointment as curator of the Jaap Kunst Collection, I have been engaged with exorcizing Kunst in this inclusive manner; he is an ancestor I communicate with. The spell of the grandness and emblematic stature of his legacy needs to be broken, but his legacy remains in need of being valued, scrutinized, and studied. Kunst was musically, conceptually, and socially entangled with those who worked with him. They might remain invisible and inaudible as equally important predecessors if we throw Kunst out with the bathwater. My work and that of my colleagues is entangled with all these actors, and seats need to be reserved at the table for them all in case they pop by. Preparing those seats is one of the tasks that the DeCoSEAS consortium has set itself, with full awareness that this task might imply giving up our own seats at some point.

This has made me think about the ethnographies and historiographies I have practiced and produced over the last twenty years. The premises I have distanced myself from rhetorically—essentialism, racism, nature-culture divides, colonialism, and anthropocentrism—continue to underlie the practices I cherish. The fact that Kunst's narrative appealed to me so much may have pointed me at this insight, which makes me feel uncomfortable and excited at the same time, all the more so since my life and work are so entangled with Kunst's on so many levels. I feel boosted, supported, and uncomfortable being part of this lineage. I feel excited about the possibilities of disentangling myself from this lineage, even if this necessitates my transferring agency over the kind and speed of such disentanglement to other parties such as the inheritors of the invocation of the *éré* from Nias. What is important to explore is whether and how such disentanglement disturbs the operation of a universalizing historiography, not only rhetorically but also practically, and what epistemic reinventions beyond objectification it facilitates in the worldwide production and dissemination of knowledge.

NOTES

1. Jaap Kunst, *Cultural Relations between the Balkans and Indonesia* (Amsterdam: Koninklijk Instituut voor de Tropen, 1954), 3.

2. Kunst, *Cultural Relations between the Balkans and Indonesia*, 4.

3. Kunst, *Cultural Relations between the Balkans and Indonesia*, 6.

4. Jaap Kunst, "A Musicological Argument for Cultural Relationship between Indonesia (probably the Isle of Java), and Central Africa," *Proceedings of the Musical Association* 62 (1935–36): 57–76; German translation, *Anthropos* 31 (1936): 131–40.

5. Kunst, *Around Von Hornbostel's Theory of the Cycle of Blown Fifths* (Amsterdam: Koninklijke Vereeniging Indisch Instituut, 1948), 4.

6. Percival Kirby, *The Musical Instruments of the Native Races of South Africa* (Johannesburg: University of the Witwatersrand Press, 1968 [1934]); Hugh Tracey, *The Evolution of African Music and Its Function in the Present Day* (Johannesburg: Institute for the Study of Man in Africa, 1961).

7. Ernst Heins, Elisabeth den Otter, and Felix van Lamsweerde, eds., *Jaap Kunst—Indonesian Music and Dance: Traditional Music and Its Interaction with the West: A Compilation of Articles (1934–1952) originally published in Dutch, with Biographical Essays* (Amsterdam: Royal Tropical Institute/University of Amsterdam, 1994), 16; Marjolijn van Roon, "Jaap Kunst, Government Musicologist: An Unusual Incident in the Colonial Political History of the Netherlands East Indies," *Oideion: The Performing Arts Worldwide* 35, no. 2 (1995): 63–84.

8. Heins, Den Otter, and Van Lamsweerde, *Jaap Kunst*, 41.

9. Felix van Lamsweerde, "Inventory of the Wax Cylinder Collection of the Tropenmuseum," in Heins, Den Otter, and Van Lamsweerde, *Jaap Kunst*, 247.

10. Susanne Ziegler, *Die Wachszylinder des Berliner Phonogramm-Archivs: Textdokumentation und Klangbeispiele* (Berlin: Staatliche Museen zu Berlin—Preußischer Kulturbesitz, 2006), 391–413.

11. Jaap Kunst, *Musicologica: A Study of the Nature of Ethnomusicology, Its Problems, Methods, and Representative Personalities* (Amsterdam: Koninklijke Vereeniging Indisch Instituut, 1950).

12. Van Lamsweerde, "Inventory of the Wax Cylinder Collection of the Tropenmuseum."

13. Ziegler, *Die Wachszylinder des Berliner Phonogramm-Archivs*.

14. Heins, Den Otter, and Van Lamsweerde, *Jaap Kunst*, 18–20.

15. Jaap Kunst, *De inheemsche muziek en de zending: Voordracht op 1 Mei 1946 gehouden voor de Zendingsschool te Oegstgeest* (Amsterdam: H. J. Paris, 1947).

16. Kunst, *Musicologica*, 20.

17. See Decolonizing Southeast Asian Sound Archives, www.decoseas.org.

Barbara Titus, "Tracing Earlines in Ethnomusicology," in *Noise as Constructive Element in Music: Theoretical and Music-Analytical Perspectives on Noise and Noise Music*, ed. Mark Delaere (London: Routledge, 2022); Titus, "The 'Attentively Silent' Presence of Jaap Kunst in the Vereniging voor Nederlandse Muziekgeschiedenis," *Tijdschrift van de Koninklijke Vereniging voor Nederlandse Muziekgeschiedenis* 68 (2018): 163–74; Titus, "Jaap Kunst dan Pentingnya Koleksi Musik Indonesia Miliknya" in *Melacak jejak Jaap Kunst: Suara dari Masa Lalu*, exhibition catalogue November 28 2019–January 10, 2020, Jakarta Museum Nasional: 10-21, 2020; meLê yamomo and Barbara Titus, "The Persistent Refrain of the Colonial Archival Logic/Colonial Entanglements and Sonic Transgressions: Sounding Out the Jaap Kunst Collection," in *Postcolonial Sound Archives: Challenges and Potentials*, ed. Rasika Ajotikar, 39–70 (2021); meLê yamomo and Barbara Titus, "Rehearsing Decolonial Curatorship of Southeast Asian Sound Archives in Europe," in *The Future of Dutch Colonial Past: Curating Heritage, Art and*

Activism, ed. Pepijn Brandon, Emma van Bijnen, Karwan Fatah-Black, Imara Limon, Wayne Modest, and Margriet Schavemaker (Amsterdam: Amsterdam University Press, 2024), 110–23.

18. Ana María Ochoa Gautier, "El reordenamiento de los sentidos y el archive sonoro," *ArteFilosofía* 11 (2011): 82–95, quoted in Miguel García, "Sound Archives under Suspicion," in *Historical Sources of Ethnomusicology in Contemporary Debate,* ed. Susanne Ziegler, Ingrid Åkesson, Gerda Lechleitner, and Susana Sardo (Newcastle upon Tyne: Cambridge Scholars Publishing, 2017), 10–20, at 11.

19. Michel Foucault, *The Archaeology of Knowledge,* trans. A. M. Sheridan Smith (London: Routledge, 2002 [1969]), quoted in García, "Sound Archives under Suspicion."

20. García, "Sound Archives under Suspicion," 14.

21. Jaap Kunst, *Music in Flores,* trans. Emile van Loo (Leiden: Brill, 1942), 42.

22. Kunst, *Cultural Relations between the Balkans and Indonesia.*

23. Vinko Žganec and Nada Sremec, *Hrvatske narodne pjesme i plesovi* [Croatian folk songs and dances] (Zagreb: Seljacka Sloga, 1951); Kunst, *Cultural Relations between the Balkans and Indonesia,* 4.

24. Leo Treitler, "The Present as History," *Perspectives of New Music* 7 (1969): 1–58, at 2; García, "Sound Archives under Suspicion," 14.

25. Kunst, *Cultural Relations between the Balkans and Indonesia,* 5, 6–7, 7–9.

26. Kunst, *Cultural Relations between the Balkans and Indonesia,* 4, 6, 7.

27. Treitler, "The Present as History," 6, 7.

28. James Clifford, *The Predicament of Culture: Twentieth-Century Ethnography, Literature and Art* (Cambridge MA: Harvard University Press, 1988); Timothy Rice, "Dancing in the Scholar's World," in *May It Fill Your Soul: Experiencing Bulgarian Music,* (Chicago: The University of Chicago Press, 1994), 3–15.

29. Kunst, *Cultural Relations between the Balkans and Indonesia,* 7 (emphasis added).

30. García, "Sound Archives under Suspicion," 14; Treitler, "The Present as History," 3, 7.

31. Dipesh Chakrabarty, *Provincializing Europe: Postcolonial Thought and Historical Difference* (Princeton, NJ: Princeton University Press, 2000); and Olivia Bloechl, "On Colonial Difference and Musical Frontiers: Directions for a Postcolonial Musicology," in *Native American Song at the Frontiers of Early Modern Music* (Cambridge, UK: Cambridge University Press, 2008), 1–32.

32. KITLV-NIMH-NIOD, "Summary of *Beyond the Pale: Dutch Extreme Violence in the Indonesian War of Independence, 1945–1949,* with the main findings of the research programme on Independence, Decolonization, Violence and War in Indonesia 1945–1950" (Amsterdam: NIOD, 2022).

33. KITLV-NIMH-NIOD, "Summary of *Beyond the Pale,*" 3.

34. Kunst, "Een reis naar Australië," 24. "Zolang over dit eens zo rustige en welvarende Indonesië Soekarno's gangster-regering haar wanbeheer voert, wil ik geen voet in dit land zetten."

35. Clara Brinkgreve, *Met Indië verbonden: Een verhaal van vier generaties, 1849–1949* (Zutphen: Walburg Pers, 2009).

36. David Van Reybrouck, *Revolusi: Indonesië en het ontstaan van de moderne wereld* (Amsterdam: De Bezige Bij, 2020), 500–5.

37. Kunst, *De inheemsche muziek en de zending,* 26.

38. Julia Byl, *Antiphonal Histories: Resonant Pasts in the Toba Batak Musical Present* (Middletown, CT: Wesleyan University Press, 2014); and David Irving, *How the World Made European Music: A Global History of Early Modern Synthesis* (forthcoming).

39. Chakrabarty in Bloechl, "On Colonial Difference and Musical Frontiers," xvi.

40. Bloechl, "On Colonial Difference and Musical Frontiers," 13, 7, 13, 6.

41. Treitler, "The Present as History," 7, 11.

42. Diana Taylor, *The Archive and the Repertoire: Performing Cultural Memory in the Americas* (Durham, NC: Duke University Press, 2003); Ann Laura Stoler, *Along the Archival Grain: Epistemic Anxieties and Colonial Common Sense* (Princeton, NJ: Princeton University Press, 2009); Ochoa Gautier, *Aurality: Listening and Knowledge in Nineteenth-Century Colombia* (Durham, NC: Duke University Press, 2014); Byl, *Antiphonal Histories*; Rachel Mundy, *Animal Musicalities: Birds, Beasts, and Evolutionary*

Listening (Middletown, CT: Wesleyan University Press, 2018).

43. Chakrabarty in Bloechl, "On Colonial Difference and Musical Frontiers," xvi.

44. Dana Rappoport, "The Long Journey of the Rice Maiden from Li'o to Tanjung Bunga: A Lamaholot Sung Narrative (Flores, Eastern Indonesia)," in *Austronesian Paths and Journeys*, ed. James J. Fox (Canberra: ANU Press, 2021), 164–65.

45. Anka Blažević, Mara Blažević, Mara Blažević, Kaja Kavrag, Anka Kurtović, Anka Petrušić, Mara Petrušić 1968."Gigetanje" from the village Debeljaci, recorded by Martin Koenig and released on *Village Music of Yugoslavia: Songs & Dances from the Adriatic, Dinara, Panonia, and Vardar Regions* (New York: Nonesuch Records, 1971). [Part of the University of Amsterdam Etnomusicologisch Centrum Jaap Kunst {ECJK} Archive: 561–6].

46. Chakrabarty quoted in Bloechl, "On Colonial Difference and Musical Frontiers 11; García, "Sound Archives under Suspicion," 11.

47. Ziegler, *Die Wachszylinder des Berliner Phonogramm-Archivs*, 395.

48. Bloechl, "On Colonial Difference and Musical Frontiers," 6.

49. Eduardo Kohn, *How Forests Think: Toward an Anthropology beyond the Human* (Berkeley, CA: University of California Press, 2013); Peter Wohlleben, *Das geheime Leben der Bäume: Was sie fühlen, wie sie kommunizieren—die Entdeckung einer verborgenen Welt* (München: Heyne Verlag, 2017).

50. Eduardo Viveiros de Castro, "Cannibal Metaphysics: Amerindian Perspectivism," *Radical Philosophy* 132 (2013): 17–28; David Graeber's proposal of radical alterity, "Radical Alterity Is Just Another Way of Saying 'Reality': A Reply to Eduardo Viveiros de Castro," *Hau: Journal of Ethnographic Theory* 5, no. 2 (2015): 1–41; and Bernd Brabec de Mori's conceptualization of the sonicoid, "Sonic Substances and Silent Sounds: An Auditory Anthropology of Ritual Songs," *Tipití: Journal of the Society for the Anthropology of Lowland South America* 13, no. 2 (2015): 25–42.

51. Bloechl, "On Colonial Difference and Musical Frontiers," 11.

52. Merlin Sheldrake, *Entangled Life: How Fungi Make Our Worlds, Change Our Minds and Shape Our Futures* (New York: Penguin Random House, 2021).

53. Caroline Bithell, "Exorcising the Ancestors? Praisesong to the Ancestors and the Post-New Nuclear Family," in *The New (Ethno)Musicologies*, ed. Henry Stobart (Lanham, MD: Scarecrow Press, 2008), 76–82.

54. yamomo and Titus, "The Persistent Refrain of the Colonial Archival Logic," 49.

55. Bithell, "Exorcising the Ancestors?," 77.

56. Bithell, "Exorcising the Ancestors?," 77, 81.

Abraham, Otto, and Erich von Hornbostel. "Vorschläge für die Transkription exotischer Melodien." *Sammelbände der Internationalen Musikgesellschaft* 11, no. 1. (October–December, 1909): 1–25.

Acri, Andrea. "Birds, Bards, Buffoons and Brahmans: (Re-)Tracing the Indic Roots of Some Ancient and Modern Performing Characters from Java and Bali." *Archipel* 82 (2014): 13–70.

———. "On Birds, Ascetics, and Kings in Central Java: 'Ramayana' Kakawin, 24.95–126 and 26." *Bijdragen tot de Taal-, Land- en Volkenkunde* 166 (2010): 475–506.

Adam, Ahmat B. *The Vernacular Press and the Emergence of Modern Indonesian Consciousness (1855–1913).* Ithaca, NY: Southeast Asia Program, Cornell University, Studies on Southeast Asia 17 (1995).

Adi, Ganug Nugroho. "Blacius Subono: An Outlandish Dalang and Musician." *Jakarta Post*, December 30, 2013.

Adler, Guido. "Umfang, Methode und Ziel der Musikwissenschaft." *Vierteljahreszeitschift für Musikwissenschaft* 1 (1885): 5–20.

Adriaanse, L. *De nieuwe koers in onze zending, of Toelichting op de zendingsorde.* Amsterdam: Kirchner, 1903.

———. *Sadrach's kring.* Leiden: Donner, 1899.

Albers, C. "De Zendingschool en hare betekenis." In *Overzicht van de Vierde Zending-Conferentie, gehouden te Batavia en te Depok van 22 tot 30 Augustus,* 112–36. Neerbosch: Snelpersdrukkerij der Weesinrichting, 1885.

Allport, Gordon W. *The Nature of Prejudice.* New York: Addison-Wesley, 1954.

Andaya, Leonard Y. *The World of Maluku: Eastern Indonesia in the Early Modern Period.* Honolulu: University of Hawai'i Press, 1993.

Anderson, Benedict. *Mythology and the Tolerance of the Javanese.* Ithaca, NY: Cornell University Press, Studies in Southeast Asia 37, 1965.

———. *Imagined Communities: Reflections on the Origin and Spread of Nationalism*. 2nd ed. London: Verso, 2006.

Anugrah, Dwi. "Wayang Jataka Berbasis Sastra" [Jataka Wayang based on literature]. *Berita Magelang* [Magelang news], December 6, 2021.

Apples, Eddy. "Missie Naar Flores: Pater Simon Buis SVD en Zijn Flores-Films, 1925–1934." *Audiovisuel Archief, Jaarboek*, 1996: 7–31.

Apriaman, Abdul Latief. "Wayang Sasak Tumbuh di Bawah Bayang Kecurigaan" [Wayang Sasak growing under the shadow of suspicion]. *Tempo*, July 23, 2019.

Aritonang, Jan Sihar. "The Encounter of the Batak People with Rheinische Missions-Gesellschaft in the Field of Education." PhD diss., University of Utrecht, 2000.

Aritonang, Jan Sihar, and Karel Steenbrink, eds. *A History of Christianity in Indonesia*. Leiden: Brill, 2008.

Arom, Simha, et al. "Typologie des techniques polyphoniques." In *Musiques: Une encyclopédie pour le XXIe siècle, tome 5: L'Unité de la musique*, edited by Jean-Jacques Nattiez, 1088–1109. Paris: Actes Sud/Cité de la Musique, 2007.

Arps, Bernard. "De kwestie van het Javaanse kerkgezang." In *Woord en Schrift in de Oost: de betekenis van zending en missie voor de studie van taal en literatuur in Zuidoost-Azië*, 1–32. Leiden: Opleiding Talen en Culturen van Zuidoost-Azië en Oceanië, Universiteit Leiden, Semaian 19, 2000.

———. "The Regulation of Beauty: J. Kats and Javanese Poetics." In *The Canon in Southeast Asian Literatures: Literatures of Burma, Cambodia, Indonesia, Laos, Malaysia, the Philippines, Thailand and Vietnam*, edited by David Smyth, 114–34. Richmond: Curzon, 2000.

———. *Tall Tree, Nest of the Wind: The Javanese Shadow-Play* Dewa Ruci *Performed by Ki Anom Soeroto. A Study in Performance Philology*. Singapore: NUS Press, 2016.

———. *Tembang in Two Traditions: Performance and Interpretation of Javanese Literature*. London: School of Oriental and African Studies, 1992.

Asmoro, Purbo. *Wayang Ilang, Dhalang Nantang* [Wayang disappears, dalangs protest]. YouTube video of streamed performance, February 18, 2022. With translation by Katherine Emerson. www.youtube.com/watch?v=-4lIH1jIlug.

Baker, Brett Charles. "Indigenous-Driven Mission: Reconstructing Religious Change in Sixteenth-Century Maluku." PhD diss., Australian National University, 2012.

Beach, Harland P., and Charles H. Fahs, eds. *World Missionary Atlas*. New York: Institute of Social and Religious Research, 1925.

Bebbington, David. *Victorian Religious Revivals: Culture and Piety in Local and Global Contexts*. New York: Oxford University Press, 2012.

Beech, Hannah. "Welcome to Nusantara." *New York Times*, May 16, 2023.

Besser, Stephan. "Die Organisation des kolonialen Wissens. 10. Oktober 1902." In *Mit Deutschland um die Welt. Eine Kulturgeschichte des Fremden in der Kolonialzeit*, edited by Alexander Honold and Klaus R. Scherpe, 271–78. Stuttgart: J. B. Metzler, 2004

Berlinski, Mischa. *Fieldwork*. New York: Atlantic, 2007.

Bibliothèque royale de Belgique. *Catalogue de la bibliothèque de F. J. Fétis, acquise par l'état belge*. Brussels: Librairie Européene C. Muquardt, 1877.

Bithell, Caroline. "Exorcising the Ancestors? Praisesong to the Ancestors and the Post-New Nuclear Family." In *The New (Ethno)Musicologies*, edited by Henry Stobart, 76–82. Lanham, MD: Scarecrow Press. 2008.

Bleker, Otto. "Ferdinand Dejean (1731–97): Surgeon of the Dutch East-India Company, Man of the Enlightenment, and Patron of Mozart." *The Historian* 78, no. 1 (2016): 57–80.

Bloechl, Olivia A. "On Colonial Difference and Musical Frontiers: Directions for a Postcolonial Musicology." In *Native American Song at the Frontiers of Early Modern Music*, 1–32. Cambridge, UK: Cambridge University Press, 2008.

Bloom, Katya, Margit Galanter, and Sandra Reeve, eds. *Embodied Lives: Touched by the Art of Amerta Movement with Suprapto Suryodarmo*. London: Karnac, 2014.

Blumhofer, Edith. "Fanny Crosby and Protestant Hymnody." In *Music in American Religious Experience*, edited by Philip V. Bohlman, Edith L. Blumhofer, and Maria M. Chow, 215–32. New York: Oxford University Press, 2006.

Body, Jack, and Yono Sukarno, eds. *Jemblung and Related Narrative Traditions of Java*. Leiden: PAN Records. PAN 2048CD, 1997. Audio CD with liner notes.

Boen, Boen. *Alkitab Wayang: Perjanjian Baru* [The Wayang Bible: The New Testament]. Jakarta: BPK Gunung Mulia, 2018.

Bohlman, Philip V. "Missionaries, Magical Muses, and Magnificent Menageries: Image and Imagination in the Early History of Ethnomusicology." *World of Music* 30 (1988): 5–27.

———. "Prologue: Again, Herder." In *Song Loves the Masses: Herder on Music and Nationalism*, by Johann Gottfried Herder, translated and edited by Philip V. Bohlman, 1–18. Berkeley: University of California Press, 2017.

———. "Representation and Cultural Critique in the History of Ethnomusicology." In *Comparative Musicology and Anthropology of Music: Essays on the History of Ethnomusicology*, edited by Bruno Nettl and Philip V. Bohlamn, 131–51. Chicago: University of Chicago Press, 1991.

Bonatz, Dominik. "'Nicht von Gestern': Megalithismus auf Nias/Indonesien." *Antike Welt*, 1 (2002): 25–32.

Bonsen, Roland, Hans Marks, and Jelle Miedema, eds. *The Ambiguity of Rapprochement: Reflections of Anthropologists on Their Controversial Relationship with Missionaries*. Nijmegan: Focaal, 1989.

Boonstra, Saskia. "Performing Islam." *Inside Indonesia* 106 (October–December, 2011): 21.

Bouws, Jan. *Solank daar musiek is . . . Musiek en musiekmakers in Suid-Afrika (1652–1982)*. Cape Town: Tafelberg, 1982.

Boxer, Charles Ralph. *The Dutch Seaborne Empire 1600–1800*. London: Hutchinson, 1965.

———. "Some Portuguese Sources for Indonesian Historiography." In *An Introduction to Indonesian Historiography*, edited by Soedjatmoko, Muhammad Ali, G. J. Resink, and G. McT. Kahin, 217–33. Ithaca, NY: Cornell University Press, 1965.

Brabec de Mori, Bernd. "Sonic Substances and Silent Sounds: An Auditory Anthropology of Ritual Songs." *Tipití: Journal of the Society for the Anthropology of Lowland South America* 13 (2015): 25–42.

Brakel-Papenhuijzen, Clara. *Dairi Stories and Pakpak Storytelling: A Storytelling Tradition from the North Sumatran Rainforest*. Leiden: Brill, 2014.

Bramantyo, Triyono. "Early Acceptance of Western Music in Indonesia and Japan." *Arts and Social Sciences Journal* 9, no. 5 (2018): 1–5.

Brandes, Jan. "Hollands bruidsfeest te Batavia, Jan Brandes, 1779–1785." Amsterdam: Rijksmuseum. www.rijksmuseum.nl/en/collection/NG-369.

Brandewie, Ernest. *In the Light of the Word: Divine Word Missionaries of North America*. Maryknoll, NY: Orbis, 2000.

Brandts Buys, J. S. "Uit de pers. De *tjantang baloeng's*—Javaansche en Balische kleppers—*Beḍåjå ketawang*—Édan-édanan." *Djåwå* 13 (1933): 258–62.

Brinkgreve, Clara. *Met Indië verbonden: Een verhaal van vier generaties, 1849–1949.* Zutphen: Walburg, 2009.

Brinner, Benjamin. "Performer Interaction in a New Form of Javanese *Wayang.*" In *Essays on Southeast Asian Performing Arts: Local Manifestations and Cross-Cultural Implications,* edited by Kathy Foley, 96–114. Berkeley: Centers for South and Southeast Asia Studies, University of California, Berkeley, 1992.

Bronwen, Douglas, and Chris Ballard, eds. *Foreign Bodies: Oceania and the Science of Race 1750–1940* Canberra: Australian National University Press, 2008.

Brossard, Sébastien de. *Dictionnaire de musique, contenant une explication des termes grecs, latins, italiens & françois les plus usitez dans la musique.* Paris: Christophe Ballard, 1703.

Bruijn, Max de. "Interior of the Lutheran Church." In *The World of Jan Brandes, 1743–1808: Drawings of a Dutch Traveller in Batavia, Ceylon and Southern Africa,* edited by Max de Bruijn and Remco Raben, 185–89. Zwolle: Waanders, 2004.

Brumund, J. F. G. *Berigten omtrent de evangelisatie van Java.* Amsterdam: Van der Heij, 1854.

Buis, Simon P., and Piet L. Beltjens. "Ria Rago." Film script. Erfgoedcentrum Nederlands Kloosterleven, 1930.

Busse Berger, Anna Maria. *Medieval Music and the Art of Memory.* Berkeley: University of California Press, 2005.

———. *Mensuration and Proportion Signs: Origins and Evolution.* Oxford: Clarendon Press, 1993.

———. *The Search for Medieval Music in Africa and Germany, 1891–1961: Scholars, Singers, Missionaries.* Chicago: University of Chicago Press, 2020.

Butler, Anthea. *White Evangelical Racism: The Politics of Morality in America.* Chapel Hill: University of North Carolina Press, 2021.

Byl, Julia. *Antiphonal Histories: Resonant Pasts in the Toba Batak Musical Present.* Middletown, CT: Wesleyan University Press, 2014

———. "Harmonic Egalitarianism in Toba Liquor Stands and Studios." In *Sounding Out the State of Indonesian Music,* edited by Andrew McGraw and Christopher J. Miller, 19–39. Ithaca, NY: Cornell University Press, 2022.

———. "Music, Convert and Subject in the North Sumatran Mission Field." In *The Oxford Handbook of Music and World Christianities,* edited by Jonathan Dueck and Suzel Reily, 33–54. New York: Oxford University Press, 2006

Cachet, F. Lion. *Een jaar op reis in dienst der Zending.* Amsterdam: Wormser, 1896.

Campbell, Joseph. *The Hero with a Thousand Faces.* Princeton, NJ: Princeton University Press, 1949.

Campo López, Antonio Carlos. "Molucas y España en el siglo XVII." In *En el archipiélago de la especiería: España y Molucas en los siglos XVI y XVII,* edited by Javier Serrano Avilés and Jorge Mojarro Romero, 38–67. Madrid: Desperta Ferro, 2021.

Capistrano-Baker, Florina H., ed. *Art of Island Southeast Asia: The Fred and Rita Richman Collection.* New York: Metropolitan Museum, 1994.

Chakrabarty, Dipesh. *Provincializing Europe: Postcolonial Thought and Historical Difference.* Princeton, NJ: Princeton University Press, 2000.

Chenoweth, Vida, and Darlene Bee. "On Ethnic Music." *Practical Anthropology* 15, no. 5 (1968): 205–12.

Cicero. *Tusculan Disputations*. Translated by J. E. King. Loeb Classical Library 141. Cambridge, MA: Harvard University Press, 1927.

Clifford, James. *Person and Myth: Maurice Leenhardt in the Melanesian World*. Durham, NC: Duke University Press, 1992.

———. *The Predicament of Culture: Twentieth-Century Ethnography, Literature and Art*. Cambridge MA: Harvard University Press, 1988.

Cohen, Mathew Isaac. "Contemporary 'Wayang' in Global Contexts." *Asian Theatre Journal* 24 (2007): 338–69.

Colín, Francisco, and Pablo Pastells. *Labor evangélica, ministerios apostolicos de los obreros de la Compañia de Jesus, fundacion, y progressos de su provincia en las Islas Filipinas. Historiados por el Padre Francisco Colín . . . Parte primera sacada de los manuscritos del Padre Pedro Chirino, el primero de la Compañia que passó de los reynos de España a estas islas, por orden, y a costa de la catholica, y real Magestad*. 3 vols. Barcelona: Henrich y Compañía, 1900–2.

Cooley, Timothy J., and Gregory Barz, eds. *Shadows in the Field: New Perspectives for Fieldwork in Ethnomusicolgy*. 2nd ed. New York: Oxford University Press, 2008.

Coolsma, S. *De zendingseeuw voor Nederlandsch Oost-Indië*. Utrecht: Breijer, 1901.

Corte-Real, Maria de São José. "Music in Fernão Mendes Pinto's *Peregrinação*." In *Portugal and the World: The Encounter of Cultures in Music*, edited by Salwa El-Shawan Castelo-Branco, 185–200. Lisbon: Publicações Dom Quixote, 1997.

Costa, Horacio de la. *The Jesuits in the Philippines, 1581–1768*. Cambridge, MA: Harvard University Press, 1961.

Coté, Joost. "Thomas Karsten's Indonesia: Modernity and the End of Europe, 1914–1945." *Bijdragen Tot de Taal-, en Volkenkunde* 170 (2014): 66–98.

Coutinho, Deepti. "Santos Passos & Motets/Tradition of Christian Sacred Music for Lent." *Goa Roots*, March 9, 2016. https://goaroots.com/santos-passos-motet-tradition-of -christian-sacred-music-for-lent/.

"Das Jahr 1921 in der Niasmission." *Berichte der Rheinischen Missionsgesellschaft* 79 (1922): 97–112.

de Baets, Peter. "Michael Ondaatje: Een Brugse connectie." *Biekorf: West-Vlaams Archief voor Geschiedenis, Archeologie, Taal- en Volkskunde* 112, no. 2 (2012): 169–70.

de Beer, Henk. "Kort historisch overzicht van de film-activiteit." Unpublished document. Erfgoedcentrum Nederlands Kloosterleven (1992).

DeCoSEAS 2021. "Decolonizing Southeast Asian Sound Archives." Research project coordinated by meLê yamomo and Barbara Titus. Available at www.decoseas.org.

Delius, Eberhard. "Die Batakkirche in der Feuerprobe." Wuppertal, VEM, Ms. 1944 (from 1939).

———. "Singende Kirche auf dem Missionsfeld." *Berichte der Rheinische Missiongesellschaft* 96 (1939): 1–17.

Denning, Michael. *Noise Uprising: The Audiopolitics of a World Musical Revolution*. London: Verso, 2015.

De Ocampo, Esteban A. *The Ternateños: Their History, Language, Customs and Traditions*. Ermita, Manila: National Historical Institute, 2007.

de Vos, F. H. "Genealogy of the Family of Gratiaen of Ceylon." *Journal of the Dutch Burgher Union* 6, no. 1 (1913): 16–21.

Dessì, Paola. "L'itinerario sonoro di Lodovico di Verthema." In *Per una storia dei popoli senza note*. Heuresis. XIII: Sezione di Arti, Musica, Spettacolo, No. 9, 105–11. Bologna: Cooperativa Libraria Universitaria (CLUEB), 2010.

Diehl, Katharine Smith. *Printers and Printing in the East Indies*. Vol. 1, *Batavia*. New Rochelle, NY: Aristide D. Caratzas, 1990.

Door een leek. *Gĕnḍing en tĕmbang. Iets over gĕnḍing en tĕmbang en over Javaansch kerkgezang*. Met re- en dupliek overgedrukt uit "De Opwekker" van 1901 en 1902. Uitgegeven door den Nederlandsch-Indischen Zendingbond. Batavia: Albrecht, 1904.

Dooren, Ine van. "De Missiefilm Ria Rago: Een Gedramatiseerd Document." *GBG Nieuws* 33 (1995): 8–16.

Doyle, Dennis. "The Concept of Inculturation in Roman Catholicism: A Theological Consideration," *U.S. Catholic Historian* 30, no. 1 (Winter 2012): 1–13

Dürr, Alfred. *The Cantatas of J. S. Bach*. New York: Oxford University Press, 2005.

Ecklund, Judith. "Paradoxes and Realities of Wayang among the Sasak of Lombok." In *Puppet Theater in Contemporary Indonesia; New Approaches to Performance Events*, edited by Jan Mrázek, 205–21. Ann Arbor: Centers for South and Southeast Asian Studies, University of Michigan, 2002.

Evangelical Lutheran Church in America. *Evangelical Book of Worship*. Minneapolis: Augsburg Fortress, 2006.

Evans, Andrew D. "Anthropology at War: Racial Studies of POWs during World War I." In *Worldly Provincialism: German Anthropology in the Age of Empire*, edited by H. Glenn Penny and Matti Bunzl, 198–229. Ann Arbor: University of Michigan Press, 2003.

Evers, Hans-Dieter. "Nusantara." *Journal of the Malaysian Branch of the Royal Asiatic Society* 89, no. 1 (2016): 3–14.

Fairley, Brian. "Vessels of Song: Ethnodoxy and the Enduring Legacy of Missionary Work." *SEM Student News* 14 (2018): 37–40.

Feener, R. Michael. "A Re-examination of the Place of al-Hallaj in the Development of Southeast Asian Islam." *Bijdragen tot de Taal-, Land- en Volkenkunde* 154, (1998): 571–92.

Fernández de León, Melchor. *Comedia famosa: La conquista de las Malucas*. Valencia: En la imprenta de la Viuda de Joseph de Orga, 1762.

———. "La gran comedia, Conquista de las Malucas." In *Primavera numerosa de muchas armonias luzientes, en doce comedias fragantes parte quarenta y seis, impressas fielmente de los borradores de los mas célebres plausibles ingenios de España*, 174v–97v. Madrid: Francisco Sanz, 1679.

Filippi, Daniele V. "'Catechismum Modulans Docebat': Teaching the Doctrine through Singing in Early Modern Catholicism." In *Listening to Early Modern Catholicism: Perspectives from Musicology*, edited by Daniele V. Filippi and Michael Noone, 129–48. Leiden: Brill, 2017.

———. "A Sound Doctrine: Early Modern Jesuits and the Singing of the Catechism." *Early Music History* 34 (2015): 1–43.

Fink, G. W. "Notizen über Musik und Gesänge der malaiischen Eingebornen auf den sundischen und molukkischen Inseln (Ostindien)." *Allgemeine musikalische Zeitung*, no. 52 (December 23, 1840): cols 1057–63.

Florida, Nancy K. *Writing the Past, Inscribing the Future: History as Prophecy in Colonial Java*. Durham, NC: Duke University Press, 1995.

Foley, Kathy. "First Things: Opening Passages in Southeast Asian Puppet Theatre." In *Puppet Theater in Contemporary Indonesia*, edited by Jan Mrázek, 271–83. Ann Arbor: Centers for South and Southeast Asian Studies, University of Michigan, 2002.

———. "The Origin of Kala: A Sundanese *Wayang Golek Purwa* Play by Abah Sunarya and Gamelan Giri Harja I." *Asian Theatre Journal* 18 (2001): 1–58.

———. "The *Ronggeng*, the *Wayang*, the *Wali*, and Islam: Female or Transvestite Male Dancers-Singers-Performers and Evolving Islam in West Java." *Asian Theatre Journal* 32 (2015): 356–86.

———. "Les Wali reduit au silence" [Silencing the walis]. In *Marionettes et Pouvoir*, edited by R. Fleury and J. Sermon, 150–70. Montpellier: Deuxième Époque, 2019.

———. "Saintly Puppet Masters and Sacred Clowning: Antinomian Religion and Patterns in Islamic Puppetry." In *Puppets and Spirit: Ritual, Religion, and Performing Objects*, edited by Claudia Orenstein and Tim Cusack, 184–96. New York: Routledge, 2023.

Fosdahl, Frank. "Wayang Wahyu Lakon *Wahyu Manunggal Sejati*" [Wayang wahyu play *Divine Power of Singular Revelation*]. April 17, 2021. YouTube video. www.youtube.com/watch?v=8ayxsml9C3c.

Fosler-Lussier, Danielle. *Music on the Move*. Ann Arbor: University of Michigan Press, 2020.

Foucault, Michel. *The Archaeology of Knowledge*. Translated by A. M. Sheridan Smith. London: Routledge, 2002. First published 1969 by Éditions Gallimard (Paris).

Frederiks, Johannes Godefridus, and F. Jos van den Branden. *Biographisch Woordenboek der noord- en zuidnederlandsche Letterkunde*. 2nd rev. ed. Amsterdam: L. J. Veen, 1892.

Fries, Eduard. "Das 'Koppensnellen' auf Nias." *Allgemeine Missionszeitschrift* 35 (1908): 73–88.

García, Francisco. *Vida y milagros de San Francisco Xavier, de la Compañia de Jesus, apostol de las Indias*. Madrid: Iuan Garcia Infanzon, 1672.

Gardner, Helen "The 'Faculty of Faith': Evangelical Missionaries, Social Anthropologists, and the Claim for Human Unity in the Nineteenth Century." In *Foreign Bodies: Oceania and the Science of Race 1750–1940*, edited by Douglas Browen and Chris Ballard, 259–82. Canberra: Australian National University Press.

García, Miguel. "Sound Archives under Suspicion." In *Historical Sources of Ethnomusicology in Contemporary Debate*, edited by Susanne Ziegler, Ingrid Åkesson, Gerda Lechleitner, and Susana Sardo, 10–20. Newcastle upon Tyne: Cambridge Scholars Publishing, 2017.

Geertz, Clifford. *Religion of Java*. Glencoe, IL: The Free Press, 1960.

Gibson-Hill, C. A. "Documents Relating to John Clunies Ross, Alexander Hare and the Early History of the Settlement on the Cocos-Keeling Islands." *Journal of the Malayan Branch of the Royal Asiatic Society* 25, no. 4 (1952): 5–306.

Gouda, Frances. *Dutch Culture Overseas: Colonial Practice in the Netherlands Indies, 1900–1942*. Jakarta: Equinox, 2008.

Gowing, Peter G. "The Legacy of Frank Charles Laubach." *International Bulletin of Missionary Research* (1983): 59–60.

Graeber, David. "Radical Alterity Is Just Another Way of Saying 'Reality': A Reply to Eduardo Viveiros de Castro." *Hau: Journal of Ethnographic Theory* 5 (2015): 1–41.

Gratiaen, Jan Frans [Gratiaen, Johannes Vranciscus]. "Redeneeringen over nuttige Muzikaale Onderwerpen, Tot onderzoek van Kenners, tot verlustiging van Geoeffende en tot onderrichting van weetgierige Muziek-liefhebbers." *Verhandelingen van het Bataviaasch Genootschap van Kunsten en Wetenschappen* 6 (1792): "Voorreeden" (1–14), contents (1–2), and main text (1–286).

Gratiaen, Jan Frans [as Gratiaen, Johannes Franciscus]. "Redeneringen over nuttige Muzikale Onderwerpen, Tot onderzoek van kenners, tot verlustiging van geoefende en tot onderrigting van weetgierige muzijk-liefhebbers. *Verhandelingen van het Bataviaasch Genootschap van Kunsten en Wetenschappen* 6, reprint (1827): 95–299.

Groeneboer, Kees. *Een Vorst onder de Taalgeleerden: Herman Neubronner van der Tuuk, Taalafgevaardigde voor Indië van het Nederlandsch Bijbelgenootschap 1847–1873.* Leiden: KITLV Uitgeverij, 2002.

Gronow, Pekka. "The Record Industry Comes to the Orient." *Ethnomusicology* 25, no. 2 (May 1981): 251–84.

Groot, Hans. *Van Batavia naar Weltevreden: Het Bataviaasch Genootschap van Kunsten en Wetenschappen, 1778–1867.* Leiden: KITLV Uitgeverij, 2009.

Guillot, C. *L'Affaire Sadrach: Un essai de christianisation à Java au XIXe siècle.* Paris: Éditions de la Maison des sciences de l'homme, 1981.

Guzzetti, Barbara J., ed. *Literacy for the New Millennium.* Westport, CT: ABC-CLIO, 2007.

Haddon, Alfred C. *Head-Hunters: Black, White, and Brown.* London: Methuen, 1901.

———. *Reports of the Cambridge Anthropological Expedition to Torres Straits.* 6 vols. Cambridge, UK: Cambridge University Press, 1901–35.

Hadiwidjojo. "Sesorahipun Pangarsa Paheman Radyapustaka 'G.P.H. Hadiwidjojo' wonten ing Walidyasana" [A speech by the head of Radyapustaka Museum 'G.P.H. Hadiwidjojo' in the Walidyasana hall], 1953. Typed manuscript.

Hall, Edward T. *The Dance of Life: The Other Dimension of Time.* New York: Anchor Books, 1984.

Hamilton, Mary, Bryan Maddox, and Camilla Addey, eds. *Literacy as Numbers.* New York: Cambridge University Press, 2015.

Hämmerle, Johannes. *Nias—Eine eigene Welt. Sagen, Mythen, Überlieferungen.* Collectianea Instituti Anthropos vol. 43. St. Augustin: Anthropos Institut und Academia Verlag, 1999.

Handojomarno Sir, S. T. *Suatu Survey Mengenai Gereja Kristen Jawi Wetan.* Malang and Jakarta: Gereja Kristen Jawi Wetan and Lembaga Penelitian dan Studi Dewan Gereja-Gereja di Indonesia. Benih yang Tumbuh 7, 1976.

Hariyadi, Mathias. "Muslim Scholar against *Wayang,* Indonesia's Traditional Theatre." *Asia News,* February 18, 2022.

Harnish, David. *Change and Identity in the Music Cultures of Lombok, Indonesia.* Leiden: Brill 2021.

______. "The Worlds of Wayang Sasak: Music, Performance, and Negotiations with Religion and Modernity." *Asian Music* 34 (2003): 91–120.

Harnish, David, and Anne Rasmussen, eds. *Divine Inspirations: Music and Islam in Indonesia.* New York: Oxford University Press, 2012.

Harris, M. "History and Significance of the Emic/Etic Distinction." *Annual Review of Anthropology* 5 (1976): 329–50.

Harthoorn, S. E. *De evangelische zending en Oost-Java: Eene kritische bijdrage.* Haarlem: Kruseman, 1863.

Hedstrom, Matthew. *The Rise of Liberal Religion: Book Culture and American Spirituality in the Twentieth Century.* New York: Oxford University Press, 2013.

Heerkens, P. "Boekbespreking: J. Kunst, Music in Flores. Leiden 1942." *Cultureel Indië* 5 (1943) 138–41.

———. *Flores: De Manggarai*. Uden: Missiehuis, 1930.

———. "Het Lied van Saka Ladja." In *Onder Palmen en Waringins: Geest en Godsdienst van Insulinde*, 30–41. Naarden: Uitgeverij in Den Toren, 1946.

———. *Het Lied van Saka Ladja*. Haarlem: Uitgeverij J.H. Gottmer, 1949.

———. *De Kinkenduut*. Tilburg: Henri Bergmans, 1940.

———. *Lieder Der Florinesen: Sammlung 140 Florinesischer Lieder und 162 Texte mit Übersetzung aus dem Sprachgebiete der Lionesen, Sikanesen, Ngada's und Manggarier*. Leiden, Netherlands: E. J. Brill, 1953.

———. "Noengoenangé van Wonga Wéa." *Cultureel Indië* 5 (1943): 1–24.

———. "Ola Wolo, de Buine Slaaf. Roman uit de Timor-Archipel." University of Amsterdam, Jaap Kunst Collection, 1938.

———. *Den Örgel*. Tilburg: Bergmans, 1938.

———. *Ria Rago: Adat-Roman Uit de Timor-Archipel*. Eindhoven: Het Poirtersfonds, 1938.

———. *Sinjo, de Slimme App*. Ende, Flores: Stenzel, 1932.

Hefner, Robert W. "Of Faith and Commitment: Christian Conversion in Muslim Java." In *Conversion to Christianity: Historical and Anthropological Perspectives on a Great Transformation*, edited by Robert W. Hefner, 99–125. Berkeley: University of California Press, 1993.

Heins, Ernst. "The Netherlands." In *Ethnomusicology: Historical and Regional Studies*, edited by Helen Myers, 101–10. New York: W. W. Norton, 1992.

Heins, Ernst, Elisabeth den Otter, Felix van Lamsweerde, eds. *Jaap Kunst—Indonesian Music and Dance: Traditional Music and its Interaction with the West. A Compilation of Articles (1934–1952) Originally Published in Dutch, with Biographical Essays*. Amsterdam: Royal Tropical Institute/University of Amsterdam, 1994.

Herle, Anita, and Jude Philp, eds. *Recording Kastom. Alfred Haddon's Journals from the Torres Trait and New Guinea, 1888 and 1898*. Sydney: Sydney University Press 2020.

Herle, Anita, and Sandra Rouse, eds. *Cambridge and the Torres Strait. Centenary Essays on the 1898 Anthropological Expedition*. Cambridge, UK: Cambridge University Press 2008.

Herzfeld, Michael. *Cultural Intimacy: Social Poetics and the Nation-State*. 2nd ed. New York: Routledge, 2005.

Heuken, Adolf. *Be My Witness to the Ends of the Earth! The Catholic Church in Indonesia before the 19th Century*. Jakarta: Cipta Loka Caraka, 2002.

———. "Catholic Converts in the Moluccas, Minahasa and Sangihe-Talaud, 1512–1680." In *A History of Christianity in Indonesia*, edited by Jan Sihar Aritonang and Karel Steenbrink, 23–72. Leiden: Brill, 2008.

Hiery, Hermann Joseph. "Schule und Ausbildung in der Deutschen Südsee." In *Die Deutsche Südsee 1884–1914. Ein Handbuch*, edited by Hermann Joseph Hiery, 198–238. Paderborn: Verlag Ferdinand Schöningh 2001.

Hodges, Robert. "'*Ganti Andung Gabe Ende*': The Changing Voice of Grief in the Pre-funeral Wakes of Toba Batak." PhD diss., University of California, Santa Barbara, 2009.

Hoedmaker, Libertus A. "The Legacy of Hendrik Kraemer." *International Bulletin of Missionary Research* 4 (1980): 60–64.

Hoekema, A. G., ed. "*Tot heil van Java's arme bevolking*": *Een keuze uit het dagboek (1851–1860) van Pieter Jansz, doopsgezind zendeling in Jepara, Midden-Java*. Hilversum: Verloren. Manuscripta Mennonitica 1, 1997.

Hollinger, David A. *Christianity's American Fate: How Religion Became More Conservative and Society More Secular*. Princeton: Princeton University Press, 2022.

——. *Protestants Abroad: How Missionaries Tried to Change the World but Changed America*. Princeton, NJ: Princeton University Press, 2017.

Holt, Fabian. *Genre in Popular Music*. Chicago: University of Chicago Press, 2007.

Hood, Mantle. *The Nuclear Theme as a Determinant of Patet in Javanese Music*. Groningen: J. B. Wolters, 1954.

Hopkins, C. Howard. *John R. Mott, 1865–1955*. Geneva: Eerdmans, 1985.

Hornbostel, Erich M. von, and Curt Sachs. "Systematik Der Musikinstrumente. Ein Versuch." *Zeitschrift für Ethnologie* 46, no. 4/5 (1914): 553–90.

Hornbostel, Erich M. von. "African Negro Music." *Africa: Journal of the International African Institute* 1 (1928): 30–62.

Hughes-Freeland, Felicia. "*Golék Ménak* and *Tayuban*: Patronage and Professionalism in Two Spheres of Central Javanese Culture." In *Performance in Java and Bali: Studies of Narrative, Theatre, Music, and Dance*, edited by Bernard Arps, 88–120. London: School of Oriental and African Studies, 1993.

Huigen, Siegfried. "Antiquarian Ambonese: François Valentyn's Comparative Ethnography." In *The Dutch Trading Companies as Knowledge Networks*, edited by Siegfried Huigen, Jan L. de Jong, and Elmer Kolfin, 361–92. Leiden: Brill, 2010.

Humburg, Martin, Domonik Bonatz, and Claus Veltmann, eds. *Im "Land der Menschen": Der Missionar und Maler Eduard Fries und die Insel Nias*. Bielefeld: Regionalgeschichte Verlag, 2003.

Huria Kristen Batak Protestan. *Buku Ende HKBP, Mar Haluaon na Gok dohot Sangap di Jahowa*. Pematangsiantar: Percetakan HKBP, 2009.

Hutajulu, Ritaony. "Analisis Struktural Musik Vokal pada Opera Batak: Dengan Pusat Perhatian pada Karya Tilhang Gultom." Bachelor's thesis, Universitas Sumatera Utara, Medan, Indonesia, 1988.

Hutchison, William R. *Errand to the World: American Protestant Thought and Foreign Missions*. Chicago: University of Chicago Press, 1987.

Huygens Instituut. "The Dutch East India Company's Shipping between the Netherlands and Asia 1595–1795: Details of Voyage 3368.3 from Texel to Ceylon" (Voyage of the *Krabbendijke*). https://resources.huygens.knaw.nl/das/detailVoyage/94441. Accessed February 28, 2023.

——. "The Dutch East India Company's Shipping between the Netherlands and Asia 1595–1795: Details of voyage 3347.1 from Rammekens to Batavia" (Voyage of the *Zeelandia*). https://resources.huygens.knaw.nl/das/detailVoyage/94441. Accessed February 28, 2023.

Ibrahim, Muhammad ibn. *The Ship of Sulaima*. Translated from the Persian by J. O'Kane. London: Routledge and Kegan Paul, 1972 [1688].

Irving, David R. M. "Ancient Greeks, World Music, and Early Modern Constructions of Western European Identity." *Studies on a Global History of Music: A Balzan Musicology Project, 2013–2015*, ed. Reinhard Strohm, 21–41. Abingdon: Routledge, 2018.

——. "The Genevan Psalter in Eighteenth-Century Indonesia and Sri Lanka." *Eighteenth-Century Music* 11, no. 2 (2014): 235–55.

——. "Global Soundscapes from the First Voyage of Circumnavigation, 1519–1522." In *Soundscapes of the Early Modern Hispanophone and Lusophone Worlds*, edited by Victor Sierra Matute, 287–312. New York: Routledge, 2025.

Jacobs, Hubert, ed. *Documenta Malucensia: I (1542–1577)*. Rome: Jesuit Historical Institute, 1974.

———, ed. *Documenta Malucensia: II (1577–1606)*. Rome: Jesuit Historical Institute, 1980.

———, ed. *Documenta Malucensia: III (1606–1682)*. Rome: Jesuit Historical Institute, 1984.

———. "Indonesia: Antigua CJ (1546–1677)." In *Diccionario histórico de la Compañía de Jesús: biográfico-temático*, edited by Charles E. O'Neill and Joaquín María Domínguez, 2015–17. Rome and Madrid: Institutum Historicum, S. I.[Societatis Iesu], Universidad Pontificia Comillas, 2001.

———, ed. *A Treatise on the Moluccas (c. 1544): Probably the Preliminary Version of Antonio Galvão's Lost História das Molucas Edited, Annotated, and Translated into English from the Portuguese Manuscript in the Archivo General de Indias, Seville by Hubert Th. Th. M. Jacobs*. Rome; St. Louis: Jesuit Historical Institute; St. Louis University, 1971.

Jans, P. [P. Jansz Sr.]. "Kerkgezang in Javaansch têmbang ten dienste der Inlandsche gemeenten." In *Overzicht van de Vierde Zending-Conferentie, gehouden te Batavia en te Depok van 22 tot 30 Augustus 1885*, 9–16. Neerbosch: Snelpersdrukkerij der Weesinrichting, 1885.

———. *Kitab Isi Masmur Papethingan Sawatawis, Tinembangaken Jawi*. Amsterdam: Sepin, 1865.

Janssen, Rolf. *We hebben gezongen en niks gehad: Muzikanten en liederen uit Midden Brabant*. Tilburg: Boekhandel Gianotten B. V., 1984.

Jenkins, J. S. "Mozart's Indian: Dr Ferdinand Dejean." *Journal of Medical Biography* 2, no. 1 (1994): 53–58.

Joch, Markus. "Der Katechismus zur Kolonialfrage. Februar 1879: Friedrich Fabri fragt: 'Bedarf Deutschland der Colonien.'" In *Mit Deutschland um die Welt. Eine Kulturgeschichte des Fremden in der Kolonialzeit*, edited by Alexander Honold and Klaus R. Scherpe. Stuttgart: J. B. Metzler, 2004.

Jones, William. "On the *Musical Modes* of the *Hindus*: Written in 1784, and since much enlarged—By the President." *Asiatick Researches: Or, Transactions of the Society, Instituted in Bengal, for Inquiring into the History and Antiquities, the Arts, Sciences, and Literature of Asia* 3 (1792): 59–87.

Kambe, Yukimi. "Viols in Japan in the Sixteenth and Early Seventeenth Centuries." *Journal of the Viola da Gamba Society of America* 37 (2000): 31–67.

Karaton Ngayogyakarta Hadiningrat. "Beksan Ajisaka Uyon-uyon Hadiluhung Jumadilakir 1954 Jimakir/1 Februari 2021."

Kartomi, Margaret. "A influência portuguesa na música da Indonésia e da Malásia." *Revista de Cultura* 26 (1997): 27–38.

———. "Appropriation of Music and Dance in Contemporary Ternate and Tidore." *Studies in Music* 26 (1992): 85–95.

———. "Is Maluku Still Musicological *Terra Incognita?* An Overview of the Music-Cultures of the Province of Maluku." *Journal of Southeast Asian Studies* 25 (1994): 141–71.

———. "Kapri: A Synthesis of Malay and Portuguese Music on the West Coast of North Sumatra." In *Cultures and Societies of North Sumatra*, edited by Rainer Carle, 351–93. Berlin: Dietrich Reimer Verlag, 1987.

———. "A Malay-Portuguese Synthesis on the West Coast of North Sumatra." In *Portugal and the World: The Encounter of Cultures in Music*, edited by Salwa El-Shawan Castelo-Branco, 289–321. Lisbon: Publicações Dom Quixote, 1997.

———. "Maluku." In *The Garland Encyclopedia of World Music*, vol. 4: *Southeast Asia*, edited by Terry Miller and Sean Williams, 812–22. New York: General Music Publishing, 1998.

———. *Matjapat Songs in Central and West Java*. Canberra: National University Press, 1973.

———. *Musical Journeys in Sumatra*. Urbana: University of Illinois Press, 2012.

———. "Portuguese Influence on Indonesian Music." In *Festschrift Christoph-Hellmut Mahling zum 65. Geburtstag*. edited by Axel Beer, Kristina Pfarr, and Wolfgang Ruf, 657–66. Tutzing: Hans Schneider, 1997.

———. "Revival of Feudal Music, Dance and Ritual in the Former 'Spice Islands' of Ternate and Tidore." In *Culture and Society in New Order Indonesia*, edited by Virginia Matheson Hooker, 184–211. Kuala Lumpur: Oxford University Press, 1993.

Kasdorf, Hans. *Gustav Warnecks missiologisches Erbe: Eine biographische-historische Untersuchung*. Basel: Brunnen, 1990.

Kats, J. "Het godsdienstig lied in de zending, uit een muzikaal oogpunt beschouwd." In *Overzicht van de Tiende Zending-Conferentie, gehouden te Buitenzorg en te Depok van 25 Augustus tot 2 September 1900*, 103–42. Batavia: Kolff, 1901.

Kempis, Thomas à. *De Navolging van Christus*. Translated by Piet Heerkens. Den Bosch: Malmberg, 1937.

Kingsolver, Barbara. *The Poisonwood Bible*. New York: Perennial, 1998.

Kipp, Rita Smith. *The Early Years of a Dutch Colonial Mission: The Karo Field*. Ann Arbor: University of Michigan Press, 1990.

Kirby, Percival. *The Musical Instruments of the Native Races of South Africa*. Johannesburg: University of the Witwatersrand Press, 1968 [1934].

Kirkendall, Andrew J. *Paolo Feire and the Cold War Politics of Literacy*. Chapel Hill: University of North Carolina Press, 2010.

Kitab Masmur. *Kitab Masmur Katembangaken Miwah Repen Greja*. Leiden: Brill, 1885.

KITLV-NIMH-NIOD. "Summary of *Beyond the Pale: Dutch Extreme Violence in the Indonesian War of Independence, 1945–1949*, with the main findings of the research programme on *Independence, Decolonization, Violence and War in Indonesia 1945–1950*." Amsterdam: NIOD, 2022.

Kloes, Andrew. *The German Awakening: Protestant Renewal after the Enlightenment*. New York: Oxford University Press, 2019.

Klotz, Sebastian. "Murray Island versus Aberdeenshire: Contextualizing the Cross-Cultural Hearing Tests of the Cambridge Anthropological Expedition to Torres Straits, 1898–1899." In *Testing Hearing. The Making of Modern Aurality*, edited by Viktoria Tkaczyk, Mara Mills, and Alexandra Hui, 77–108. Oxford: Oxford University Press 2020.

Koenig, Martin, comp. *Village Music of Yugoslavia: Songs & Dances from the Adriatic, Dinara, Panonia and Vardat Regions*. New York: Nonesuch Records, 1971.

Koch, Lars-Christian. "Images of Sound: Erich M. von Hornbostel and the Berlin Phonogram Archive." In *The Cambridge History of World Music*, edited by Philip V. Bohlman, 475–97. Cambridge, UK: Cambridge University Press 2013.

Kohn, Eduardo. *How Forests Think: Toward an Anthropology Beyond the Human*. Berkeley: University of California Press, 2013.

Koster, G. L. "*Hikayat Tanah Hitu*: A Rare Local Source of 16th and 17th Century Moluccan History." *Review of Culture* 28 (2008): 133–42.

———. "How Malay Is the Ambonese Chronicle Hikayat Tanah Hitu?" Research Gate, July 7, 2021. www.researchgate.net/publication/353039754_How_Malay_is_the_Ambonese _chronicle_Hikayat_Tanah_Hitu. Accessed May 29, 2022.

Kozok, Uli. "On Writing the Not-to-Be-Read: Literature and Literacy in a Precolonial 'Tribal' Society." *Bijdragen tot de Taal-, Land- en Volkenkunde* 156 (2000): 33–55.

Kruithof, Maryse J. "Zaaiers, zaait in Gods naam voort! Carel Poensen, het leven van een zendeling-etnoloog (1836–1919)." PhD diss., Erasmus Universiteit Rotterdam, 2010.

Kunst, Jaap. *Around Von Hornbostel's Theory of the Cycle of Blown Fifths*. Amsterdam: Koninklijke Vereeniging Indisch Instituut, 1948.

———. *The Cultural Background of Indonesian Music*. Amsterdam: Indisch Instituut, 1949.

———. *Cultural Relations Between the Balkans and Indonesia*. Amsterdam: Royal Tropical Institute, 1954.

———. *De inheemsche muziek en de zending: Voordracht, op 1 Mei 1946 gehouden voor de Zendingsschool te Oegstgeest*. Amsterdam: H. J. Paris, 1947.

———. "Een reis naar Australië (15 mei—28 augustus 1959)." Unpublished manuscript. Jaap Kunst Archive, University of Amsterdam.

———. "Indigenous Music and the Christian Mission." In *Indonesian Music and Dance: Traditional Music and its Interaction with the West*, edited by Ernst Heins, Elisabeth den Otter, Felix van Lamsweerde, and Maja Frijn, 57–87. Amsterdam: Royal Tropical Institute, 1994.

———. *Music in Flores: A Study of the Vocal and Instrumental Music among the Tribes Living in Flores*. Leiden: Brill, 1942.

———. *Music in Java*. 3rd enlarged ed. 2 vols. The Hague: Martinus Nijhoff, 1973.

———. *Music in Nias*. Translated by Mrs. Carrière-Lagay. Leiden: Brill, 1939.

———. *Musicologica: A Study of the Nature of Ethnomusicology, its Problems, Methods, and Representative Personalities*. Amsterdam: Koninklijke Vereeniging Indisch Instituut, 1950.

———. "A Musicological Argument for Cultural Relationship between Indonesia (Probably the Isle of Java), and Central Africa." *Proceedings of the Musical Association* 62 (1935–36): 57–76.

Lach, Donald F., and Edwin J. Van Kley. *Asia in the Making of Europe*. 3 vols, 9 books. Chicago: University of Chicago Press, 1965–93.

Lagemann, H. "Missionar auf Nias." *Tijdschrift voor Indische taal-, land- en volkenkunde*, Teil 48. Koninklijk Bataviaasch Genootschap van Kunsten en Wetenschappen, 1906, 341–407.

Laksono, Paschalis Maria. *Tradition in Javanese Social Structure*. Translated by E. G. Koentjoro. Yogyakarta: Gadjah Mada University Press, 1986.

Lamsweerde, Felix van. "Inventory of the Wax Cylinder Collection of the Tropenmuseum." In *Jaap Kunst—Indonesian Music and Dance: Traditional Music and its Interaction with the West. A Compilation of Articles (1934–1952)*, edited by Ernst Heins, Elisabeth den Otter, and Felix van Lamsweerde, 247–73. Amsterdam: Royal Tropical Institute/University of Amsterdam, 1994.

Langdon, J. H. "The Erectines of Asia." In *Human Evolution*, 391–418. Switzerland: Cham, 2022.

Laubach, Frank Charles. *The People of the Philippines: Their Religious Progress and Preparation for Spiritual Leadership in the Far East*. New York: George H. Doran, 1925.

———. *Towards a Literate World*. New York: Columbia University Press, 1938.

———. "Why There Are Vagrants." PhD diss., Columbia University, 1916.

Laugrand, Frédéric B., and Olivier Servais, eds. *Du missionnaire à l'anthropologue: Enquête sur une longue tradition en compagnie de Michael Singleton*. Paris: Karthala, 2012.

Lavelle, Lise. *Amerta Movement of Java 1986–1997: An Asian Movement Improvisation*. PhD diss., Lund University, Centre for Languages and Literature, 2006.

Lembaga Kebudayaan Betawi. "Kekawin." Betawi Cultural Institute. www.kebudayaanbe tawi.com/.

Lenocker, Tyler. "The Mission Theory of Hendrik Kraemer." Boston University, School of Theology, History of Missiology (digital humanities project). www.bu.edu/missiology /missionary–biography/i-k/kraemer-hendrik-1888–1965/.

Leonardo de Argensola, Bartolomé. *Conquista de las Islas Malucas*. Madrid: Alonso Martin, 1609.

———. *The Discovery and Conquest of the Molucco and Philippine Islands: Containing Their History, Ancient and Modern, Natural and Political: Their Description, Product, Religion, Government, Laws, Languages, Customs, Manners, Habits, Shape, and Inclinations of the Natives. With an Account of Many Other Adjacent Islands, and Several Remarkable Voyages through the Streights of Magellan, and in Other Parts. Written in Spanish by Bartholomew Leonardo de Argensola, Chaplain to the Empress, and Rector of Villahermosa. Now Translated into English: And Illustrated with a Map and Several Cuts*. London: 1708.

Lingga, Hotben. "Pentas 'The Story of Buku Ende: Hymns from the Bataklands' Sukses di Gelar di JCC, Jakarta." *GramediaPost*, September 7, 2015.

Lobato, Manuel. "Os *mardicas* de Ternate e os crioulos de origem portuguesa nas Filipinas. Um olhar interdisciplinar sobre as relações entre identidade e língua." In *Tópicos transatlânticos: Emergência da Lusofonia num mundo plural*, edited by Silvério da Rocha-Cunha, Noémi Marujo, Cláudia Teixeira, Marco Martins, Paulo Rodrigues and Maria do Rosario Borges, 55–67. Évora: Universidade de Évora—Escola de Ciências Sociais, 2012.

Lockard, Craig. *Southeast Asia in World History*. New York: Oxford University Press, 2009.

López-Gay, Jesús. *La liturgia en la misión del Japón del siglo XVI*. Rome: Libreria dell'Università Gregoriana, 1970.

Luschan, Felix von. "Anleitung für ethnographische Beobachtungen und Sammlungen in Afrika und Ozeanien." *Zeitschrift für Ethnologie* (Sonderabdruck) 36 (1904). https:// echo.mpiwg-berlin.mpg.de/ECHOdocuView?url=/permanent/vlp/lit39587/&pn=3.

Lustig, Jacob Wilhelm. *Inleiding tot de muzykkunde: Uit klaare, onwederspreekelyke gronden, de innerlyke geschapenheid, de oorzaaken van de zonderbaare uitwerkselen, de groote waarde, en 't regte gebruik der muzykkonst aanwyzende*. Groningen: printed for the author by Hindrik Vechnerus, 1751.

———. *Twaalf redeneeringen over nuttige Muzikaale Onderwerpen*. Amsterdam: A. Olofsen, 1756.

———. *Inleiding tot de muzykkunde: Uit klaare, onwederspreekelyke gronden, de innerlyke geschapenheid, de oorzaaken van de zonderbaare uitwerkselen, de groote waarde, en 't regte gebruik der muzykkonst aanwyzende*. Amsterdam: A. Olofsen, 1758.

———. *Inleiding tot de muziekkunde*. 2nd ed. Groningen: Hindrik Vechnerus, 1771.

Manhart, Thomas M. "A Song for Lowalangi: The Inculturation of Catholic Mission and Nias Traditional Arts with Special Respect to Music." PhD diss., National University of Singapore, 2004.

Manusama, Zacharias J. "Hikayat Tanah Hitu: Historie en sociale structuur van de Ambonse eilanden in het algemeen en van Uli Hitu in het bijzonder tot het midden der zeventiende eeuw." PhD diss., University of Leiden, 1977.

Marchand, Suzanne. "Priests among the Pygmies: Wilhelm Schmidt and the Counter-Reformation in Austrian Ethnology," in *Worldly Provincialism: German Anthropology in the*

Age of Empire, edited by H. Glenn Penny and Matti Bunzl, 283–316. Ann Arbor: University of Michigan Press, 2003.

Marcocci, Giuseppe. *The Globe on Paper: Writing Histories of the World in Renaissance Europe and the Americas*. Translated by Richard Bates. New York: Oxford University Press, 2020.

Martin, Stephen. "The Symbolic Portrait of Mozart's Patron Dr. Ferdinand Dejean." *Hektoen International: A Journal of Medical Humanities* 10, no. 4 (2018). https://hekint.org/2018/04/12/symbolic-portrait-mozarts-patron-dr-ferdinand-dejean/.

Martins, Maria Odete Soares. *A missionação nas Molucas no século XVI: Contributo para o estudo da acção dos Jesuítas no Oriente*. Lisboa: Centro de história de Além-Mar, Universidade Nova de Lisboa, Facultade de Ciências Sociais e Humanas, 2002.

Mary, André, and Gaetano Ciarcia, eds. *Ethnologie en Situation Missionaire*. Les Carnets de Bérose 12. *BEROSE International Encyclopedia of Histories of Anthropology*. Martin Monferran, 2019.

Mason, David E. *Frank C. Laubach, Teacher of Millions*. Minneapolis: T. S. Denison, 1967.

Masroer Ch Jb. "Spiritualitas Islam dalam Budaya Wayang Kulit Masyarakat Jawa dan Sunda" [Islamic spirituality in the wayang kulit culture of Java and Sunda]. *Jurnal Ilmiah Sosiologi Agama* [Journal of sociology of religion] 9 (2015): 38–61.

Massil, S. W. "The History of the National Library of Indonesia: The Bibliographical Borobudur." *Libraries & Culture* 24, no. 4 (1989): 475–88.

Mataram Surya Visi Ltd and Universitas Amikom. "Hikayat Ajisaka di Flickfair Los Angeles" [Story of Ajisaka at Flickfair Los Angeles]. *News MSV Studio*. Accessed November 12, 2021 http://msvstudio.co.id/news-id/7379727/hikayat-ajisaka-di-flickfair-los-angeles/.

Mattheson, Johann. *Der Musicalische Patriot*. Hamburg, 1728.

Maugham, W. Somerset. *Rain and Other Stories*. New York: Grosset and Dunlap, 1921.

McLean, Mervyn. "Oceania." In *Ethnomusicology: Historical and Regional Studies*, edited by Helen Myers, 392–400. New York: W. W. Norton, 1993.

McGuire, Meredith B. *Lived Religion: Faith and Practice in Everyday Life*. New York: Oxford University Press, 2008.

Medhurst, W. H. *China: Its State and Prospects, with Especial Reference to the Spread of the Gospel*. London: Snow, 1838.

Medina, Nestor. *Christianity, Empire and the Spirit: (Re)Configuring Faith and the Cultural. Theology and Mission in World Christianity*, Vol. 11. Leiden: Brill, 2018.

Melk-Koch, Marion. *Auf der Suche nach der menschlichen Gesellschaft: Richard Thurnwald*. Veröffentlichung des Museums für Völkerkunde Berlin, Neue Folge 46. Berlin: Staatliche Museen Preußischer Kulturbesitz, 1989.

Menzel, Gustav. *Die Rheinische Mission*. Wuppertal: Verlag der Vereinigten Evangelischen Mission, 1978.

Merien & Raja. "Be'odong" and "Barassi hama." Sung by Merien and Raja in Riangkroko (Northeastern Flores), recorded by Jaap Kunst in July or August 1930. Wax cylinder 185 in the Jaap Kunst Sound Collection, University of Amsterdam.

Messner, Gerald Florian. "Jaap Kunst Revisited; Multipart Singing in Three East Florenese Villages Fifty Years Later: A Preliminary Investigation." *World of Music* 31, no. 2 (1989): 3–51.

Michaud, Jean. *"Incidental" Ethnographers: French Catholic Missions on the Tonkin-Yunnan Frontier, 1880–1930*. Leiden: Brill, 2007.

Michener, James A. *Hawaii*. New York: Fawcett, 1959.

Mission Press di Si Antar. *Umpama Angka na Masa ni Habatahon*. Pematang Siantar: Rongkoman Rhein, 1903.

Moen, J. L. "Het Buddhisme op Java en Sumatra in Zijn Laatste Boei Periode." *Tijdschrift van de Bataviaasch Genootschap van Kunsten en Wetenschappen* 64 (1924): 521–79.

Mojarro, Jorge. "Los molucos en el *Códice Boxer*, 1592." In *En el archipiélago de la especiería: España y Molucas en los siglos XVI y XVII*, edited by Javier Serrano Avilés and Jorge Mojarro Romero, 291–93. Madrid: Desperta Ferro, 2021.

Monteiro, Maria Isabel Lopes. "Instrumentos e instrumentistas de sopro no século XVI português." Master's thesis, Universidade Nova de Lisboa, 2010.

Mühlhäusler, Peter. "Die deutsche Sprache im Pazifik." In *Die Deutsche Südsee 1884–1914. Ein Handbuch*, edited by Hermann Joseph Hiery, 239–62. Paderborn: Verlag Ferdinand Schöningh 2001.

Mundy, Rachel. *Animal Musicalities: Birds, Beasts, and Evolutionary Listening*. Middletown, CT: Wesleyan University Press, 2018.

Murdyantoro, D. Danan. "Belajar Gamelan=Bikin Ngantuk?" *Warta Musik* [28], no. 2 (2003): 11–12.

Murillo Velarde, Pedro. *Historia de la provincia de Philipinas de la Compañía de Jesús: Segunda parte, que comprehende los progresos de esta provincia desde el año de 1616 hasta el de 1716*. Manila: en la Imprenta de la Compañía de Jesús, por D. Nicolas de la Cruz Bagay, 1749.

Mutsaers, Lutgard. "Jan Frans Gratiaen: Michael Ondaatje's Ancestor from Flanders." *The Low Countries* 21 (2013): 284–85.

Myers, Helen, ed. 1993. *Ethnomusicology: Historical and Regional Studies*. New York: W. W. Norton.

"Naam lyst der heeren Directeuren, Dirigeerende en andere Leden van het Bataviaasch Genootschap der Kunsten en Weetenschappen &c." [February 7, 1791]. *Verhandelingen van het Bataviaasch Genootschap van Kunsten en Wetenschappen* 5 (1790): first section, 37–64.

"Naam lyst der heeren Directeuren, Dirigeerende en andere Leden van het Bataviaasch Genootschap der Kunsten en Weetenschappen &c." [February 17, 1792]. *Verhandelingen van het Bataviaasch Genootschap van Kunsten en Wetenschappen* 6 (1792): first section, 25–50.

Naam-boekje van de wel. ed. Heeren der Hooge Indische Regeeringe, gequalificeerde persoonen, enz. en bedienden op Batavia; Mitsgaders de Respective Gouverneurs, Directeurs, Commandeurs en Opperhoofden op de Buiten Comptoiren van Nederl. India, zoo als dezelve ultimo September 1759. in wezen zyn bevonden. Als meede alle de Gouverneurs Generaal, zedert het jaar 1610. Nevens de hooge en mindere Collegien en Bediendens op de Buyten Comptoiren van Nederlands India. Amsterdam: Cornelis Wilt, 1760.

Nettl, Bruno. *The Study of Ethnomusicology: Thirty-Three Discussions*. Champaign: University of Illinois Press, 2015.

Niemeijer, Hendrik E. "The Free Asian Christian Community and Poverty in Pre-Modern Batavia." In *Jakarta–Batavia: Socio-Cultural Essays*, edited by Kees Grijns and Peter J. M. Nas, 75–92. Leiden: KITLV Press, 2000.

Niessen, Sandra. *Rangsa ni Tonun: A Film about the Sacred Batak Weaving Tradition, behind the Scenes*. Osterbeek and Jakarta: Bergoord Publishing, 2013.

Nieuwe Tilburgsche Courant. "Pater P. Heerkens, SVD Overleden: Een Fijnbesnaard Dichter van Het Tilburgsche Dialect," January 29, 1944.

Niles, Don. "Comments," *Papua New Guinea (1904–1909): The Collections of Rudolf Pöch, Wilhelm Schmidt, and Josef Winthuis,* OEAW PHA, CD 9. Tondokumente aus dem Phonogrammarchiv der Österreichischen Akademie der Wissenschaften, Gesamtausgabe der Historischen Bestände 1899–1950, 2000. CD booklet, 17–142.

———. "The Contribution of the Berlin Phonogramm-Archiv to the Study of Papua New Guinea Musics." In *Music Archiving in the World: Papers Presented at the Conference on the Occasion of the 100th Anniversary of the Berlin Phonogramm-Archiv,* edited by Gabriele Berlin and Artur Simon, 189–200. Berlin: Verlag für Wissenschaft und Bildung, 2002.

Nocentelli, Carmen. *Empires of Love: Europe, Asia, and the Making of Early Modern Identity.* Philadelphia: University of Pennsylvania Press, 2013.

Noll, Johannes. "Die falsche Götzen machen zu Spott." *Berichte der Rheinischen Missionsgesellschaft* 85 (1928): 98–99.

Nortier, C. W. *Een horlogemaker en een landheer: De eerste Christus-getuigen in Oost-Java.* Den Haag: Voorhoeve. *Lichtstralen op de akker der wereld* 55 (1954).

———. *Van zendingsarbeid tot zelfstandige kerk in Oost-Java.* N.p.: Uitgegeven vanwege den Zendingsstudie-Raad door de Drukkerij van de Stichting Hoenderloo, 1939.

Ochoa Gautier, Ana María. *Aurality: Listening and Knowledge in Nineteenth-Century Colombia.* Durham, NC: Duke University Press, 2014.

———. "El reordenamiento de los sentidos y el archive sonoro." *ArteFilosofía* 11 (2011): 82–95.

Okazaki, Yoshiko. "Liturgical Music among the Toba Batak People of North Sumatra: The Creation of a New Tradition." *Crossroads* 12 (1998): 55–74.

———. "Music, Identity, and Religious Change among the Toba Batak People of North Sumatra." PhD diss., University of California, Los Angeles, 1994.

Ollé, Manel, and Joan-Pau Rubiés, eds. *El Códice Boxer: Etnografía colonial e hibridismo cultural en las Islas Filipinas.* Barcelona: Publicacions i Edicions de la Universitat de Barcelona, 2020.

Ondaatje, Michael. *Running in the Family.* London: Picador, 1984.

Onghokham. "The Residency of Madiun: Priyayi and Peasant in the Nineteenth Century." PhD diss., Yale University, 1975.

Overzicht van de Tiende Zending-Conferentie, gehouden te Buitenzorg en te Depok van 25 Augustus tot 2 September 1900. Batavia: Kolff, 1901.

Pasaribu, Rianti Mardalena. *Mengembangkan Musik Liturgi Khas Indonesia: Perjalanan Hidup dan Karya-karya Karl-Edmund Prier.* Yogyakarta: Kanisius, 2015.

Pedersen, Paul. *Batak Blood and Protestant Soul: The Development of National Batak Churches in North Sumatra.* Grand Rapids, MI: William B. Eerdmans, 1970.

Peirce, Charles. "The Fixation of Belief." In *Writings of Charles Peirce: A Chronological Edition, Vol. 3, 1872–1878,* edited by Christian W. Kloesel, et al. Bloomington: Indiana University Press, 1986.

Pels, Peter. "Anthropology and Mission: Towards a Historical Analysis of Professional Identity." In *The Ambiguity of Rapprochement: Reflections of Anthropologists on Their Controversial Relationship with Missionaries,* edited by Roland Bonsen, Hans Marks, and Jelle Miedema, 77–100. Nijmegen: Focaal, 1989.

Pike, K. L. *Language in Relation to a Unified Theory of the Structures of Human Behavior.* 2nd ed. The Hague: Mouton, 1967.

Pires, Tomé. *The Suma Oriental of Tomé Pires: An Account of the East, from the Red Sea to Japan, Written in Malacca and India in 1512–1515*. Edited and translated by Armando Cortesão. 2 vols. London: Hakluyt Society, 1944.

Pleyte, Cornelis Marinus. "Singa Mangaradja de Heilige Koning der Bataks." *Bijdragen tot de taal-, land- en volkenkunde* (January 1903): 34.

Pöch, Rudolf. "Zweiter Bericht über meine phonographischen Aufnahmen in Neu-Guinea (Britisch Neu-Guinea vom 7. Oktober 1905 bis zum 1. Februar 1906)," in *Sitzungsberichte der Mathematisch-Naturwissenschaftlichen Classe der Kaiserlichen Akademie der Wissenschaften*, Wien, 2.Abt-a-116, Band (1907): 801–17 (no. 10 of Mitteilungen der Phonogramm-Archivs-Kommission der kaiserlichen Akademie der Wissenschaften in Wien.

Poensen, Carel. "De Wajang." *Mededeelingen van wege het Nederlandsch Zendelinggenootschap* vol. 16 (1872): 59–115, 204–22, 233–80, 353–67; vol. 17 (1873): 138–64.

———. "Mattheus Aniep (Eene Bijdrage tot de kennis der geschiedenis van de zending op Oost-Java)." *Mededeelingen van wege het Nederlandsche Zendelinggenootschap* 24 (1880): 333–91.

Poeze, H. A. "J. Kats 1875–1945." In *De wajang poerwa: Een vorm van Javaans toneel*, edited by J. Kats. 13–47. Dordrecht en Cinnaminson: Foris, 1984.

Pols, Hans. "Psychological Knowledge in a Colonial Context: Theories on the Nature of the 'Native Mind' in the Former Dutch East Indies." *History of Psychology* 10 (2007): 111–31.

Poplawska, Marzanna. "Christian Music and Inculturation in Indonesia." PhD diss., Wesleyan University, 2008.

———. *Performing Faith: Christian Music, Identity and Inculturation in Indonesia*. NY: Routledge, 2020.

———. "Wayang Wahyu as an Example of Christian Forms of Shadow Theatre." *Asian Theatre Journal* 21 (2004): 194–202.

Prier, Karl-Edmund, SJ. "Aransemen untuk Lagu Pentatonis." *Warta Musik* 24, no. 6 (1999): 171–74.

———. *Inkulturasi Musik Liturgi*. PML A-66. Yogyakarta: Pusat Musik Liturgi, 1999.

———. *Inkulturasi Musik Liturgi, I*. Edisi revisi. PML A-84. Yogyakarta: Pusat Musik Liturgi, 2014 [1999].

———. *Inkulturasi Musik Liturgi, II*. PML A-82. Yogyakarta: Pusat Musik Liturgi, 2014.

———. *Inkulturasi Musik Liturgi, III*. PML A-86. Yogyakarta: Pusat Musik Liturgi, 2019.

———. *Inkulturasi Musik Liturgi, IV*. PML A-93. Yogyakarta: Pusat Musik Liturgi, 2021.

———. *Inkulturasi Nyanyian Liturgi*. PML A-45. Yogyakarta: Pusat Musik Liturgi, 1993.

———. "Kriteria Penilaian Nyanyian." *Warta Musik* [29], no. 1 (2004): 19–20.

———. "Lagu Anak yang Bercacat." *Warta Musik* [28], no. 2 (2003): 48–49.

———. "Lagu yang Tidak Bercacat" *Warta Musik* [28], no. 3 (2003): 82–83.

———. "Madah Bakti—Edisi 2000 Terbit Akhir Oktober." *Warta Musik* 25, no. 6 (2000): 184–85.

———. "Menemukan Spiritualitas Pelayanan dalam Bermusik," *Warta Musik* [29], no. 6 (2004): 177–80.

———. "Mengiringi Lagu Batak Toba dengan Organ." *Warta Musik* 25, no. 5 (2000): 139–41.

———. "Musik Gereja dalam Peralihan." *Warta Musik* [28], no. 6 (2003): 170–73.

———. *Ordinarium Batak Toba: Buku Iringan Organ. Hasil Lokakarya Komposisi Musik Liturgi, Pematang Siantar, 1986. Aransemen Karl-Edmund Prier*. PML 200-I. Yogyakarta: Pusat Musik Liturgi, 2011.

———. *Perjalanan Musik Gereja Katolik Indonesia, Tahun 1957–2007* [The journey of Indonesian [Catholic] Church music from years 1957–2007]. PML A-79. Yogyakarta: Pusat Musik Liturgi, 2008.

Proosdij-ten Have, Loekie van, and Marjolijn van Roon. *Jaap Kunst, Correspondence 1920–1940: An Annotated Index*. Amsterdam: Proosdij/Van Roon, 1992.

Purba, Mauly. "'Adat ni Gondang': Rules and Structure of the 'Gondang' Performance in Pre-Christian Toba Batak 'Adat' Practice." *Asian Music* 34, no.1 (2002/03): 67–109.

———. "From Conflict to Reconciliation: The Case of the 'Gondang Sabangunan' in the Order of Discipline in the Toba Batak Protestant Church." *Journal of Southeast Asian Studies* 36 (2005): 207–33.

Pusat Musik Liturgi. *Hasil Lokakarya Komposisi Musik Liturgi, 26 Nop.–2 Des. 1990, di Mataloko, Flores*. Workshop document. PML 1990.

———. *Hasil Lokakarya Komposisi Musik Liturgi III, tanggal 17 s/d 25 April 1997 di Mataloko, Flores*. Workshop document. PML 1997.

———. *Hasil Lokakarya Komposisi Musik Liturgi, 1–7 April 2000 di Kemah Tabor, Mataloko, Flores*. Workshop document. PML, 2000.

———. *Hasil Lokakarya Komposisi Musik Liturgi Gaya Rote-Ndao-Nagekeo, 15–22 Juni 2003 di Mataloko, Flores*. Workshop document. PML 2003.

———. *Himpunan Materi Lokakarya Komposisi Musik Liturgi . . . 20–27 Oktober 1996 di Rumah Retret Efata, Ruteng, Flores*. Workshop document. PML 1996.

———. *Kidung Adi: Buku Sembahyangan saha Kekidungan: Buku Umat*. PML 66-U. Yogyakarta: Pusat Musik Liturgi, 1983.

———. *Lokakarya Komposisi Musik Liturgi 27 Oktober–2 November 1998, Detusoko*. Workshop document. PML, 1998.

———. *Madah Bakti: Buku Doa dan Nyanyian Umum: Edisi Pokok dengan Lampiran*. PML 55-U. Yogyakarta: Pusat Musik Liturgi, 1980.

———. *Madah Bakti: Buku Doa dan Nyanyian: Edisi 2000*. PML 144-U. Yogyakarta: Pusat Musik Liturgi, 2000.

———. *Madah Bakti Suplemen: Buku Nyanyian untuk Melengkapi Madah Bakti*. PML 105-P. Yogyakarta: Pusat Musik Liturgi, 1992.

Putnam, Robert D. *E. Pluribus Unum*: Diversity and Community in the Twenty-First Century: The 2006 Johan Skytte Prize Lecture" *Scandinavian Political Studies* 39, no. 2: 137–74.

Putnam, Robert, and David Campbell. *American Grace: How Religion Divides and Unites Us*. New York: Simon and Schuster, 2010.

Quentmeier, J. "Das Gesangbuch der Batakkirche." *Berichte der Rheinischen Missionsgesellschaft* 98 (1941): 52–56.

Quinn, George. *Bandit Saints of Java*. Melton Mowbray: Monsoon Books, 2019.

Raffles, Thomas Stamford. *The History of Java: In Two Volumes*. London: Black, Parbury, and Allen, 1817.

Ranggasutrasna, Ki Ngabehi, et al. *Serat Tjentini*. Betawi: Firma Ruygrok, 1915.

Rappoport, Dana. "The Long Journey of the Rice Maiden from Li'o to Tanjung Bunga: A Lamaholot Sung Narrative (Flores, Eastern Indonesia)." In *Austronesian Paths and Journeys*, edited by James J. Fox, 161–92. Canberra: ANU Press, 2021.

———. *Indonésie, Toraja: funérailles et fêtes de fécondité*. Compact disc. Chant du Monde CNR 2741004. Paris, 1995.

Reenders, H., ed. *De gereformeerde zending in Midden Java, 1859–1931: Een bronnenpublicatie*. Zoetermeer: Boekencentrum, 2001.

Reid, Anthony. *Southeast Asia in the Age of Commerce, 1450–1680*. Vol. 1, *The Lands below the Winds*. New Haven, CT: Yale University Press, 1988.

Reily, Suzel Ana, and Jonathan Dueck, eds. *The Oxford Handbook of Music and World Christianities*. Oxford: Oxford University Press, 2016.

Rheinberger, Hans-Jörg, and Michael Hagner, eds. *Die Experimentalisierung des Lebens: Experimentalsysteme in den biologischen Wissenschaften, 1850/1950*. Berlin: Akademie Verlag, 1993.

Rice, Timothy. "Dancing in the Scholar's World." In *May It Fill Your Soul: Experiencing Bulgarian Music*, 3–15. Chicago: University of Chicago Press, 1994.

Ricklefs, M. C. *Polarising Javanese Society: Islamic and Other Visions (c. 1830–1930)*. Leiden: KITLV Press, 2007.

Ridjali. *Historie van Hitu: Een Ambonse geschiedenis uit de zeventiende eeuw*. Edited and translated by Hans Straver, Christiaan van Fraassen, and Jan van der Putten. Utrecht: Landelijk Steunpunt Educatie Molukkers, 2004.

Rinallo, Diego, et al. *Consumption and Spirituality*. New York: Routledge, 2013.

Rinkes, D. A. *Nine Saints of Java*. Translated by H. M. Froger. Edited by A. Gorden. Kuala Lumpur: Malaysian Sociological Research Institute, 1996.

Robb, J. Wesley. "Hendrik Kraemer versus William Ernest Hocking." *Journal of Bible and Religion*, 29 (1961): 93–101.

Rook, Emilie. "Complex Centers and Powerful Peripheries: Catholicism, Music, and Identity Politics in Indonesia." PhD diss., University of Pittsburgh, 2020.

Roon, Marjolijn van. "Jaap Kunst, Government Musicologist: An Unusual Incident in the Colonial Political History of the Netherlands East Indies." *Oideion: The Performing Arts Worldwide* 35 (1995): 63–84.

Rosenkranz, Gerhard. *Das Lied der Kirche in der Welt*. Berlin: Verlag Haus und Schule, 1951.

Rouse, Sandra. "Haddon, Missionaries and 'Men of Affairs.'" *Cambridge Anthropology* 21, no. 1 (1999): 9–27.

Ruiz Jiménez, Juan. "Bautismo de la princesa de Bacan en la isla de Ternate (1559)." *Paisajes sonoros históricos (c.1200–c.1800)*. Historical Soundscapes (website), January 8, 2021, http://historicalsoundscapes.com/evento/1256/ternate/es.

Sá, Artur Basílio de, ed. *Documentação para a história das missões do padroado português do Oriente. Insulíndia 3.º vol. (1563–1567)*. Lisbon: Agencia Geral do Ultramar: Divisão de Publicações e Biblioteca, 1955.

Salam, Solichin. *Sekitar Wali Songo* [Regarding the Nine Wali]. Yogyakarta: Menara Kudus, 1960.

Sánchez Marcos, Fernando. "*Conquista de las Malucas* (1609): Texto y contexto de una historia marítima." In *El mar en los siglos modernos*, edited by Manuel-Reyes García Hurtado, Domingo L. González Lopo, and Enrique Martínez Rodríguez, 685–97. Santiago de Compostela: Xunta de Galicia, 2009.

Sánchez Pons, Jean-Nöel. "Misón y dimisión: Las Molucas en el siglo XVII entre Jesuitas portugueses y españoles." In *Jesuitas e imperios de Ultramar. Siglos XVI–XX*, edited by Alexandre Coello de la Rosa, Javier Burrieza, and Doris Moreno, 81–101. Madrid: Sílex, 2012.

Santoso, Soewito, trans. and ed. [Mpu Tantular]. *Sutasoma: A Study in Javanese Wajrayana*. New Delhi: International Academy of Indian Culture, 1975.

Scarfe, Brigitta, and Muhamad Hasbi. "The Significance of Place in the Musical Practice of Two Biola Players in Riau Islands Province." In *Performing the Arts of Indonesia: Malay Identity and Politics in the Music, Dance and Theatre of the Riau Islands*, edited by Margaret Kartomi, 152–68. Copenhagen: NIAS Press, 2019.

Scheurleer, Daniel François. *Catalogus der muziekbibliotheek van D. F. Scheurleer*. The Hague: Printed by Gebr. Giunta d'Albani, 1893.

Schmidt, Pater Wilhelm, P. G. Schmidt, and P. J. Hermes, "Die Sprachlaute und ihre Darstellung in einem allgemeinen linguistischen Alphabet/Les sons du langage et leur représentation dans un alphabet linguistique general." *Anthropos* 2, no. 2. (1907): 282–329.

Schrag, Brian, and Neil R. Coulter. "Response to 'Ethnomusicology as Tool for the Christian Missionary.'" *European Meetings in Ethnomusicology* 10 (2003): 98–108.

Schreiner, Lothar. "Nommensen in His Context: Aspects of a New Approach. In *Cultures and Societies of North Sumatra*, edited by Rainer Carle, 179–87. Berlin: Dietrich Reimer Verlag, 1987.

Seebass, Tilman. "Presence and Absence of Portuguese Musical Elements in Indonesia: An Essay on the Mechanisms of Music Acculturation." In *Portugal and the World: The Encounter of Cultures in Music*, edited by Salwa El-Shawan Castelo-Branco, 227–51. Lisbon: Publicações Dom Quixote, 1997.

Serrano Avilés, Javier, and Jorge Mojarro Romero, eds. *En el archipiélago de la especiería: España y Molucas en los siglos XVI y XVII*. Madrid: Desperta Ferro, 2021.

Setyanto, Agus Handi. *Wayang Katholik: Cara Cerdas Berkatese* [Catholic wayang: A smart mode of catechism]. Yogyakarta: Pt. Kanisius, 2017.

Setyanto, Agus Handi, Wisma Nugraha, Dr. Soetarno. "Sajian Ki Blacius Subono: Mediasi Kisah Alkitab Wayang Wahyu Lakon Hana Caraka Nabi Elia" [Ki Blacius Subono's Presentation: Mediation of Bible Stories "Wayang Wahyu Play Hana Caraka"], Universitas Gajah Mada, 2016.

Sheldrake, Merlin. *Entangled Life: How Fungi Make Our Worlds, Change Our Minds and Shape Our Futures*. New York: Penguin Random House, 2021.

Simanungkalit, D. *Hulehon ma Tuhan tu Ho: Gemengde Koor*. Pearaja: Departement Naposobulung HKBP, 1988.

Simon, Artur. "Gondang, Gods and Ancestors: Religious Implications of Batak Ceremonial Music." *Yearbook for Traditional Music* 25 (1993): 81–88.

Sinaga, Ancietus B. "*Madah Bakti*: An Experiment in the Inculturation of Liturgical Music." *East Asian Pastoral Review* 30, no. 2 (1993): 120–44.

Shelemay, Kay Kaufman. *The Garland Library of Readings in Ethnomusicology: Ethnomusicological Theory and Method*. New York: Garland, 1990.

Smeding, Henrik. "Bezoekreis naar de gemeenten in Kediri, Madioen en Modjokerto, gedaan van 9 tot 29 Julij 1859, door de zendelingen S.K Harthoorn en H. Smeding." *Mededeelingen van wege het Nederlandsche Zendinggenootschap* 5 (1861): 120–50, 245–86.

———. "Enkele Opmerkingen env rage over het zendingswerk op Java." *Mededeelingen van wege het Nederlandsche Zendinggenootschap* 6 (1862): 235–84.

Smelik, Jan. "Orgelgebruik in de protestantse kerkdienst tussen 1886 en 1938. Deel vier: Kerktoonsoorten en ritmisch zingen." *Het Orgel* 115 (2019): 3–11.

Soewandi, R. M. *Djedjèrèngan bab: Beksa Tajoeb, Bondhan, Tuwin Wirèng* [Description of Tayuban, Bondhan, and Wiring Dance]. Typed manuscript. Yogyakarta: 1938,

Sommer, Ernst. "Johann Matthäus Meyfart und sein Lied 'Jerusalem du hochgebaute Stadt.'" *Jahrbuch für Liturgik und Hymnologie* 7 (1962): 149–57.

Spiller, Henry. *Archaic Instruments in Modern West Java, Indonesia: Bamboo Murmurs*. New York: Routledge, 2023.

———. *Erotic Triangles: Sundanese Dance and Masculinity in West Java*. Chicago: University of Chicago Press, 2010.

———. *Javaphilia: American Love Affairs with Javanese Music and Dance*. Oʻahu: University of Hawaiʻi Press, 2015.

———. "Lou Harrison's Music for Western Instruments and Gamelan: Even More Western than It Sounds." *Asian Music* 39 (2009): 31–52.

———. "University Gamelan Ensembles as Research." In *Mapping Landscapes for Performance as Research: Scholarly Acts and Creative Cartographies*, edited by Shannon Rose Riley and Lynette Hunter, 171–78. Hampshire: Palgrave Macmillan, 2009.

Spoorman, Rein. "Tradition and Creative Inspiration: Musical Encounters of the Moluccan Communities in the Netherlands." In *Recollecting Resonances: Indonesian-Dutch Musical Encounters*, vol. 288 of *Verhandelingen van het Koninklijk Instituut voor Taal-, Land- en Volkenkunde*, edited by Bart Barendregt and Els Bogaerts, 281–96. Leiden: Brill, 2014.

Stoler, Ann Laura. *Along the Archival Grain: Epistemic Anxieties and Colonial Common Sense*. Princeton, NJ: Princeton University Press, 2009.

Storch, Christian. "How the Pagans Became 'Convinced' about Christianity: Four Conclusions on the Relationship between Music and the Missions in Early Colonialism." In *Música discurso poder*, edited by Maria do Rosário Girão Santos and Elisa Maria Lessa, 221–34. Ribeirão: Ediçoes Húmus, 2012.

———. "The Influence of Portuguese Musical Culture in Southeast Asia in the Sixteenth and Seventeenth Centuries." In *Portuguese and Luso-Asian Legacies, 1511–2011*, vol. 2, *Culture and Identity in the Luso-Asian World: Tenacities and Plasticities*, edited by Laura Jarnagin, 208–22. Singapore: Institute of Southeast Asian Studies, 2012.

———. "Wege portugiesischer Musikkultur nach Südostasien im Kontext der europäischen Expansionspolitik des 16. und 17. Jahrhunderts." In *Migration und Identität: Wanderbewegungen und Kulturkontakte in der Musikgeschichte*, 69–83. Kassel: Bärenreiter-Verlag, 2013.

Strategier, P. E. M. "De taal der hartstochten: De visie van drie achttiende-eeuwse Nederlandse schrijvers op muziek en haar relatie met de dichtkunst." PhD diss., University of Amsterdam, 2001.

Strom, Jonathan. *German Pietism and the Problem of Conversion*. University Park: University of Pennsylvania Press, 2017.

Stumpf, Carl. "Das Berliner Phonogrammarchiv." *Internationale Wochenschrift für Wissenschaft, Kunst und Technik* 22 (February 1908): 225–46.

Stutterheim, W. F. "A Thousand Years Old Profession in the Princely Courts of Java." In *Studies in Indonesian Archaeology*. The Hague: Martinus Nijhoff, 1956 [1935], 91–103.

Sumarsam. *Gamelan: Cultural Interaction and Musical Development in Central Java*. Chicago: University of Chicago Press, 1995.

———. "Inner Melody in Javanese Gamelan Music." *Asian Music* 7 (1975): 3–13.

Suratno. "Studi Tentang Lakon Wahyu Dalam Pakeuran Wayan6 Kultt [*sic*] Purwa Di Surakarta" [A study of wahyu plays in the Surakarta-style puppetry in the last decade]. *Harmonia: Journal of Arts Research and Education* 5, no. 1 (2004): 194–200.

Suryadinata, Leo, Evi Nurvidya Arifin, and Aris Ananta. *Indonesia's Population: Ethnicity and Religion in a Changing Political Landscape*. Singapore: ISEAS, 2003.

Susilomadyo, Wedana. "Macapat from the Kraton Yogyakarta: Classic Poems for a Contemporary Catastrophe. Translated by Nyi MJ. Reninawangmataya. *Balungan* 14 (2020): 49–53.

Sutarjo. "*Wayang Sadat* in Javanese Culture." In *Proceedings of the International Seminar Tri Matra: Exploring and Identifying the Dynamics and Its Challenges of Cultural Transformation*, 2005. https://portal.uns.ac.id/javanologi/wp-content/uploads/sites/26/2018/05/wayang-sadat-in-javanese-culture.pdf.

Sutarman, Soediman Partonadi. *Sadrach's Community and Its Contextual Roots: A Nineteenth Century Javanese Expression of Christianity*. Amsterdam: Rodopi, 1990.

Sykes, Jim, and Julia Byl, eds. *Sounding the Indian Ocean: Musical Circulations in the Afro-Asiatic Seascape*. Berkeley: University of California Press, 2023.

Tambunan, Jubelando O. "Berteologi Melalui Nyanyian: Kajian Peran Buku Ende Membangun Spiritual Jemaat Geraja." *Clef: Jurnal Musik dan Pendidikan Musik* 2 (2021): 11–18.

Taussig, Michael. *Mimesis and Alterity: A Particular History of the Senses*. New York: Routledge, 1993.

Taylor, Diana. *The Archive and the Repertoire: Performing Cultural Memory in the Americas*. Durham, NC: Duke University Press, 2003.

Taylor, Jean Gelman. *The Social World of Batavia: Europeans and Eurasians in Colonial Indonesia*. 2nd ed. Madison: University of Wisconsin Press, 2009.

The, Lian, and Paul W. Van der Veur. *The Verhandelingen van het Bataviaasch Genootschap: An Annotated Content Analysis*. Athens: Ohio University, Center for International Studies, 1973.

Tiemersma, L. "Het kerkgezang en de Maleische psalmbundels." In *Overzicht van de Negende Zending-Conferentie, gehouden te Buitenzorg en te Depok van 20 tot 28 Augustus 1898*, 26–55. Batavia: Kolff, 1898.

Tilhang Gultom Group. *Batak Music*. Ethnic Folkways Records FE 4357, 1976. Vinyl LP.

Titus, Barbara. "The 'Attentively Silent' Presence of Jaap Kunst in the Vereniging voor Nederlandse Muziekgeschiedenis" *Tijdschrift van de Koninklijke Vereniging voor Nederlandse Muziekgeschiedenis* 68 (2018): 163–74.

———. "Tracing Earlines in Ethnomusicology." In *Noise as Constructive Element in Music: Theoretical and Music-Analytical Perspectives on Noise and Noise Music*, edited by Mark Delaere. New York: Routledge, 2022.

Tjoa-Bonatz, Mai Lin. "Idols and Art: Missionary Attitudes toward Indigenous Worship and Material Culture on Nias, Indonesia, 1904–1920." In *Casting Faiths: Imperialism and the Transformation of Religion in East and Southeast Asia*, edited by Thomas David Dubois, 105–28. Basingstoke: Palgrave Macmillan, 2009.

———. "Missionare und Kunst: Ein Spannungsfeld zwischen Kulturzerstörung und Kulturerhalt." *Indonesien Magazin Online*, May 2, 2016. www.indonesienmagazin.de/index.php/wissen/152-missionare-und-kunst.

Tkaczyk, Viktoria. *Thinking with Sound: A New Program in the Sciences and Humanities around 1900*. Chicago: University of Chicago Press, 2023.

Tobing, Philip O. L. *The Structure of the Toba-Batak Belief in the High God*. Amsterdam: Jacob van Campen, 1956.

To'Liman-Turalir, Julie. "Why Historic Recordings Are of Value to the Tolai People Today." In *Music Archiving in the World: Papers Presented at the conference on the Occasion of the 100th Anniversary of the Berlin Phonogramm-Archiv*, 55–58. Berlin: Verlag für Wissenschaft und Bildung, 2002.

Tracey, Hugh. *The Evolution of African Music and Its Function in the Present Day*. Johannesburg: Institute for the Study of Man in Africa, 1961.

Treitler, Leo. "The Present as History." *Perspectives of New Music* 7 (1969): 1–58.

Twain, Mark. *Innocents Abroad*. New York: American Publishing, 1869.

Ungaran, Syahrul Munir. "Wayang Wahyu, Kisah Alkitab yang Disajikan dalam Bentuk Wayang." *Kompas*, 2017. https://regional.kompas.com/read/2017/04/23/09314321/wayang.wahyu.kisah.alkitab.yang.disajikan.dalam.bentuk.wayang.

Utami, Ayu. *Manjali dan Cakrabirawa*. Jakarta: Kepustakaan Populer Gramedia, 2019.

Valentijn, François. *Oud en nieuw Oost-Indiën, vervattende een naaukeurige en uitvoerige verhandelinge van Nederlands mogentheyd in die gewesten, benevens eene wydluftige beschryvinge der Moluccos, Amboina, Banda, Timor, en Solor, Java, en alle de eylanden onder dezelve landbestieringen behoorende, het Nederlands comptoir op Suratte, en de levens der Groote Mogols*. 5 vols. Dordrecht; Amsterdam: Joannes van Braam; Gerard Onder de Linden, 1724–26.

Vallier, John Bellarmine. "Ethnomusicology as Tool for the Christian Missionary." *European Meetings in Ethnomusicology* 10 (2003): 85–97.

Van Akkeren, Philip. *Sri and Christ: A Study of the Indigenous Church in East Java*. London: Lutterworth, 1970.

van Bemmelen, Sita Thama. "Good Customs, Bad Customs in North Sumatra." PhD diss., Vrije Universiteit Amsterdam, 2012.

van den End, Th. *De Nederlandse Zendingsvereniging in West-Java, 1858–1963: Een bronnen-publicatie*. Leiden: Brill: 1991.

van der Geest, Sjaak. "Anthropologists and Missionaries: Brothers under the Skin," *Man*, New Series 25 (1990): 588–601.

van der Molen, Willem. "Hoe heeft zulks kunnen geschieden? Het begin van de Javaanse typografie." In *Woord en Schrift in de Oost: De betekenis van zending en missie voor de studie van taal en literatuur in Zuidoost-Azië*, edited by Willem van der Molen and Bernard Arps, 132–62. Leiden: Opleiding Talen en Culturen van Zuidoost-Azië en Oceanië, Universiteit Leiden, 2000.

van der Putten, Jan. "A Collection of Unstandardised Consistencies? The Use of Jawi Script in a Few Early Malay Manuscripts from the Moluccas." In *Creating Standards: Interactions with Arabic Script in 12 Manuscript Cultures*, edited by Dmitry Bondarev, Alessandro Gori, and Lameen Souag, 217–36. Berlin: De Gruyter, 2019.

———. "In the Fringe of the Page: The Malay Tale of Hitu from Its Margins." In *Teks, naskah dan kelisanan: Festschrift untuk Prof. Achadiati Ikram*, edited by T. Pudjiastuti, T. Christomy and A. Ikram, 399–416. Depok: Yayasan Pernaskahan Nusantara, 2011.

Van Dijk, K., and P. Nas. "Dakwah and Indigenous Culture: The Dissemination of Islam." *Bijdragen tot de Taal-, Land- en Volkenkunde* 154 (1998): 218–35.

Van Hoëvell, W. R. "Javaansche christenen te Soerabaija." *Tijdschrift ter Bevordering van Christelijken Zin in Neêrland's Indië* 1(1847): 164–73.

———. *Reis over Java, Madura en Bali in het midden van 1847*. Vol. 1. Amsterdam: Van Kampen, 1849.

Van Reybrouck, David. *Revolusi: Indonesië en het ontstaan van de moderne wereld*. Amsterdam: De Bezige Bij, 2020.

Van Rhijn, L. J. *Reis door den Indischen Archipel, in het belang der evangelische zending*. Rotterdam: Wijt, 1851.

Vandenberghe, An. "Entre Mission et Science: La Recherche Ethnologique Du Pére Wilhelm Schmidt SVD et Le Vatican (1900–1939)." *Missions et Sciences Sociales* 19 (2006): 15–36.

Vetter, Roger. "Review Work: Indonesian Music and Dance—Traditional Music and Its Interaction with the West: A Compilation of Articles (1934–1952)." *Asian Music* 29, no. 1 (1997), 125–82.

Villiers, John. "'A Truthful Pen and an Impartial Spirit': Bartolomé Leonardo de Argensola and the *Conquista de las Islas Malucas*." *Renaissance Studies* 17 (2003): 449–73.

Viveiros de Castro, Eduardo. "Cannibal Metaphysics: Amerindian Perspectivism." *Radical Philosophy* 132 (2013): 17–28.

Vlekke, Bernard H. M. *Nusantara: A History of the East Indian Archipelago*. 1st ed. Netherlands: Ayer, 1943.

Voorhoeve, Petrus. *Codices Batacici*. Leiden: Universitaire Pers Leiden, 1977.

Vormann, Franz. "Tänze und Tanzfestlichkeiten der Monumbo-Papua (Deutsch-Neuguinea)." *Anthropos* 6, no. 2. (1911): 411–27.

Vormann, Franz, and P. Wilhelm Scharfenberger, *Die Monumbo-Sprache*. Vol. 1, *Grammatik und Wörterverzeichnis*. Vienna(?): Mechitharisten-Buchdruckerei, 1914.

Vugt, Joos van, and Marie-Antoinette Willemsen, eds. *Bewogen Missie: Het Gebruik van Het Medium Film Door Nederlandse Kloostergemeenschappen*. Hilversum, Netherlands: Uitgeverij Verloren, 2012.

Wahyudi, Yohanes. "Inkulturasi Musik Liturgi Gaya Lio." *Warta* Musik [42] (2017): 152–55.

Wallace, Alfred Russel. *The Malay Archipelago: The Land of the Orang-Utan and the Bird of Paradise. A Narrative of Travel, with Studies of Man and Nature*. 2nd ed. 2 vols. London: Macmillan, 1869.

Warneck, Johannes. *Die Religion der Batak: Ein Paradigma für die animistische Religionen des Indischen Archipels*. Gottingen: Vandenhoeck & Ruprecht, 1909.

———. "Eine Gabe der deutschen Christenheit an die Völker." *Berichte der Rheinischen Missionsgesellschaft* 93 (1936): 215–18.

Warta Musik, Tim Redaksi, eds. "Inkulturasi di Lio." *Warta Musik* [26] (2001): 39.

———. "Apakah gamelan harus klasik?" *Warta Musik* [28] (2003): 5-6.

Weintraub, Andrew. "The Sound and Spectacle of Dangdut Koplo: Genre and Counter-Genre in East Java, Indonesia." *Asian Music* 44, no. 2 (Summer/Fall 2013): 160–94.

Weiss, Sarah. "Review of: Indonesian Music and Dance—Traditional Music and Its Interaction with the West. A Compilation of Articles (1935-1952), by Jaap Kunst." *Yearbook for Traditional Music* 31 (1999): 130–31.

Werkmeister, S. "Die verhinderte Weltsprache. 16. Dezember 1915: Adalbert Baumann präsentiert 'Das neue, leichte Weltdeutsch.'" In *Mit Deutschland um die Welt. Eine Kulturgeschichte des Fremden in der Kolonialzeit*, edited by Alexander Honold and Klaus R. Scherpe, 464–72. Stuttgart: J. B. Metzler, 2004.

Wessing, Robert. "Bamboo, Rice, and Water." In *The Garland Encyclopedia of World Music*. Vol. 4, *Southeast Asia*, edited by T. E. Miller and S. Williams, 47–54. New York: Garland, 1998.

White, David Gordon. *Kiss of the Yoginï: "Tantric Sex" in Its South Asian Contexts*. Chicago: University of Chicago Press, 2003.

Wicki, Josef, ed. *Documenta Indica I (1540-1549)*. Rome: Monumenta Historica Societatis Iesu, 1948.

———, ed. *Documenta Indica III (1553-1557)*. Rome: Monumenta Historica Societatis Iesu, 1954.

———, ed. *Documenta Indica IV (1557–1560)*. Rome: Monumenta Historica Societatis Iesu, 1956.

Wilkens, J. A. "Séwåkå,een Javaansch gedicht met eene vertaling en woordenboek." In *Tijdschrift voor Nederlandsch-Indië*, 381–461. https://play.google.com/books/reader?id=IJYKAAAAYAAJ&pg=GBS.PA382&hl=en.

Widiyanto, Danar. "Wahyu Cakraningrat, Sebuah Filosofis untuk Merebut Kekuasaan" [Wahyu Cakraningrat, a philosophy to seize power]. *KRyogya.com*, May 6, 2018.

Wijayanto, Gustriya Sukodoyo, and Wilis Rengganiasih Endah Ekowati. "Development of Jātaka Puppet Videos as Learning Media for Adi Sekha Students at Adhicitta Buddhist Sunday School." *Jurnal Pencerahan* [Journal of enlightenment] 14 (2021): 13–28.

Willemsem, Marie-Antoine. "In Memoriam Jilis A. J. Verheijen, SVD: A Collector's Life." *Bijdragen tot de Taal-, Land- en Volkenkunde*, 154, no. 1 (1998): 1–12.

Winter, F. W. *Tembang Jawa nganggo musik kanggo ipamulanggan Jawa*. Vol. 1. Kantor Pangetjapan Gupremén, 1874.

Wohlleben, Peter. *Das geheime Leben der Bäume: Was sie fühlen, wie sie kommunizieren—die Entdeckung einer verborgenen Welt*. München: Heyne Verlag, 2017.

Woodfield, Ian. *English Musicians in the Age of Exploration*. Stuyvesant: Pendragon, 1995.

Xavier, Francis. *The Letters and Instructions of Francis Xavier*. Translated and edited by M. Joseph Costelloe. St. Louis, MO: Institute of Jesuit Sources, 1992.

yamomo, meLê, and Barbara Titus. "The Persistent Refrain of the Colonial Archival Logic/Colonial Entanglements and Sonic Transgressions: Sounding Out the Jaap Kunst Collection." *The World of Music* 10 (Postcolonial Sound Archives: Challenges and Potentials, 2021), 39–70.

Yampolsky, Philip. *Music of Nias and North Sumatra*. Music of Indonesia, 4. Compact disc. Smithsonian Folkways Recordings, SF40420. Washington, DC, 1992.

———. *Vocal and instrumental music from East and Central Flores*. Music of Indonesia, 8. Compact disc. Smithsonian Folkways Recordings, SF40424. Washington, DC, 1995.

Yasadipura, R. N. *The Book of Cabolèk*. Translated and edited by S. Soebardi. The Hague: Nijhoff, 1975.

Žganec, Vinko, and Nada Sremec. *Hrvatske narodne pjesme i plesovi* [Croatian folk songs and dances]. Zagreb: Seljacka Sloga, 1951.

Ziegler, Susanne. *Die Wachszylinder des Berliner Phonogramm-Archivs: Textdokumentation und Klangbeispiele*. Veröffentlichungen des Ethnologischen Museums Berlin, Neue Folge 73, Abt. Musikethnologie, Medien-Technik und Berliner Phonogramm Archiv XII. Berlin: Staatliche Museen zu Berlin—Preußischer Kulturbesitz, 2006.

Zimmer, Georg. "Erwünschte Nachricht aus Borneo." *Berichte der Rheinischen Missionsgesellschaft* 9 (1846): 275–77.

Zoetmulder, P. J. *Pantheism and Monism in Javanese Suluk Literature: Islamic and Indian Mysticism in an Indonesian Setting*. Leiden: KITLV Press, 1994.

Zuidervaart, Huib J., and Rob H. van Gent. "'A Bare Outpost of Learned European Culture on the Edge of the Jungles of Java': Johan Maurits Mohr (1716–1775) and the Emergence of Instrumental and Institutional Science in Dutch Colonial Indonesia." *Isis* 95, no. 1 (2004): 1–33.

CONTRIBUTORS

BERNARD ARPS is professor of Indonesian and Javanese language and culture at Leiden University, where he teaches area studies theory, cultural politics in Southeast Asia (using performance genres as case material), literatures of South and Southeast Asia, and Javanese language in/as culture. He has published widely on Javanese and Indonesian song, popular music, and puppetry. His most recent book is *Tall Tree, Nest of the Wind: A Study in Performance Philology* (NUS Press, 2016).

ANNA MARIA BUSSE BERGER is distinguished professor emerita at the University of California, Davis. Her books include *Mensuration and Proportion Signs: Origins and Evolution* (Oxford University Press, 1993), *Medieval Music and the Art of Memory* (University of California Press, 2005), and *The Search for Medieval Music in Africa and Germany, 1891–1961: Scholars, Singers, Missionaries* (University of California Press, 2020). She is an honorary member of the American Musicological Society and has won major awards from the American Musicological Society, the Society for Music Theory, and the Society for Ethnomusicology.

JULIA BYL thinks about how an expansive, worldwide music history can register local meaning. She teaches on Treaty 6 Territory at the University of Alberta, as associate professor of music. She has written on Toba Batak music in *Antiphonal Histories* (Wesleyan University Press, 2014) and has edited, with Jim Sykes, *Sounding the Indian Ocean* (University of California Press, 2023). Her current project is a collaborative study on music, the individual, and institutional membership in Timor-Leste, one of world's youngest countries. Julia has also directed and edited a documentary, *Poets in the Living Room*, about the extraordinary musical and poetic lives of Saleem and Regula Burckhardt Qureshi.

KATHY FOLEY is research professor and distinguished professor emerita of performance play and design at University of California, Santa Cruz and past president of Union International de la marionette-USA. She edited *Asian Theatre Journal* (2005–18) and was one of the first non-Indonesian *dalang* to perform in the Indonesian National Wayang Festival (Pekan Wayang Indonesia). She has taught at Chulalongkorn University, University of Hawai'i, and University of Malaya and has been supported by Fulbright, Asian Cultural Council, Institute of Sacred Music/Yale, and East-West Center grants. In 2022, she guest edited the first issue of *Puppetry International Research* https://pirjournal.commons.gc.cuny.edu/puppet-research-international-1-no-1/.

DAVID A. HOLLINGER is a former president of the Organization of American Historians and an elected member of the American Philosophical Society and the American Academy of Arts and Sciences. His nine books include *Science, Jews, and Secular Culture* (Princeton University Press, 1996), *After Cloven Tongues of Fire* (Princeton University Press, 2013), *Protestants Abroad* (Princeton University Press, 2017), and *Christianity's American Fate* (Princeton University Press, 2022). He is Preston Hotchkis Professor of History Emeritus at the University of California, Berkeley.

DAVID R. M. IRVING is an ICREA research professor affiliated to the Institució Milà i Fontanals de Recerca en Humanitats (IMF), CSIC, Barcelona, a corresponding fellow of the Australian Academy of the Humanities, and honorary senior fellow at the Melbourne Conservatorium of Music, University of Melbourne. He is the author of *Colonial Counterpoint: Music in Early Modern Manila* (Oxford University Press, 2010) and *The Making of European Music in the Long Eighteenth Century* (Oxford University Press, 2024), coeditor of the journal *Eighteenth-Century Music*, and co-general editor of *A Cultural History of Western Music* (Bloomsbury, 2024).

ESTELLE JOUBERT is associate professor of musicology at the Fountain School of Performing Arts, Dalhousie University. Her research interests include computational musicology, global histories of musics in the early modern period, and opera studies. She is author of *German Opera and Enlightenment Philosophy: The Politics of Sensation* (Cambridge University Press, 2024) and, together with David R. M. Irving, coeditor of *A Cultural History of Music in the Age of Enlightenment* (Bloomsbury, 2023). Her current research includes a project on musics in the Cape Colony, Southern Africa, 1497–1910, and with Austin Glatthorn, she is coeditor of the forthcoming *Cambridge History of German Opera to the Early Nineteenth Century*.

SEBASTIAN KLOTZ is professor of transcultural musicology and the historical anthropology of music at Humboldt University Berlin. In 2017, he initiated the Erich von Hornbostel Audio Emergence Lab (HAEL). He was the leader of the Sounding Cities project, which explores auditory transformations in Berlin, Chicago, and Kolkata (with Philip Bohlman/Chicago and Lars-Christian Koch/Berlin; published by LIT-Verlag in 2018); and he is in charge of a long-term editorial project, *The Correspondence of Felix Mendelssohn Bartholdy*. He is academic advisor to the *Lautarchiv* and has co-curated the exhibition *Listening to the World* (Berlin 2018).

EMILIE ROOK is an ethnomusicologist based in Pittsburgh, PA. She holds a master of arts in religion from Yale Divinity School and the Yale Institute of Sacred Music (2015) and a doctorate in music from the University of Pittsburgh (2020). Emilie's scholarship deals with issues of power, identity politics, and religion, particularly in Indonesia. She currently works as an independent researcher, occasional adjunct professor, and full-time parent to her young children.

HENRY SPILLER is an ethnomusicologist whose research focuses on Sundanese music and dance from West Java, Indonesia, on gender and sexuality, and on gamelan music and the West. His books include *Erotic Triangles: Sundanese Dance and Masculinity in West Java* (University of Chicago Press, 2010), *Javaphilia: American Love Affairs with Javanese Music and Dance* (University of Hawai'i Press, 2015), and *Archaic Instruments in Modern West Java: Bamboo Murmurs* (Routledge, 2023), as well as the Routledge textbook *Focus: Gamelan Music of Indonesia* (now in a 2022 third edition, with new coauthor Elizabeth Clendinning). He is professor emeritus at the University of California, Davis, where, beginning in 2005, he taught world music classes and graduate seminars and directed the Department of Music's gamelan ensemble.

SUMARSAM is a Winslow-Kaplan Professor of Music at Wesleyan University. He is the author of *Gamelan: Cultural Interaction and Musical Development in Central Java* (University of Chicago Press, 1995), *Javanese Gamelan and the West* (University of Rochester Press, 2013), and *The In-Between in Javanese Performing Arts: History and Myth, Interculturalism and Interreligiosity* (Wesleyan University Press 2024). As a gamelan musician and a keen amateur *dhalang* (puppeteer) of Javanese wayang puppet play, he performs, conducts workshops, and lectures throughout the United States, Australia, Europe, and Asia.

BARBARA TITUS is associate professor of cultural musicology at the University of Amsterdam. She is the author of two books: *Recognizing Music as an Art Form* (Cornell University Press, 2016) and *Hearing Maskanda* (Bloomsbury Academic, 2022). She is the coeditor of the journal *The World of Music*. Barbara studied musicology at Utrecht University (The Netherlands) and gained her doctorate from Oxford University (UK). Barbara is the curator of the Jaap Kunst Sound Collection at the University of Amsterdam and the project leader and first principal investigator of the JPICH-funded project Decolonizing Southeast Asian Sound Archives (DeCoSEAS) that renegotiates established understandings of heritage curation.

DUSTIN WIEBE is a musicologist (PhD, Wesleyan University) with research interests in Southeast Asian music history, theory, and performance practice. He writes regularly on these topics, and his publications are found in noted journals and academic presses. From 2020 to 2022, Dr. Wiebe served as Luce Postdoctoral Fellow at the University of California, Davis. Previously, he has held positions at the University of Georgia (visiting faculty) and the University of Manitoba (research scholar). Dustin is also a dedicated guitar pedagogue, having studied at the Royal Conservatory of Music in Toronto and the Eastman School of Music (MM). He is presently a music teacher at Morello Park Elementary in the San Francisco Bay Area.

PHILIP YAMPOLSKY has studied the music of Indonesia and its neighbors since 1970. He recorded and edited the twenty-volume *Music of Indonesia* CD series (Smithsonian Folkways Recordings, 1991–99) and wrote the annotations for most of them. From 2000 to 2006, he was program officer in arts and culture for the Jakarta office of the Ford Foundation. His research focus since 2011 has been singing in rural Timor (both the Indonesian half and the independent Republic of Timor-Leste). Another long-standing line of his research is the representation, misrepresentation, and non-representation of traditional Indonesian and Timorese music genres in commercial media, beginning with the era of 78-rpm gramophone records and extending up to the present day.

Founded in 1893,
UNIVERSITY OF CALIFORNIA PRESS
publishes bold, progressive books and journals
on topics in the arts, humanities, social sciences,
and natural sciences—with a focus on social
justice issues—that inspire thought and action
among readers worldwide.

The UC PRESS FOUNDATION
raises funds to uphold the press's vital role
as an independent, nonprofit publisher, and
receives philanthropic support from a wide
range of individuals and institutions—and from
committed readers like you. To learn more, visit
ucpress.edu/supportus.